ELEMENTARY CHINESE

ELEMENTARY CHINESE

SECOND EDITION

Shau Wing Chan

(SHOÙJUNǴ CH'EŃ)

STANFORD UNIVERSITY PRESS

STANFORD, CALIFORNIA

This edition is a completely revised and reset version of the text first published in 1951. An earlier version, entitled *Chinese Reader for Beginners,* was published in 1942.

Stanford University Press
Stanford, California
Copyright © 1951, 1959 by the Board of Trustees
of the Leland Stanford Junior University
Printed in the United States of America
ISBN 0-8047-0413-9
This edition first published 1959
Reprinted 1961, 1966, 1971

to

S.Y., STANLEY, WALLY

PREFACE to the Second Edition

This edition differs from the first edition in only two major respects other than its appearance: (1) the typographical errors and inconsistencies of the first edition have been corrected; (2) lists of simplified characters and character components now in use in mainland China have been added for the reader's convenience. It is hoped that the present edition will prove useful to beginning students of Chinese.

SHAU WING CHAN

Stanford, California
August 30, 1959

PREFACE to the First Edition

Since the publication of my *Chinese Reader for Beginners* several years ago, I have received many friendly and constructive suggestions with a view to making it a more effective tool in the teaching of modern Chinese to students in this country. The general feeling has been that the *Reader* could have contained more adequate notes on grammar, more extensive reading material, and a more liberal use of romanization so as to furnish the student better guidance not only in pronunciation but also in understanding the syntactical structure of the material used.

I have made every possible effort to incorporate such sound advice in the writing of this new volume, which I hope will eventually replace the *Reader*. Consequently, though the basic pedagogical pattern of the *Reader* is retained in the present work, its vocabulary has been thoroughly rearranged and somewhat enlarged, its reading material made more extensive, its notes on grammar made fuller, and its use of romanization made more liberal. It is my belief that this work will provide enough material for a beginning course in Chinese on the college level meeting five hours a week and lasting throughout the academic year. A course conducted on a less intensive basis will most likely find it rather difficult to finish the sixty lessons contained herein. In that case, the instructor in charge of the course will have to make other arrangements that will best suit the needs of his students.

It may be pointed out here that the system of romanization used throughout this work is basically the Wade-Giles system, with the omission of the following diacritical marks: ˆ (over the letter "e") and ˘ (over the letter "u" when it is preceded by "tz"). The umlaut, however, is retained over the letter "u" to indicate a modified phonetic value for the vowel. Moreover, instead of resorting to superior Arabic numerals, [1], [2], [3], [4], placed immediately after the romanized syllables, I have used the following marks, ⁻, ´, ˇ, `, to indicate the four tones in modern Chinese, and they are placed directly over the last letters of the syllables. A syllable without any such mark over its last letter is to be construed as neutral.

I am indebted to those who have so generously given me constructive advice from time to time. I feel particularly grateful to Dr. Yuen Ren Chao of the University of California, Berkeley, California, for having kindly gone over the whole manuscript, pointing out inaccuracies and making helpful suggestions and corrections as he went along. Also, I am grateful to my wife for her patient assistance and encouragement during the preparation of the work. I alone, however, am to be held responsible for any shortcoming or inadequacy.

Shau Wing Chan

Stanford, California
January 1951

CONTENTS

INTRODUCTION

I. THE CHINESE LANGUAGE

Chinese is an independent member of a huge family of languages known as Indo-Sinitic, which includes Tai, Tibetan, Burmese, and the languages of the Bodo-Naga-Kachin, Miao, Lolo, and Mon-Khmer groups. As a written language it has produced a very extensive and venerable literature and played a culturally important role in eastern Asia. As a spoken language in its existing dialectal variations it is, in terms of geographical coverage, probably the most extensive language of the world. In terms of numerical strength, it is second only to English.

Although Chinese is reputedly one of the oldest of living languages, we are not at all certain about its age, since the larger question of the origin of the Chinese people still remains unsettled. According to Chinese traditional accounts, the rudiments of Chinese writing were first conceived by Fúhsī (伏羲), one of the legendary rulers, whose reign has traditionally been placed in the twenty-ninth century B.C., after he had seen some mystical signs on the back of a horse dragon which had emerged from the Yellow River. He ordered his minister, Ts'ang Chieh (倉頡), to execute those signs in the form of written symbols, and these symbols became the high ancestors of Chinese writing. It should be pointed out that interesting though this legend may sound, it appears to have been a much later attempt to account for the origin of Chinese writing, and as long as it is yet to be substantiated with verifiable data, it should be regarded only as a legend. However, authentic specimens of the earliest type of Chinese writing, dating back at least to the middle of the second millennium of the pre-Christian era, have been unearthed. The style in which the writing was done is not too primitive; a number of the originally pictorial and ideographic characters had by that time ceased to be pictographic representations of concrete objects and direct symbols of ideas, and had become logographs, or conventionalized visual symbols of spoken words. The fact that these early specimens display such elegance of form and such a vast vocabulary range—estimated to exceed two thousand words—seems to favor the supposition that centuries of growth and cultivation preceded them. It is therefore reasonable to suggest that Chinese has had a continuous history of evolution for at least three and a half millennia.

Throughout these many centuries of growth, Chinese has experienced various kinds of change and development and has been exposed to the influences of foreign cultures as a result of the numerous contacts of the Chinese with non-Chinese peoples. The history of the Chinese language may be divided into the following four main periods, each with certain characteristics of its own: the Archaic Period, from remote antiquity to about A.D. 500; the Ancient Period, from about A.D. 500 to 900; the Middle

Period, from A.D. 900 to 1200; the Modern Period, from 1200 to the present. Aside from the various changes in pronunciation and in the style of writing, the Chinese language has never made any extensive borrowing from any foreign language, and its basic features as a literary medium have remained practically unaltered. For this reason, the language of the Confucian classics of the pre-Christian era remains perfectly intelligible to the lettered Chinese of today, although they have to read the contents of these works aloud according to modern dialectal pronunciation, since their knowledge of ancient Chinese pronunciation is extremely meager and none too positive. But at any rate, a Chinese student of today wishing to study the literary monuments of his country produced in the past does not have to face the same linguistic difficulties which will confront an English-speaking student who wishes to study *Beowulf* or *The Canterbury Tales*, or a French-speaking student who wishes to study the *Chanson de Roland*.

II. WRITTEN AND SPOKEN CHINESE

In our brief discussion of Chinese the peculiar relationship between Chinese as it is written and as it is spoken must be pointed out. In the case of alphabetical languages, most significant phonetic changes in their spoken forms will be revealed in their written counterparts. It is possible for a word such as "hlāford," phonetically pronounced as written in *Beowulf*, for example, to be now phonetically pronounced and written as "lord." Chinese uses a script that does not lend itself readily to recording such phonetic changes. There is no such revealing change recorded in written Chinese, which is meant primarily for the satisfaction of the eye, whereas spoken Chinese definitely attempts to satisfy the ear. For this reason the writing system of Chinese can remain uniform throughout China and eastern Asia despite the great variations which spoken Chinese has developed. For the same reason we may say that written Chinese has no standard pronunciation of its own because there has never been developed in China a standard spoken language, or we may better say that written Chinese has as many standards of pronunciation as there are Chinese dialects, many of which are bafflingly different from one another. The same passage from, let us say, the *Book of History*, or the same poem by Lǐ Pó or Tù Fù of the eighth century, will sound quite different when it is read by a native of Peiping, Shanghai, Amoy, or Canton. In a loose sense we may admit that there was a "standard" spoken Chinese in imperial times, known to the West as Mandarin, which was a sort of official language (kuañhuà, 官話), but its use was limited to officialdom and its value varied from time to time as the political capital was shifted from place to place. It was at best an artificial tongue and should not be compared with the local dialects, which have been living tongues and whose popularity and tenacious hold are not limited to the uneducated segments of the local population. This peculiar relationship between written and spoken Chinese should be borne in mind if the significance of recent efforts exerted by Chinese intellectual leaders to bring about a national spoken language (kuóyǔ, 國語) is to be fully grasped.

III. MODERN CHINESE DIALECTS

Speaking of the dialects in China, it is extremely difficult to trace with certainty their origin and the underlying reasons accounting for their birth. It may be said with reasonable safety, however, that they were already in existence during the Archaic Chinese period, that they did not stem from the same source, and that not all of them have living direct descendants. But judging from the major living dialects in use in China now, despite their differences in pronunciation, in the choice of the most commonly used words, and in grammar, they still reveal sufficient common traits to show that they are descendants of closely related, if not the same, high ancestors.

The major modern Chinese dialects may be divided into the following six groups: Mandarin, Wu, Kan-Hakka, Min, Canton, and Hsiang. The Mandarin group may be further divided into three subgroups: Northern, Southern, and Southwestern. The Northern subgroup is spoken in Manchuria, north China proper, Sinkiang, Kansu, and parts of Hupeh, Anhwei, and Kiangsu provinces. The dialect of Peiping is the best-known member of this subgroup. The Southern subgroup is spoken along the lower Yangtze region in parts of the provinces of Anhwei, Kiangsu, and Hupeh. The Southwestern subgroup is spoken in Szechuan, Yunnan, Kweichow, and parts of Hupeh and Kwangsi provinces. The Wu group, which includes the dialects of Shanghai, Wenchow, and Soochow, is spoken in Kiangsu, Chekiang, and eastern Kiangsi provinces. The Kan-Hakka group is spoken in southern Kiangsi and parts of Kwangtung provinces. The Min group, which includes the dialects of Foochow, Amoy, and Swatow, is spoken in northern Fukien and eastern Kwangtung provinces, Hainan Island, and Leichow Peninsula. The Cantonese group is spoken principally in Kwangtung and Kwangsi provinces. The Hsiang group is spoken principally in Hunan province. Besides these major groups, there are certain isolated dialects spoken in southern Anhwei, Hunan, and northeastern Kwangsi provinces. On the basis of this sketchy geographical outline of the major dialectal groups, it is apparent that the most active dialectal belt in China starts from the lower Yangtze region, sweeping southeastward along the coast until it reaches the Indo-Chinese border.

These dialects are characterized generally by their having preserved or dropped the final consonants -m, -p, -t, -k of ancient Chinese, by their having retained or unvoiced the ancient voiced initials b', d', g', dz', etc., and by the number of tones they possess more or less as a result of whether or not they have preserved the ancient Chinese "entering" or abrupt tone. The Mandarin, Wu, and Hsiang groups have dropped the ancient finals, but the Kan-Hakka, Min, and Cantonese groups have retained them. As to the ancient voiced initials, the Mandarin, Kan-Hakka, Min, and Cantonese groups have unvoiced them, but the Wu and Hsiang groups have preserved them. As to the number of tones each of these dialectal groups possesses, it ranges from four for Northern Mandarin to eight or nine for Cantonese. Southern Mandarin has five tones, while Wu, Kan-Hakka, Min, and Hsiang have six to seven.

IV. THE CHINESE CHARACTERS

The Chinese system of writing consists of numerous symbols or characters, many of which, in the earliest stage of their history, were merely
pictographic in form. As the need increased for symbols conveying abstract
as well as concrete ideas, difficult or impossible to pictorialize, ideographic
and suggestive characters were invented. Still later, other methods were
resorted to for the creation of new characters to meet the ever increasing
needs. It·may be pointed out here that all the written characters are
complete units in themselves, uninflectional in form, conveying a complete
idea, and monosyllabic in sound. Their shape may vary according to the
style in which they are written. Seven styles of writing have been
developed. The oldest of them all is known as Chiákŭweń (甲骨文), or
Oracle Bone writing, typified by the inscriptions on animal leg or shoulder
bones and tortoise shells of the Shang (商) Dynasty, traditionally dated
1766–1122 B.C. The next in age is the Tà Chuaǹ (大篆), or Great Seal style,
typified by the inscriptions on bronzes of the Chou (周) Dynasty, 1122–221
B.C. In the following dynasty, the Ch'iń (秦), 221–206 B.C., the Hsiaŏ
Chuaǹ (小篆), or Small Seal style, and the Lì Shū (隸書), or Official style,
were developed. The K'aĭ Shū (楷書), or Model style, Hsiń Shū (行書),
or Running style, and Ts'aŏ Shū (草書), or Cursive style, were developed
during the course of the Haǹ (漢), 206 B.C.-A.D. 221, and Chiǹ (晉), A.D.
265–420, dynasties. The last-named style is actually a kind of shorthand
writing. The following table will show the main characteristics of these
seven styles of writing:

Character Meaning	Oracle Bone	Great Seal	Small Seal	Official	Model	Running	Cursive
Horse	馬	馬	馬	馬	馬	馬	馬
To hit the mark, middle	中	中	中	中	中	中	中
Short-tailed bird	隹	隹	隹	佳	隹	隹	隹
Moon	月	月	月	月	月	月	月
Crosswalks; To Walk	行	行	行	行	行	行	行

Chinese characters have traditionally been broadly classified into six
categories. The first category is called Hsiańhsiń (象形), or pictographic,
which comprises characters that in their ancient forms were mere pictures
of concrete objects. These are easy to understand, and a few examples will

suffice: 🐟 from which is later developed 魚 (yǔ, "fish"); ⌒⌒ from which is later developed 山 (shañ, "mountain"); ⊙ from which is later developed 日 (jiḣ, "sun"); ☽ from which is later developed 月 (yüeḣ, "moon"); 🐴 from which is later developed 馬 (mǎ, "horse").

The second category is called Chiḣshiḣ (指事), or diagrammatic or indicative. In this category we find characters which by their very form indicate the idea or ideas they are meant to convey: 一 (ī, "one"); 二 (erḣ, "two"); 三 (sañ, "three"); 上, which comes from older forms ᷄ and ⊥ (shànġ, "up"); 下, which comes from older forms ᷅ and 丅 (hsià, "down").

The third category is called Huìi (會意), or suggestive, and comprises characters which are formed on the basis of association of ideas suggested by their constituent simple elements. Thus, 明 (ming, "bright") is formed by 日 (jiḣ, "sun") and 月 (yüeḣ, "moon") to suggest brightness; 安 (añ, "peace") suggests the idea of peace or security by placing 女 (nǚ, "woman"), from an older form 𠥇, pictorializing a woman kneeling—revealing her inferior position—under 宀 (mień, "roof"), from an older pictorial form 𠆢; 林 (liḣ, "forest") suggests the abundance of trees by doubling 木 (mù, "tree"), formerly written 𣎵. It may be noted that the characters of these first three categories form much less than half of the total number of characters.

The fourth category is known as Chiǎchieḣ (假借), or borrowed characters, that is, characters adopted for new words on the basis of identity of sound. Thus, 來, formerly written 𣏾, a picture of a stalk of growing grain or wheat, was originally a character for some kind of grain or wheat. Later there was coined the word "laí," meaning "to come." Instead of creating a new character for the latter word, 來, on account of its identity of pronunciation, was simply "borrowed" for that purpose, after realizing how difficult it was to convey the idea of "coming" in pictorial or even suggestive writing. Similarly, 難 (nań), originally the character for a kind of desert bird, was borrowed for the new homophonous word meaning "difficult," and 萬 (waḣ), originally a picture of a scorpion in its earlier forms 𧒥, 𧒟, 𧑒, was borrowed for the new homophonous word meaning "ten thousand."

The fifth category is known as Hsinġshenġ (形聲), or Hsieḣshenġ (諧聲), or phonetic compounds. Each of the characters in this group is formed by two elements, a signific and a phonetic. The former determines the meaning, the latter furnishes the clue to pronunciation. Thus, 洋 (yanġ, "ocean") is formed by 氵, a variant form of 水 (shuī, "water") for forming compounds, and 羊 (yanġ, "sheep"); 銅 (t'unġ, "copper, bronze") is compounded of a signific, 金 (chiñ, "metal"), and a phonetic, 同 (t'unġ, "same, similar"). In this category we also find compounds which are formed from characters which have acquired extended meanings. For example, 文 (weń) originally meant "line, pattern," but has acquired the extended meanings of "writing, literature, culture." In order to distinguish the original meanings from the extended figurative ones, 紋 (weń), with 糸 (szū, "silk") as its signific, was coined to convey the former literal meanings, while 文 retains the extended figurative ones. Words in this category are by far the most numerous of all the six categories.

The last category is known as Chuanchù (轉注), or characters which time and usage have extended or declared analogous in meaning. It includes characters having identical significs and somewhat similar meanings but different phonetics, such as 老 (laŏ), 考 (k'aŏ), 耄 (maò), 耆 (ch'í), and 耋 (tieh), all meaning "old age." This group is extremely small in size.

V. TONES

Chinese as a language is noted for its paucity of vocables. As has often been pointed out, even the Cantonese dialect, which is probably the richest in monosyllabic combinations, has less than eight hundred in all, while Northern Mandarin has about half of that number, or approximately four hundred. This paucity results in the existence of many homonyms in the language. The student can notice for himself, even within the limited vocabulary range of this book, that homonyms occur in Chinese with fairly persistent regularity. For instance, the monosyllable "shih" stands for many words written with different characters meaning time, to lose, ten, rock, city, to begin, to be, poetry, world, to gather, to try, affair, history, room, real, scholar, to recognize. Similarly, the monosyllable " i " stands for words written with different characters meaning one, clothes, medicine, suitable, to doubt, chair, by means of, already, easy, idea, the right thing to do, to translate, to discuss. A phenomenon like this is quite apt to create uncertainty and confusion. It may be pointed out that the context sometimes will help determine the meaning intended, but in most cases the number of homonyms is too numerous to depend comfortably on contextual implication alone.

Such a state of uncertainty and confusion, however, is remedied by a system of tones which functions so as to distinguish the various musical accents with which a monosyllable can be pronounced, thereby reducing the extent of possible confusion of meanings. Thus, when the monosyllable "shih" is pronounced, for instance, in a high level tone, it may stand for words meaning to lose, poetry; in a high rising tone, for words meaning ten, time, to recognize, rock, to gather, real; in a low dipping tone, for words meaning to begin, history; in a high falling tone, for words meaning to be, affair, room, to try, world, city, scholar. Similarly, when the monosyllable " i " is pronunced in a high level tone, it stands for words meaning one, clothes, medicine; in a high rising tone, for words meaning suitable, to doubt; in a low dipping tone, for words meaning chair, by means of, already; in a high falling tone, for words meaning easy, idea, to discuss, the right thing to do, to translate. With the aid of the tone system, then, the uncertainty and confusion caused by the existence in Chinese of homonyms is only to a certain extent remedied. In order further to reduce the extent of uncertainty and confusion, Chinese has to employ various types of elucidative devices, which the student will see for himself as he is going through the lessons and notes of this book, and which require too much space even for a brief discussion here.

According to Barnard Karlgren,[1] these tones in Chinese are the outcome of the elision of ancient prefixes denoting parts of speech long extinct. Tones or musical accents existed in the prehistoric Indo-European language but are preserved only in Swedish, Norwegian, Serbo-Croatian, and Lithuanian among its daughter languages; none of these languages, however, employs tones to the same extent that Chinese does.

Categorically speaking, there are four tones in Chinese, known as P'ing (平) or Level or Even; Shang (上) or Rising; Ch'ù (去) or Falling or Departing; and Jù (入) or Entering or Abrupt. Then each of these four tones is split on two different levels, one high, the other low in pitch, so that there are altogether eight tonal variations for a given monosyllable. These tonal variations are designated Upper or High Level, Low Level, Upper or High Rising, Low Rising, Upper or High Falling, Low Falling, Upper or High Abrupt, Low Abrupt. These tones did not come into existence all at the same time, but were in a state of gradual and continual evolution to meet changing needs. Up to the third century of the pre-Christian era, only the Level, Rising, and Abrupt tones were employed. During the next eight hundred years or so, the Falling tone was gradually developed. It has already been pointed out that not all of these tones, with their high and low variations, are preserved in all the modern Chinese dialects. Cantonese has preserved them all, while Northern Mandarin, upon which China's National Language, or Kuóyǔ (國語), is based, has preserved only four of the eight tonal variations; other dialects have preserved five, six, or seven. Therefore it must be remembered that the four tones of Kuóyǔ are not the same as the four original tones of ancient Chinese.

The four tones of Northern Mandarin or Kuóyǔ for stressed syllables are: (1) the First tone or 陰平 (Yiñp'ing, "High Level"); (2) the Second tone or 陽平 (Yangp'ing, "High Rising"); (3) the Third tone or 上聲 (Shangsheng or Shangsheng, "Low Dipping"); (4) the Fourth tone or 去聲 (Ch'ùsheng, "High Falling"). Throughout this text the four tones are graphically indicated over the last letter of a syllable in romanized orthography by tone marks ˉ, ´, ˇ, `, instead of the superior Arabic numerals [1], [2], [3], [4], regularly used in the Wade system of romanization. From now on, for the sake of convenience, they will be referred to as the first, second, third, and fourth tones. These tones are concretely presented in the following musical notations, each of the digits beneath them representing a relative pitch of the scale:

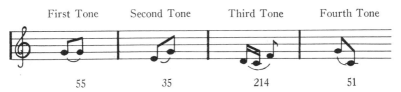

First Tone	Second Tone	Third Tone	Fourth Tone
55	35	214	51

[1] *Sounds and Symbols in Chinese*, pp. 29-30.

It must be borne in mind that no Chinese monosyllable is meant to be uttered as a pure musical note or combination of musical notes in any set key starting from a set position within an octave. The choice of key and notes above is merely arbitrary. The speaking voice, in manipulating the above note combinations, must glide from one pitch to another as in a portamento. The total range of pitch of these tones depends on the sex and mood of the speaker and may therefore vary to the extent of a tone or a tone and a half.

VI. STRESS

The description of the qualities of the four tones in the foregoing section is true only when a syllable is spoken in isolation and stressed. When a group of syllables is spoken in succession, however, the tone qualities of some of them are often so changed that they no longer can be identified acccording to their original characteristics. Such changes are caused primarily by two major factors: stress and the position of the syllables in a phrase or sentence.

By stress is meant the emphasis of utterance given certain syllables as they stand in relation to other syllables within a phrase or sentence. It will be sadly misleading to think that in actual conversation all the elements of a Chinese sentence are spoken with the same amount of accentual force and duration. The truth of the matter is that some syllables receive more stress and are longer in duration than others. A stressed syllable in Chinese is spoken with relative loudness and given full duration for its delivery, while its characteristic tone quality is reproduced distinctly and without any modification.

It is possible to say that there are primary, secondary, and even tertiary stresses in Chinese. Generally speaking, all monosyllabic but syntactically independent or free words are fully stressed. In the case of most dissyllabic syntactical words, the initial syllable receives the secondary stress, while the primary stress falls on the final one. There are, however, a relatively small number of dissyllabic syntactical words with a tonic accent on the initial syllable. The student will have to learn these more or less as exceptions. In the case of syntactical words of three or more syllables, the secondary stress falls on the initial syllable, the tertiary stress on the medial syllable or syllables, and the primary stress on the final one.

VII. NEUTRAL TONE

An unstressed syllable when spoken lacks the loudness, the full delivery duration, and the distinct characteristic tone quality, whatever that may be. In actual practice it is merely glided over lightly in a nondescript tone which has been called the "neutral" tone. A syllable in any of the four tones can be neutral in tone. Although it is quite difficult to work out any hard and fast rule for determining the occurrence of atonic syllables in a phrase or sentence, it may nevertheless be pointed out that generally all particles, interjections, pronouns following verbs, and other words which in themselves do not possess any important concrete meaning are to be dealt with as atonic syllables.

According to Dr. Yuen Ren Chao of the Academia Sinica and University of California, Berkeley, California, the pitch of these atonic syllables is "determined by the preceding syllable."[2] After a syllable in the first tone, e.g., 他的 (T'āte, "his, her, hers"), it is half-low in pitch. After a syllable in the second tone, e.g., 誰的 (Shuíte, "whose"), it is medium in pitch. After a syllable in the third tone, e.g., 我的 (Wŏte, "my, mine"), it is half-high in pitch. After a syllable in the fourth tone, e.g., 大的 (Tàte, "that which is big, big one"), it is low in pitch. Using the 1-to-5 range of the four tones as a criterion, a low pitch corresponds to 1; a half-low, to 2; a medium, to 3; a half-high, to 4.

When a neutral tone syllable follows another one, its pitch depends on that of the preceding one. Its pitch is low if the pitch of the preceding neutral tone syllable is medium, half-low, or low: 拿出來 (Nách'ulai, "to bring or take out"—35-3-1); 伸出來 (Shench'ulai, "to stretch out"—55-2-1); 笑起來 (Hsiaòch'ilai, "to begin to laugh"—51-1-1). Its pitch is half-low if that of the preceding neutral tone syllable is half-high: 走出來 (Tsouch'ulai, "to walk or come out"—21[4][3]-4-2). All neutral tone syllables or words are indicated by a dot below them in the character text and by the omission of the tone mark over them in the romanized portions of this work.

As to the neutral tone syllable or syllables in compounds, they have to be checked in dictionaries which record such tonal phenomena, such as *A Chinese-English Dictionary*, by R. H. Matthews (Revised American Edition, Harvard University Press, 1943); *The Five Thousand Dictionary*, by C. H. Fenn (Revised American Edition, Harvard University Press, 1943); and *Concise Dictionary of Spoken Chinese*, by Yuen Ren Chao and Lien Sheng Yang (Harvard University Press, 1947).

VIII.   TONE SANDHI

Tone sandhi is the change in the quality of tones of syllables when they are spoken in succession; it is brought about partly by stress and partly by the positions occupied by the syllables within a phrase or a sentence. How stress can affect the tone qualities of syllables in unstressed positions and how it has given rise to the neutral tone has already been discussed above. We have yet to show the tone changes which happen to stressed syllables in relation to the position they occupy. Tone sandhi of Northern Mandarin is fairly simple and may be stated as follows:

[2] "Tone and Intonation in Chinese," *Bulletin of the National Research Institute of History and Philology* (Shanghai: Academia Sinica, 1933), IV, Part 2, 129. I am also indebted to Dr. Chao for his introductory material dealing with tones in Matthews' *Chinese-English Dictionary* (Revised American Edition, 1943), and for his *Mandarin Primer* (Cambridge: Harvard University Press, 1948), which contains a succinct treatment of the neutral tone.

[3] For this tonal phenomenon, see "Tone Sandhi ' below.

1. A syllable in the third tone, followed immediately by another in any other tone but that, loses its rising pitch and retains merely its low falling quality. For example, the first syllable of 好説 (Haŏshuō, "good to say"), 好人 (Haŏ jeń, "good person"), and 好看 (Haŏk'aǹ, "good to look at, pretty") is to be pronounced not in the regular low dipping tone (214), but in a half-low falling pitch (21). This is also true even when a third-tone syllable is followed by an atonic syllable, e.g., 椅子 (Ĭtzu, "chair"), 我們 (Wŏmen, "we, us"), 你們 (Nĭmen, "you"). Such third-tone syllables are still marked " ˇ " throughout the romanized portions of this work.

2. A syllable in the third tone followed immediately by another in the same tone becomes second or high rising. Thus, 很好, "very good," is to be pronounced "heń haŏ"; 老手 "old hand, expert," as "laó shoŭ." In certain compounds consisting of a stressed syllable in the third tone followed by an unstressed one which is originally in the same tone but which is not a particle without any important concrete meaning and hence still feels the effect of its original tone despite its atonic position, the first syllable goes through a tone change somewhat similar to but not quite identical with the second tone; for inasmuch as the syllable has acquired the high rising quality of the second tone, it still retains some of the glottal stricture characteristic of the third tone. For the convenience of graphic indication, however, such syllables are still marked with " ´ " over them. Thus, 小姐, "unmarried young lady, Miss," and 等你, "to wait for you," are marked "hsiaóchieh" and "teń ni," respectively. When three or more stressed syllables in the third tone come together, they must be examined in the light of the grammatical structure of the sentence in which they are found. If they belong together to form a conversational unit, there are two ways to handle them. One is to alternate the use of the second and third tones on such syllables. The other is to change all such syllables except the last to the second tone. Thus, 我有手, "I have hands," and 我也有手, "I also have hands," may be said as "Wŏ yú shoŭ" and "Wó yeń yú shoŭ" or "Wó yú shoŭ" and "Wó yeń yú shoŭ," respectively. The second way is followed in this work. If they are not to be spoken together, as 你有手, 我也有手, "You have hands [and] I also have hands," the first three and the last four syllables must be dealt with separately. Note that the third and seventh syllables retain their original third tone because they are both at the end of a conversational unit. All third tone syllables undergoing such tone sandhi are marked " ´ " in the romanized portions of this work.

3. In the case of trisyllabic words or phrases, if the first syllable is in either the first or second tone, the second syllable in the second tone, and the third in any of the four tones, then the second tone of the second syllable is changed to the first. Thus, 西紅柿, "tomatoes," actually is pronounced "hsī-hungshih," although its second syllable is originally in the second tone. But this type of tone sandhi occurs only in fairly speedy conversation. Therefore, in the romanized portions of this work, this type of tone change is not indicated.

4. When two syllables in the fourth tone come together, the falling

quality of the first syllable is arrested at the middle point of the pitch range and so the syllable sounds more like a 53 rather than 51. 現在 (Hsièntsài, "now") and 會議 (Huiì, "conference, meeting") are examples of this type of tone sandhi, which also is not indicated in the romanized portions of this work.

IX. CHINA'S KUÓYŬ OR NATIONAL LANGUAGE

The fact that there has been no standard spoken Chinese and that there are many dialectal variations has already been pointed out and briefly discussed. The truth of the matter is that despite the fact that the major modern Chinese dialects reveal enough common traits to indicate close kinship among them, some of them, at least when spoken, are quite different from one another—as different, let us say, as French is from Italian or Spanish, or as Dutch is from English. It is true that written Chinese is quite uniform throughout the country and has created no difficulty at all for lettered Chinese in communicating ideas regardless of their own dialectal affiliation, since its uniformity has transcended all dialectal barriers. However, it is chiefly meant for the eye rather than for the tongue and ear and has to be read before it can be fully comprehended. Therefore it has its obvious limitations. Furthermore, the written characters are of such a nature that they do not and cannot adapt themselves so readily to new needs or changing circumstances as can spoken Chinese, and hence the writing system of Chinese as a whole is quite conservative and detached from the swiftly changing experiences of the Chinese people. Under such circumstances, a native of Canton finds it extremely difficult to converse with a native of Amoy or Shanghai or Peiping, and vice versa, on account of dialectal difficulties. Just imagine a native of San Francisco being unable to communicate orally with a native of San Diego, California, or Portland, Oregon, or Salt Lake City, Utah, or Phoenix, Arizona, or New York, and you will be able to realize the awkwardness of the situation and the urgent necessity for the Chinese people to have some sort of commonly understood and spoken language.

The Chinese themselves must undoubtedly have long felt the need for such a language. As early as 1911, after the revolution which converted China from a monarchy into a republic, the Chinese Ministry of Education, feeling keenly the need for a common national language for the effective operation of a modern democratic state, took the initiative in launching a movement to unify the spoken languages of the country. It organized a group of language experts and educators to find means of unifying Chinese pronunciation. They devised a group of thirty-nine phonetic alphabets (注音字母, Chùyiñ tzùmŭ) which were later increased to forty and then reduced again to thirty-seven. In 1918 a Preparatory Commission for the Unification of the National Language was appointed by the Ministry. The Commission adopted in the following year the pronunciation of the dialect of Peiping as the standard for the National Language. In April 1920 the Chinese government ordered that the phonetic alphabets be renamed Phonetic

Symbols (注音符號, Chùyiñ fúhaò), and strongly urged all government employees as well as teachers and students of the schools throughout the country to learn and master and promote these symbols as effective means to combat dialectal difficulties and illiteracy. In 1930 the first government decree on the promotion of these symbols was issued on a nation-wide basis by requiring the publishers of popular reading materials and newspapers to print the symbols beside the traditional characters in order that such materials would be self-pronouncing. In 1935 the Ministry of Education made a special appropriation to the Chung Hwa Book Company of Shanghai for the manufacture of four complete sets of character-phonetic types, which were later supplied to Chinese publishing concerns so that all textbooks for primary and mass-education schools would carry the phonetic symbols alongside the traditional characters. In November 1940 the Committee for the Promotion of a Phonetic System, under the auspices of the Ministry of Education, began publishing a folk newspaper once every three days for the benefit of school children and the semi-illiterate masses who had mastered the phonetic symbols. The paper carried news of the war in China as well as world news and other items of vital interest.

While the Chinese government was launching the movement to unify pronunciation, a group of farsighted intellectual leaders, headed by Dr. Hu Shih and others, in 1917 started the Literary Revolution, a movement advocating the use of the vernacular language, that is, Mandarin, as a new medium of literary expression. They urged that the conservative, artificial, and stereotyped literary language be relegated to the realm of dead languages and that the modern, realistic, and living vernacular, China's Kuóyŭ or National Language, be substituted. At first they ran into very strong opposition, but it gradually lessened in intensity and severity. Before very long the movement found enthusiastic followers, and with the support of the Ministry of Education, which was already pushing with vigor the Unification of the National Language Movement, new textbooks written in Mandarin were ordered for China's school children. New plays, new novels and short stories, new poetry, and scientific treatises were written in the new language.

The leaders chose Mandarin as the basis of the new National Language because it was the most widely spoken dialect of China. Disregarding the slight differences in pronunciation, vocabulary, and grammar among its three main varieties, Mandarin is spoken in approximately three-fourths of the territory of China proper. It is the only Chinese dialect that has produced an extensive literature of genuine artistic value, literary perfection, and popular appeal. It is the language of China's great novelists and dramatists. This body of literature, it is true, was once frowned upon by scholars and literary critics because it was written not in the traditional literary language, which for centuries was the only accepted norm in the eyes of the Chinese literati, but in the living language of the Chinese people. Since the Literary Revolution, however, both the novel and the drama have been restored to their rightful places in the Chinese literary pantheon, and they are now regarded as two of the most important integral parts of China's literary achievement.

Despite the fact that the pronunciation of the Peiping dialect has been adopted as the criterion for China's new National Language, the Peiping dialect must not be considered identical with the latter. Kuóyǔ is different from the dialect of Peiping in that it has, according to the Preparatory Commission for the Unification of the National Language, tried to be a sort of common linguistic meeting ground for every Chinese and has avoided the extreme colloquialism of any given region. It is true that up to now, in those parts of China where the local dialects—different from the Kuóyǔ standards of pronunciation, vocabulary, and grammar—are still spoken universally, the teaching of the National Language in the schools seems to be just another subject in the curriculum, and there is no indication as yet that the local dialects are being supplanted. It is also true that the National Language is hardly used at all by the government and commercial organizations in the transaction of their routine business—owing, no doubt, to the firmly entrenched position of the traditional language. Nevertheless, it may be said that there has been a growing awareness on the part of the Chinese people, regardless of their professional and dialectal interests, of the existence of this common language. It has been successful in leveling off some of the minor dialectal differences within the north China area; and even in regions where an extremely complicated dialect pattern exists, or where the citizenry is clinging tenaciously to the local dialects, Kuóyǔ, when used as a medium of oral communication, is beginning to attract more and more attention. It is certainly true that in the Cantonese dialect area more and more people are learning to speak the National Language. Newspapers throughout China are devoting more space to their vernacular sections, and some are even writing their editorial columns in the vernacular.

For the benefit of the beginning Western student, the basic difference between Kuóyǔ and the traditional language may be pointed out here. Whereas the latter can hardly be spoken as it is written, or fully understood even in dialectal pronunciation, the former can be spoken and understood as it is written, and vice versa. The traditional is noted for its conciseness, frequently leaving out many things which would ordinarily be expressed and thus creating a sort of sketchiness or even ambiguity. Such ambiguous terseness makes it necessary for its readers to fill in the missing elements as they go along in their reading before they can feel reasonably safe in ascertaining the intended meaning. Kuóyǔ, as a rule, tries to avoid such ambiguity and sketchy pithiness by phrasing its expressions with adequate verbal clarity and by adhering to a more or less fixed sentence pattern, so that a sentence written in it can actually be read aloud and understood by its hearers. It is true that both literary Chinese and Kuóyǔ depend largely on word order for indicating the functions of words in a sentence as well as the relationships between them, but there is a much stronger and more regular tendency in Kuóyǔ to use auxiliary or elucidating words as guiding marks for the same purpose than in literary Chinese.

X. RECENT LANGUAGE REFORMS

Following closely the movements to unify the National Language and to champion the vernacular language as a new medium of literary and scientific expression was a series of attempts to reform written Chinese. The leaders of these language reform movements all felt that the Chinese language as they themselves had learned it was too difficult and time-consuming and that something had to be done to the language before the Chinese masses could acquire enough of it to meet their daily minimum needs. They further argued that it would take a person years and years of studying the many thousands of characters and the many complicated rules regarding usage before he could be efficient in the language, and that since this was the case, it was small wonder China's rate of illiteracy was frightfully high. They came to the conclusion that the Chinese language system as a whole should be radically modified and made practical so that it could be placed within the grasp and understanding of the average Chinese citizen. It was with such a hope in mind that they proceeded with their reforms.

One type of reform strongly advocated the use of phonetic symbols as an aid to enable the illiterate to read. The sole function of these symbols, as has already been pointed out, is phonetic, and in so far as they are used as a guide to correct pronunciation in accordance with the standard of Kuóyǔ, they are only helpful to those who have not yet acquired such a knowledge. They cannot possibly add anything to the task of making the Chinese language system simpler or more readily accessible to the masses. But the leaders of this movement believed that the sole reason why an average illiterate adult could not read was that he did not know the pronunciation for the characters and that if, with the aid of these symbols, he could be enabled to get their proper pronunciation, it would be relatively easy for him to identify the characters with the spoken words for which they stood. However, the end result of this movement did not entirely tally with the fervent expectations of its leaders.

Other reformers advocated the alphabetization of the Chinese language. Those who supported this movement believed that the Chinese ideographic writing was simply a great barrier that should be done away with completely, that it was mainly responsible for China's high rate of illiteracy, and that it should be replaced by an alphabetical writing system which would be much easier for the illiterate masses to master.

The use of Latin alphabets for the transcription of Chinese sounds has had a lengthy history dating back to the year 1598, when Matteo Ricci, a Jesuit missionary to China, worked out the first systematic form of spelling for the then current Mandarin sounds on the basis of the pronunciation of his native language. From then on there were other romanization systems worked out by others in the light of the needs of other Western languages—French, English, German, Russian, Spanish, etc. The most widely used system among English-speaking peoples is that designed by Sir Thomas Wade (1818–95), who served for many years as a member of the British Legation in Peking (now Peiping), and then modified by Herbert

A. Giles. The system now is known as the Wade-Giles system, and with certain slight modifications, it is the system used in the romanized portions of this work. In 1928 the Chinese Ministry of Education adopted the Guoyeu Romatzyh (國語羅馬字, Kuóyǔ Lómǎtzù) as a variant form of the phonetic symbols. It was the joint effort of several Chinese scholars, with the greatest share of credit belonging to Dr. Yuen Ren Chao, although he himself very modestly transferred it to Dr. Lin Yutang.[4] Its distinguishing feature is that instead of indicating the tones by the use of diacritical marks or figures, it does so by the use of different letters: *mai* (second tone), "to bury"; *mae* (third tone), "to buy"; *may* (fourth tone), "to sell." The effectiveness of tonal spelling as an instrument of teaching has been amply demonstrated by Dr. W. Simon and Dr. Chao himself. Between 1929 and 1931 there was another system of romanization worked out for the same purpose. It was devised mainly by Professor A. Dragunov, primarily for teaching the illiterate Chinese in the Soviet Far East to read and write, and is known as Latinxua (拉丁化, Lātinghuà) or Latinization of the Chinese language. This system uses twenty-four letters of the English alphabet, leaving out "q" and "v," for the transcription of Northern Mandarin sounds, and has no indication of tones, except in a few sporadic cases. The latter feature is generally considered its most serious shortcoming because the basic word-forming elements in Chinese are consonants, vowels, and tones, and if any of these basic elements is left out in any system of romanization meant for Chinese, it can hardly serve the purpose for which it is designed.[5]

A third type of reform advocated the simplification of the Chinese characters. Its leaders felt that many Chinese characters in fairly common use have too many strokes; they would be not only difficult for China's masses to learn and memorize, but time-consuming and effort-wasting for even the educated to write. With this view in mind, they devised a simplified system of writing whereby complicated characters would be written in much simpler forms by reducing their strokes to a practicable minimum. Thus, 學 (hsüeh, "to learn") becomes 孚; 鐵 (t'ieh, "iron") becomes 铁; 無 (wú [literary Chinese], "not to have") becomes 乇; 麗 (lì, "elegant, graceful") becomes 冏; etc. The two specimens of traditional and simplified writing on p. xxvi will give our readers a better idea as to how much time and effort can be saved by the simplified writing system. The specimens are based on a passage from the Confucian classic, *Tà Hsüeh* (*Treatise on Great Learning*).[6]

[4] *Mandarin Primer*, p. 11.

[5] See *Mandarin Primer*, pp. 11-13. See also the informative article, "The Alphabetization of Chinese," by John De Francis, *Journal of the American Oriental Society*, 63-64 (1943), 225-40. Dr. De Francis feels that the indication of tones in romanized Chinese is not as important as it generally is deemed to be on account of the polysyllabicity of spoken Chinese; this feature, and the context, will be just as effective as tones in ruling out ambiguity and confusion in meanings of certain words. He is also in favor of alphabetizing Chinese as the only answer to China's high illiteracy rate.

[6] See *Chientzù lunchí* (簡字論集, *Essays on Simplified Writing*), by Ch'en Kuangyaó (陳光垚) (Shanghai: Commercial Press, 1931), p. 70.

Traditional Writing

大學之道,在明明德,在新民,在止於至
善.知止而后有定,定而后能靜,靜而后能
安,安而后能慮,慮而后能得.

Simplified Writing

大学之道,左明〃德,左亲民,左止于至
善.知止而后有定,〃而后乚静,〃而后乚
安,〃而后乚虑,〃而后乚汤.

(Translation: "What the Great Learning teaches, is—to illustrate
illustrious virtue; to renovate the people; and to rest in the highest excellence.   The point where to rest being known, the object of pursuit is
then determined; and, that being determined, a calm unperturbedness may
be attained to.   To that calmness there will succeed a tranquil repose.   In
that repose there may be careful deliberation, and that deliberation will be
followed by the attainment of the desired end."—James Legge.)

On the problem of recent language reform, mention must be made of
what the Communists in China have been trying to achieve in this direction.[7]
Since its seizure of power on the Chinese mainland in the autumn of 1949,
the Communist regime has been making persistent efforts in language
reform for the realization of three basic goals.   The first goal is the simplification of Chinese written characters by reducing their strokes — populariz-
ing existing abbreviated forms, introducing new simplified component
elements, substituting homophonous characters with fewer strokes, standard-
izing and regularizing abbreviated forms used in ordinary cursive writing,
etc.   The second goal is the adoption of Mandarin as spoken in Peiping as
the standard national spoken language (普通話, p'ūt'unġhuà).   The third
goal is the introduction of a latinized phonetic alphabet which will for
many years to come coexist with the written characters and will be used
primarily for reducing the high rate of illiteracy, speeding up the task of
elementary education, giving the Chinese language a larger degree of
adaptability to scientific research, providing a more effective system of
indexing and classifying documents, etc.

Although it is true that on the basis of their three chief objectives the
Chinese Communists have so far advanced nothing sensationally different

[7] For a more detailed treatment, see the excellent article by Harriet C. Mills,
"Language Reform in China: Some Recent Developments," *The Far Eastern Quarterly,*
XV (1956), 517–40, and *China's Language Reform* by Tao-tai Hsia (New Haven: The
Institute of Far Eastern Languages, Yale University, 1956).

from the suggestions of earlier proponents of language reform, the effect of the persistence and vigor with which they have been imposing their program of language reform on the people, most noticeably as of now in the direction of simplified characters, should not be underestimated. Late in 1955 the Ministry of Education of the Communist government ordered all schools and government agencies connected with education to adopt the simplified characters already promulgated. Since 1956 more and more newspapers and popular magazines, as well as learned journals, have been using the simplified characters, commonly printed in horizontal lines reading from left to right. Although the use of simplified characters is not yet uniform, it seems certain that as soon as enough new fonts of them become available, the "obsolete" characters will disappear altogether from Communist Chinese publications.

It is impossible to predict what the Communists will do next to the Chinese language in the name of reform. As for how successful and satisfactory their present measures will turn out to be, only time can tell. One thing is certain: some reform is desirable. Traditional Chinese, with its archaisms, its formidable vocabulary, its intricate rules of syntax and grammar, and its resistance to change, can hardly be expected to fulfill the needs of the Chinese people for a practical and living language. Yet this does not necessarily mean that China's great cultural records of the past have to be forgotten or despised. It is earnestly hoped that any future language reform in China will not purposely ignore or destroy the country's colorful cultural heritage, but will do everything possible to perpetuate this heritage in the collective memory of the Chinese people.

PRONUNCIATION OF CHINESE
According to the Wade-Giles Romanization System

For the representation of the consonants, vowels, diphthongs, and triphthongs of Peiping Mandarin, the Wade-Giles system of romanization uses twenty-one letters of the English alphabet, plus a German ü, a circumflexed ê, and a buzzing ŭ—twenty-four letters in all. It also uses an apostrophelike sign ' after certain letters and combinations of letters to indicate aspiration. The five English letters not used at all in the system are b, d, q, v, and x. Four letters, g, r, z, and u, are never used initially. The four tones are indicated by the use of superior Arabic numerals, $^1, ^2, ^3, ^4$, which are placed immediately after each syllable. It is well to bear in mind that not all of the English letters used in the system retain their English phonetic values. Some of them do, others do not.

In this book the diacritical marks ^ and ˘ over the letters e and u, respectively, have been omitted and the initial consonant combination "ss" is merged with "sz" for obvious orthographical and phonetic reasons. The Arabic numerals are replaced by tone marks ¯, ´, ˘, `, which, instead of being placed immediately after a syllable, are placed directly over the last letters of syllables, whatever they are, depending upon the tones of the syllables in question. A syllable in the neutral tone has no tone mark over it at all.

The three constituents of a basic Chinese syllable are the initial, or beginning sound, the final, or remainder of the syllable, and a tone, or musical quality in which the entire syllable is to be uttered. The number of initials and finals in Peiping Mandarin is relatively small. The student is strongly urged, therefore, to master them as soon as possible. Before listing the initials one by one, we may group them, by the various ways in which they are articulated, into six different categories: (1) Labials: f, m, p, p'; (2) Dental stops, nasal, and lateral: t, t', n, l; (3) Dental sibilants: ts, ts', tz, tz', s, sz; (4) Retroflexes: ch, ch', sh (never before i or ü), j; (5) Palatals: ch, ch', hs (only before i or ü); (6) Gutturals: k, k', h. Note that the retroflexes are articulated by having the tip of the tongue curled back until it touches the back of the alveolus and by eliminating lip action.

In the following table are listed all the initials and finals of Peiping Mandarin:

INITIALS

ch (before i or ü), as " j " (less the voiced effect) in " jeer."

ch' (before i or ü), as " ch " (but stronger) in " cheese."

ch (before a, e, o, or u), as " dr " (less the voiced effect) in " draw " (with tongue curled far back and without lip action).

ch' (before a, e, o, or u), as " tr " (but stronger) in " trawl " (with tongue curled far back and without lip action).

f, as " f " in " fee."

h, as "ch" in German "ach." Note that "h" is velar, not glottal as in English.

hs, as "sh" (but slightly more front) in "sheen."

j, as "r" in American pronunciation of "run" (with tongue curled far back and without lip action).

k, as "k" in American pronunciation of "sky."

k', as "k" (but stronger) in "Kansas."

l, as "l" in "late."

m, as "m" in "mad."

n, as "n" in "now."

p, as "p" in American pronunciation of "spray."

p', as "p" (but stronger) in "power."

s, as "s" (but more front) in "sister."

sh (before a, e, ih, o, or u), as "sh" in "shall" (with tongue curled far back and without lip action).

sz (only before ŭ, spelled "u" in this book) has the same value as "s."

t, as "t" in American pronunciation of "stem."

t', as "t" (but stronger) in "time."

ts (before a, e, o, or u), as "dz" in "adz."

ts' (before a, e, o, or u), as "ts" (but stronger) in "seats."

tz (before ŭ, spelled "u" in this book), has same value as "ts."

tz' (before ŭ, spelled "u" in this book), has same value as "ts'."

w, as "w" in "want."

y, as "y" in "yonder."

FINALS

a, as "a" in "father."

ai, as "ai" in "aisle."

an, as "a" and "n" in "barn."

ang, as "a" and "ng" in "darning."

ao, as "ow" in "how."

e (spelled ê originally), as "u" (but longer) in "us."

ei, as "ei" in "deign."

en, as "en" in "open."

eng, as "ung" in "sung" (but with the lengthened "u" of "us" dominating the sound).

erh, as "er" in "herb."

i, as "i" in "machine."

ia, as "e" and "a" in "he argues."

iang, as "e," "a," and "ng" in "he's darning."

iao, as "e" and "ow" in "the owl."

ieh, as "e" and "e" in "he edits."

ien, as "e" and "en" in "he ends."

ih (only after ch, ch', j, and sh) is like a vocalized "r." The way to pronounce, for example, "shih" is to say "sh" and then immediately say the vocalized "r."

in, as " in " in " machine."

ing, as " ee " and " ng " in " seeing."

iu, as " eu " in " feud."

iung, as " e " and " oo " and " ng " in " he's wooing."

o (after the gutturals k, k', and h, and as a separate syllable in itself) is like " e," but after other consonants it is like " uo."

ou, as " ou " in " soul."

u, as " u " in " rule."

ua, as " oo " and " a " in " too ardent."

uai, as " wo " and " ai " in " two aisles."

uan, as " uan " in " Don Juan."

uang, as " wo," " a," and " ng " in " two darning needles."

uei (only after k, k'), as " o " and " ai " in " to aid."

ui (never after k, k') is like " uei."

un, as " oon " in " noon."

ung, as " oo " and " ng " in " wooing."

uo, as " o " and " o " in " to order " (the last " o " not quite as rounded).

ü, as " ee " in " lee " (articulated with fully rounded lips).

u (spelled originally " ŭ," used only after sz, tz, tz') is used to show the buzzing quality of the initial. The way to pronounce " tzu," for example, is to say " tz " and then immediately vocalize it by keeping the tip of the tongue at the back of the teeth with lips open and retracted.

VOCABULARY CHARACTERS

(Wŏ)
I, me

(Yŭ)
To have; there is, there are

(Nĭ)
You

(Pū)
Not, no

(T'ā)
He, him; she, her; it (See Note 4)

(Meí) Also written 没.
Not, no

(Men)
(Pluralizing suffix for pronouns)

(Yeĥ)
Also, too; still; even

(Te)
(Subordinative particle)

(Jeń)
Man, person, people, human being

(Shiĥ)
To be; correct!

(Shū)
Book

COMPOUNDS

我 的 (Wŏte) My, mine

你 們 (Nĭmen) You [plural]

你 的 (Nĭte) Your, yours

他 們 (T'āmen) They, them

他 的 (T'āte) His, her, hers

我們的 (Wŏmente) Our, ours

我 們 (Wŏmen) We, us

你們的 (Nĭmente) Your, yours

他們的 (T'āmente) Their, theirs

1

READING MATERIAL

1. 我 是 人.	4. 我 沒 有 書.
2. 你 們 也 是 人.	5. 你 也 沒 有 書.
3. 他 有 書.	6. 書 是 我 們 的.

7. 書 不 是 你 們 的.

8. 書 也 不 是 他 們 的.

9. 你 是 不 是 人?	13. 他 有 書 沒 有?
10. 我 是 人.	14. 他 沒 有 書.
11. 書 是 人 不 是?	15. 你 有 書 沒 有?
12. 書 不 是 人.	16. 我 也 沒 有 書.

ROMANIZED TEXT OF READING MATERIAL

1. Wǒ shih jeń.	9. Nǐ shih pushih jeń?
2. Nǐmen yeḥ shih jeń.	10. Wǒ shih jeń.
3. T'ā yǔ shū.	11. Shū shih jeń pushih?
4. Wǒ meí yǔ shū.	12. Shū pū shih jeń.
5. Ní yeḥ meí yǔ shū.	13. T'ā yǔ shū meiyu?
6. Shū shih wǒmente.	14. T'ā meí yǔ shū.
7. Shū pū shih nǐmente.	15. Ní yǔ shū meiyu?
8. Shū yeḥ pū shih t'āmente.	16. Wó yeḥ meí yǔ shū.

NOTES

1. Nouns in Chinese, unlike most nouns in English, do not undergo any change in form to show number. They look alike whether they are used in the singular or plural. Whether a noun is to be understood as being used in the singular or plural sense can usually be figured out on the basis of whether a singular or plural number is used along with it or by the implication in the context. In sentence 1 above, for instance, the singular use of 人 is clearly implied in the context by the singular subject 我, and in sentence 2, the plural use of the same noun, by the plural subject 你們. However, the implication carried in the context is sometimes not altogether clear. For instance, in sentences 3, 6, 7, and 8 above, 書 may be construed either in the singular or plural. Such an indifferent use of nouns with reference to number may puzzle the student especially when the question of translating such sentences into English comes up, since the majority of

nouns in English have to be inflected to show number. Apparently in such Chinese sentences it is the thing named by the noun, not the quantity of it, that is important. It does not make much difference whether the noun is to be rendered into English in the singular or plural form. Very often, even under such circumstances, the situational context will make it clear whether a noun so used is to be construed in the singular or plural.

In this connection it may be pointed out that no article is required for nouns in Chinese and that usually word order will to a large extent determine whether a noun is used with a definite or indefinite reference. When a noun is in the subject position, its reference is usually definite, whereas one in the object position refers to something indefinite. Thus, 人有書 may be rendered into English as "The man has a book," "The man has books," or " The men have books," etc. If the noun in object position is to have a definite reference, then it is usually preceded by a demonstrative or some similar modifier. By relying on the linguistic or situational context, whether a noun is used definitely or otherwise can as a rule be ascertained.

2. Though 們 was originally the pluralizing suffix for pronouns, its function has been extended to a number of nouns denoting persons, such as 朋友們 (p'enǵyumen, "friends"), 學生們 (hsüehshengmen, "students"), 工人們 (kunḡjeńmen, "laborers"), etc. However, the use of 們 to pluralize nouns denoting persons is really unnecessary except possibly when these nouns are used in the plural number in the vocative case. It may be interesting to point out the fact that 們 is used in some places in North China to pluralize "nouns denoting animals and things" as well.[1] Examples of this extended use of 們 can be found in the works of prominent modern Chinese writers.

3. In the dialect of Peiping there are the polite forms 您 (niń) and 他 (t'añ) for the second and third person singular pronouns, respectively. 您 probably comes from 你老人家, "You, an aged person" (hence, a person deserving respect), and 他 is coined by analogy of 您. Both 您 and 他 have no plural form. There is also an inclusive form 咱(偺)們 (tsámen, "we," including the person or persons addressed) for the first person plural. However, since these forms are hardly used at all outside of Peiping, they are not used in this text.

4. 她, "she, her" and 牠(它), "it," may, for the sake of convenience, be pronounced like 他. Their use is optional rather than grammatically necessary, although there is a tendency among modern Chinese writers to use them in their works pretty consistently. For our purpose, use 他 for both "he" and "she" and 他的 for both "his" and "her, hers." "It" and the neuter "they" are ordinarily left out if the sense is clear enough to warrant their omission, or else replaced by the nouns for which they stand. If 他 is used for "it," it is limited only to the objective position, whereas 他 們 is not to be used for the neuter "they" or "them" in any position.

---

[1] C. W. Mateer, *Mandarin Lessons* (Revised Edition; Shanghai, 1908), p. 783.

5. Both 沒 and 不 are negative particles, but they are used differently. Use 沒 to negate the verb 有 and 不 to negate all the other verbs.

6. Note that in an interrogative sentence in Chinese the inverted word order is not used. There are several common ways to ask a question in Chinese. One is to state an idea positively and then repeat it (usually just the main verb) in the negative. The repetition may be placed immediately after the main verb or at the end of the statement. For examples, see sentences 9, 11, 13, and 15 in the Reading Material above. Since in Chinese there is no exact equivalent for the all-purpose words "yes" or "no," the most practical way to answer affirmatively such a question is to repeat the positive elements of the question, and negatively, the negative elements of it. For samples, see sentences 10, 12, 14, and 16 in the Reading Material above.

7. Both 不 and 一 (see Lesson Two) are to be pronounced in the high falling tone as "pù" and "ì," respectively, when they precede a syllable in the high even tone " ˉ ", or high rising tone " ´ ", or low falling-rising tone " ˇ ", but in the high rising tone as "pú" and "í," respectively, when they precede a syllable in the high falling tone " ` ". Thus, 不吃, "not to eat," is to be pronounced as "pù ch'iħ"; 不來, "not to come," as "pù laí"; 不好, "not (to be) good," as "pù haǒ"; but 不大, "not (to be) big," as "pú tà." Similarly, 一天, "one day," is to be pronounced as "ì t'ieñ"; 一年, "one year," as "ì nień"; 一里, "one li" (distance measure roughly equivalent to a third of a mile), as "ì li"; but 一次, "one time, once," as "í tz'ù." When 不 and 一 are used alone, or when they occur at the end of a phrase or statement, they retain their basic high even tone. Since both words have such peculiar tonal behavior, and since they are used so frequently, it is strongly urged that the student familiarize himself with these tonal modifications and be able to handle them properly in any situation. For the sake of ease of identification, however, they are invariably written as "pū" and "ī," respectively, in our romanized text.

ORAL EXERCISES

A. Say the following in Chinese:

1. My; his; our; their?
2. My book; your book; his book?
3. I have books.
4. I don't have books.
5. Do you have books?
6. Men are not books.
7. I am a man.
8. He also is a man.

B. Render the following into English:

1. Wǒmente shū; t'āmente shū.
2. Wǒmen yǔ shū, nǐmen yeh yǔ shū.
3. T'ámen shiħ jeń pushih?
4. T'āmen shiħ jeń.
5. Nǐmen shiħ jeń pushih?
6. Wǒmen yeh shih jeń.
7. Shū pū shiħ nǐte, yeǐ pū shiħ wǒte.
8. Nǐ meí yǔ shū, wó yeh meí yǔ shū.

WRITTEN EXERCISES

A. Transcribe Section B, above, in Chinese.

B. Render the following into English:

1. 你 們 有 書;他 們 也 有 書.
2. 他 們 沒 有 書,我 們 也 沒 有 書.
3. 你 們 有 書 沒 有 ?
4. 我 們 沒 有 書.
5. 他 們 有 沒 有 書 ?
6. 他 們 也 沒 有 書.
7. 你 有 他 的 書 沒 有 ?
8. 我 有 他 的 書.

C. Render the following into Chinese:

1. I have books; you also have books.
2. We do not have books; they also do not have books.
3. I am a man; you also are a man.
4. We have our books; you [plural] have your books.
5. My books are not your books; your books are not my books.
6. My books are mine; their books also are mine.

VOCABULARY CHARACTERS

(Haŏ)
Good, well

(Ī)
A, an, one [*]

(Tà)
Big, large, huge, great

(Liǎng) Also written 两.
Two, a couple of [*]

(Hsiaŏ)
Small, little, tiny

(Sañ)
Three [*]

(Ko) Also written
箇;个.
(Classifier used exten-
sively with nouns
denoting persons and
things. See Note 1.)

(Szù)
Four [*]

(Chiĥ)
(Classifier for animals,
fowls, parts of the
body, boats, etc.)

(Shoŭ)
Hand

(Peň)
(Classifier for books and
documents); root,
origin [*]; this [*]¹

(Ma)
(Interrogative particle);
(suffix of manner)

¹Attention! When a character in the Vocabulary is marked with [*] after its meaning in English, it is to be understood that it is not a free form and is introduced
primarily for forming compounds with other characters. The student is warned against
using such characters singly according to the meaning or meanings given.

6

READING MATERIAL

1. 人 大,書 小.
2. 我 的 書 好,他 的 書 好 不 好?
3. 他 有 好 書 麼?
4. 他 沒 有 好 書.
5. 大 書 是 我 的,小 書 也 是 我 的.
6. 一 個 人 有 兩 隻 手,兩 個 人 有 四 隻 手.
7. 你 有 一 本 好 書,他 有 三 本 好 書.
8. 我 有 四 本 書,兩 本 大 的,兩 本 小 的.
9. 好 書 是 你 的,不 好 的 書 也 是 你 的 麼?
10. 一 本 大 書 是 我 的,一 本 小 書 是 他 的.

ROMANIZED TEXT OF READING MATERIAL

1. Jeń tà, shū hsiaŏ.
2. Wŏte shū haŏ, t'āte shū haŏ puhao?
3. T'ā yú haŏ shū ma?
4. T'ā meí yú haŏ shū.
5. Tà shū shih̄ wŏte, hsiaŏ shū yeh̆ shih̄ wŏte.
6. Īko jeń yú lianğchih̄ shoŭ, lianğko jeń yŭ szùchih̄ shoŭ.
7. Ní yŭ īpeń haŏ shū, t'ā yŭ sañpeń haŏ shū.
8. Wó yŭ szùpeň shū, lianğpeň tà te, lianğpeň hsiaŏ te.
9. Haŏ shū shih̀ nīte, pū haŏ te shū yeh̆ shih̀ nīte ma?
10. Īpeň tà shū shih̀ wŏte, īpeń hsiaŏ shū shih̀ t'āte.

NOTES

1. Chinese nouns possessing individual entity mostly require the use

of a classifier (or "numerative" or "numerary adjunct" as it has been vari-
ously called), which is interposed between the number or demonstrative
and the noun. Some nouns have their own special classifiers while others
do not. "One man" is 一個人, "two hands," 兩隻手, "three books," 三本書,
etc. 個, on account of its extensive use, is regarded as a sort of universal
classifier. That is to say that it is used not only with nouns which do not
have their own classifiers and abstract nouns, such as "problem," "condition," "affair," etc., but also with nouns which have their own classifiers.
The student should as early as possible learn Chinese nouns together with
their proper classifiers, and observe, in particular, the ones with which 個
is most commonly used. A classifier is used before a noun when the
latter is preceded by a numeral or demonstrative.

   2.   In Chinese when an adjective is used predicatively, it absorbs the
function of the copula 是. This fact accounts for the absence of 是 in such
constructions. Sentence 1, above, may be translated into English as "The
man is big; the book is small" or "The men are big; the books are small,"
etc. Adjectives are negated by 不, which immediately precedes them. In
asking a question of the type dealt with in Note 6 of Lesson One, the
repetition involved will affect the adjective since it absorbs the function of
the copula 是, which is left out entirely. When 是 is used together with
a predicate adjective, either the sentence ends with the subordinative particle
的, which means that the entire predicate construction is substantive, or it
is used primarily for the sake of emphasis, contrast, or concession.

   3.   Another way of asking a question in Chinese is to use the interrogative particle 麼 at the end of an indicative statement. For examples,
see sentences 3 and 9, above. Note the absence of any repetition in this
type of question. As a final interrogative particle in a question, 麼 may
also be written 嗎, but for the compound 甚麼, "what?" (see Lesson Three,
below), do not use 嗎 interchangeably with 麼.

   4.   兩 is much more often used as an adjective to mean "two" or "a
couple" in modern Chinese than 二 (erh, "two"), which will be introduced
in Lesson Eleven, and which is used primarily to stand for the numeral
"two." For our present purpose, use 兩 to translate the adjective "two"
unless otherwise noted.

   5.   In sentence 8, above, note its elliptical construction after the first
comma. If written out in full that part of the sentence should have read
兩本書是大的書；兩本書是小的書. It is quite common in Chinese to drop
a noun, if the context is clear enough to justify that, by retaining merely
its classifier to avoid redundancy. So, instead of 兩本書, merely 兩本 will
suffice. For the same reason it is equally common to drop a predicate noun,
if the sense of the sentence is not impaired, by retaining the subordinative
particle 的, which comes before it. (See sentences 6, 7, and 8 in Lesson
One and sentences 5, 9, and 10 above.) Even the copula 是 may frequently
be omitted in this type of construction, as it is in the present case, for
greater word economy.

   6.   Note that the subordinative particle 的 is used with 不好 "not

good, bad, poor," which is treated as a dissyllabic adjective, and which usually requires the use of 的 between itself and the noun modified to avoid possible ambiguity of meaning.

7. For the peculiar tonal behavior of 一, see Note 7 of Lesson One.

ORAL EXERCISES

A. Say the following in Chinese :
1. One hand ; two books ; three men.
2. My hand ; my big hands ; my two big hands.
3. Four big books ; three small books ; two small hands.
4. Have you [any] hands ?
5. Yes, I have hands. I have two hands.
6. Is the man well ?
7. Yes, he is well.
8. The large books are mine.

B. Render the following into English :
1. Wǒmen yǔ shū, nǐmen meí yǔ shū.
2. Nǐmente shū haǒ, t'āmente shū pū haǒ.
3. Nǐmente shoǔ tà puta ?
4. Wǒmente shoǔ tà.
5. T'āmente shū haǒ puhao ?
6. T'āmente shū pū haǒ.
7. Wó yú liangǧchǐh shoǔ, ní yeh́ yú liangǧchǐh shoǔ ma ?
8. Wó yeh́ yú liangǧchǐh shoǔ.

WRITTEN EXERCISES

A. Transcribe Section B, above, in Chinese.

B. Render the following into English :

1. 他 們 的 書 大; 我 們 的 書 小.
2. 大 書 是 他 們 的; 小 書 是 我 們 的.
3. 一 個 人 有 書; 兩 個 沒 有.
4. 好 人 有 好 書 麼 ?
5. 好 人 有 好 書, 也 有 不 好 的 書.
6. 他 們 的 好 書 大 麼 ?
7. 他 們 的 好 書 不 大.
8. 他 們 的 小 書 好, 大 書 也 好.

C. Render the following into Chinese:

1. Are you [plural] well?
2. Yes, we are well; are you well, too?
3. I am well, too.
4. The good book is neither large nor[2] small.
5. My two hands are big; his two hands are small.
6. Your hands are big; are your books big, too?
7. They have three books: one is good; two are poor.
8. One man has two small books; two men have four small books.

[2] Render "neither . . . nor" as "not . . . not . . ."

VOCABULARY CHARACTERS

(Shem̀)
Also written 什.
What? [*]

(Maó)
Hair (on body), fur, feathers; ten cents [*]; (a surname)

(Chè)
This [*]; this thing

(Ch'ien)
Lead (metal)

(Nǎ)
Which [*] Also written 哪.
(Nà)
That [*]; that thing

(Kang)
Steel

(Hsieh)
Some, a little [*]

(Chǐh)
Paper

(Pǐ)
Writing implement

(Chang)
(Classifier for paper, tables, bedding, pictures, etc.); (a surname)

(Chǐh)
(Classifier for writing brushes and similar slender objects)

(Shuí)
Who? whom? anybody

COMPOUNDS

甚 麼 (Shem̀ma) What? Any, anything

一 些 (Īhsieh) Some

這 些 (Chèhsieh) These

這 個 (Chèko) This, this one

那 個 (Nàko) That, that one

那 些 (Nàhsieh) Those

那 些 (Nǎhsieh) Which ones?

那 個 (Nǎko) Which? Which one?

毛 筆 (Maópǐ) Writing brush

鉛 筆 (Ch'ienpǐ) Pencil

鋼 筆 (Kangpǐ) Pen

誰 的 (Shuíte) Whose? Anybody's

11

READING MATERIAL

1. 這是甚麼？這個是甚麼？
2. 這是筆,這個是筆.
3. 那是甚麼？那個是甚麼？
4. 那是紙.那個是紙.
5. 這些是甚麼筆？
6. 這些是毛筆.
7. 那些鉛筆是誰的？
8. 那些鉛筆是我的.
9. 你有兩枝鋼筆,沒有紙.
10. 他有四張紙,沒有鋼筆.
11. 誰有紙,沒有筆？
12. 我有紙,沒有筆.
13. 這本書是我的,這張紙是你的.
14. 這些鉛筆是他的,那些毛筆
也是他的.
15. 這兩本書大,那三本書小.
16. 這個好,那個不好.
17. 是這個不是？是那個不是？
18. 不是這個,也不是那個.
19. 那個是你的？那個是他的？
20. 那些書是我的？那些筆是
他的？

ROMANIZED TEXT OF READING MATERIAL

1. Chè shih shemma? Chèko shih shemma?
2. Chè shih pī. Chèko shih pī.
3. Nà shih shemma? Nàko shih shemma?
4. Nà shih chih. Nàko shih chih.
5. Chèhsieh shih shemma pī?
6. Chèhsieh shih maópī.
7. Nàhsieh ch'ienpī shih shuíte?
8. Nàhsieh ch'ienpī shih wŏte.
9. Ní yú liangchih kanpī, meí yú chih.
10. T'ā yŭ szùchang chih, meí yŭ kanpī.
11. Shuí yú chih, meí yú pī?
12. Wó yú chih, meí yú pī.
13. Chèpen shū shih wŏte, chèchang chih shih nìte.
14. Chèhsieh ch'ienpī shih t'āte, nàhsieh maópí yeh shih t'āte.
15. Chè liangpen shū tà, nà sanpen shū hsiaŏ.
16. Chèko haŏ, nàko pū haŏ.
17. Shih chèko pushih? Shih nàko pushih?
18. Pū shih chèko, yeh pū shih nàko.
19. Năko shih nìte? Năko shih t'āte?
20. Nàhsieh shū shih wŏte? Năhsieh pī shih t'āte?

NOTES

1. A third way to ask a question in Chinese is to use an interrogative pronoun or adjective. Note that the normal, rather than the inverted, word order is used. For examples, see sentences 1, 3, 5, 7, and 11 above.

2. Use the classifier with a noun when the latter is qualified by the demonstrative adjective 這 or 那. The reason for so doing is that the presence of the numeral 一 is clearly implied and understood. However, when a noun is qualified by 這些 or 那些, the use of the classifier becomes optional and common practice leaves it out. For an example, see sentence 14 above. When 這 and 那 are followed by a plural number, they remain singular in form. In sentence 15 above, 這兩本書 means "these two books" and 那三本書 means "those three books."

3. The student will probably notice that sentences 9, 10, 11, and 12 look somewhat queer to him in structure, though their meaning can be easily and clearly grasped. He will feel that judging them as sentences, especially in the light of sentence structure in English, some part of speech is lacking. It may be pointed out here, however, that Chinese sentences as a whole are more informal or fragmentary in structure. For instance, when two nouns, or two verbs, or two adjectives are used together, they do not necessarily have to be joined by a connective particle. Sentence 9 above, if translated literally into English, will read, "He has two pens, [does] not have [any] paper." According to the grammatical requirements

of English, either a semicolon has to be used after "pens" and the understood subject of the second clause, "he," written out after the semicolon, or some sort of coordinating conjunction has to be introduced to link together the two verbs "to have" and "not to have" in the predicate, before the sentence can be considered grammatically acceptable. This is not the case with sentences in Chinese. If the meaning is reasonably clear from the context, even the subject, or the verb, or the object, or some other equally essential part may be left out. This is done frequently not only in colloquial Chinese, but in narrative, descriptive, or expository writings as well. Such a practice must be constantly borne in mind.

4. The interrogative pronoun 誰 is inflected like the personal pronouns, but unlike the latter, it has no plural form.

5. Note that 甚麼 and 誰 may be used as indefinite pronouns, and that when so used, they mean "anything" and "anybody," respectively. When it is used unemphatically in this capacity, 甚麼 becomes neutral in tone in both syllables.

6. 這 or 這個 and 那 or 那個 are the reduced forms of 這一個東西 (tunghsi), "this one thing," and 那一個東西, "that one thing." When these demonstrative pronouns are used as the subject of a copulative verb the meaning of which is to be completed by a predicate noun, it makes no difference whether 這 or 這個, or 那 or 那個 is used for "this" and "that," respectively. However, if they are used as the subject of a copulative verb the meaning of which is to be completed by a predicate adjective, or as the object of a verb, or as the predicate noun of a copulative verb, then only 這個 and 那個 will be used. "This is a book" is 這是書 or 這個是書, and "That is paper" is 那是紙 or 那個是紙; but "This is good, and that is not good" is 這個好, 那個不好, "I want this, and he wants that" is 我要 (yaò) 這個, 他要那個; and "It is this, not that" is 是這個, 不是那個.

這個 and 那個 are used to mean "this one" and "that one," respectively, when the speaker is indifferent to or not interested in the category to which the noun involved belongs. If he is anxious to clarify the category of the noun involved, 個 is to be replaced by the special classifier, whatever it may be. For instance, if the noun involved is 書, then 本 should take the place of 個. "I have this one [book], not that one" is 我有這本, 沒有那本.

7. The grammatical subject "it" is not expressed in Chinese. "Is it they?" becomes 是他們麼 or 是他們不是? Cf. Note 4, Lesson One.

ORAL EXERCISES

A. Say the following in Chinese:

1. One writing brush; two pencils; three sheets of paper; four pens.
2. This pen; that pencil; these writing brushes; those books.
3. These two men; those four sheets of paper.
4. Whose hands? whose books? whose paper?
5. What are these?
6. These are books.

7. What are those?
8. Those are pens.
9. Whose hands are these?
10. Those are their hands.

B. Render the following into English:

1. Ní yŭ sheḿma?
2. Wŏ meí yŭ shemma.
3. T'ā shih̀ shuí?
4. Chè shih̀ shuíte ch'ieñpī?
5. Nàhsieh maópí haŏ ma?
6. Shuí yŭ shū, meí yú pī?
7. T'ā yŭ shū, meí yú pī.
8. Nàhsieh kanḡpī shih̀ wŏte, pū shih̀ t'āte.
9. Chèko tà puta? Nàko hsiaŏ puhsiao?
10. Chèko pū tà, nàko pū hsiaŏ.

WRITTEN EXERCISES

A. Transcribe Section B, above, in Chinese.

B. Render the following into English:

1. 他有甚麼筆?

2. 他沒有甚麼筆.

3. 那些不好的書是他們的麼?

4. 不是他們的, 是你們的.

5. 誰沒有紙?

6. 他沒有.

7. 那三枝鉛筆是誰的? 是你的麼?

8. 是他的, 不是我的.

9. 這是甚麼? 是鋼筆不是?

10. 是鉛筆, 不是鋼筆.

C. Render the following into Chinese:

1. I have two good writing brushes and also have two poor ones.
2. Those books are not mine; they are his.
3. Whose paper do you have?

   4. I do not have anybody's paper.
   5. These two pencils are good ; are those two also good ?
   6. One is good and one is not good.
   7. Those three big books are good : one is mine ; one is yours ; one is his.
   8. These people have good books; and they have good writing brushes, too.
   9. Is it you [plural] ? Is it they ?
   10. It is we, not they.

VOCABULARY CHARACTERS

(Tsaì)
To be present; to be in, on, at

(Lǐ)
Also written 裡.
Inside [*]

(Hěn)
Very, quite

(Shuō)
To speak, to talk, to say

(Chūng)
Middle [*]

(Kuó)
Country, nation, state, kingdom

(Meǐ)
Beautiful, pretty;
(for transliterating similar sounds)

(Huì)
To know how, to be able, can; to meet; to be likely; meeting, society, association

(Mínǵ)
To understand [*]; bright, clear [*]; dawn [*]

(Paí)
White; plain [*]; vain;
(a surname)

(Huà)
Spoken words, spoken language; dialect [*]

(K'aǹ)
To look at; to consider

COMPOUNDS

明白 (Mínǵpai) To understand

這裏 (Chèli) Here

那裏 (Nàli) There

那裏 (Nǎli) Where?

中國 (Chūnḡkuo) China (Middle Kingdom)

中國紙 (Chūnḡkuo-chiȟ) Chinese paper

中國人 (Chūnḡkuo-jeń) The Chinese people; a Chinese person

中國書 (Chūnḡkuo-shū) Chinese book

中國筆 (Chūnḡkuo-pǐ) Chinese writing brush

17

中國話 (Chungkuo-huà) The Chinese spoken language

看 書 (K'an-shū) To read (a book silently)

説 話 (Shuō-huà) To speak, to talk

美 國 (Meĭkuo) The United States of America, America

美國人 (Meĭkuo-jén) The American people ; an American

美國書 (Meĭkuo-shū) An American book

美國筆 (Meĭkuo-pĭ) An American pen

美國紙 (Meĭkuo-chiĥ) American paper

美國話 (Meĭkuo-huà) The American (spoken) language

好 看 (Haŏk'àn) Good looking, pretty

好 説 (Haŏshuō) Good to speak, say, etc.

READING MATERIAL

1. 那 裏 有 中 國 書,這 裏 沒 有 中 國 書.

2. 中 國 人 説 中 國 話,美 國 人 説 美 國 話.

3. 他 的 中 國 筆 在 那 裏? 他 的 中 國 筆 在 這 裏.

4. 我 會 説 話,你 會 不 會?

5. 那 些 人 看 書,這 些 人 不 看 書.

6. 我 説 中 國 話,你 們 明 白 不 明 白?

7. 你 説 中 國 話,我 們 不 很 明 白.

8. 他 的 手 裏 有 書,你 的 手 裏 有 紙.

9. 你 在 這 裏 看 書,我 在 這 裏 看 你 看 書.

10. 這 些 大 書 很 美,那 些 大 書 也 很 美.

11. 我 的 書 很 好 看, 你 的 書 很 不
好 看.

12. 中 國 人 不 會 看 美 國 書, 美 國
人 也 不 會 看 中 國 書.

ROMANIZED TEXT OF READING MATERIAL

1. Nàli yŭ Chunḡkuo-shū, chèli meí yŭ Chunḡkuo-shū.
2. Chunḡkuo-jeń shuō Chunḡkuo-huà, Meĭkuo-jeń shuō Meĭkuo-huà.
3. T'āte Chunḡkuo-pĭ tsaì năli? T'āte Chunḡkuo-pĭ tsaì chèli.
4. Wŏ huì shuō-huà, nĭ huì puhui?
5. Nàhsieh jeń k'aǹ-shū, chèhsieh jeń pū k'aǹ-shū.
6. Wŏ shuō Chunḡkuo-huà, nĭmen minḡpai pumingpai?
7. Nĭ shuō Chunḡkuo-huà, wŏmen pū heň minḡpai.
8. T'āte shoúli yŭ shū, nĭte shoúli yú chiň.
9. Nĭ tsaì chèli k'aǹ-shū, wŏ tsaì chèli k'aǹ ni k'aǹ-shū.
10. Chèhsieh tà shū heń meĭ, nàhsieh tà shū yeň heń meĭ.
11. Wŏte shū heń haŏk'aǹ, nĭte shū heň pū haŏk'aǹ.
12. Chunḡkuo-jeń pū huì k'aǹ Meĭkuo-shū, Meĭkuo-jeń yeň pū huì k'aǹ Chunḡkuo-shū.

NOTES

1. Observe very carefully the difference in tone when 那 is used interrogatively.

2. The basic difference in meaning between 在 and 有 should be distinguished. 在 denotes presence, whereas 有 indicates possession or availability. "The people are here" is to be rendered into Chinese as 人在這裏 and "There are people here" as 這裏有人. Use 在 whenever "to be" is used to denote presence, and 有 whenever "to have" or "there is" or "there are" is used to indicate possession or availability.

3. It may be pointed out that whereas in English "there is" or "there are" is commonly used to begin a sentence with in order to indicate availability, such is not the common practice in Chinese. Take the sentence "There are people here" as an illustration. Instead of saying 有人在這裏, which is a literal and understandable translation, Chinese prefers to alter the construction of the sentence so that 有, by analogy of the construction used to indicate possession, such as 我有書, "I have books," follows the subject. The result is 這裏有人, "This place [here] has people." Note how 這裏, "here," an adverb in the English sentence, has been converted into a noun used nominatively in the Chinese.

4. The verb "to be" is not to be always rendered into Chinese by 是. When it is used as a copula linking two nouns which equate with each other,

it is correct to use 是. For instance, "He is a good man" may be rendered as 他是好人, or "This is a book," as 這是書. But when "to be" is used to denote presence, an attribute, or a state of mind, 是 may not be used. 在 is used to denote presence (see Note 2 above), while for denoting an attribute or state of mind no copula is required, since all adjectives used predicatively absorb the function of it (see Note 2, Lesson Two).

5. Many verb compounds in Chinese, such as 說話, 看書, etc., are formed by a verb plus an object which is necessary to complete the action expressed by the verb. Whereas in English it is possible to use a verb such as "speak" or "read" in isolated sentences intransitively, it is impossible to do so in Chinese, which demands the inclusion of the object. For "he speaks," we will have to say 他說話, "He speaks words," and for "You cannot read" [if by "read" it is meant to read a book], 你不會看書 [You cannot read books].

6. Western proper names may be rendered into Chinese usually by one of two processes, namely, translation and transliteration. The former calls for the rendering of the basic idea, if there is any, of the original into Chinese; the latter is an attempt to approximate the syllable or syllables of the original by the use of Chinese characters having somewhat similar sounds and it is resorted to when either the original has no meaning to be translated or its meaning is such that it defies translation. With these two processes in mind, the student can study the Western proper names introduced in subsequent lessons with a view to seeing which process has been used in rendering them into Chinese. As to 美國 being the Chinese equivalent of "U.S.A.," it is a shortened, and hence conversationally preferred, form of 美利堅合眾國 (meīlichieñ hóchung̀kuó), "The United States of America," which is the "official" name.

ORAL EXERCISES

A. Say the following in Chinese:
1. I speak; he speaks; you also speak.
2. I read [books]; you read; he also reads.
3. What does he say?
4. What do you read?
5. Where is he? He is here.
6. Where are you? I am here, too.
7. Is she pretty?
8. She is very pretty.
9. Do you understand? Don't you understand?
10. I am a Chinese; he also is a Chinese.
11. He speaks Chinese; you don't speak Chinese.
12. Do they have Chinese books?
13. They don't; they have American books.
14. There is a Chinese writing brush here.
15. Whose is the pretty American pen? It is mine.

B. Render the following into English:

1. Nǎli yǔ shū?
2. Chèli yǔ shū.
3. Nàhsieh shih̀ sheḿma shū?
4. Nàhsieh shih̀ Meǐkuo-shū.
5. Nǐ huì shuō Chunḡkuo-huà puhui?
6. Wǒ huì shuō Chunḡkuo-huà.
7. Meǐkuo-huà haǒshuō puhaoshuo?
8. Meǐkuo-huà heń haǒshuō.
9. T'āmente Chunḡkuo-shū tsaì chèli putsai?
10. T'āmente Chunḡkuo-shū pū tsaì chèli, tsaì nàli.

WRITTEN EXERCISES

A. Transcribe Section B, above, in Chinese.

B. Render the following into English:

1. 中國人說中國話;美國人說美國話.

2. 你們說美國話,我們不明白.

3. 中國人有中國筆;美國人沒有中國筆.

4. 他會看中國書,不很會說中國話.

5. 美國在那裏? 美國在這裏.

6. 你明白他說甚麼不明白?

7. 這兩本書,那一本好看?

8. 他們的手裏有甚麼?

9. 這些人會說甚麼話?

10. 那些美國人在那裏看甚麼?

C. Render the following into Chinese:

1. This Chinese can speak American; that American can speak Chinese.
2. He says those American books are very good to read.

3. They speak Chinese : I cannot understand what they say.
4. The Chinese are in China ; the Americans are in America.
5. There is a very pretty book in his hand.
6. China is very big ; America, too, is very big.
7. China has people ; America, too, has people.
8. Some Chinese speak American ; some Americans, too, speak Chinese.
9. There is no Chinese here ; there is no American there.
10. Can those Chinese read American books? No, they cannot.

Lesson FIVE

A Review Lesson

CHARACTERS

You have learned the following characters from the previous four lessons. They are grouped here for your convenience in reviewing them according to the number of strokes they have. Do you know how they are properly written? Do you know how they are pronounced? Can you tell readily what they mean? Can you write them from memory? Review them carefully and thoroughly until you feel reasonably sure that you can answer all the questions above positively.

Number of Strokes	Characters	Pronunciation and Tone	Meaning	Lesson Reference
One	一	Ī	A, an, one	2
Two	人	Jeń	Man, person, people, human being	1
Three	也	Yeh̆	Also, too; still; even	1
	大	Tà	Big, large, huge, great	2
	小	Hsiaŏ	Small, little, tiny	2
	三	Sañ	Three	2
Four	不	Pū	Not, no	1
	手	Shoŭ	Hand	2
	毛	Maó	Hair, fur, feathers; ten cents; (Chinese surname)	3
	中	Chunḡ	Middle	4
Five	他	T'ā	He, him; she, her; it	1
	本	Peň	(Classifier for books and documents); origin, root; this	2
	四	Szù	Four	2
	白	Paí	White, plain; vain; (a surname)	4
Six	有	Yŭ	To have; there is, there are	1

Number of Strokes	Characters	Pronunciation and Tone	Meaning	Lesson Reference
Six	好	Haǒ	Good, well	2
	在	Tsaì	To be present	4
Seven	我	Wǒ	I, me	1
	你	Nǐ	You	1
	沒	Meí	Not, no	1
	那	Nà	That thing; that	3
	那	Nǎ	Which?	3
Eight	的	Te	(Subordinating particle)	1
	兩	Liǎng	Two, a couple of	2
	些	Hsieh̄	Some, a little	3
	枝	Chih̄	(Classifier for writing brushes and similar slender objects)	3
	明	Miń	To understand; bright, clear; dawn	4
Nine	是	Shih̀	To be; correct!	1
	甚	Sheḿ	What?	3
	很	Heň	Very, quite	4
	美	Meǐ	Pretty; (for transliterating similar sounds)	4
	看	K'aǹ	To look at; to consider	4
Ten	們	Men	(Pluralizing suffix for pronouns)	1
	書	Shū	Book	1
	個	Ko	(Classifier used extensively with nouns denoting persons and things)	2
	隻	Chih̄	(Classifier for animals, fowls, parts of the body, boats, etc.)	2
Eleven	這	Chè	This thing; this	3

Number of Strokes	Charac- ters	Pronuncia- tion and Tone	Meaning	Lesson Reference
Eleven	張	Chāng	(Classifier for paper, tables, bed- ding, pictures, etc.); (a surname)	3
	紙	Chǐh	Paper	3
	國	Kuó	Country, nation, state, kingdom	4
Twelve	筆	Pǐ	Writing implement	3
Thirteen	鉛	Ch'ien	Lead	3
	裏	Lǐ	Inside	4
	會	Huì	To know how; to be able, can; to meet; to be likely; meeting, society, association	4
	話	Huà	Spoken words; spoken language, dialect	4
Fourteen	麼	Ma	(Interrogative particle); (suffix of manner)	2
	說	Shuō	To speak, to talk, to say	4
Fifteen	誰	Shuí	Who? whom? anybody	3
Sixteen	鋼	Kāng	Steel	3

ORAL DRILL

A. Say the following in Chinese:

What?	Where?
Who?	Whose?
There	Here
Our	Their
Which pen?	Which person?
Which hand?	Which pencil?
Your [plural]	One book
Two men	Four Chinese writing brushes
Three hands	These Chinese
Those Americans	These two Chinese books
Those three American pens	Three pieces of paper
Is there?	Isn't there?
Is it good?	Isn't it good?

Is it big?	Is it pretty?
Do you know how?	Don't you know how?
Do you understand?	Don't you understand?
Do you have?	Don't you have?
I don't have	I don't understand
I also am not	I also don't have
I also don't look at	They are not here.

B. Answer the following in Chinese:

1. Ní haŏ ma?
2. Ní yŭ shū meiyu?
3. Shih t'āmen pushih?
4. T'āmen yŭ meiyu?
5. Nimen shih Meĭkuo-jeń ma?
6. T'āmen mińgpai wo shuō sheńma pumingpai?
7. Nàhsieh shih sheńma jeń?
8. Nĭmen huì shuō sheńma huà?
9. Wŏte shoúli yŭ sheńma?
10. Shuí huì k'aǹ Chunğkuo-shū?

WRITING DRILL

A. Transcribe the following in Chinese. If possible, have each of the following orally delivered before transcribing.

1. Wó yú shoŭ, yeh́ yŭ shū.
2. Wŏmente shū haŏ, nĭmente shū yeh́ haŏ.
3. Nàhsieh Meĭkuo-jeńte shoŭ tà puta?
4. Heń tà, t'āmente shū yeh́ heň tà.
5. Nimente kanğpí hsiaŏ, wŏmente ch'ieńpĭ pū hsiaŏ.
6. T'āmen pū huì shuō Chunğkuo-huà, nĭmen huì puhui?
7. T'ā k'aǹ-shū, nĭ k'aǹ puk'an?
8. T'ā huì shuō-huà, nĭ huì puhui?
9. Nĭ shuō t'amen meĭ pumei?
10. Wŏ shuō t'amen heń meĭ, nĭmen yeh́ heń meĭ.

B. Render what you have transcribed from above into English.

C. Render the following into Chinese:

We are human beings. You [plural] also are human beings. We are Americans. You are Chinese. We speak American, read American books, and have American pens. We also have American paper. You speak Chinese, read Chinese books, and have Chinese writing brushes. You also have Chinese paper. We do not quite know how to speak Chinese and to read Chinese books. You do not quite know how to speak American and read American books. You speak Chinese, and we do not quite understand. We speak American; do you understand?

VOCABULARY CHARACTERS

(Shaǹg)
On, above, up [*]; to ascend

(Hsià)
Below, down, under [*]; to descend

(Waì)
Outside [*]

(Sŏ)
(Classifier for buildings); that which [*]

(Tzŭ)
Son, child [*]
(Tzu)
(Noun suffix)

(Faǵ)
House, building [*]

(Ch'ień)
Front; before [*]

(Hoù)
Rear; after [*]

(T'oú)
Head; first; (classifier for some animals); (noun suffix)

(Tĭ)
Bottom [*]

(Pă)
To grasp, to hold in the hand [*]; (classifier for chairs, knives, fans, etc.)

(Chō)
Also written 桌.
Table [*]

(Ĭ)
Chair [*]

COMPOUNDS

上頭 (Shaǹgt'ou) Upper surface, top, above

底下 (Tĭhsia) Underneath, below, following

外頭 (Waìt'ou) Outside

裏頭 (Lĭt'ou) Inside

前頭 (Ch'ieńt'ou) Front

後頭 (Hoùt'ou) Rear, back

房子 (Faǵtzu) House, building

棹子 (Chōtzu) Table

書棹子 (Shū-chōtzu) Desk

椅子 (Ĭtzu) Chair

READING MATERIAL

1. 這 是 一 所 房 子, 那 也 是 一 所
房 子 不 是?
2. 不 是, 那 是 一 張 棹 子.
3. 棹 子 前 頭 的 是 甚 麼?
4. 棹 子 前 頭 的 是 椅 子.
5. 那 把 椅 子 是 我 們 的 不 是?
6. 是 我 們 的, 你 說 美 不 美?
7. 很 美, 棹 子 也 很 美.
8. 房 子 裏 頭 有 人, 有 棹 子, 也 有
椅 子.
9. 棹 子 上 頭 有 甚 麼?
10. 棹 子 上 頭 有 書, 有 筆, 也 有 紙.
11. 椅 子 後 頭 有 中 國 筆, 底 下 沒
有 中 國 筆.
12. 房 子 裏 頭 有 人, 外 頭 沒 有 人.

ROMANIZED TEXT OF READING MATERIAL

1. Chè shih īsŏ faŋtzu, nà yeh shih īsŏ faŋtzu pushih?
2. Pū shih, nà shih īchaŋ chōtzu.
3. Chōtzu ch'ieńt'ou te shih sheḿma?
4. Chōtzu ch'ieńt'ou te shih ītzu.
5. Nàpá ītzu shih wŏmente pushih?
6. Shih wŏmente, nĭ shuō meĭ pumei?
7. Heń meĭ, chōtzu yeh heń meĭ.
8. Faŋtzu lit'ou yŭ jeń, yŭ chōtzu, yeh yú ītzu.
9. Chōtzu shaŋt'ou yŭ sheḿma?
10. Chōtzu shaŋt'ou yŭ shū, yú pī, yeh yú chih.
11. Ĭtzu hoùt'ou yŭ Chuŋkuo-pī, tĭhsia meí yŭ Chuŋkuo-pī.
12. Faŋtzu lit'ou yŭ jeń, waìt'ou meí yŭ jeń.

NOTES

1. Words denoting position, location, and direction are used postpositively in Chinese, that is, after the noun to which they are related. "On the table" becomes 桌子上頭, "under the chair," 椅子底下, "in the house," 房子裏頭, etc. This particular usage is quite unlike that of English and must therefore be always borne in mind. In the later lessons Chinese words belonging to the same category should be similarly dealt with. Note that 裏頭 and 上頭 when joined to a noun become neutral in tone in both of their syllables. Thus, 裏頭有人 is to be pronounced as "Lǐt'ou yǔ jeń," but 房子裏頭有人 is to be pronounced "Fang̊tzu lit'ou yǔ jeń." However, usually this does not apply to 前頭 or 後頭.

2. 子, which means "son" or "child," is often used in modern Chinese as a sort of diminutive noun suffix to imply smallness either actual or imputed in token of affection, but not necessarily always so. When so used it is always neutral in tone. There are other similarly used noun suffixes which will be introduced in the later lessons. When used with monosyllabic nouns, these suffixes will transform them into dissyllabic words. In spoken Chinese such compounds are less likely to be misunderstood for something else or to cause confusion in meaning between homophonous words.

3. 頭 as a suffix is added to a great number of nouns in Chinese. Apparently it was at first attached to nouns denoting objects possessing a head, or bulk resembling a head. Then in the course of time the practice of using it as a noun suffix became so common that it was extended to other nouns not within those categories. Thus it is now possible to have dissyllabic words such as 裏頭, 上頭, 前頭, 後頭, etc.

ORAL EXERCISES

A. Say the following in Chinese:
   1. One table, two chairs, three houses.
   2. One big house, two small chairs, three small desks.
   3. In front of the house; in back of the house.
   4. On my chair; on your desk; under his table.
   5. What [sort of] table is this?
   6. This is a desk.
   7. Whose chairs are these?
   8. Whose are the books on the table?
   9. He is in the house.
   10. There is nobody in back of my house.

B. Render the following into English:
   1. T'ā pū tsaì fang̊tzu lit'ou.
   2. Shuí tsaì waìt'ou?
   3. Nǐ ch'ień t'ou yǔ sheńma?
   4. Ǐtzu shangt'ou yǔ jeń.
   5. Chōtzu tǐhsia yǔ sheńma?
   6. Nà liang̊chang̊ shū-chōtzu shih shuíte?

7. Chè szùpá ïtzu haǒ puhao?
8. T'ā yǔ shū, meí yǔ shū-chōtzu.
9. Shuí tsaì lit'ou k'aǹ-shū?
10. Faṅgtzu lit'ou meí yǔ jeń shuō-huà.

WRITTEN EXERCISES

A. Transcribe Section B, above, in Chinese.

B. Render the following into English:

1. 我 在 你 前 頭, 你 在 我 後 頭.

2. 那 些 人 在 房 子 裏 頭 看 中 國 書.

3. 這 些 不 好 看 的 椅 子 是 他 的,
不 是 我 的.

4. 房 子 外 頭 的 人 是 不 是 美 國 人?

5. 不 是, 他 們 是 中 國 人.

6. 那 把 椅 子 上 頭 的 鋼 筆 是 誰 的?

7. 他 們 有 四 所 房 子: 三 所 大 的;
一 所 小 的.

8. 他 在 那 裏? 他 在 底 下 看 書.

9. 那 本 書 上 頭 有 紙, 底 下 沒 有 紙.

10. 這 張 書 棹 子 好, 那 張 不 好.

C. Render the following into Chinese:

1. I have four books on your desk.
2. He has three chairs in my house.
3. What is there in front of you?
4. My pen is on your Chinese book.
5. There is some Chinese paper under that chair.
6. Who is inside that little house?
7. The people outside can speak Chinese.
8. I read at the back of your house.
9. There are two tables [and] four chairs there.
10. In front of you there are two Chinese.

Lesson *SEVEN*

VOCABULARY CHARACTERS

(Chiñ)
Now, present [*]

(Tsó)
Yesterday [*]

(T'ieñ)
Heaven, sky; day

(Wŭ)
The noon hour (11 a.m. to 1 p.m.) [*]

(Laí)
To come

(Ch'ù)
To go; to remove, to do away with [*]

(Le)
(The perfective suffix; modal particle)

(Taò)
To arrive, to reach, to go to; to (toward); until

(Ts'unǵ)
From

(Chiā)
Home, family

(Ch'enǵ)
City; city wall

(Yaò)
To want; to have to; important [*]; shall, will

COMPOUNDS

今天 (Chiñt'ien) Today

昨天 (Tsót'ien) Yesterday

明天 (Mingt́'ien) Tomorrow

上午 (Shangẁu) Forenoon; morning

下午 (Hsiàwŭ) Afternoon

上來 (Shangĺai) To come up

上去 (Shangch́'ü) To go up

下來 (Hsiàlai) To come down

下去 (Hsiàch'ü) To go down

在家 (Tsaìchiā) To be at home

不要 (Pūyaò) Don't! Mustn't!

今天上午 (Chiñt'ien shangẁu) This morning; this forenoon

今天下午 (Chiñt'ien hsiàwŭ) This afternoon

國家 (Kuóchiā) State; country

31

READING MATERIAL

1. 你今天要到那裏去？
2. 我今天要到他的家裏去．
3. 你的家在那裏？
4. 我的家在城裏．
5. 那個人是從那裏來的？
6. 他是從中國來的．
7. 明天上午你在家不在？
8. 在,我明天上午不到城裏去了．
9. 昨天下午他來了沒有？
10. 他沒來;你去了沒有？
11. 我去了,那裏一個人也沒有．
12. 今天上午到這裏來看你的人,是從那裏來的？
13. 他們是從城裏來的．
14. 那些美國人要甚麼？
15. 他們不要甚麼．
16. 你要看書,不要說話！
17. 不要上去了,他下來了．
18. 我去了,你去不去？
19. 他昨天看的書好不好？ 很好．
20. 我說的話是甚麼話？ 是中國話．

21. 中 國 是 甚 麼? 中 國 是 一 個
國 家.

22. 美 國 是 甚 麼? 美 國 也 是 一
個 國 家.

ROMANIZED TEXT OF READING MATERIAL

1. Nĭ chiñt'ien yaò taò năli ch'ü?
2. Wŏ chiñt'ien yaò taò t'ate chiāli ch'ü.
3. Nĭte chiā tsaì năli?
4. Wŏte chiā tsaì ch'engli.
5. Nàko jeń shih̀ ts'ung năli lai te?
6. T'ā shih̀ ts'ung Chungkuo lai te.
7. Mingt'ien shangwú nĭ tsaì chiā putsai?
8. Tsaì, wŏ mingt'ien shangwú pū taò ch'engli ch'ü le.
9. Tsót'ien hsiàwŭ t'ā laíle meiyu?
10. T'ā meí laí; nĭ ch'ùle meiyu?
11. Wŏ ch'ùle, nàli ĭko jeń yeh̀ meí yŭ.
12. Chiñt'ien shangwú taò chèli lai k'an̄ ni te jeń, shih̀ ts'ung năli lai te?
13. T'āmen shih̀ ts'ung ch'engli lai te.
14. Nàhsieh Meïkuo-jeń yaò shemma?
15. T'āmen pū yaò shemma.
16. Nĭ yaò k'an̄-shū, pūyaò shuō-huà!
17. Pūyaò shangch'ü le, t'ā hsiàlai le.
18. Wŏ ch'ù le, nĭ ch'ù puch'ü?
19. T'ā tsót'ien k'an̄ te shū haŏ puhao? Heń haŏ.
20. Wŏ shuō te huà shih̀ shemma huà? Shih̀ Chungkuo-huà.
21. Chungkuo shih̀ shemma? Chungkuo shih̀ ĭko kuóchiā.
22. Meïkuo shih̀ shemma? Meïkuo yeh̀ shih̀ ĭko kuóchiā.

NOTES

1. Adverbs of time derived originally from nouns, like "today," "yesterday," etc., in English can be placed either before or after the predicate verb. In Chinese all such adverbs precede the predicate verb. It does not matter much, however, whether they precede or follow the subject.

2. When 要 is used as a future auxiliary with a principal verb the action of which has to do with volition or strong desire on the part of the subject, it can be rendered into English as "shall" or "will." When it is used as an auxiliary with a principal verb to show determination or necessity, it has the same effect of "have to; ought to; must" in English. The student will have to distinguish these differences himself from the context.

3. Whenever "to come" or "to go" is followed by an adverb of place serving as the goal of the motion of coming or going in English, such a construction must be rendered into Chinese by the use of 到 or 往 (wǎng, "to proceed toward") and 來 or 去, with the adverbial element placed between them. "To come here" is 到這裏來; "to go there" is 到那裏去; etc. Note the neutral tone of 來 and 去 in such constructions.

4. As a perfective suffix 了 (derived from the verb 了, liǎo, "to complete, to end, to finish") indicates the completion of an action, whether recent or in the past. When so used it follows immediately the verb which it affects: 來了, "came; to have come"; 去了, "went; to have gone." Note that "did not come" or "not to have come" is 沒來 or 沒有來, and "did not go" or "not to have gone" is 沒去 or 沒有去, and that in both cases 了 is left out. The thing to bear in mind is that the positive and negative constructions for indicating a completed action (roughly approximating the simple past and perfect tenses of English) are structurally different. The fact that 了 is dropped from the negative construction is sufficient to establish the fact that it is not a past or perfect tense sign in Chinese. The truth of the matter is that Chinese verbs have no tense at all.

In asking a question of the type of presenting alternatives involving a completed action, care must be exercised that both the positive and negative forms be correctly handled. If the verb in the negative repetition comes at the end of the statement, it is often dropped by retaining 沒有: 他來了沒有, "Did he come? Has he come?"; 他去了沒有, "Did he go? Has he gone?" Of course one can also resort to the use of 麼 in such cases without bothering with the repetitive process: 他來了麼? 他去了麼? A verb referring to the past and taking a quantified object takes as a rule the perfective suffix 了: 我看見了三本書, "I saw three books; I have seen three books."

Very often 了 is used to indicate the completion of an action prior to the beginning of another in the same sentence and resembles the pluperfect or perfect participial constructions. Thus, 他說了話就看書 may be rendered into English as "After he had spoken, he read," or "Having spoken, he read," etc.

As a modal particle 了 occupies the final position in a clause or sentence and may be used in connection with a changed situation to indicate determination (我不去了, "I am not going!" [Before the situation had changed, I thought I could go].), confirmation (昨天沒來的人是你了, "The person who did not come yesterday is you." [All along I thought it was you, but now I am positive it is you.]), command or request (你們不要說話了, "Don't talk!"), hypothetical assertion (要是 ["Should, if," see Note 1, Reading Drill, Lesson Forty], 他來了我就去, "If he came, I would go."), and completed action for the progress of narration (他們回家去了, "They went home.").

When 了 is used as a perfective suffix it precedes the object, quantified or otherwise, of the verb: 他說了話就看書 or 我看見了三所房子, "I saw three houses, I have seen three houses"; but when it is used as a modal particle it follows the object: 他說了話就看書了 or 我看見了三所房子了.

It is possible, however, if the object is not quantified, to say either 我看見了房子了 or simply 我看見房子了, but 我看見了房子 ordinarily is not to be construed as a complete utterance. Compare it with 他看了書 of 他看了書就説話 and the incompleteness of this type of utterance will be obvious.

When the perfective suffix and the modal particle 了 come right next to each other, they are merged together into one: 他回去[了]了 "He has returned, he has gone back."

5. Note that in sentences 5 and 6 above the predicate noun 人 has been left out, and that this very common type of sentence in Chinese, which consists primarily of two nouns equating with each other and linked by a copulative verb, may be loosely used to imply a completed action, which ordinarily requires in English a verb in the past tense or perfect tense to express. The difference in emphasis between 他是從中國來的[人], "He is a person who has come from China," and 他從中國來了, "He came from China," is that the former sentence is more concerned with the subject whereas the latter one is more interested in indicating the completed action expressed by the verb (cf. "He is from China" and "He came from China"). The fact that the person is already at the scene of conversation or his coming from China can already be established at the time of conversation certainly implies that his coming from China is already a thing of the past. Hence, 他是從中國來的 may be rendered into English as "He came from China." However, 的, which is clearly a subordinative particle in this case, should not be regarded as a device for forming the past tense, as has commonly been suggested.

6. In Chinese there is no relative pronoun as such. However, the restrictive functions of the widely used relative pronouns in English can be fulfilled in Chinese by the use of the subordinative particle 的, which indicates the relation of the noun immediately following it to the elements subordinated to the noun itself, as 昨天來的人, "the man who came yesterday"; 不會説中國話的人, "the men who cannot speak Chinese"; 你看了的書, "the book [or books] which you have read"; etc. Observe the basic difference in construction between English and Chinese. In English the relative pronoun invariably stands immediately after its antecedent and heads the entire clause containing it, whereas in Chinese 的 has no antecedent and comes at the very end of the clause but immediately before the noun to which the clause is subordinated. When a relative pronoun is used nonrestrictively it may be rendered into Chinese by the use of the pivotal object-subject, that is, a noun used as the object of a preceding verb and as the subject of a following one, as 我有一本好書在棹子上頭, "I have a good book, which is on the table."

7. 來 and 去 are very often placed after a verb to indicate the direction of action expressed by the latter. Whereas 來 indicates an action moving toward the speaker (hither), 去 indicates one moving away from him (thither). When so used, both 來 and 去 become neutral in tone and form with the verb to which they are appended what we call "directional

compounds," as 上來, "to come up"; 上去, "to go up"; 下來, "to come down"; 下去, "to go down"; etc. Such a directional compound may be appended to yet another action verb to form a longer compound of the same nature, as 拿 (ná), "to hold in the hand" (see Lesson Eight); 上來, "to bring up [here]"; 拿下來, "to bring down [here]"; 拿上去 "to take up [there]"; 拿下去 "to take down [there]"; etc. For other similar compounds of this type, see Lesson Eight. Note that in such compounds only the main action verb retains its own tonal qualities, while the directional elements have all become atonic.

8. A Chinese imperative sentence in the affirmative is formed by the use of a verb either with or without the subject, and in the negative by the use of an additional auxiliary, 不要, which comes before the main verb. "Speak Chinese!" is 説中國話 or 你説中國話, but "Don't speak Chinese!" is 不要説中國話 or 你不要説中國話.

9. It is true that according to the normal word order in Chinese the transitive precedes its object. Not infrequently, however, the object is placed, for the sake of emphasis, in the "exposed" position, preceding the verb and sometimes even the subject, as 中國話我會説, "Chinese I can speak"; 不好的書我不看, "Books that are not good I don't read"; etc. For even greater emphasis, sometimes 也 or 都 (toū, "all, invariably") is used to intensify the verb, as 甚麼書我都看, "I read *any* book"; 一本中國書我也沒有, "I don't have a *single* Chinese book."

10. Adverbs of place usually precede action verbs. Thus, "He goes to the city today" becomes 他今天到城裏去; "He reads here," 他在這裏看書; etc.

ORAL EXERCISES

A. Say the following in Chinese:
1. Tomorrow afternoon; yesterday morning; this afternoon.
2. I want books; I don't want any pencil.
3. Do you want that house? Does he want to read?
4. Are you going?[1] Is he coming?[1]
5. Where are they going?[1]
6. Did you read? Did he speak?
7. Did you come here? Did you go there?
8. He is going[1] to America.
9. Did he go to China?
10. Did they come? Have they gone?
11. He came from the city.
12. Read! Speak! Come! Go!
13. Don't read! Don't speak! Don't come!
14. Don't come here! There isn't anybody here.
15. The man who didn't come yesterday will come tomorrow.

[1] Render it as though the simple verb had been used.

B. Render the following into English:

1. T'ā pū shih ts'ung ch'engli lai te.
2. T'āmen tsót'ien taò Meïkuo ch'ü le.
3. Nĭ yaò k'aǹ-shū puyao?
4. Wǒ pū yaò k'aǹ-shū, wǒ yaò shuō-huà.
5. Wǒ ch'ieńt'ou te fangtzu pū heň tà.
6. Yaò taò ch'engli ch'ü te jeń pū tsaì chèli!
7. T'ā mingt'ien shaǹgwǔ laí pulai?
8. Wǒ tsót'ien meí ch'ù, wǒ mingt'ien ch'ù.
9. Nĭmen mingt'ien laí k'aǹ-shū pulai?
10. Pū shih nĭte shū yeň pū shih wǒte, shih t'āte.

WRITTEN EXERCISES

A. Transcribe Section B, above, in Chinese.

B. Render the following into English:

1. 有書的人不看書;沒有書的人要看書.

2. 昨天上午我看書;下午沒看.

3. 在那裏看書的美國人到中國來了四天.

4. 會上去不會下來的人是誰?

5. 他昨天下午到城裏去了.

6. 那個大城裏頭有很多房子;有些大,有些小.

7. 明天我不來了,你來不來.

8. 在你前頭的桌子好看麽?

9. 說中國話,不要說美國話.

10. 他們今天上午看的書是你的,不是我的.

C. Render the following into Chinese:
1. Whose is the desk in front of two big chairs in your home?
2. It is mine; the two big chairs in back of it are also mine.
3. Who is the person who doesn't understand the Chinese I speak?
4. The person who reads good books is here today.
5. He came from America; I also came from America.
6. Don't come down! He is up there.
7. There isn't a single Chinese in that big house.
8. Have they gone to America? No, they haven't.
9. Don't go there! Those people are in the city today.
10. Come here tomorrow afternoon! He will be home tomorrow.

Lesson EIGHT

VOCABULARY CHARACTERS

 (Tŏ)
Many ; much
(Tó)
How ? How !

 (Keĭ)
To give ; to ; for

 (Shaŏ)
Few ; little

 (T'inḡ)
To listen

 (Chieǹ)
To see, to meet ; to perceive [*]

 (Tsoŭ)
To walk ; to go away

 (Teĭ) Must
(Té) To get ; to obtain ; to be done, to be ready
(Te) (Particle indicating potentiality, capability, or manner in which an action is achieved)

 (Hsieĕ)
To write

 (Tzù)
Written character ; word

 (Ch'ū)
To emerge ; to put forth, to issue

 (Ná)
To hold in the hand

 (Chiǹ)
To enter ; to advance [*]

COMPOUNDS

多少 (Tŏshaŏ) How many? How much?

看見 (K'aǹchien) To see

聽見 (T'inḡchien) To hear

拿來 (Nálai) To bring

拿去 (Nách'ü) To take

出來 (Ch'ūlai) To come out

出去 (Ch'ūch'ü) To go out

進來 (Chiǹlai) To come in

進 去 (Chìnch'ü) To go in

拿進來 (Náchinlai) To bring in

拿進去 (Náchinch'ü) To take in

拿出來 (Nách'ulai) To bring out

拿出去 (Nách'uch'ü) To take out

寫下來 (Hsiehhsialai) To write down

寫出來 (Hsiehch'ulai) To write out

走進來 (Tsoŭchinlai) To come in

走進去 (Tsoŭchinch'ü) To go in

寫 字 (Hsieh-tzù) To write characters)

説出來 (Shuōch'ulai) To speak out ; to utter

走出來 (Tsoŭch'ulai) To come out

走出去 (Tsoŭch'uch'ü) To go out

READING MATERIAL

1. 我 看 得 見 你 的 房 子, 看 不 見 你 的 書.

2. 你 聽 得 見 聽 不 見 那 些 美 國 人 説 中 國 話?

3. 我 出 來, 你 進 去; 他 出 去, 我 進 來.

4. 我 給 你 一 本 中 國 書 好 不 好?

5. 昨 天 他 拿 了 甚 麼 來 給 你 們?

6. 房 子 外 頭 的 人 多, 房 子 裏 頭 的 人 少.

7. 我 看 得 見 很 多 會 説 美 國 話 的 中 國 人.

8. 你 拿 了 我 的 鉛 筆 進 去 給 誰?

9. 你 出 去 拿 一 把 椅 子 進 來 給 我.

10. 他 寫 字 寫 得 很 好.

11. 那 些 中 國 字 寫 得 不 很 好.

12. 你不要説中國話出來給他們聽.

13. 我給他們寫這些中國字出來好不好?

14. 他們有多少美國書？ 他們有很多美國書.

15. 他要走了, 你出來不出來?

16. 他拿了甚麼出來？ 你拿了甚麼進去?

17. 那個中國字你説得出來説不出來?

18. 誰走進來了？ 你看得見看不見?

19. 他説出來了, 你聽不見麼?

20. 他走不出來, 我要進去看看他.

ROMANIZED TEXT OF READING MATERIAL

1. Wŏ k'ańtechień nite fańtzu, k'ańpuchień nite shū.
2. Nĭ t'ińgtechień t'ingpuchien nàhsieh Meĭkuo-jeń shuō Chuńgkuo-huà?
3. Wŏ ch'ūlai, nĭ chińch'ü; t'ā ch'ūch'ü, wŏ chińlai.
4. Wó keí ni īpeň Chuńgkuo-shū haŏ puhao?
5. Tsót'ien t'ā nále sheńma lai keí nimen?
6. Fańtzu waìt'ou te jeń tō, fańtzu lit'ou te jeń shaŏ.
7. Wŏ k'ańtechień heň tō huì shuō Meĭkuo-huà te Chuńgkuo-jeń.
8. Nĭ nále wote ch'ieńpĭ chinch'ü keī shuí?
9. Nĭ ch'ūch'ü ná īpá ītzu chinlai keí wo.
10. T'ā hsieh-tzù hsiehte heń haŏ.
11. Nàhsieh Chuńgkuo-tzù hsiehte pū heń haŏ.
12. Nĭ pūyaò shuō Chuńgkuo-huà ch'ulai keī t'amen t'iń.
13. Wó keī t'amen hsieh chèhsieh Chuńgkuo-tzù ch'ulai haŏ puhao?
14. T'āmen yŭ tōshaó Meĭkuo-shū? T'āmen yú heň tō Meĭkuo-shū.

15. T'ā yaò tsoŭ le, nĭ ch'ūlai puch'ulai?
16. T'ā nále sheḿma ch'ulai? Nĭ nále sheḿma chinch'ü?
17. Nàko Chunḡkuo-tzù nĭ shuōtech'ulai shuopuch'ulai?
18. Shuí tsoŭchinlai le? Nĭ k'aṅtechieṅ k'anpuchien?
19. T'ā shuōch'ulai le, nĭ t'inḡpuchieṅ ma?
20. T'ā tsoŭpuch'ulai, wŏ yaò chiṅch'ü k'aṅk'an t'a.

NOTES

1. The compound 多少 actually offers a choice between two alternatives: "many" or "much" and "few" or "little." When it is used in a direct question it means "how many, how much?"; but when it is used in an indirect question, it may be rendered into English as "[whether] many or few, much or little." When 多 or 少 is used attributively in Chinese it is generally rounded out by the insertion of 很 before it, as for "I have many houses" the Chinese will usually say 我有很多房子. See also sentence 7 of Reading Material above.

2. Quite a number of verb compounds in Chinese are formed by two verbs, one of which asserts an action while the other indicates the result of it. Such compounds may be called "resultative compounds." Take 看見 as an example. 看 means "to look at" and asserts the action, while 見, meaning "to perceive," indicates the result of the action. Hence the compound is to be taken to mean to look at something until it is perceived by the organs of sight, hence, "to see." 聽見 is another compound of the same type, meaning to listen to something until it is perceived by the organ of hearing, hence, "to hear." All resultative compounds take the particle 得 (neutral in tone), which is inserted between their two component elements, to indicate potentiality or capability, and the negative particle 不 to show the lack of the same. Thus, 看得見 means "to be able to see, can see, capable of seeing," etc., whereas 看不見 means "unable to see, cannot see, incapable of seeing," etc.

3. The basic meaning of 出 is "to emerge"; of 拿, "to hold in the hand"; of 進, "to enter." However, as soon as these verbs are joined to 來 and 去 to form directional compounds they begin to correspond to English verb groups consisting of a verb plus a very closely related abverb or preposition, as 出來, "to come out"; 出去, "to go out"; 拿來, "to bring [hither]"; 拿去, "to take [thither]"; 進來, "to come in"; 進去, "to go in"; 拿出來, "to bring out"; 拿出去, "to take out"; etc. If and when such directional compounds take a direct object, it is placed immediately after the action verb or, if the compounds have two directional elements, between the latter. Thus we say, 拿一本書來, "to bring a book hither"; 拿一本書出來 or 拿出一本書來, "to bring a book out, to bring out a book." If and when such compounds take an indirect object as well, the latter is placed after the directional element or elements, but is immediately followed by 給 (see Note 4 below), as 他拿了一本書來給我, "He brought me a book; he brought a book to me."

4. When the verb 給, "to give," takes both a direct and an indirect object, the latter usually precedes the former. For an example, see sentence 4 of Reading Material above. However, 給 in its verbal capacity may be used to perform the functions of the English prepositions "to" (action toward) and "for" (in place of). When it performs the function of "to," together with the indirect object, it is placed after the main verb; when it performs the function of "for," together with the indirect object, it is placed before the main verb. Thus, "I write a letter to you" is 我寫信給你, but "I write a letter for you" is 我給你寫信. This distinction, however, is not always observed in Peiping. The result is that 我給你寫信 may mean "I write a letter to you" or "I write a letter for you." The situational context, of course, will help make clear which of the two meanings is intended by the speaker.

5. It has been pointed out that verb compounds such as 看書, 説話, 寫字, etc., which are formed by a verb plus its cognate object, cannot be used in isolated sentences intransitively by merely omitting their objects (cf. Note 5, Lesson Four). The way to use such a verb-object compound intransitively in isolated sentences is to state the compound in full and then repeat the verbal element of it, as 他寫字寫得很好, "He writes very well."

6. Adverbs of manner and of degree and measure in Chinese usually follow the verbs, adverbs, or adjectives they qualify and are introduced by the particle 得.

7. The verb 寫 in sentence 11 of the Reading Material above is to be understood as in the passive voice. The reason is that if it were used actively, then 字 would have to be regarded as the performer of the act of writing, something which is impossible and does not make sense. Moreover, had that been the case, an object of the verb 寫 would have been given. This type of seemingly active construction is used in Chinese to perform the function of the passive in which the agent performing the action is not mentioned. The sentence may be rendered into English as "Those Chinese characters are not very well written." In this connection it may be helpful to point out the fact that in Chinese the passive construction as such does not exist, and so whenever and wherever possible, the active construction should be resorted to in definite preference to the passive. For a fuller discussion of the passive construction, see Note 1, Lesson Thirty-four.

8. The expression 好不好 is frequently used at the end of a statement to indicate that the speaker is awaiting approval and can be rendered into English simply as "Will it do?" Sentence 13 above means something like "Will it do for me to write out these Chinese characters for them?"

9. In the language of Peiping, 得, pronounced as "tei," is often used as a sort of auxiliary verb meaning "to have to, must," etc. For example, 你得去 means "You must [have to] go"; 你得看書, "You must [have to] read." When so used, 得 is limited only to affirmative statements. Cf. 要.

10. A look at the construction of sentences 5, 8, 9, and 12 above will reveal the fact that there are in each of them two verbs used one after the other without any connective between them in the predicate. Whereas

such a construction is not permissible grammatically in English—in which the usual practice is to turn the second verb into an infinitive, introduced with or without the sign "to"—it is frequently used in Chinese. The verbs so used may or may not take an object, as 我要去, "I want go—I want to go"; 我叫他來, "I ask he come—I ask him to come"; 我給他寫信, "I give he write letter—I write a letter for him"; etc.

ORAL EXERCISES

A. Say the following in Chinese:
  1. Can you see? Can you see me? Can't you see me?
  2. Did you hear? Did you hear me speak? Can you hear?
  3. I read, he writes. I say it out, you write it down.
  4. He didn't write yesterday.
  5. I have many pencils. I can take them out for you to look at.
  6. They gave me a piece of paper.
  7. There are very few books here.
  8. Bring that to me! Take it to him!
  9. Don't bring this in! Take it out!
  10. Come in to write!
  11. Go out to read!
  12. Take these books out to them!
  13. Write this for him!
  14. Don't say it out! Write it down!

B. Render the following into English:
  1. Wó hsiehle sañko tzù, ni k'añtechieñ ma?
  2. T'ā keí ni nách'ulai hǎo puhao?
  3. Ni huì hsieh tōshaǒko Chungkuo-tzù?
  4. Waìt'ou te jeñ tō puto? T'āmen yaò chiñlai puyao?
  5. Wǒmen yaò chiñch'ü k'añ-shū le.
  6. Wǒ t'ingchienle t'a shuō shemma le.
  7. T'āmen tsót'ien meí ná shemma lai.
  8. Shuí nále nimente ch'ieñpǐ ch'ü le?
  9. Ni pūyaò tsoǔ, t'ā chiñlai le.
  10. T'ā shuōle nàko tzù ch'ulai keí women t'ing le.
  11. Ni shuō te huà, wǒ t'ingpuchieñ.

WRITTEN EXERCISES

A. Transcribe Section B, above, in Chinese.

B. Render the following into English:

1. 在那裏看書的美國人不會說中國話.

2. 我 昨 天 拿 了 三 本 書 出 去 給 他 們 看.

3. 他 聽 不 見 我 在 這 裏 說 甚 麼.

4. 我 給 你 拿 這 個 出 去; 你 給 我 拿 那 個 進 來.

5. 那 些 美 國 人 說 中 國 話 說 得 好 不 好?

6. 說 得 很 好; 他 們 寫 中 國 字 也 寫 得 很 好.

7. 房 子 裏 頭 有 多 少 人 看 書, 有 多 少 人 寫 字?

8. 我 看 見 很 多 人 進 來, 很 少 人 出 去.

9. 他 進 去 看 書; 我 出 來 寫 字.

10. 不 要 走, 他 要 拿 鉛 筆 出 來 給 你 了.

C. Render the following into Chinese:

1. Did you hear yesterday where he said he was going?
2. He writes on the desk which you say is not mine.
3. How many books can you see in that little house?
4. That is very well said. Have you heard it?
5. I saw him come in and saw him go out.
6. Do not write these two words for them!
7. These are the words written by me[1] yesterday morning.
8. Bring the pens on that table to me!
9. I heard him say he wanted to go to the city.
10. I was home reading: he was home writing.

[1] Use the relative clause construction.

Lesson NINE

VOCABULARY CHARACTERS

叫 (Chiaò)
Also written 叫.
To name, to call, to order, to ask, to cause

怎 (Tseṁ)
How [*], why [*]

告 (Kaò)
To tell, to announce [*]

訴 (Sù)
To tell [*]

問 (Weǹ)
To ask, to question, to inquire

請 (Ch' inǧ)
To invite, to request; please

錢 (Ch'ień)
Money; a cash; (a surname)

知 (Chiḣ)
To know [*]

道 (Taò)
Way, path; doctrine [*]

報 (Paò)
To report [*]; to requite [*]; newspaper

信 (Hsiǹ)
Letter; to believe [*]; to trust [*]

封 (Fenǧ)
To seal; (classifier for letters)

COMPOUNDS

多 麼 (Tóma) How? How!

怎 麼 (Tseṁma) How? Why?

這 麼 (Chèma) Thus, in this way, such

那 麼 (Nèma) Thus, in that way, such, that being the case, then

告 訴 (Kaòsu) To tell, to inform

請 問 (Ch'inǧ weǹ) I beg to ask, permit me to ask, may I ask

知 道 (Chiḣtao) To know

信 封 (Hsiǹfenǧ) Envelope

問 問 (Weǹwen) To ask [casually]

看 看 (K'aǹk'an) To take a look

說 說 (Shuōshuo) To say or speak a little

寫 寫 (Hsieḣhsieh) To write a little

中 國 錢 (Chunǧkuo-ch'ień) Chinese money

美 國 錢 (Meǐkuo-ch'ień) American money

有 錢 (Yǔ-ch'ień) Wealthy, rich

46

READING MATERIAL

1. 請 問 這 個 中 國 話 叫 甚 麼?
2. 這 個 中 國 話 叫 椅 子.
3. 那 個 中 國 話 叫 書 麼?
4. 不, 那 個 中 國 話 叫 報.
5. 我 要 問 問 你, 他 是 誰?
6. 我 不 知 道 他 是 誰.
7. 這 個 中 國 字 怎 麼 寫? 請 你 寫 寫 給 我 們 看.
8. 這 個 中 國 字 這 麼 寫. 你 們 看 看, 寫 好 了.
9. 書 棹 子 上 頭 的 兩 封 信 是 誰 的?
10. 我 不 知 道 是 誰 的, 我 要 問 問 他.
11. 請 你 告 訴 我, 你 有 中 國 錢 沒 有.
12. 我 沒 有 中 國 錢, 我 有 美 國 錢, 你 要 不 要?
13. 不 要 了, 美 國 錢 我 也 有.
14. 他 昨 天 寫 的 中 國 字 有 多 大?
15. 有 這 麼 大, 沒 有 那 麼 大.
16. 他 叫 你 拿 信 封 來, 你 得 給 他 拿 來.
17. 我 沒 聽 見 他 叫 我 拿 甚 麼 來.
18. 那 是 誰 的 書, 你 知 道 麼?

ROMANIZED TEXT OF READING MATERIAL

1. Ch'inğ wèn chèko Chunğkuo-huà chiaò sheḿma?
2. Chèko Chunğkuo-huà chiaò ìtzu.
3. Nàko Chunğkuo-huà chiaò shū ma?
4. Pū, nàko Chunğkuo-huà chiaò paò.
5. Wŏ yaò wènwen ni, t'ā shih̆ shuí?
6. Wŏ pū chih̆tao t'a shih̆ shuí.
7. Chèko Chunğkuo-tzù tseḿma hsieh̆?   Ch'inğ ni hsieh̆hsieh keí women
k'aǹ.
8. Chèko Chunğkuo-tzù chèma hsieh̆.   Nı̆men k'aǹk'an, hsieh̆haŏ le.
9. Shū-chōtzu shangt'ou te lianğfenğ hsiǹ shih̆ shuíte?
10. Wŏ pū chih̆tao shih̆ shuíte, wŏ yaò wènwen t'a.
11. Ch'inğ ni kaòsu wo, ní yŭ Chunğkuo-ch'ień meiyu.
12. Wŏ meí yŭ Chunğkuo-ch'ień, wó yú Meĭkuo-ch'ień, nı̆ yaò puyao?
13. Pū yaò le, Meĭkuo-ch'ień wó yeh̆ yŭ.
14. T'ā tsót'ien hsieh̆ te Chunğkuo-tzù yŭ tó tà?
15. Yŭ chèma tà, meí yŭ nèma tà.
16. T'ā chiaò ni ná hsiǹfenğ lai, ní teí keĭ t'a nálai.
17. Wŏ meí t'inğchien t'a chiaò wo ná shemma lai.
18. Nà shih̆ shuíte shū, nı̆ chih̆tao ma?

NOTES

1. Leaving out 請問, which is only a parenthetical clause anyway, the remainder of sentence 1 of the Reading Material above is definitely to be understood as active in construction though it may best be rendered into English in the passive. 這個, the object of 叫, has been transposed to the "exposed" position, apparently for emphasis. Literally, the remainder of the sentence means "this thing the Chinese spoken language calls what?"; hence, "what is this thing called in Chinese?"

2. 不 in sentence 4 above means "It isn't so!" It is used for answering negatively a question which does not lend itself quite readily to the usual treatment of answering it by repeating the negative alternative it presents.

3. Chinese verbs, particularly monosyllabic action verbs, are often reduplicated to indicate their transitory aspect, with the neutral tone resulting on the repeated syllable, as 問問, 看看, etc. Structurally speaking, they are the reduced forms of 問一問, 看一看, "to ask [casually], to ask a question," and "to take a look," respectively, which consist of a verb plus its object. Since 一 occupies a phonetically weak position, it is often absorbed in actual conversation by the syllable following, hence the reduced forms. Note that these reduplicated verbs are never used in negative statements.

4. The verb 請, "to invite," etc., may often be used to begin an imperative sentence, in order to indicate politeness on the part of the person making the request, thus approximating the function of "please" in English. 請進來 or 請你進來 means "Please come in!"

5. 好 is often used with action verbs to form resultative compounds to indicate the satisfactory completion of the action expressed by them, as 寫好, "to write [until] completed," hence, "to finish writing." To indicate ability or capability and the lack of it 得 and 不 are used, respectively (cf. Note 2, Lesson Eight), as 寫得好 and 寫不好, meaning "to be able to finish writing; to be capable of completing the writing" and "to be unable to finish writing; to be incapable of completing the writing." Incidentally, 寫得好 may also be taken to mean "to be well written" (see Note 6, Lesson Eight). The context will make it clear which meaning is intended. But 寫不好 cannot be construed as "to be not well written," which, of course, should be 寫得不好.

6. 多 as an adverb of degree and measure may be used for interrogative or exclamatory purposes. 有多大 in sentence 14 above literally means "to have how much bigness," hence, "to be how big." But 多大 or 多麼大 can also mean "How big!" depending on the context. Note the difference in tone when 多 is used in either of these two ways. 麼 in 多麼, 這麼, 那麼, 怎麼, etc., is a suffix of manner and is never written 嗎.

7. Note that 那麼 is pronounced "nèma," probably by analogy of 這麼 "chèma" and probably because of the fact that the initial "m" of 麼 has the tendency of "raising" the low vowel "a" of 那 into an "e."

ORAL EXERCISES

A. Say the following in Chinese:

1. Please tell me! Please ask [order] him!
2. Don't tell him! Don't let [give] him know!
3. Ask him [casually]! Don't ask him!
4. Ask [invite] him to come in! Ask them not to go out today!
5. How is it said? How is it written?
6. It is said that way. It is written this way.
7. What is this called? What is that called?
8. May I ask who they are? May I ask what that is?
9. Why didn't he come? Why didn't you go?
10. Please read the newspapers a little! Please don't read the newspapers!

B. Render the following into English:

1. Nǐ yaò sheḿma? Wǒ yaò īko hsìnfeṅg.
2. "Hsìnfeṅg" Meǐkuo-huà tseḿma shuō?
3. T'āte fanġtzu yǔ tó tà?
4. Ch'inġ ni shuōshuo Chunġkuo-huà keǐ t'amen t'īng.
5. Nǐ yaò k'aṅk'an t'a hsieḣhaǒ te hsìn ma?
6. T'āmen k'aṅle tsót'ien te paò meiyu?
7. Meí k'aṅ, tsót'ien te paò pū tsaì chèli.
8. Chiñt'ien shanġwǔ t'ā kaòsule shuí?
9. Nǐ chiḣtao "shū-chōtzu" Meǐkuo-huà tseḿma shuō ma?
10. Chiḣtao, wó yeʰ chiḣtao "ch'ień" Meǐkuo-huà tseḿma shuō.

WRITTEN EXERCISES

A. Transcribe Section B, above, in Chinese.

B. Render the following into English:

　　1. 你 怎 麼 不 去 問 問 不 看 書 的
人 要 看 甚 麼 ?

　　2. 請 你 告 訴 我, 誰 叫 他 拿 昨 天
的 報 來 的 ?

　　3. 這 裏 有 四 封 信: 兩 封 是 給 你
的; 兩 封 是 給 他 的.

　　4. 我 沒 有 中 國 錢; 你 去 問 問 他
有 沒 有 好 不 好 ?

　　5. 他 不 會 寫 那 個 字; 請 你 寫 給
他 看 看.

　　6. 我 不 知 道 那 個 美 國 話 叫 甚 麼.

　　7. 我 寫 好 信 了, 沒 有 信 封. 你 有
沒 有 ?

　　8. 我 要 出 去 了; 請 他 明 天 來.

　　9. 他 不 知 道 誰 有 美 國 錢; 不 要
問 他.

　　10. 請 你 寫 信 的 人 來 了; 叫 他 進
來 好 不 好 ?

C. Render the following into Chinese:

1. Have you read the letter which I wrote you yesterday?
2. I have not; I do not know that you wrote me yesterday.
3. He is the one who brought you the newspapers this morning.
4. Please tell me who the man who wants American money is.

5. Do you know whether he can speak Chinese?

6. I do not know; why do you not ask him?

7. How much American money do you have? How much Chinese money do you want?

8. I have a great deal of American money. I want very little Chinese money.

9. Please bring me the big envelope on the table.

10. Please tell me whether he is from China.

Lesson TEN

A Review Lesson

CHARACTERS

Number of Strokes	Characters	Pronunciation and Tone	Meaning	Lesson Reference
Two	了	Le	(The perfective suffix; modal particle)	7
Three	上	Shaṅg	On, above; up; to ascend	6
	下	Hsià	Below, down, under; to descend; next	6
	子	Tzŭ / Tzu	Son, child / (Noun suffix)	6 / 6
Four	今	Chiñ	Now, present	7
	天	T'ieñ	Heaven, sky; day	7
	午	Wŭ	The noon hour (11 a.m. to 1. p.m.)	7
	少	Shaǒ	Few; little	8
Five	外	Waì	Outside	6
	去	Ch'ǜ	To go; to remove, to do away with	7
	出	Ch'ū	To emerge; to put forth, to issue	8
	叫	Chiaò	To name; to call; to order; to cause; to ask	9
Six	字	Tzù	Written character; word	8
	多	Tŏ / Tó	Many, much / How? How much?	8 / 8
Seven	把	Pă	To grasp; to hold in the hand; (classifier for chairs, knives, fans, etc.)	6
	見	Chieǹ	To see, to meet; to perceive	8
	走	Tsoŭ	To walk; to go away	8
	告	Kaò	To tell; to announce	9
Eight	所	Sŏ	(Classifier for buildings); that which	6

52

Number of Strokes	Characters	Pronunciation and Tone	Meaning	Lesson Reference
Eight	底	Tǐ	Bottom	6
	房	Fanǵ	House, building	6
	來	Laí	To come	7
	到	Taò	To arrive, to reach; to go to; to (toward); until	7
	知	Chiħ	To know	9
Nine	前	Ch'ień	Front; before	6
	後	Hoù	Rear; after	6
	城	Ch'enǵ	City; city wall	7
	要	Yaò	To want; to have to; important; shall, will	7
	怎	Tsem̌	How? why?	9
	信	Hsiǹ	Letter; to believe, to trust	9
	封	Fenḡ	To seal; (classifier for letters)	9
Ten	家	Chiā	Home, family	7
	昨	Tsó	Yesterday	7
	拿	Ná	To hold in the hand	8
Eleven	從	Ts'unǵ	From	7
	得	Té	To get, to obtain; to be done; to be ready	8
	得	Te	(Particle indicating capability, potentiality, or manner in which an action is achieved)	8
		Teǐ	Must	8
	問	Weǹ	To ask, to inquire, to question	9
Twelve	棹	Chō	Table	6
	椅	Ǐ	Chair	6

Number of Strokes	Characters	Pronunciation and Tone	Meaning	Lesson Reference
Twelve	進	Chìn	To enter ; to advance	8
	給	Keǐ	To give ; to ; for	8
	訴	Sù	To tell	9
	報	Paò	To report ; to requite ; newspaper	9
Thirteen	道	Taò	Way, path ; doctrine	9
Fifteen	寫	Hsieň	To write	8
	請	Ch'ǐng	To invite ; to request ; please	9
Sixteen	頭	T'oú	Head ; first ; (classifier for some animals) ; (noun suffix)	6
	錢	Ch'ień	Money ; a cash ; (a surname)	9
Twenty-two	聽	T'ǐng	To listen	8

ORAL DRILL

A.   Say the following in Chinese.   (The items in this section are arranged in dialogue form. Results can best be attained by having two persons participating in it, one doing the questioning, the other the answering. They can reverse their roles at any logical point.)

What?	Nothing!
Who?	You!
Whose?	His.
Where?	Here.
Which one?	This one.
Which book?	That book.
What do you have?	I haven't anything.
What do you want?	I don't want anything.
Who are you?	I am . . .
Whom do you see?	I see you.
Whom do you also see?	I also see them.
What language do they speak?	They speak American.
What language do you speak?	I speak Chinese.
Do they speak American well?	They speak it very well.
Is the Chinese he speaks good?	It is not very good.
What is this?	That is a newspaper.
Is it your newspaper?	No, it is his.

What is that?	That is a house.
Whose house is it?	It is theirs.
Where are you going?	I am going home.
Where is your house?	It is in the city.
Is the city large?	It is very large.
Are the people there numerous?	Very numerous.
Áre you going today?	Yes, I am.
Did they go?	No, they didn't.
Can you see me?	Yes, I can see you.
Can you hear them?	No, I can't hear them.
How do you write that word?	I don't how to write it.
Is it all right for me to go in?	It is. Please go in.
How is it that you don't know?	I haven't heard it.
Did he come out?	Yes, he did.
Have they gone?	No, they haven't.
Where is he from? America?	No, he is from China.
Where did they go?	They went to America.
How many houses do you see?	I see very many houses.
Are they big houses?	No, they are very small ones.
What is that called?	That is called a table.
What is "chair" called in Chinese?	"Chair" is called "ïtzu" in Chinese.
What is "kangpï" called in American?	"Kangpï" is called "pen" in American.
How many chairs are there in that house?	There are four chairs in that house.
Where is my newspaper?	It is on that table.
Is it a Chinese newspaper?	No, it is an American paper.
Can you read an American paper?	Yes, I can read it. I also can read a Chinese newspaper.
I want to ask you. Is that your money?	No, it isn't. I don't know whose it is.
Do you know how to write the Chinese character [for] money?	Yes, I do. I'll write it for you to see.
Do you understand what those people said yesterday?	Yes, they said they wanted some big envelopes.
Do you understand the Chinese I speak?	Yes, I do. You speak it very well.

B. Answer the following in Chinese :

1. T'ā hsieh te tzù ni k'antechien k'anpuchien?
2. Ni shuō Chungkuo-huà t'ā t'ingtechien t'ingpuchien?
3. Wŏmen yaò k'an te shū shih pushih Meïkuo-shū?
4. Tsót'ien meí laí te jeń yú Meïkuo-ch'ień meiyu?
5. T'ā chiaò ni ná shemma ch'uch'ü keï t'a k'an?
6. Nimen yaò t'a ná shemma paò chinlai?
7. Chōtzu shangt'ou te hsin shih shuíte?
8. Nàhsieh Chungkuo-tzù shih shuí keí ni hsiehhsialai te?

9.   Chèko Chunḡkuo-tzù nǐ yaò hsieȟch'ulai keǐ shuí k'aǹ?
10. Wǒ meí ná ch'ień lai, nǐ kaòsule t'a meiyu?

WRITING DRILL

Write out your Chinese version of Section A of Oral Drill above.

READING DRILL

After reading the following, render it into English:

那所房子裏頭有四個人。房子中有兩張桌子。桌子上頭有很大的一些書，一些報。這些書是中國書，一些是美國書；一些報是中國報，一些是美國報。

中國人會說中國話，會看中國書，也會看中國報。美國人會說美國話，會看美國書，也會看美國報。

你看，美國人拿出一些錢來給中國人。中國人告訴美國人，"我們是中國人，要中國錢。你們有中國錢沒有？"美國人說，"我們是美國人，沒有中國錢。我們會寫美國字。我們有鉛筆，也有鋼筆。你們要鉛筆不要？要鋼筆不要？"一個中國人說，"鉛筆好，鋼筆不好。我要鉛筆。"一個中

國 人 說,"我 說 鋼 筆 好,鉛 筆 不 好.我
不 要 鉛 筆,要 鋼 筆." 要 鉛 筆 的 中 國
人 得 了 一 枝 鉛 筆,要 鋼 筆 的 中 國
人 得 了 一 枝 鋼 筆.

VOCABULARY CHARACTERS

二 (Erh)
Two [*]

五 (Wŭ)
Five [*]

六 (Liù)
Six [*]

七 (Ch'ī)
Seven [*]

八 (Pā)
Eight [*]

九 (Chiŭ)
Nine [*]

十 (Shih)
Ten [*]

老 (Laŏ)
Old, aged; always [*]

月 (Yüeh)
Moon [*]; month

年 (Nień)
Year

禮 (Lĭ)
Propriety; rite

拜 (Paì)
To worship; to pay
respect to, to call on [*]

幾 (Chĭ)
How many? several,
a few

號 (Haò)
Number; mark, sign [*]

COMPOUNDS

前天 (Ch'ieńt'ien) Day before
yesterday

後天 (Hoùt'ien) Day after tomorrow

大前天 (Tà-ch'ieńt'ien) Three
days ago

大後天 (Tà-hoùt'ien) Three
days hence

今年 (Chiññien) This year

去年 (Ch'ùnien) Last year

明年 (Mińnien) Next year

前年 (Ch'ieńnien) Year before
last

後年 (Hoùnien) Year after
next

大前年 (Tà-ch'ieńnien) Three
years ago

大後年　(Tà-hoùnien) Three years hence

這個月　(Chèkoyüeh) ⎫ This
本　月　(Peňyüeh) ⎭ month

上　月　(Shangyüeh) Last month

下　月　(Hsiàyüeh) Next month

一　月　(Īyüeh) January

二　月　(Erhyüeh) February

三　月　(Sañyüeh) March

四　月　(Szùyüeh) April

五　月　(Wǔyüeh) May

六　月　(Liùyüeh) June

七　月　(Ch'īyüeh) July

八　月　(Pāyüeh) August

九　月　(Chiǔyüeh) September

十　月　(Shiňyüeh) October

十一月　(Shiňiyüeh) November

十二月　(Shiňerhyüeh) December

禮　拜　(Lǐpai) Week

這個禮拜　(Chèko lǐpai) This week

上禮拜　(Shang-lǐpai) Last week

下禮拜　(Hsià-lǐpai) Next week

禮拜天　(Lǐpaìt'ieñ) Sunday

禮拜一　(Lǐpaìī) Monday

禮拜二　(Lǐpaìerh) Tuesday

禮拜三　(Lǐpaìsañ) Wednesday

禮拜四　(Lǐpaìszù) Thursday

禮拜五　(Lǐpaìwǔ) Friday

禮拜六　(Lǐpaìliù) Saturday

天　天　(T'ieñt'ieñ) Every day

年　年　(Nieňnieň) Every year

十　一　(Shiňī) Eleven

十　二　(Shiňerh) Twelve

十　三　(Shiňsañ) Thirteen

十　四　(Shiňszù) Fourteen

十　五　(Shiňwǔ) Fifteen

十　九　(Shiňchiǔ) Nineteen

二　十　(Erhshiň) Twenty

二十一　(Erhshihī) Twenty-one

二十九　(Erhshihchiǔ) Twenty-nine

三　十　(Sañshiň) Thirty

四　十　(Szùshiň) Forty

九　十　(Chiǔshiň) Ninety

九十九　(Chiǔshihchiǔ) Ninety-nine

十　幾　(Shiňchī) Ten-odd, ten plus a few

幾　十　(Chīshiň) Several tens; how many tens?

幾　號　(Chīhaò) What day of the month?

幾月 (Chǐyüeh) What month of the year?   禮拜幾 (Lipaìchī) What day of the week?

老人 (Laǒ jeń) Elderly person

READING MATERIAL

一年有十二個月. 這十二個月叫一月, 二月, 三月, 四月, 五月, 六月, 七月, 八月, 九月, 十月, 十一月, 十二月. 一月, 三月, 五月, 七月, 八月, 十月, 十二月, 這七個月是有三十一天的. 四月, 六月, 九月, 十一月, 這四個月是有三十天的. 二月是有二十八天.

一個禮拜有七天. 這七天叫禮拜一, 禮拜二, 禮拜三, 禮拜四, 禮拜五, 禮拜六, 禮拜天.

今天是禮拜三. 昨天是禮拜二. 明天是禮拜四. 後天是禮拜五. 前天是禮拜一. 大前天是禮拜天. 大後天是禮拜六.

今天是幾號? 今天是九號. 今天是幾月幾號? 今天是五月八號. 昨天是五月九號. 明天是五月十號. 後天是五月十一號. 前天是五月

今天是禮拜四。昨天是禮拜幾？明天是禮拜幾？本月是五月，上月是幾月？

一個禮拜有七天，兩個禮拜有十四天。三個禮拜有多少天？三個禮拜有二十一天。五個禮拜有多少天？五個禮拜有三十五天。一年有十二個月，三年有多少個月？三年有三十六個月。八年有多少個月？八年有九十六個月。

上禮拜六是七月一號。今天是七月三號，禮拜一。下禮拜一是七月十號。下禮拜三是七月幾號？上禮拜四是幾月幾號？

ROMANIZED TEXT OF READING MATERIAL

Ī nień yǔ shih́erh̀ko yüeh̀. Chè shih́erh̀ko yüeh̀ chiaò īyüeh, erh̀yüeh, sañyüeh, szùyüeh, wǔyüeh, liùyüeh, ch'īyüeh, pāyüeh, chiŭyüeh, shih́yüeh, shih́īyüeh, shih́erh̀yüeh. Īyüeh, sañyüeh, wǔyüeh, ch'īyüeh, pāyüeh, shih́yüeh, shih́erh̀yüeh, chè ch'īko yüeh̀ shih̀ yǔ sañshihī t'ień te. Szùyüeh, liùyüeh, chiŭyüeh, shih́īyüeh, chè szùko yüeh̀ shih̀ yǔ sañshih́ t'ień te. Erh̀yüeh, chèiko yüeh̀ shih̀ yǔ erh̀shihpā t'ień te.

Ī nień yú wǔshih́erh̀ko lipaì. Īko lipaì yǔ ch'ī t'ień. Chè ch'ī t'ień chiaò lipaì, lipaìerh̀, lipaìsañ, lipaìszù, lipaìwǔ, lipaìliù, lipaìt'ień.

Chiñt'ien shih̀ lipaìsañ. Tsót'ien shih̀ lipaìerh̀. Mińgt'ien shih̀ lipaìszù. Hoùt'ien shih̀ lipaìwǔ. Ch'ieńt'ien shih̀ lipaì. Tà-ch'ieńt'ien shih̀ lipaìt'ień. Tà-hoùt'ien shih̀ lipaìliù.

Chiñt'ien shih̀ chīhaò? Chiñt'ien shih̀ chiŭhaò. Chiñt'ien shih̀ chīyüeh chīhaò? Chiñt'ien shih̀ wǔyüeh chiŭhaò. Tsót'ien shih̀ wǔyüeh pāhaò. Mińgt'ien shih̀ wǔyüeh shih́haò. Hoùt'ien shih̀ wǔyüeh shih́īhaò. Ch'ieńt'ien

shiĥ wŭyüeh ch'ihaò.   Tsót'ien shiĥ lïpaìszù.   Chiñt'ien shiĥ lïpaìchï?
Mingt'ien shiĥ lïpaìchï?   Peňyüeh shiĥ wŭyüeh.   Shangyüeh shiĥ chïyüeĥ?
   Ïko lïpaì yŭ ch'ï t'ieñ.   Liangko lïpaì yŭ tōshaŏ t'ieñ?   Liangko lïpaì yŭ
shiĥszù t'ieñ.   Sañko lïpaì yŭ tōshaŏ t'ieñ?   Sañko lïpaì yŭ erhshihï t'ieñ.
Wŭko lïpaì yŭ tōshaŏ t'ieñ?   Wŭko lïpaì yŭ sañshihwŭ t'ieñ.   Ï nień yŭ
shiĥerĥko yüeĥ, sañ nień yŭ tōshaŏko yüeĥ?   Sañ nień yŭ sañshihliùko yüeĥ.
Pā nień yŭ tōshaŏko yüeĥ?   Pā nień yú chiūshihliùko yüeĥ.
   Shang-lïpaìliù shiĥ ch'ïyüeh ïhaò.   Chiñt'ien shiĥ ch'ïyüeh sañhaò, lïpaìï.
Hsià-lïpaìï shiĥ ch'ïyüeh shiĥhaò.   Hsià-lïpaìsañ shiĥ ch'ïyüeh chïhaò?
Shang-lïpaìszù shiĥ chïyüeh chïhaò?

NOTES

1. 月 and 禮拜 take 個 as their classifier. Without this classifier, the
use of 月 with a number will result in referring to the calendar months of
the year, e.g., 三月 (the third moon) is "March," and 八月 (the eighth moon)
is "August," whereas 三個月 is "three months" and 八個月 is "eight
months." A variant form of 一月 for "January" is 正 [chenḡ] 月. In
designating the days of the first decade of any month, it is also possible
to use 初 [ch'ū] "the beginning" plus the numerals 1 to 10. Thus April 5
may be designated as 四月五號 or 四月初五, and May 10, as 五月十號 or
五月初十. Note that when 初 is used, 號 is dropped. Note also that in
naming the days of the month, the cardinal numbers are used in Chinese.

2. 天 and 年 are used in Chinese without any classifier.

3. Since the days of the week and of the month as well as the months
of the year are designated by the use of cardinal numbers in Chinese, it is
understandable that 幾 ("how many," hence, "which number") is used in
place of 甚麼 ("what") when one wants to find out about the day of the
week or the month, or the month of the year. In phrasing questions of
this type, one may use the full form or the abbreviated form, leaving out
是, e.g., 今天是幾號 or 今天幾號, "what day [of the month] is today?"

4. When 幾 is used interrogatively it is not interchangeable with 多
少, though both mean "how many." Use 幾 when the number involved in
the anticipated answer is smaller than ten. Otherwise, use 多少.

5. There is no difference in construction between a declarative statement in which 幾 is used with the meaning of "a few" or "several" and an
interrogative one in which 幾 is used with the meaning of "how many."
In other words, when a sentence such as 我有幾本書 is spoken, it may
mean "I have several books" or "How many books [but less than ten] do I
have?" The student will have to depend on the context or the manner in
which the sentence is spoken in order to ascertain whether it is declarative
or interrogative and understand it accordingly.

6. For the difference in usage between 兩 and 二, review Note 4, Lesson
Two, above. Note that 二 alone is used for forming any number containing
a "2" in it. Thus, "12" is 十二; "20," 二十; "22," 二十二; "32," 三十二;

etc. 兩 is not used for this purpose at all except "200," 兩百; "2,000," 兩千; "20,000," 兩萬, which are based apparently on "a couple of hundred," "a couple of thousand," and "a couple of ten thousand," respectively. See Note 6, Lesson Twenty-two.

7. 十幾 may be used for any number between 12 and 20 (13 to 19 inclusive) and 幾十 for any round number between 20 and 100 (30 to 90 inclusive).

ORAL EXERCISES

A.   Say the following in Chinese:

1.   Six months; nine months; eight weeks; five weeks; seven days.
2.   Yesterday; last week; next month; day after tomorrow; year before last; year after next; last year; tomorrow.
3.   Nineteen; thirteen; eleven; fifteen; seventeen; twenty; twenty-three; thirty-nine; fifty-two; sixty-six; seventy-one; eighty-four; ninety-eight.
4.   May; August; March; January; September; February 22; March 11; July 4; October 10; December 7.
5.   Thursday; Wednesday; Tuesday; Sunday; Friday; Saturday; Monday.
6.   Last Friday; next Wednesday; next Sunday; last Saturday.
7.   What day of the month is today?
8.   What day of the week is today?
9.   What month is this?
10.   How many weeks are there in a year?

B.   Render the following into English:

1.   Tà-ch'ient'ien shih pushih lipaisañ?
2.   Chèko yüeh yǔ tōshaǒ t'ieñ?
3.   Chiñt'ien shih chīyüeh chǐhaò?
4.   Tsót'ien shih lipaìchī?
5.   Hsiàyüeh wǔhaò nǐmen yaò taò nǎli ch'ü?
6.   T'āmen mingt'ien yaò taò Meǐkuo ch'ü.
7.   Tà-hoùt'ien wǒ laí, nǐ laí pulai?
8.   Liangǧko yüeh yú chīko lǐpaì?
9.   Szù nień yǔ tōshaǒko yüeh?
10.   Nàhsieh tà tzù shih t'āmen ch'ient'ien hsieh te ma?
11.   Nàko laǒ jeń shih shuí? Shih pushih ts'ung Chungǧkuo lai te?
12.   Wǒ chiaò ni k'an-shū, ní teī k'an-shū.

WRITTEN EXERCISES

A.   Transcribe Section B, above, in Chinese.

B.   Render the following into English:

1. 你們誰知道下禮拜三是幾月幾號？

2. 前天到這裏來的人說他有幾本中國書.

3. 我叫你上禮拜三來; 你沒來.

4. 請你告訴我一年有多少個禮拜.

5. 外頭有十幾個老人要走進來.

6. 昨天他拿了幾十本書來給我看.

7. 大後天他們要到城裏去.

8. 那兩個中國人去年三月三號到美國來的.

9. 他要看五月二十七號的報.

10. 我天天進去; 你天天出來.

C. Render the following into Chinese:

1. Did those Chinese people go day before yesterday?
2. What day of this month will they go to China?
3. He comes here every day to read and write.
4. Last Friday I saw two Americans who could speak Chinese go in.
5. Whom did you see yesterday walk out from the inside?
6. I go this year; you go next year.
7. This month is September; the next month will be October.
8. He will go to the city next Sunday to see you.
9. There are eighty-two books in that house; thirty-seven are mine and forty-five are his.
10. These several scores [tens] of Chinese characters are written by him.

Lesson TWELVE

VOCABULARY CHARACTERS

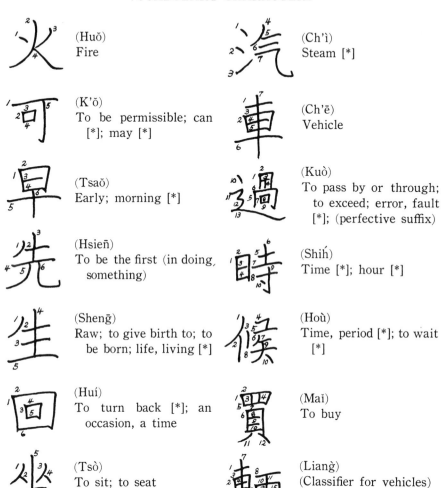

(Huǒ)
Fire

(K'ǒ)
To be permissible; can [*]; may [*]

(Tsaǒ)
Early; morning [*]

(Hsieñ)
To be the first (in doing something)

(Shenḡ)
Raw; to give birth to; to be born; life, living [*]

(Huí)
To turn back [*]; an occasion, a time

(Tsò)
To sit; to seat

(Ch'ì)
Steam [*]

(Ch'ē)
Vehicle

(Kuò)
To pass by or through; to exceed; error, fault [*]; (perfective suffix)

(Shiñ)
Time [*]; hour [*]

(Hoù)
Time, period [*]; to wait [*]

(Maǐ)
To buy

(Liàng)
(Classifier for vehicles)

COMPOUNDS

先生 (Hsieñsheng) Sir; Mr.; teacher

汽車 (Ch'ìch'ē) Automobile

可是 (K'ǒshih) But, however

回來 (Huílai) To come back

回去 (Huích'ü) To go back

時候 (Shiñhou) Time

65

火 車　(Huŏch'ē) Train

過 去　(Kuòch'ü) To pass over;
　　　　the past

聽 説　(T'inḡshuō) To hear
　　　　people say, to hear it
　　　　said

坐 車　(Tsò-ch'ē) To ride in a
　　　　vehicle

坐 下　(Tsòhsia) To sit down

坐得下　(Tsòtehsià) Capable of
　　　　sitting down, ca-
　　　　pable of seating

坐不下　(Tsòpuhsià) Incapable
　　　　of sitting down, in-
　　　　capable to ride well

請 坐　(Ch'inḡtsò) Please be
　　　　seated

好 坐　(Haŏtsò) Good to ride in
　　　　or sit on; to ride well

回 信　(Huí-hsìn) To answer a
　　　　letter

回 家　(Huí-chiā) To return
　　　　home, to go home

進 城　(Chìn-ch'enǵ) To go to
　　　　the city

READING MATERIAL

1. 張 先 生, 這 輛 大 汽 車 是 誰 的?

2. 白 先 生, 是 我 的. 你 説 好 看 不
好 看?

3. 我 説 好 看 得 很. 那 輛 小 的 也
是 你 的 麼?

4. 不 是, 那 輛 小 的 是 錢 先 生 的.

5. 張 先 生 的 汽 車 是 從 那 裏 買
回 來 的?

6. 是 從 美 國 買 回 來 的.

7. 好 坐 不 好 坐?

8. 很 好 坐.

9. 張 先 生 甚 麼 時 候 回 中 國 來 的?

10. 去 年 三 月 十 五 號 回 來 的. 白
先 生 到 美 國 去 過 沒 有?

11. 去 過, 五 年 前 去 過 一 回.

12. 白 先 生 説 美 國 的 汽 車 多 不 多?

13. 很 多, 可 是 人 沒 有 中 國 的 多.
張 先 生 説 是 不 是?

14. 是, 美 國 的 人 沒 有 中 國 的 多.

15. 張 先 生 在 美 國 的 時 候, 坐 過
火 車 沒 有?

16. 坐 過, 美 國 的 火 車 也 很 多. 白
先 生, 時 候 不 早 了, 我 要 回 家 去 了.
明 天 見.

17. 明 天 見, 明 天 見.

ROMANIZED TEXT OF READING MATERIAL

1. Chanḡ hsiensheng, chèliang̀ tà ch'ìch'ē shih̀ shuíte?
2. Paí hsiensheng, shih̀ wŏte. Nǐ shuō haŏk'aǹ puhaokan?
3. Wŏ shuō haŏk'aǹteheň. Nàliang̀ hsiaŏ te yeh̀ shih̀ nǐte ma?
4. Pū shih̀, nàliang̀ hsiaŏ te shih̀ Ch'ień hsiengshengte.
5. Chanḡ hsiengshengte ch'ìch'ē shih̀ ts'uń nǎli maīhuilai te?
6. Shih̀ ts'uń Meīkuo maīhuilai te.
7. Haŏtsò puhaotso?
8. Heń haŏtsò.
9. Chanḡ hsiensheng sheḿma shih̀hou huí Chunḡkuo lai te?
10. Ch'ùnien sañyüeh shih̀wŭhaò huílai te. Paí hsiensheng taò Meīkuo ch'ükuo meiyu?
11. Ch'ùkuo, wŭ nień ch'ień ch'ùkuo īhuí.
12. Paí hsiensheng shuō Meīkuote ch'ìch'ē tō puto?
13. Heň tō, k'ŏshih jeń meí yǔ Chunḡkuote tō. Chanḡ hsiensheng shuō shih̀ pushih?
14. Shih̀, Meīkuote jeń meí yǔ Chunḡkuote tō.
15. Chanḡ hsiensheng tsai Meīkuo te shih̀hou, tsòkuo huŏch'ē meiyu?
16. Tsòkuo, Meīkuote huŏch'ē yeh̀ heň tō. Paí hsiensheng, shih̀hou pū tsaŏ le, wŏ yaò huí-chiā ch'ü le. Minḡt'ien chien.
17. Minḡt'ien chieǹ, mingt'ien chien.

NOTES

1. When 先生 is used as an honorific title, it is placed after, not before, the person's name or surname. Thus, "Mr. Chanḡ" becomes 張先生. In

formal conversation the Chinese often resort to the use of the third person
to replace the second.   Note that when 先生 follows a surname or personal
name, it is neutral in tone in both of its syllables.

2. 好看得很 in sentence 3 above means the same as 很好看, but is
considered more emphatic.

3. When 回來 and 回去 are used together with an adverb of place
which serves as the goal of the action of returning, they are split up by
the place named.   For example, see sentence 9 above.

4. The perfective suffix 過, derived from the verb 過, "to pass by or
through," is used to indicate that the action expressed by the verb which
it follows did happen or has happened once in the past.   Thus, 看見過
means "did see once before, to have seen once before," 聽見過, "did hear
once before, to have heard once before," etc.   The negative form of 看見過
is 沒(有)看見過, "never saw before, to have never seen before."   The difference between 了 and 過 as perfective suffixes is that the former refers
to a given moment in the past when an action was completed, whereas the
latter refers to a completed action in terms of the past experience as a
whole.

5. The way to make a comparison in Chinese when the inferior member
precedes the superior one is to use 沒有 after the former and the appropriate
adjective or adverb after the latter.   See sentences 13 and 14 above.   For
ways to make other types of comparison, see Notes 1, 2, 3, and 4 of Lesson
Seventeen, and Note 2 of Lesson Eighteen.

6. The difference in meaning between 時候 and 回 is that the former
connotes measured or measurable duration, whereas the latter connotes a
recurrent occasion.   時候 is like the French word *temps*, and 回, *fois*.

7. 明天見 means "See you tomorrow."

8. The relative adverb of time, "when," is rendered into Chinese by
the use of the subordinative particle 的 plus 時候.   Literally, it means "the
time of."   Note that 的時候 comes invariably at the end of the subordinate
clause containing it rather than at the beginning, as is the case with
English.

9. In ordinary usage all adverbial clauses of time and adverbial clauses
of condition precede the principal clauses to which they are joined to form
complex sentences in Chinese.   Although it is possible to say in English,
"When he walked out of the house I had already returned" or "I had already
returned when he walked out of the house," depending on the difference in
emphasis, it is only possible to state the same idea in Chinese in the first
form, that is, having the adverbial clause of time precede the principal
clause, "I had already returned."

ORAL EXERCISES

A. Say the following in Chinese:

1. An automobile; a good-looking automobile; a good-riding automobile;
an American automobile.

2. He rides on a vehicle; he rides on a train; you ride in an automobile.

3. Automobiles do not ride as well as trains.
4. Sir, please be seated! Sir, please come in!
5. What does he want to buy?
6. I will come back tomorrow afternoon.
7. Mr. Chang̊ is going back this afternoon.
8. Don't sit here! Don't come back!
9. When he writes I read; when he reads I write.
10. He has never ridden on vehicles.

B. Render the following into English:

1. Nĭ k'an̊chienkuo huŏch'ē meiyu?
2. Chè sānliang̊ ch'ìch'ē pū shih̊ nĭte.
3. T'ā shuō-huà te shih̊hou wŏ k'an̊-shū, t'ā k'an̊-shū te shih̊hou wó hsieh̊-tzù.
4. Ch'ień hsiensheng, ch'ing̊ chin̊lai tsòtso.
5. T'ā huílai le, nĭ yaò huích'ü ma?
6. T'āmente ch'ìch'ē haŏtsò puhaotso?
7. Ch'ìch'ē meí yú huŏch'ē tà.
8. Nĭmen wŭko jeń tsòtehsià tsopuhsia?
9. Wŏ ch'ūch'ü te shih̊hou meí k'an̊chien ni.
10. T'ā pū chih̊tao nimen tsót'ien shem̊ma shih̊hou huílai te.

WRITTEN EXERCISES

A. Transcribe Section B, above, in Chinese.

B. Render the following into English:

1. 我沒看見過你們的汽車,聽說很好坐.

2. 白先生,請進來看看我們昨天買的書.

3. 昨天誰給你們買了三輛汽車?

4. 今天他來看你的時候,你到那裏去了?

5. 火車裏頭有很多人,也有很多椅子.

6. 你們上禮拜進城去,是坐甚麼車去的?

7. 我 們 是 坐 火 車 去 的.

8. 張 先 生 回 中 國 來 了 沒 有？

9. 錢 先 生 沒 有 到 美 國 去 過.

10. 他 會 説 中 國 話, 可 是 不 會 寫

中 國 字.

C.   Render the following into Chinese:

1.   Mr. Ch'ień, please come in, Mr. Pai is at home.
2.   Tomorrow he will go to the city by train.
3.   Do you know when he will come home?
4.   No, but I know when he went out.
5.   The Chinese I speak is not as good as the Chinese you speak.
6.   I have never heard him speak American.
7.   There are two automobiles here: one is yours, one is his.
8.   He wants to buy an automobile but he has no money.
9.   Sir, have you ever been to China?
10.   Yes, I have. I went to China year before last.

VOCABULARY CHARACTERS

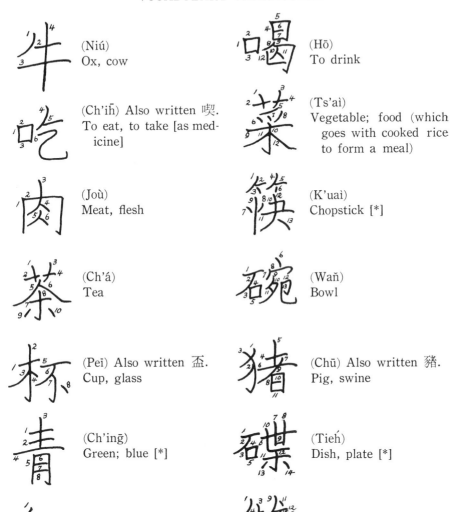

(Niú)
Ox, cow

(Hō)
To drink

(Ch'iħ) Also written 喫.
To eat, to take [as med-
icine]

(Ts'ai)
Vegetable; food (which
goes with cooked rice
to form a meal)

(Joù)
Meat, flesh

(K'uaì)
Chopstick [*]

(Ch'á)
Tea

(Waň)
Bowl

(Peī) Also written 盃.
Cup, glass

(Chū) Also written 豬.
Pig, swine

(Ch'inḡ)
Green; blue [*]

(Tieħ)
Dish, plate [*]

(Hunǵ)
Red [*]

(Shuanḡ)
A pair, a couple; even

(Faǹ)
Cooked rice; food; meal

71

COMPOUNDS

吃 飯 (Ch'ih̄-fàn) To eat a meal, to eat food

喝 茶 (Hō-ch'á) To drink tea

筷 子 (K'uaìtzu) Chopsticks

牛 肉 (Niújoù) Beef

猪 肉 (Chūjoù) Pork

飯 碗 (Fànwǎn) Rice bowl

茶 杯 (Ch'ápeī) Teacup

青 菜 (Ch'inḡts'aì) Green vegetables

碟 子 (Tiéhtzu) Dish, plate, saucer

青 茶 (Ch'inḡch'á) Green tea

紅 茶 (Hunḡch'á) Black tea

中國飯 (Chunḡkuo-fàn) Chinese meal, Chinese food

中國菜 (Chunḡkuo-ts'aì) Chinese food

中國茶 (Chunḡkuo-ch'á) Chinese tea

美國飯 (Meĭkuo-fàn) American meal, American food

美國菜 (Meĭkuo-ts'aì) American food

美國茶 (Meĭkuo-ch'á) American tea

好 吃 (Haŏch'ih̄) Good to eat, good eating

好 喝 (Haŏhō) Good to drink, good drinking

READING MATERIAL

1. 這個是甚麼？
2. 這個是飯碗.
3. 那個也是飯碗麼？
4. 不是,那個是茶杯.
5. 這個中國話叫甚麼？
6. 這個中國話叫"筷子."
7. 這雙筷子是誰的？
8. 是他們的.
9. 那個中國話叫甚麼？
10. 那個中國話叫"碟子."
11. 你今天吃過飯沒有？

12. 沒 吃 過, 可 是 喝 過 茶.

13. 你 喝 了 甚 麼 茶? 是 紅茶 不 是?

14. 不 是 紅 茶, 是 青 茶.

15. 你 說 中 國 飯 好 吃 不 好 吃?

16. 很 好 吃, 美 國 飯 也 很 好 吃.

17. 這 裏 有 甚 麼?

18. 有 一 碟 子 牛 肉, 也 有 一 碟 子

青 菜.

19. 沒 有 猪 肉 麼?

20. 沒 有, 也 沒 有 紅 茶.

21. 紅 茶 好 喝 不 好 喝?

22. 不 好 喝, 青 茶 好 喝.

23. 他 一 天 吃 幾 碗 飯?

24. 他 一 天 吃 三 四 碗 飯.

25. 你 昨 天 喝 了 幾 杯 茶?

26. 我 喝 了 四 五 杯 茶.

ROMANIZED TEXT OF READING MATERIAL

1. Chèko shih shemma?
2. Chèko shih faǹwaň.
3. Nàko yeh shih faǹwaň ma?
4. Pū shih, nàko shih ch'ápeī.
5. Chèko Chungkuo-huà chiaò shemma?
6. Chèko Chungkuo-huà chiaò "k'uaìtzu."
7. Chèshuang k'uaìtzu shih shuíte?
8. Shih t'āmente.
9. Nàko Chungkuo-huà chiaò shemma?
10. Nàko Chungkuo-huà chiaò "tiehtzu."
11. Nǐ chiňt'ien ch'ihkuo faǹ meiyu?
12. Meí ch'ihkuo, k'ŏshih hōkuo ch'á.
13. Nǐ hōle shemma ch'á? Shih hungch'á pushih?

14. Pū shih̀ hunǵch'á, shih̀ ch'inḡch'á.
15. Nǐ shuō Chunḡkuo-fan̄ haŏch'iň puhaoch'iň?
16. Heń haŏch'iň, Meǐkuo-fan̄ yeń heń haŏch'iň.
17. Chèli yǔ sheḿma?
18. Yǔ ītieh́tzu niújoù, yeń yǔ ītieh́tzu ch'inḡts'aì.
19. Meí yǔ chūjoù ma?
20. Meí yǔ, yeň meí yǔ hunǵch'á.
21. Hunǵch'á haŏhō puhaoho?
22. Pū haŏhō, ch'inḡch'á haŏhō.
23. T'ā ī t'ieñ ch'iň chíwaň fan̄?
24. T'ā ī t'ieñ ch'iň sañ-szùwaň fan̄.
25. Nǐ tsót'ien hōle chīpeī ch'á?
26. Wǒ hōle szù-wǔpeī ch'á.

NOTES

1. 碗, 碟, and 杯 are used as measure words in sentences 18, 23, 24, 25, and 26 above. Note that when they are used in this new capacity their own classifier is not used even though a definite number is present. Compare 一碗飯, "one bowl of rice," 一杯茶, "one cup of tea," and 一碟子青菜, "one dish of vegetables," with 一個飯碗, "one bowl," 一個茶杯, "one teacup," and 一個碟子, "one dish."

2. When two consecutive numbers are used in a Chinese expression to show a slight uncertainty or an approximation, the conjunction "or" is not necessary, as 三四碗飯 in sentence 24 above, which means simply "three or four bowls of rice."

3. The printed forms of "chū," "pig, swine," are 猪 and 豬.

ORAL EXERCISES

A. Say the following in Chinese:
1. Please give me a cup of green tea.
2. These are my chopsticks; those are yours.
3. Do you want those Chinese rice bowls?
4. No, but I want these American dishes.
5. Is pork good to eat?
6. It is very good to eat.
7. This teacup is not very big, but very pretty.
8. He drinks green tea; I drink black tea.
9. Yesterday he bought me some beef.
10. Please bring me a dish of green vegetables.

B. Render the following into English:
1. Chanḡ hsiensheng, chèli yǔ Chunḡkuo-fan̄ ch'iň meiyu?
2. Ch'ień hsiensheng, yǔ, k'ŏshih pū heń haŏch'iň.
3. Chèli te Meǐkuo-fan̄ haŏch'iň ma?
4. Haŏch'iňteheń, nǐ meí ch'iňkuo ma?

5. Meí ch'iṅkuo, nǎli yú Meǐkuo-faṅ ch'iḥ, wó yeḥ pū chiṅtao.
6. Nǐ chiṅt'ien hsiàwǔ yaò chiṅ-ch'eṅg ch'ü maǐ sheṁma?
7. Maǐ saṅko faṅwǎn, szùko tieḥtzu.
8. Chuṅḡkuo-ch'á ní maǐ pumai?
9. Wǒ meí yú heṅ tō ch'ień, Chuṅḡkuo-ch'á pū maǐ le.
10. Wó yeḥ meí yú heṅ tō ch'ień, k'ōshih wǒ yaò maǐ Chuṅḡkuo-ch'á.

WRITTEN EXERCISES

A. Transcribe Section B, above, in Chinese.

B. Render the following into English:

1. 昨天白先生請張先生在家裏吃飯.

2. 我不知道"牛肉"美國話怎麼說.

3. 中國人吃了飯喝青茶; 美國人吃了飯喝紅茶.

4. 他拿了你的筷子出去給那些美國人看.

5. 誰說牛肉沒有豬肉好吃?

6. 棹子上頭有三雙筷子, 三碗飯, 四碟子菜, 三杯茶.

7. 他一天喝七八杯茶, 你說多不多?

8. 你今天甚麼時候坐汽車到城裏去買中國青茶?

9. 你告訴了他誰拿了他的碟子進去沒有?

10. 請你給我看看他昨天買的茶杯.

C. Render the following into Chinese:

1. The green tea is not mine; it is his.
2. Whose rice bowl do you see on that table?
3. These chopsticks are not as good as those.
4. We eat Chinese meals; they eat American meals.
5. Last week we bought some very nice green vegetables.
6. Last Friday I saw him buy five or six teacups in the city.
7. I can see three Chinese eating American meals in the house.
8. Chinese eat pork; Americans eat beef.
9. Two or three years ago I bought him five or six very large dishes.
10. Yesterday I did not drink any tea. Did you?

VOCABULARY CHARACTERS

刀 (Taō)
Knife

做 (Tsò)
To make; to be; to act as; to do

叉 (Ch'ā)
Fork [*]; pitchfork

晚 (Wǎn)
Evening [*]; late, tardy

太 (T'ai)
Too, excessively; a married woman, wife [*]

够 (Koù) Also written 夠, 彀.
Sufficient, enough

水 (Shuǐ)
Water

都 (Toū) Printed form 都.
All, invariably

包 (Paō)
Dumpling [*]; package; to wrap; to include [*]; (a surname)

麵 (Mièn) Also written 麪.
Flour [*]

奶 (Naǐ)
Milk

罷 (Pa) Also written 吧.
(A modal particle)
(Pà)
To cease, to finish

再 (Tsai)
Again

謝 (Hsieh)
To thank; thanks [*]; (a surname)

COMPOUNDS

早上 (Tsaǒshang) Morning, morning time

中飯 (Chungfàn) ⎫ Noon meal,
午飯 (Wǔfàn) ⎬ lunch

晚上 (Wǎnshang) Evening, evening time

早飯 (Tsaǒfàn) Breakfast, morning meal

麵包 (Miènpaō) Bread

晚飯 (Wǎnfàn) Evening meal, dinner

刀子 (Taōtzu) Knife

77

叉 子 (Ch'ātzu) Fork

刀 叉 (Taōch'ā) Knives and forks

謝 謝 (Hsiehhsieh) Thank you, thanks

做 飯 (Tsò-fàn) To cook a meal

做 菜 (Tsò-ts'aì) To cook food

外 國 (Waìkuo) Foreign country

外國人 (Waìkuo-jeń) Alien, foreigner

外國話 (Waìkuo-huà) Foreign spoken language

外國飯 (Waìkuo-fàn) Foreign meal

外國菜 (Waìkuo-ts'aì) Foreign food

太 太 (T'aìt'ai) Mrs., wife, married lady

水 杯 (Shuǐpeī) Water glass

牛 奶 (Niúnaǐ) Cow's milk

再 見 (Tsaì chieǹ) Good-bye! See you again!

有 些 (Yǔhsieh̄) Some

READING MATERIAL

1. 你 們 今 天 早 上 吃 了 甚 麼?

2. 我 們 今 天 早 上 吃 了 早 飯.

3. 你 們 早 飯 吃 了 甚 麼, 喝 了 甚 麼?

4. 吃 了 麵 包, 喝 了 牛 奶.

5. 你 們 午 飯 晚 飯 也 吃 麵 包 麼?

6. 不 吃 麵 包, 我 們 吃 飯, 吃 肉, 吃 青 菜.

7. 在 裏 頭 做 飯 的 人 是 誰?

8. 是 錢 太 太. 他 很 會 做 飯.

9. 他 中 國 飯 外 國 飯 都 會 做 麼?

10. 都 會, 做 得 都 很 好 吃.

11. 這 把 刀 子 是 你 的 不 是?

12. 不 是 我 的, 是 謝 先 生 的.

13. 那 把 叉 子 是 外 國 人 的 不 是?

14. 不 是, 也 是 謝 先 生 的.
15. 這 些 外 國 人 都 會 說 中 國 話 不 會?
16. 不 都 會, 有 些 會, 有 些 不 會.
17. 你 喝 的 是 牛 奶 不 是?
18. 不 是 牛 奶, 也 不 是 茶, 是 水.
19. 這 些 碗, 碟 子, 筷 子 都 是 他 的 麼?
20. 都 不 是 他 的, 是 我 的. 你 要 碟 子 不 要?
21. 不 要 碟 子, 我 要 筷 子.
22. 你 要 幾 雙 筷 子?
23. 我 要 兩 雙.
24. 你 家 裏 有 四 個 人, 兩 雙 不 夠 罷?
25. 夠 了, 我 有 兩 雙 在 家 裏 了.
26. 那 麼 你 拿 這 兩 雙 好 的 回 去 罷.
27. 很 好, 謝 謝, 明 天 再 見.
28. 明 天 再 見.

ROMANIZED TEXT OF READING MATERIAL

1. Nǐmen chiñt'ien tsaŏshang ch'iȟle sheḿma?
2. Wǒmen chiñt'ien tsaŏshang ch'iȟle tsaŏfaǹ.
3. Nǐmen tsaŏfaǹ ch'iȟle sheḿma, hōle sheḿma?
4. Ch'iȟle mieǹpaō, hōle niúnaǐ.
5. Nǐmen wǔfaǹ waňfaǹ yeȟ ch'iȟ mieǹpaō ma?
6. Pū ch'iȟ mieǹpaō, wǒmen ch'iȟ-faǹ, ch'iȟ joù, ch'iȟ ch'iñgts'aì.
7. Tsaì lǐt'ou tsò-faǹ te jeń shiȟ shuí?
8. Shiȟ Ch'ień t'aìt'ai. T'ā heň huì tsò-faǹ.
9. T'ā Chuñgkuo-faǹ waìkuo-faǹ toū huì tsò ma?
10. Toū huì, tsòte toū heň haŏch'iȟ.

11. Chèpă taōtzu shih̀ nīte pushih?
12. Pū shih̀ wŏte, shih̀ Hsieh̀ hsienshengte.
13. Nàpă ch'ātzu shih̀ waìkuo-jeńte pushih?
14. Pū shih̀, yeh̀ shih̀ Hsieh̀ hsienshengte.
15. Chèhsieh waìkuo-jeń toū huì shuō Chunḡkuo-huà puhui?
16. Pū toū huì, yŭhsieh̀ huì, yŭhsieh̀ pū huì.
17. Nĭ hō te shih̀ niúnaĭ pushih?
18. Pū shih̀ niúnaĭ, yeh̀ pū shih̀ ch'á, shih̀ shuĭ.
19. Chèhsieh wań, tieh̀tzu, k'uaìtzu toū shih̀ t'āte ma?
20. Toū pū shih̀ t'āte, shih̀ wŏte. Nĭ yaò tieh̀tzu puyao?
21. Pū yaò tieh̀tzu, wŏ yaò k'uaìtzu.
22. Nĭ yaò chīshuanḡ k'uaìtzu?
23. Wŏ yaò lianḡshuanḡ.
24. Nĭ chiāli yŭ szùko jeń, lianḡshuanḡ pū koù pa?
25. Koù le, wó yú lianḡshuanḡ tsaì chiāli le.
26. Nèma nĭ ná chè lianḡshuanḡ haŏ te huich'ü pa.
27. Heń haŏ, hsieh̀hsieh, mińt'ien tsaì chieǹ.
28. Mińt'ien tsaì chieǹ.

NOTES

1. When 罷 is used as a modal particle, it may indicate conjecture on the part of the speaker expressed interrogatively or mild or polite command. When so used it is simply tacked on to the end of a statement. For examples, see sentences 24 and 26 above. A command without 罷 at the end of it is to be understood as strong and obligatory.

2. Note the different positions in which 都 is used in sentences 16 and 20 above. In the former, 不 qualifies 都; in the latter, 都 qualifies 不.

ORAL EXERCISES

A. Say the following in Chinese:
1. Too good; too small; too early; too late.
2. In the morning I read; in the evening you read.
3. He will go abroad [to foreign countries] next year.
4. Mrs. Chanḡ, Mr. Ch'ień is not coming this evening.
5. I want a knife; I don't want a fork.
6. We all don't know how to cook a meal.
7. He drinks tea; I drink water.
8. Go out! Go home! Don't come here again!
9. Is the bread yours? Where did you buy it?
10. Don't go out in the evening! I will come again tomorrow evening.

B. Render the following into English:
1. Chanḡ hsiensheng Chanḡ t'aìt'ai toū huì tsò-faǹ.
2. Nĭmen mińt'ien tsaŏshang ch'ǜ maĭ mieǹpaō puch'ǜ?
3. Wŏ yaò ch'ih̄ waìkuo-faǹ, pū yaò ch'ih̄ Chunḡkuo-faǹ.

4. T'ā tsót'ien hsieň te tzù toū shiȟ chèma tà te.
5. Chunḡkuo-huà te "koù" [enough] tzù shiȟ chèma hsieȟ te pushiȟ?
6. Nĭ shuō te huà wǒ meí t'inḡchien, ch'inǵ ni tsaì shuōshuo.
7. Nĭ ī t'ień ch'iȟ sańwaň faǹ koù pukou?
8. Nàhsieh waìkuo-jeń yŭ taōch'ā, wŏmen meí yŭ.
9. Ch'inǵ ni ná chèhsieh shū huich'ü pa, wǒ pū tsaì k'aǹ le.
10. Maó hsiensheng, tsaì chieǹ, wǒ minǵt'ien tsaōshang tsaì laí.

WRITTEN EXERCISES

A. Transcribe Section B, above, in Chinese.

B. Render the following into English:

1. 我昨天喝水喝得太多了.
2. 這個字你寫得不好,請再寫一回.
3. 那些外國人在那裏做甚麼?
4. 他們在那裏做外國菜給我們吃.
5. 太晚了,你們回去罷.
6. 他們都要到外頭去看看那些外國人.
7. 這些中國字都是他們昨天晚上寫的.
8. 中國人喝茶;外國人喝牛奶.
9. 白先生,我要走了,明天再見.
10. 我昨天買的刀叉,都在這裏.

C. Render the following into Chinese:

1. Mr. Hsieȟ says he wants to invite you for [to eat] dinner tomorrow night.
2. I can speak Chinese but I can't speak [any] foreign language.
3. Please come here to cook a meal for those foreigners.
4. I want to buy some knives and forks to give to Mr. Chanḡ.

    5. In the morning I eat bread; in the evening I eat rice.

    6. He is not going abroad next year.

    7. Thank you, Mr. Paí; I have eaten enough foreign meals.

    8. The bread is his; the knives are also his.

    9. Please ask them what they want to drink [at] dinner this evening.

    10. Please again drink [some] black tea; the water here is not very good to drink.

CHARACTERS

Number of Strokes	Characters	Pronunciation and Tone	Meaning	Lesson Reference
Two	二	Erh̀	Two	11
	七	Ch'ī	Seven	11
	八	Pā	Eight	11
	九	Chiŭ	Nine	11
	十	Shih́	Ten	11
	刀	Taō	Knife	14
Three	叉	Ch'ā	Fork; pitchfork	14
Four	五	Wŭ	Five	11
	六	Liù	Six	11
	月	Yüeh̀	Moon; month	11
	火	Huŏ	Fire	12
	牛	Niú	Ox, cow	13
	太	T'aì	Too, excessively; a married woman; wife	14
	水	Shuĭ	Water	14
Five	生	Shenḡ	Raw; to give birth to; to be born; life, living	12
	可	K'ŏ	To be permissible; can, may	12
	包	Paō	Dumpling; package; to wrap; to include; (a surname)	14
	奶	Naĭ	Milk	14
Six	年	Nień	Year	11

Number of Strokes	Characters	Pronunciation and Tone	Meaning	Lesson Reference
Six	先	Hsieñ	To be the first (in doing something)	12
	老	Laŏ	Old, aged; always	11
	早	Tsaŏ	Early; morning	12
	回	Huí	To turn back; an occasion, a time	12
	吃	Ch'iħ	To eat, to take (as medicine)	13
	肉	Joù	Meat, flesh	13
	再	Tsaì	Again	14
Seven	汽	Ch'ì	Steam	12
	車	Ch'ē	Vehicle	12
	坐	Tsò	To sit, to seat	12
Eight	杯	Peī	Cup, glass	13
	青	Ch'inğ	Green, blue	13
Nine	拜	Paì	To worship, to pay respect to, to call on	11
	紅	Hunǵ	Red	13
Ten	時	Shiħ	Time, hour	12
	候	Hoù	Time, period; to wait	12
	茶	Ch'á	Tea	13
Eleven	猪	Chū	Pig, swine	13
	做	Tsò	To make; to be; to act as; to do	14
	夠	Koù	Sufficient, enough	14
	都	Toū	All, invariably	14
Twelve	幾	Chĭ	How many? several, a few	11

Number of Strokes	Characters	Pronunciation and Tone	Meaning	Lesson Reference
Twelve	買	Maǐ	To buy	12
	喝	Hō	To drink	13
	飯	Faǹ	Cooked rice; food; meal	13
	菜	Ts'aǐ	Vegetable, food	13
	晚	Waň	Evening; late, tardy	14
Thirteen	號	Haò	Number, mark, sign	11
	過	Kuò	To pass by or through; to exceed; error, fault; (perfective suffix)	12
	筷	K'uaì	Chopsticks	13
	碗	Waň	Bowl	13
Fourteen	碟	Tieň	Dish, plate	13
Fifteen	輛	Liaǹg	(Classifier for vehicles)	12
	罷	Pa / Pà	(Modal particle) / To cease, to finish	14 / 14
Seventeen	禮	Lǐ	Propriety, rite	11
	謝	Hsieň	To thank, thanks; (a surname)	14
Eighteen	雙	Shuāng	A pair, a couple; even	13
Twenty	麵	Mieǹ	Flour	14

ORAL DRILL

A. Say the following in Chinese. (The items in this section are arranged in dialogue form. Results can best be attained by having two persons participating in it, one doing the questioning, the other the answering. They can reverse their roles at any logical point.)

Is it you?	It isn't I.
Is it they?	It isn't they either.
Who is it then?	It is you.
Have they come?	Yes, they have.
Have they come back?	No, they haven't.

Has he come back to America?	Yes, he has.
Have they ever been abroad?	No, they haven't, but I have.
Which country have you been to?	I have been to China.
When did you go to China?	I went there four or five years ago.
What did you see when you were there?	I saw a great many people and houses.
What did you buy when you were there?	I bought some Chinese books, chopsticks, and rice bowls.
Did you understand the Chinese spoken by the Chinese?	No, I didn't understand even one word.
Did all the Chinese understand the American you spoke?	Not all of them understood; some did, and some didn't.
When did you come back to America from China?	I came back two or three years ago.
Will you go to China again?	I will go again next year.
What month next year will you go?	I will go in May [of] next year.
I am going. Are you?	I am going, too.
When he reads, do you also read?	When he reads, I don't read; I write.

B. Render the following into English:

1. T'ā tsoŭlech'ulai le.
2. Wó tsoŭlechinch'ü le.
3. Nàko Chungkuo-tzù nĭmen toū yaò hsiehhsialai.
4. Chèpá itzu t'aì hsiaŏ, tsòpuhsià liangko jeń.
5. T'āmen mingt'ien yaò huítaò chèli lai.
6. Hsieh hsiensheng maĭle ichang waìkuo-paò huilai, k'ŏshih pū huì k'aǹ.
7. Ch'ień t'aìt'ai chiñt'ien yaò maĭ ihsieh ch'ingts'aì hui chiāli ch'ü.
8. Nàhsieh waìkuo-jeń ch'ieńt'ien tsaŏshang nále sheńma huich'ü?
9. Chèli yú heň tō chūjoù, nĭmen yaò puyao?
10. Nàli yŭ īko shuĭpeī, ch'ing ni keī t'a īpeī shuĭ pa.

C. Write out your Chinese version of Section A of Oral Drill, above.

D. Transcribe Section B of Oral Drill, above, in Chinese.

E. Render the following into Chinese:

One chair	One word
Two tables	Two letters
Three newspapers	Three houses
Four men	Four days
Five automobiles	Five dishes
Six pens	Six pairs of chopsticks
Seven rice bowls	Seven foreigners
Eight months	Eight bowls of rice
Nine years	Nine cups of tea
Ten weeks	Ten knives

READING DRILL

After reading the following, render it into English:

張子中先生：

你好。我沒寫信給你三個禮拜了。上禮拜四晚上白先生、白太太請我吃飯，飯都很好吃。白先生吃得太多，也喝牛奶，白太太喝青茶；我也喝青茶。他們說外國先生很多。白太太告訴我，他們要到美國去。他寫信給你了。

錢先生、錢太太禮拜二都請白先生、白太太到他家吃飯。白太太做青菜、包包子；錢太太做青菜、包包子。他們三號住¹在美國候，請白太太們坐火車去。

白先生今年說到美國去買書，三個禮拜。他說給我買三本書；下午二時候，我告訴他，請他給我買書。下禮拜二你請白先生、白太太到你家去。十二月在中國很好，你要麼告訴我。這本書很好，我家……再見。

　　　　　　　　　　謝明道

---

¹ 住 (chù) "to reside," see Lesson 16.

VOCABULARY CHARACTERS

(Chiù)
Then, thereupon, consequently

(Ǐ)
By [*]; with [*]; by means of [*]

(Chù)
To reside, to live at; to hold fast, to hold on to [*]

(Yiñ)
Reason [*]; cause [*]

(Weì)
For [*], on account of [*], for the sake of [*]
The printed form may look like 為.

(Chiaō)
To teach, to instruct
(Chiaò)
Teaching, religion [*]

(Hsüeh)
To learn, to study; learning [*]

(Wań)
To finish; to complete

(Tuì)
To correspond; to face; to check by comparing; opposite

(Ts'ò)
Wrong; error [*], mistake [*]

(Hsieñ)
Now [*]; to appear [*], to manifest [*]

(Chù)
Sentence [*]; (classifier for sentences, phrases, etc.)

(Ch'ǐ)
To rise [*], to raise [*]; to begin, to start

COMPOUNDS

可 以 (K'ói) May, can; possible or permissible

所 以 (Sói) Therefore, hence, so

以 前 (Ǐch'ień) Before (this time), ago, formerly, previously

以 後 (Ǐhoù) Afterwards, later

88

句 子　(Chǜtzu) Sentence

因 为　(Yīnwèi) Because, on account of

為甚麼　(Weìshemma) Why? For what?

現 在　(Hsièntsaì) Now, at present

不 錯　(Pūts'ò) Not wrong; not bad

對不起　(Tuìpuch'ì) I am sorry

就 是　(Chiùshih) Even if

READING MATERIAL

1. 你 們 會 說 美 國 話 不 會 ？

2. 很 對 不 起, 不 會 說.

3. 為 甚 麼 你 們 不 學 ？

4. 因 為 沒 有 人 教 我 們, 所 以 沒 有 學. 你 知 道 有 誰 可 以 教 我 們 麼 ？

5. 知 道, 謝 先 生 可 以 教 你 們, 因 為 他 在 美 國 住 過 很 多 年, 美 國 話 說 得 很 好.

6. 可 是 現 在 謝 先 生 不 在 這 裏 了; 你 可 以 教 我 們 麼 ？

7. 可 以, 那 麼 我 就 教 你 們 罷. 我 先 說 一 句 美 國 話 出 來, 你 們 聽 完 了 就 把 那 句 話 學 說, 好 不 好 ？

8. 很 好, 請 你 說 罷.

9. 我 說 完 了, 你 們 都 聽 見 了 罷 ？

10. 聽 見 了, 可 是 我 們 不 明 白.

11. 我 可 以 告 訴 你 們 ... 現 在 明 白 了 麼 ？

12. 明白了, 謝謝.

13. 好, 現在請你們把那句話說出來給我聽, 看看你們說得對不對.

14. 好, 我們現在說了, 請你聽聽 ...說得對不對?

15. 不對, 你們說錯了, 再說一回罷!

16. 這一回說得對了麼?

17. 對是對了, 可是說得不很好, 請再說一回...這回說得很不錯了...今天我教了你們說十句美國話, 你們都明白, 都說得很不錯. 明天我再教你們說十句, 好不好?

18. 很好, 一天學十句, 那麼三個月以後, 我們就會說很多句美國話了.

19. 你們住在那裏?

20. 住在城裏.

21. 我也住在城裏. 現在我要回家去了. 我們明天見.

22. 明天見.

ROMANIZED TEXT OF READING MATERIAL

1. Nimen huì shuō Meǐkuo-huà puhuì?
2. Heň tuìpuch'ǐ, pū huì shuō.
3. Weìsheḿma nimen pū hsüeḣ?

4. Yiñweì meí yŭ jeń chiaō women, sói meí yŭ hsüeń. Nī chihtao yŭ shuí k'ói chiaō women ma?

5. Chihtao, Hsieh hsiensheng k'ói chiaō nimen, yiñweì t'ā tsaì Meĭkuo chùkuo heñ tō nień, Meĭkuo-huà shuōte heń haŏ.

6. K'ŏshih hsieñtsaì Hsieh hsiensheng pū tsaì chèli le; nĭ k'ói chiaō women ma?

7. K'ói, nèma wŏ chiù chiaō nimen pa. Wŏ hsieñ shuō īchù Meĭkuo-huà ch'ulai, nimen t'iñgwańle chiù pă nàchù huà hsüeń shuō, haŏ puhaŏ?

8. Heń haŏ, ch'iń ni shuō pa.

9. Wŏ shuōwań le, nīmen toū t'iñgchienle pa?

10. T'iñgchien le, k'ŏshih wŏmen pū miñgpai.

11. Wŏ k'ói kaòsu nimen . . . Hsieñtsaì miñgpaile ma?

12. Miñgpai le, hsiehhsieh.

13. Haŏ, hsieñtsaì ch'iń nimen pă nàchù huà shuōch'ulai keí wo t'iñg, k'ańk'an nimen shuōte tuì putui.

14. Haŏ, wŏmen hsieñtsaì shuō le, ch'iń ni t'iñgt'ing . . . Shuōte tuì putui?

15. Pū tuì, nīmen shuōts'ò le, tsaì shuō ī huí pa!

16. Chèi huí shuōte tuì le ma?

17. Tuì shih tuì le, k'ŏshih shuōte pū heń haŏ, ch'iñg tsaì shuō ī huí . . . Chè huí shuōte heń pūts'ò le . . . Chiñt'ien wŏ chiaōle nimen shuō shihchù Meĭkuo-huà, nīmen toū miñgpai, toū shuōte heń pūts'ò. Miñgt'ien wŏ tsaì chiaō nimen shuō shihchù, haŏ puhao?

18. Heń haŏ, ī t'ieñ hsüeń shihchù, nèma sañko yüeh īhoù, wŏmen chiù huì shuō heń tōchù Meĭkuo-huà le.

19. Nīmen chù tsaì năli?

20. Chù tsaì ch'eñgli.

21. Wó yeń chù tsaì ch'eñgli. Hsieñtsaì wŏ yaò huí-chiā ch'ü le. Wŏmen miñgt'ien chieñ.

22. Miñgt'ien chieñ.

NOTES

1. 對不起 (or 住), which literally means "to face without being able to remain standing [or firm]," is used to express regret on the part of the speaker, and hence it is tantamount in effect to saying "I am sorry!" There is the positive form, 對得起, but it is not used except for questioning or for the purpose, probably, of vindicating oneself in a strong argument involving one's intentions or conscience.

2. 就 can be used to show either temporal or logical sequence. But observe the fact that it always comes after, never before, the subject, as is often the case with English.

3. 就 is often used to lend more emphasis to the copula 是, and may be taken to mean "precisely, simply, just," depending on the construction of the sentence. If we say 我就是左先生, it may be rendered into English as "I am precisely [simply, just] Mr. Tsŏ." Since the insertion of "precisely,"

"simply," or "just" does not add materially to the meaning of the statement in English, 就 may be left out in the English translation. Do not confuse 就 followed by 是 with the compound 就是, "even if." When the latter is used it is intensified by 都 or 也, which precedes the predicate verb. For example, see sentence 6 of the Written Exercises in this lesson.

4. The verb 完, "to finish, to complete," is often used with an action verb to form a resultative compound to indicate the termination of the action expressed by the latter, as 吃完, 説完, 寫完, 喝完, etc. They may be rendered into English as "to finish eating," "to finish saying," "to finish writing," and "to finish drinking."

5. The verb 把, "to grasp, to hold in the hand," is often used to help indicate that the action expressed by the main verb following it in relation to the direct object is one of execution or disposal. It may be called an "auxiliary" verb in the sense that it does help out the main verb by indicating the nature of the latter's action, not by completing, as is the case with auxiliary verbs in English, the grammatical form of the main verb with regard to voice, mood, or tense. When 把 is used in this capacity in a sentence, the direct object of the main verb is so transposed that it precedes not only the indirect object, but the main verb as well (see Note 4, Lesson Eight), as 我把書給你 (cf. 我給你書). However, it must not be taken for granted that the direct object of any transitive verb in any active sentence can be similarly transposed. If the main verb expresses a mental act or a receptive phenomenon, 把 cannot be used: thus 我愛他, "I love him," and 我看見他, "I see him," cannot be restated as 我把他愛 and 我把他看見. Again, if the action expressed by the main verb cannot possibly alter the object, 把 should not be used: thus 他上樓, "He goes upstairs," cannot be restated as 他把樓上. Finally, if the main verb happens to be 有 or 在, the 把 construction is not to be used: thus 你有錢, "You have money," and 我在家, "I am at home," cannot be restated as 你把錢有 and 我把家在. It may be added that 把 is never used with any verb without a complement.

6. In sentence 17 above, the expression 對是對了, "[as to being] correct, [the thing in question] is correct," may be translated into English simply as "it is correct" with an emphatic "but" following it immediately, and it is used to show concession on the part of the speaker. Other adjectives may be similarly treated in this concessive construction.

7. 不錯 is frequently used to mean "good" (cf. English "not bad" in current use). Thus 説得很不錯 in sentence 17 above may be taken to mean "quite well spoken." 錯 can be freely appended to action verbs to form resultative compounds to indicate that a mistake or error has been made.

8. 一天 in sentence 19 above means "one day," but it may also mean "a whole day long" or "all day long." For example, 我昨天一天在家裏看書 means "I stayed home all day long yesterday reading."

9. 以前 and 以後, like 前頭 and 後頭 (see Lesson Six), are to be used postpositively. Both are used to show temporal relationships, whereas 前頭 and 後頭 are used only to show spatial ones.

10. In order to breach the external hiatus in compounds such as "k'ói" (可以) and "sói" (所以), the "i" must be pronounced like the "y" in "yea" or "yeast."

11. When 爲甚麼 is used unemphatically, its last two syllables become neutral in tone, 爲甚麼 (weishemma). Cf. Note 5, Lesson Three.

ORAL EXERCISES

A. Say the following in Chinese:

1. Two years before; five months before; eight days afterwards; three weeks afterwards.
2. Why? Why don't you go? Why didn't you come? Where do you live?
3. I am sorry! I didn't know you couldn't speak American.
4. Will it do for you to give me that book?
5. When? Now! Right? Yes, right! No, not right!
6. You may return home now. Do you live here?
7. Can you write that word for us?
8. That house is good, but it is not big enough.
9. Last night he taught us to say that sentence.
10. He has finished reading yesterday's newspaper.

B. Render the following into English:

1. Yiñweì t'ā meí laí, sói wǒ meí ch'ǜ.
2. T'ā shuō ni pū hō-ch'á, t'ā chiù pū chih-fàn.
3. Nàko jeń maǐle paò huilai chiù ch'ih-fàn.
4. Ni k'aǹts'ò le, nàko pū shih "t'ieñ" [sky] tzù.
5. Wǒ náts'òle shū lai, weìshemma ní yeh meí kaòsu wo?
6. T'ā chiù shih chiaò ni chiñch'ü k'aǹ-shū te jeń.
7. Wǒ tsót'ien meí chiaō t'a shuō, sói t'ā hsieǹtsaì pū huì shuō.
8. Shih nień ich'ień t'ā chiaōkuo women hsieh Chungkuo-tzù.
9. Ni shuō te huà heñ tuì, sói t'ā meí tsaì laí le.
10. T'ā tsót'ien waňshang chiaò wo kaòsu ni szù nień ihoù tsaì taò nàli ch'ü.

WRITTEN EXERCISES

A. Transcribe Section B, above, in Chinese.

B. Render the following into English:

1. 你們學中國話學了兩個月，可是說得很不錯了.

2. 你們有書就要看書，沒有書就要寫字.

3. 張先生兩個月以前要買汽車,可是現在不買了.

4. 不錯,他是美國人,可是他很會說中國話.

5. 現在不早了,為甚麼你不回家去做晚飯?

6. 就是他有錢也不要再買昨天的報.

7. 我不知道他昨天為甚麼沒去,也不知道你為甚麼沒來.

8. 我說一句中國話,你說一句美國話,好不好?

9. 請你把他昨天給你的書拿出來.

10. 你們都要把這些字寫出來給謝先生看看.

C. Render the following into Chinese:

1. [If] you have money, then I can buy that house for you.
2. It is very late now, why don't you go back?
3. Please have all of these words written down.
4. Please say that sentence again for[1] him to hear.
5. He asked me last night why you didn't go.
6. Please tell him that because I had no automobile, I didn't go.
7. Sorry, I didn't know you had finished writing the letter for Mrs. Paí.
8. Having finished eating breakfast, he taught us to speak Chinese.
9. What you said was not quite correct because you hadn't heard what he said.
10. Two years ago he came here; now, he is in China.

[1] Use the verb 給.

VOCABULARY CHARACTERS

快 (K'uaì) Fast, quick; happy [*]

慢 (Maǹ) Slow

長 (Ch'anǵ) Long

短 (Tuaň) Short

高 (Kaō) Tall, high, lofty; (a surname)

低 (Tī) Low, base

兒 (Erh́) Son, child [*] (Erh) (Noun suffix)

點 (Tieň) Also written 點. Dot, speck, point; a little; to light (as a fire or lamp)

還 (Haí) Still, yet

最 (Tsuì) (Sign of the superlative)

新 (Hsiñ) New

舊 (Chiù) Old

比 (Pǐ) To compare

更 (Kenǵ) (The comparative sign)

COMPOUNDS

快 車 (K'uaìch'ē) Fast train; express train

慢 車 (Maǹch'ē) Slow train; local train

天 天 (T'ieñt'ieñ) Every day

人 人 (Jeńjeń) Everybody

年 年 (Nieńnień) Every year

上 回 (Shaǹghui) The last time

下 回 (Hsiàhui) The next time

還 是 (Haíshih) Whether; or; after all

95

這 兒	(Chèrh) Here, this place	那 兒	(Nǎrh) Where? Which place?
兒 子	(Erhtzu) Son	比一比	(Pǐipi) To make a comparison
一點兒	(Ītiǎrh) A little, a bit	比得上	(Pǐteshang) Capable of comparing with
那 兒	(Nàrh) There, that place	比不上	(Pǐpushang) Incapable of comparing with

從 前 (Ts'unǵch'ień) Formerly

READING MATERIAL

1. 你今天甚麼時候要到城裏去?

2. 我今天下午去. 你去不去?

3. 我不去了.

4. 為甚麼不去?

5. 因為我沒有汽車, 所以不去.

6. 你昨天坐的汽車不是你的麼?

7. 從前是我的, 可是我把汽車給了我的兒子了.

8. 那麼為甚麼不坐火車去?

9. 火車走得太慢罷? 比不上汽車那麼快!

10. 我說火車比汽車還要快; 我今天也要坐火車去.

11. 你要坐的火車是快車還是慢車?

12. 是快車, 上禮拜我坐過一回, 比汽車好坐得多.

13. 慢車你坐過沒有？
14. 沒坐過，可是張先生告訴我汽車比慢車快一點兒．
15. 慢車好坐不好坐？
16. 還好坐，可是坐慢車的人太多了．
17. 你今天進城要看看錢先生的新房子麼？
18. 要，可是我不知道那一所新房子是他的．你可以告訴我麼？
19. 可以，最高的新房子就是他的了．
20. 謝謝；你看得見我們前頭的三張書棹子麼？
21. 看得見，一張是白先生的，一張是謝先生的，一張是毛先生的．書棹子很長，毛先生的比白先生更長，謝先生的最長．
22. 火車到了，我們明天再見罷．
23. 好，明天再見．

ROMANIZED TEXT OF READING MATERIAL

1. Nǐ chiñt'ien sheṁma shiḥhou yaò taò ch'enǵli ch'ü?
2. Wǒ chiñt'ien hsiàwǔ ch'ù. Nǐ ch'ù puch'ü?
3. Wǒ pū ch'ù le.
4. Weìsheṁma pū ch'ù?
5. Yiñweì wǒ meí yǔ ch'ìch'ē, sói pū ch'ù.
6. Nǐ tsót'ien tsò te ch'ìch'ē pū shiḥ nǐte ma?

7. Ts'uńgch'ień shih̀ wŏte, k'ŏshih wó pă ch'ìch'ē keīle wote erh̀tzu le.

8. Nèma weìshem̀ma pū tsò huŏch'ē ch'ü?

9. Huŏch'ē tsoūte t'aì maǹ pa? Pǐpushanġ ch'ìch'ē nèma k'uaì!

10. Wŏ shuō huŏch'ē pǐ ch'ìch'ē haí yaò k'uaì; wŏ chiñt'ien yeh̀ yaò tsò huŏch'ē ch'ü.

11. Nǐ yaò tsò te huŏch'ē shih̀ k'uaìch'ē haíshih maǹch'ē?

12. Shih̀ k'uaìch'ē, shanġ-lǐpaì wŏ tsòkuo ī huí, pǐ ch'ìch'ē haŏtsòtetō.

13. Maǹch'ē nǐ tsòkuo meiyu?

14. Meí tsòkuo, k'ŏshih Chanḡ hsiensheng kaòsu wo ch'ìch'ē pǐ maǹch'ē k'uaì ītiărh.

15. Maǹch'ē haŏtsò puhaotso?

16. Haí haŏtsò, k'ŏshih tsò maǹch'ē te jeń t'aì tō le.

17. Nǐ chiñt'ien chiǹ-ch'enġ yaò k'aǹk'an Ch'ień hsienshengte hsiñ fanġtzu ma?

18. Yaò, k'ŏshih̀ wŏ pū chih̀tao năisō hsiñ fanġtzu shih̀ t'āte. Nǐ k'ói kaòsu wo ma?

19. K'ói, tsuì kaō te hsiñ fanġtzu chiù shih̀ t'āte le.

20. Hsieh̀hsieh, nǐ k'aǹtechieǹ women ch'ień t'ou te sañchanḡ shū-chōtzu ma?

21. K'aǹtechieǹ, īchanḡ shih̀ Paí hsienshengte, īchanḡ shih̀ Maó hsienshengte, īchanḡ shih̀ Hsieh̀ hsienshengte. Paí hsienshengte shū-chōtzu heǹ ch'anġ, Maó hsienshengte kenġ ch'anġ, Hsieh̀ hsienshengte tsuì ch'anġ.

22. Huŏch'ē taò le, wŏmen minġt'ien tsaì chieǹ pa.

23. Haŏ, minġt'ien tsaì chieǹ.

NOTES

1. To make a comparison in Chinese when the superior member precedes the inferior, the common way is to use 比, "to compare," after the former and the appropriate adjective or adverb after the latter. Thus, when we say 火車比汽車好坐, we mean that the train rides better than the automobile. (Cf. Note 5, Lesson Twelve, above.)

2. Another way of making a comparison in Chinese when the inferior member precedes the superior is to use 比不上 or 比不得. 我比不上你, "I am not to be compared with you," means by implication "I am not as good as you," Similarly, 我寫的字比不上你寫的 means "The words written by me [which I have written] are not as good as those written by you." (Cf. Note 5, Lesson Twelve, above.)

3. 更 is the sign of comparison, but it is not used except when the positive is present or clearly implied. When so used it precedes immediately the adjective or adverb compared.

4. Frequently the positive is used in Chinese in place of the comparative. This is true of a comparison in which a choice has to be made between the two members with reference to the adjective or adverb under comparison. If we want to determine, for instance, which is shorter, my pencil or his ink pen, or who is taller, you or I, we will say in Chinese, 我的鉛筆短還是他的鋼筆短 or 你高還是我高? The repetition of the ad-

jective compared depends on the construction. For "Which of these two books is larger?" we simply say 這兩本書那一本大?

5. 天天, 人人, 年年, and a few other similar reduplicated noun compounds carry with them the implication of "every" or "all," according to context. It must not be taken for granted that this reduplication process can be made to work with all or most other nouns in Chinese. However, if it is reasonably clear from the context, it is possible for the same effect to be achieved by the reduplication of the classifier of the noun involved. For example, the sentence, "There are very many books here; every one of them is a good book," may be rendered into Chinese as 這裏有很多書, 本本都是好的. Similarly, "He has four automobiles; every one of them is new" will become 他有四輛汽車, 輛輛都是新的. Note that 都 or 也 is used for the sake of intensifying the implication that no exception exists in the situation. The omission of the noun in the above cases after the reduplicated classifier is simply for the sake of avoiding redundancy. In a sporadic sentence in which no noun has been used before the reduplicated classifier, it is necessary to insert one after it. Thus, 這裏個個人都會寫中國字 means "Everybody here knows how to write Chinese characters." Note also that the reduplicated noun or classifier retains its own tone.

6. 兒, "son, child," like 子 (Note 2, Lesson Six, above), is a sort of diminutive suffix which in present-day usage is not necessarily limited to nouns which indicate smallness either actual or imputed in token of affection. Though it is written as a separate character when so used, it is not pronounced as a full syllable. It is so weakened that it sounds like a final " r " (transliterated in this text as " 'rh "). When it immediately follows a syllable ending in -ien, it causes the final " n " of the preceding syllable to drop and the vowel " e " to become " a." Thus, "ī tieň erh," 一點兒, becomes "ītiǎrh."

7. The difference in connotation between 老 and 舊, both meaning "old," is that the former carries with it the implication of "advanced in years," whereas the latter implies "antiquated" or "not new." In usage, 老 is the opposite of 少 (shaò), "young in years," while 舊 is the opposite of 新. Generally, 老 is used with animate objects while 舊 is used with inanimate objects. Thus we say 老人, 老朋友, 老馬, "old horse," 老樹, "old trees," but 舊汽車, 舊房子, 舊書, etc.

ORAL EXERCISES

A. Say the following in Chinese:
1. I want to drink a little tea.
2. Every book here is very small.
3. He goes to the city every day.
4. They are a little taller than we.
5. Which of these two houses is larger?
6. He is better than I, but not as good as you.
7. The Chinese characters written by Mr. Paí are best written.

8. His son writes most slowly.
9. The express train is a great deal faster than the local train.
10. Is it you or he? It is he, not I.

B. Render the following into English:

1. Chèko pǐ nàko haǒ. Nàko pīpushang̀ chèko.
2. Wǒmen sañko jeń t'ā tsuì yǔ-ch'ień.
3. T'ā shuō ni pū yaò chèma hsiaǒ te, yaò tà ītiǎrh te.
4. Shuí kaòsu ni Chanḡ t'aìt'ai mingt'ien yaò tsaǒ ītiǎrh huích'ü?
5. Yǔ hsiñ te chiù pū yaò chiù te jeń shih nǐ haíshih t'ā?
6. T'āmen hsüeh́le Chunḡkuo-huà sañ nień, k'ǒshih hsieǹtsaì haí pū huì shuō.
7. Shang̀hui nǐ taò Chunḡkuo ch'ü te shih́hou, t'ā haí meí yǔ ch'ìch'ē.
8. Nàhsieh waìkuo-jeń taò Meǐkuo ch'ükuo chǐ huí?
9. Ch'inǧ t'amen ná haǒ ītiǎrh te shū lai keī Ch'ień t'aìt'ai k'aǹ.
10. Meǐkuote ch'ìch'ē ī nień pǐ ī nień haǒk'aǹ.
11. Ch'inǵ ni pá women k'aǹ te shū pǐipi.
12. Wǒte fanǵtzu pīpushang̀ nite, yeh́ pīpushang̀ t'ate.

WRITTEN EXERCISES

A. Transcribe Section B, above, in Chinese.

B. Render the following into English:

1. 你上回進城去是坐汽車去的,還是坐火車去的?

2. 那些美國人年年也到中國去一回.

3. 我的房子比你的高,可是沒有他的高.

4. 這些中國人個個都不會說美國話,可是還會看一點兒美國書.

5. 現在還早一點兒,請你再坐坐.

6. 他今天給我們的信裏頭有很多的新字,個個我們都沒看見過.

7. 他 們 今 天 都 到 這 裏 來 看 書,
看 完 了 書 就 看 報.

8. 最 好 請 你 叫 他 明 天 再 到 這
兒 來 教 我 們 說 中 國 話.

9. 他 昨 天 晚 上 對 我 們 說 的 話,
有 一 點 兒 不 很 對.

10. 這 些 筷 子 太 長; 你 有 短 一 點
兒 的 沒 有?

C. Render the following into Chinese:

1. The express train is much longer than the local train.
2. Everybody has come, but still he doesn't speak.
3. Water is good to drink; milk is better to drink; tea is best to drink.
4. Is this American money Mr. Paō's or Mr. Chanḡ's?
5. He has spoken that sentence three times, but I still don't understand it.
6. He wants to buy a little beef for Mrs. Ch'ien.
7. I heard that he wrote very slowly, but read very fast.
8. He came a little late last night.
9. The local train travels a little slower than my new automobile.
10. He is the wealthiest man among the eight of us here.
11. He is very tall; I cannot compare with him.
12. He is very rich; I am not as wealthy as he is.

VOCABULARY CHARACTERS

 (Keñ)
To follow, to accompany;
and; with

 (Yàng)
Manner, appearance [*];
sort, kind; sample [*]

 (Jèn)
To recognize [*]; to ad-
mit [*]

 (Shiń or Shìh)
To know [*], to recog-
nize [*], to be ac-
quainted with [*]

 (P'eń)
Friend [*], companion [*]

 (Yŭ)
Friend [*], companion [*]

 (Yīng)
(For transliterating similar sounds); heroic [*]

 (Fà)
(For transliterating simi-
lar sounds)
(Fá)
Method [*], device [*]

 (Ó) or (Ò)
(For transliterating similar sounds)

 (Weń)
Written language [*];
writing [*]; literature
[*]

 (Hsiàng)
To resemble; like, similar

 (Juń)
Easy [*]; (a surname)

 (Ì)
Easy [*]

 (Nań)
Difficult

COMPOUNDS

一 樣 (Īyang) One manner, same, similar

樣 子 (Yàngtzu) Appearance, looks

這 樣 (Chèyang) }

這麼樣 (Chèmayang) } In this way, thus

102

那 樣	(Nàyang̀)	In that way, thus	
那麼樣	(Nèmayang̀)		
怎 樣	(Tsěmyang̀)	In what way, how?	
怎麼樣	(Tsěmmayang̀)		

認 識 (Jènshih) To know, to recognize, to be acquainted with

識 字 (Shíh-tzù) To be literate

學 問 (Hsüéhwèn) / 學 識 (Hsüéhshih) } Learning

見 識 (Chiènshih) Knowledge (from experience)

朋 友 (P'engýu) Friend, comrade

英 國 (Yinḡkuo) England, Great Britain

英 文 (Yinḡweń) English written language

英 國 人 (Yinḡkuo-jeń) British people or person

英 國 話 (Yinḡkuo-huà) Spoken English

俄 國 (Ókuo) Russia

容 易 學 (Junǵihsüeń) Easy to learn

俄 文 (Óweń) Russian written language

俄 國 人 (Ókuo-jeń) Russian people or person

俄 國 話 (Ókuo-huà) Spoken Russian

法 國 (Fàkuo) France

法 文 (Fàweń) French written language

法 國 人 (Fàkuo-jeń) French people or person

法 國 話 (Fàkuo-huà) Spoken French

中 文 (Chunḡweń) Written Chinese

文 學 (Weńhsüeń) Literature

文 字 (Weńtzù) Writing

容 易 (Junǵi) Easy

好好兒的 (Haŏhaōrhte) Nicely; attentively

快快兒的 (K'uaìk'uārhte) Promptly, instantly

慢慢兒的 (Maǹmārhte) In a leisurely manner

難 學 (Nańhsüeń) Difficult to learn

READING MATERIAL

這裏有很多人，有些是中國
人，有些是美國人，有些是英國人，
有些是法國人。有些人我認識，有
些人我不認識。他們説的話不一

我們美國的話，很像英國的話，也像法國的話。英文、法文、中文都學，學中文、學英文、學法文都難，就中文說，中文、俄文、美文，說話容易，寫字難。

說中國話的是中國人，說國話像中文。他們都是中國人，說國話、說美國話。美國人說美文，俄國話很難，俄國的字叫俄文，最難。

說美國話的是美國人，說話不俄，英文不俄，中文、法文的字，不對也不學，法文的說話，可以不可。

以說美國話是英文，美國話是話文的國英，學話易兒也好，可是中文是學的好，可是難，也易。

我是中國人，說國話是法國話，說法國的國美，英為也人，這有好，俄不我樣，英學、學英文，容易一文文。

是中國人，說國話像中文，因以有易。沒們學，以一英學、學比比。

可是朋友是英國人，不說法文，所以容易是我也容易，所以文學比比。

這樣的。國是俄，像很叫俄的，最字的文。容易了，英跟文文。

ROMANIZED TEXT OF READING MATERIAL

Chèli yú heň tō jeń, yŭhsieh̆ shih̆ Chunḡkuo-jeń, yŭhsieh̆ shih̆ Meĭkuo-jeń, yŭhsieh̆ shih̆ Yinḡkuo-jeń, yŭhsieh̆ shih̆ Fàkuo-jeń. Yŭhsieh̆ jeń wǒ jeńshih, yŭshieh̆ jeń wǒ pū jeńshih. T'āmen shuō te huà pū īyang̀, k'ŏshih wǒ k'ói shuō, t'āmen toū shih̆ wǒmente p'eng̊yu.

Chunḡkuo-jeń shuō te huà shih̆ Chunḡkuo-huà, Meĭkuo-jeń shuō te shih̆ Meĭkuo-huà, Yinḡkuo-jeń shuō te shih̆ Yinḡkuo-huà, Fàkuo-jeń shuō te shih̆ Fàkuo-huà, Ókuo-jeń shuōte shih̆ Ókuo-huà. Meĭkuo-huà heň hsiang̀ Yinḡkuo-huà, k'ŏshih heň pū hsiang̀ Chunḡkuo-huà, yeh̆ heň pū hsiang̀ Fàkuo-huà keň Ókuo-huà.

Chunḡkuote weńtzù chiaò Chunḡweń, Fàkuote chiaò Fàweń, Yinḡkuote chiaò Yinḡweń, Ókuote chiaò Óweń. Yiňweì Meĭkuote weńtzù heň hsiang̀ Yinḡkuote, sói yeh̆ chiaò Yinḡweń, pū chiaò Meĭweń.

Yŭ jeń shuō hsüeh̆ Chunḡweń tsuì nań, hsüeh̆ Yinḡweń tsuì jung̊i. Chèchù huà shih̆ pū tuì te. Wǒ shuō weńtzù shih̆ meí yŭ jung̊ihsüeh̆ te, yeh̆ meí yŭ nańhsüeh̆ te. Wǒmen haŏhaŏrhte hsüeh̆, Chunḡweń yeh̆ haŏ, Yinḡweń yeh̆ haŏ, Óweń yeh̆ haŏ, Fàweń yeh̆ haŏ, chiù toū jung̊ihsüeh̆. Pū haŏhaŏrhte hsüeh̆, chiù toū nańhsüeh̆ le. Sói wǒmen k'ói shuō, hsüeh̆ Chunḡweń keň hsüeh̆ Yinḡweń īyang̀ jung̊i, yeh̆ k'ói shuō hsüeh̆ Chunḡweń keň hsüeh̆ Yinḡweń īyang̀ nań, pū k'ói shuō hsüeh̆ Chunḡweń pĭ hsüeh̆ Yinḡweń nań, yeh̆ pū k'ói shuō hsüeh̆ Chunḡweń pĭ hsüeh̆ Yinḡweń jung̊i.

NOTES

1. Adverbs and adjectives which are used as free words can, for the sake of intensification or emphasis, be reduplicated whether they are monosyllabic or dissyllabic. In the case of monosyllabic ones the repeated syllable results in the first tone regardless of the tone of the original syllable, whereas in the case of dissyllabic ones, each syllable is duplicated, resulting in the recovery of tone on the part of the second syllable if the latter is in the neutral tone. It is customary, though optional, to add 的 at the end of these reduplicated forms, as 快快兒的 (k'uaìk'uārhte), reduplicating 快; 慢慢兒的 (maǹmārhte), reduplicating 慢; 好好兒的 (haŏhaŏrhte), reduplicating 好; 清清楚楚的 (ch'inḡch'inḡch'úch' úte) reduplicating 清楚 (ch'inḡch'u) [see Lesson Forty-seven]. The added 的 is often written 地 (tì) by many modern Chinese writers, who also choose to use 底 (tǐ) as the sign of the possessive in place of 的, which is used exclusively by them as the subordinative particle. In ordinary conversation, 地 and 底 are neutral in tone and unstressed, like 的, so that they sound rather alike. This use of 地 and 底 is not followed in this text.

2. When a comparison is made in which the two members to be compared are on an equal footing, the 跟 ··· 一樣 formula may be used. One member is placed before 跟 and the other member after it, but before 一樣. Then the comparison can be completed by adding the appropriate adjective or adverb, as the case may be. Thus, "I am as good as you"

becomes 我跟你一樣好; "He can write as fast as you," 他寫字寫得跟你一樣快. Another way of making this type of comparison is to use 有 [see Note 5 of Lesson Twelve]. Thus, "I am as good as you" may be rendered also as 我有你[那麼]好, and "He can write as fast as you" as 他寫字寫得有你[那麼]快. The use of 那麼 is optional.

3. When 跟 is used between two nouns or pronouns it seems to create some resemblance by the position it occupies to the conjunction "and" or the preposition "with" in English. The truth is that it still performs its function as a verb. Thus, 這本書跟那本書都是我的, which may indeed be translated into English as "This book and that book are both mine," literally means "This book following that book all [that is, both] are mine"; or 我跟你去, which may be rendered into English as "I go with you, you and I go," literally means "I following you go." Therefore, do not use 跟 to join together two verbs, adjectives, adverbs, prepositions, etc.

4. The way to present hypothetical alternatives in Chinese is to use 也好 in a series intensified by 都; these 也好's may be rendered into English by something like "Regardless of whether . . . or" or "No matter whether . . . or," as 你也好，他也好，我也好，我們都會説中國話, "Regardless of whether it is you, he, or I, we all know how to speak Chinese."

5. Note that 識 in 識字 is to be pronounced in the second tone (shih-tzù), of whereas in the other compounds introduced, 識 is to be pronounced in the neutral tone.

6. The difference in connotation between 知道 and 認識 should be pointed out here. 知道, literally "to know the way," implies having knowledge of the person, thing, or situation, whereas 認識 involves acquaintance or the ability to recognize or identify.

7. The adjectives 難 and 容易, like 好, are rather frequently used before action verbs to form compounds to indicate difficulty and ease, respectively, with reference to the action expressed by the verb following them, as 難學, "difficult to learn"; 難看 "ugly"; 難寫, "difficult to write"; 容易學, "easy to learn"; 容易寫, "easy to write"; etc.

ORAL EXERCISES

A. Say the following in Chinese:
1. Is it difficult? Is it easy?
2. Is the Russian he speaks good?
3. Are those Frenchmen literate?
4. Have you any English friends?
5. Don't say French is more difficult to learn than English.
6. I don't speak Russian as well as he does.
7. I know who that Chinese is, but I am not acquainted with him.
8. A literate person can read newspapers.
9. Your new house is quite like our old house.
10. When you eat [meals] you have to eat slowly.

B. Render the following into English:

1. Nĭ k'aǹ t'ate yanḡtzu shuō t'a shih̀ Ókuo-jeń pushih?
2. Chunḡkuo yú heň tō pū shih̀-tzù te jeń.
3. Ch'ień t'aìt'aite p'engyu ch'ùnien sañyüeh taò Yinḡkuo ch'ü le.

4. Ókuo tà haíshih Meǐkuo tà?
5. Chiaò Paí hsiensheng k'uaìk'uārhte laí, Chanḡ t'aìt'ai yaò tsoǔ le.
6. Nàhsieh Yinḡkuo-jeń toū shih̀ heń yŭ hsüeh́weǹ te.
7. Wǒ huì hsieh Óweń, yeh̀ huì shuō Ókuo-huà.
8. T'ā keñ nite p'engyu toū yaò maǐ ch'ìch'ē.
9. Fàkuo-huà junǵishuō, k'ǒshih nań shuōtehaǒ.
10. T'āte Meǐkuo p'engyu yaò taò Chunḡkuo ch'ü hsüeh́ Chunḡkuo weńhsüeh́.

WRITTEN EXERCISES

A. Transcribe Section B, above, in Chinese.

B. Render the following into English:

1. 那個英國人很像是一個有學問的人.

2. 他告訴我美國報比俄國報容易看得明白.

3. 不識字的人, 有書也好, 有報也好, 都不會看.

4. 你還有一年在美國住, 就要快快兒的把美國話學好了.

5. 我明年要到俄國去學俄文, 你說好不好?

6. 你跟法國人說話的時候, 要說法國話.

7. 那些桌子跟椅子都不是我的, 不要拿走.

8. 這 些 中 國 字, 我 知 道 不 是 你 寫 的.

9. 你 們 說 的 中 國 話 很 不 錯, 很 難 說 誰 說 得 比 誰 好.

10. 他 認 識 昨 天 來 教 我 們 英 文 的 美 國 人 麼?

C. Render the following into Chinese:

1. That character is written in this way, not in that way.
2. There are more Russians who can speak English than Americans who can speak Russian.
3. My Chinese friend, Mr. Tsŏ, is a very learned person.
4. I have a French newspaper here, but I can't read it.
5. There are not as many literate people in China as in America.
6. With whom did he say last night [that] he wanted to go to France?
7. He has studied the Chinese written language for three years, but the characters he knows [by recognition] are not very many.
8. You are quite like him; both of you have foreign friends.
9. How many years did your friend say he had lived in England?
10. It is very difficult for me to tell you whether he is coming back today.

Lesson NINETEEN

VOCABULARY CHARACTERS

條 (T'iaó)
(Classifier for long and narrow things)

等 (Tenğ)
To wait; class, grade [*]

着 (Che) Also written 著.
(Progressive suffix)

分 (Feñ)
To divide, to distinguish; a tenth of an inch; a small fraction; a degree; a cent
(Feñ) Part, share

刻 (K'ò)
Time [*]; quarter of an hour

舖 (P'ù) Also written 鋪.
Shop [*], store [*]

用 (Yung̀)
To use, to employ; use

路 (Lù)
Road, path

離 (Lí)
To be distant from; to leave [*]

開 (K'aī)
To open; to run (as a store); to start or drive a vehicle

站 (Chàn)
To stand [*]; station [*]

半 (Pàn)
Half

鐘 (Chunğ)
Bell; clock

遠 (Yüañ)
Far, distant

近 (Chìn)
Near; recent [*]

久 (Chiŭ)
A long time

109

COMPOUNDS

舖 子　(P'ùtzu) Shop, store

錢 舖　(Ch'ieńp'ù) Money shop

書 舖　(Shūp'ù) Book shop, bookstore

離 開　(Lík'ai) To leave

開 車　(K'aī-ch'ē) To start or drive a vehicle

開汽車　(K'aī ch'ìch'ē) To drive an automobile

十 分　(Shińfeñ) Extremely, very

一分鐘　(Īfeñ chuñg) One minute

一刻鐘　(Īk'ò chuñg) A quarter hour

一點鐘　(Ītień chuñg)

一個鐘頭　(Īko chuñgt'oú)　} One hour

半 年　(Pàn nień) Half a year

半個月　(Pànko yüeh) Half a month

半 天　(Pàn t'ień) Half a day

上半天　(Shàng-pant'ien) Forenoon

下半天　(Hsià-pant'ien) Afternoon

多 半　(Tōpàn) The majority

一路...一路　(Īlù...ilù)

一頭兒...一頭兒　(Īt'oúrh...it'oúrh)　}

On the one hand... on the other hand

火車站　(Huŏch'ē-chàn) Railway station

走 路　(Tsoŭ-lù) To walk, to go on foot

上 車　(Shàng-ch'ē) To entrain, to ascend a vehicle

下 車　(Hsià-ch'ē) To detrain, to get down from a vehicle

近 來　(Chìnlaí) Recently, lately

有 用　(Yŭ-yùng) To be useful

站起來　(Chànch'ilai) To stand up

快 要　(K'uaì yaò) Soon, about to

幾點鐘　(Chítień chuñg) What time (by the clock)? several hours

READING MATERIAL

1. 張 先 生 在 外 頭 等 着 你 了, 你 不 知 道 麼?

2. 不 知 道, 他 等 着 我 要 做 甚 麼?

3. 他 說 要 跟 你 坐 火 車 到 城 裏 去.

4. 到 城 裏 去 做 甚 麼?

5. 去買些中國書回來看．

6. 他不可以在這兒買麼？

7. 可以，可是這兒的中國書舖不多，中國書沒有城裏的那麼多，所以要到城裏去買．

8. 城裏的書舖離火車站遠不遠？

9. 不很遠，最近的走路走十五分鐘就到了．你今天甚麼時候回來？

10. 下半天回來．火車幾點鐘開，你知道麼？

11. 知道，下午十二點十五分開．

12. 現在幾點鐘了？

13. 上午十一點四十五分了．

14. 那麼我還有半個鐘頭．從這兒到火車站要用幾分鐘？

15. 開汽車去要用五分鐘，走路去要用七八分鐘，現在我出去好不好？

16. 不要罷．張先生進來了，我出去跟他到火車站去，請先進去．

17. 你們走路去還是開汽車去？

18. 走 路 去, 我 們 可 以 慢 慢 兒 的
走, 到 了 火 車 站 就 買 一 張 報, 買 完
報 就 上 車. 我 們 可 以 一 頭 兒 看 報,
一 頭 兒 等 火 車 開.

19. 那 麼 我 在 這 兒 等 你 回 來 好,
還 是 先 回 家 去, 今 天 晚 上 再 來 好?

20. 先 回 家 去, 晚 上 再 來 好, 因 為
在 這 兒 等 我 回 來, 就 要 等 得 太 久 了.

21. 好, 我 就 先 回 家 去, 今 天 晚 上
再 來 罷.

22. 很 好, 今 天 晚 上 再 見.

23. 今 天 晚 上 再 見.

ROMANIZED TEXT OF READING MATERIAL

1. Chanḡ hsiensheng tsaì waìt'ou tenğche ni le, nĭ pū chih̄tao ma?
2. Pū chih̄tao, t'ā tenğche wo yaò tsò shem̄ma?
3. T'ā shuō yaò ken̄ ni tsò huŏch'ē taò ch'eńgli ch'ü.
4. Taò ch'eńgli ch'ü tsò shem̄ma?
5. Ch'ü maï hsien̄ Chunḡkuo-shū huilai k'aǹ.
6. T'ā pū k'ói tsaì chèrh maï ma?
7. K'ói, k'ŏshih chèrh te Chunḡkuo-shū meí yŭ ch'eńgli shūp'ùte nèma tō, sói yaò taò ch'eńgli ch'ü maï.
8. Ch'eńgli te shūp'ù lí huŏch'ē-chaǹ yüǎn puyüǎn?
9. Pū hen̄ yüǎn, tsuì chiǹ te tsoŭ-lù tsoŭ shihwŭfen̄ chunḡ chiù k'ói taò le. Nĭ chih̄t'ien shem̄ma shih̄hou huílai?
10. Hsià-pant'ien huílai. Huŏch'ē chítien̄ chunḡ k'aī, nĭ chih̄tao ma?
11. Chih̄tao, hsiàwŭ shiher̄htien̄ shihwŭfen̄ k'aī.
12. Hsieǹtsaì chítien̄ chunḡ le?
13. Shang̀wŭ shih̄ītien̄ szùshihwŭfen̄ le.
14. Nèma wŏ haí yŭ paǹko chunḡt'oú. Ts'uńg chèrh taò huŏch'ē-chaǹ ch'ü yaò yung̀ chĭfen̄ chunḡ?
15. K'aī ch'ìch'ē ch'ü yaò yung̀ ch'i-pāfen̄ chunḡ, tsoŭ-lù ch'ü yaò yung̀ erh̄shihwŭfen̄ chunḡ. Hsieǹtsaì wŏ ch'ūch'ü ch'inḡ Chanḡ hsiensheng chiǹ-lai haŏ puhao?

16. Pū yaò ch'ǜ le, wǒ ch'ūch'ü keñ t'a taò huǒch'ē-chaǹ ch'ü pa.
17. Nǐmen tsoǔ-lù ch'ü haíshih k'aī ch'ìch'ē ch'ü?
18. Tsoǔ-lù ch'ü, wǒmen k'ói maǹmārhte tsoǔ, taòle huǒch'ē-chaǹ chiù maǐ īchanḡ paò, maǐwaǹ paò chiù shang̀-chē. Wǒmen k'ói īt'oúrh k'aǹ-paò, īt'oúrh tenḡ huǒch'ē k'aī.
19. Nèma wǒ tsaì chèrh tenḡ ni huílai haǒ, haíshih hsieñ huí-chiā ch'ü, chiñt'ien waǹshang tsaì laí haǒ?
20. Hsieñ huí-chiā ch'ü, waǹshang tsaì laí haǒ, yiñweì nǐ tsaì chèrh tenḡ wo huílai, chiù yaò tenḡte t'aì chiǔ le.
21. Haǒ, wǒ chiù hsieñ huí-chiā ch'ü, chiñt'ien waǹshang tsaì laí pa.
22. Heń haǒ, chiñt'ien waǹshang tsaì chieǹ.
23. Chiñt'ien waǹshang tsaì chieǹ.

NOTES

1. 着, as a suffix, is used immediately after a verb to indicate the progressive action expressed by the latter; it is simila. in function to the "ing" ending of verbs in English.

2. Note the dropping of the noun suffix 子 in 錢舖 and 書舖 as a result of the type of shop having been made specific.

3. Time by the clock is expressed in Chinese by 點 for the hour, 刻 for the quarter hour, and 分 for the minute, as 一點鐘, "one o'clock," 一點一刻, "quarter past one," 一點二十分, "one twenty," etc. For the half-hour, 半 is used in addition to 鐘, as 一點半, "half past one." Note that except for being precise about it, 鐘 may often be left out, as 下午三點 or 下午三點鐘, "3:00 p.m.," 一點二十五分 or 一點二十五分鐘, "one twenty-five," etc. Antemeridian and postmeridian hours are differentiated by the use of 上午 and 下午, respectively, but in Chinese these precede rather than follow the so-called "clock time," as 下午四點三十五分, "4:35 p.m.," 上午三點五十七分, "3:57 a.m.," etc. When one wants to know the time by the clock, one merely asks 幾點鐘了, "How many dots of the clock?" i.e., "What time is it?" Note that the quarter hours and the minutes are not referred to in the question at all.

4. 一點鐘 means "one hour" too. 點 serves as a measure word. It may be used interchangeably with 一個鐘頭 for this purpose. For "half an hour" one may say either 半點鐘 or 半個鐘頭, and for "three quarters of an hour," 三刻鐘.

5. When 拿 or 用 is the first of verbs used in a series with its own object to indicate the means whereby the action expressed by the verb following is performed, it may be rendered into English by "with" or "by means of," as 他拿手吃東西, "He eats things with [his] hands," 我用鉛筆寫字, "I write [words] with pencils."

ORAL EXERCISES

A. Say the following in Chinese:

1. May we entrain here? May we detrain here? May we stand here?

2. Where is the railway station? Where may we stand to wait for the train?

3. When will the train leave this morning?

4. Do you know how to drive an automobile?

5. Is there any money shop in this city?

6. It is 7:35 p.m. now.

7. They will come back at ten o'clock tomorrow morning.

8. The bookstore is very far from the railway station.

9. We came here on foot. They went there by automobile.

10. The train will arrive this afternoon.

B. Render the following into English:

1. Ch'enǵli yú heň tō p'ùtzu, yŭhsieȟ tà, yŭhsieȟ pū tà.

2. Haí yŭ īko-paǹ chungt'oú ts'unǵ ch'enǵli lai te huŏch'ē chiù yaò taò le.

3. Nimen pūyaò īt'oúrh k'aǹ-shū, īt'oúrh shuō-huà.

4. Chèt'iaó lù pǐ nàt'iaó lù tà, k'ŏshih meí yŭ nàt'iaó lù ch'anǵ.

5. Nǐ shuō tsoŭ-lù ch'ü k'uaì haíshih tsò huŏch'ē ch'ü k'uaì?

6. Nǐmen yunǵ maópí hsieȟ-tzù haŏ puhao?

7. Huŏch'ē-chaǹ lit'ou yú heň tō waìkuo-jeń.

8. Mínǵt'ien shanǵ-pant'ien wŏ yaò lai k'aǹ ni.

9. Ch'ienṕ'ù meí yŭ shūp'ù nèma tà, k'ŏshih lit'ou te jeń pǐ shūp'ù lit'ou te jeń tō.

10. Huŏch'ē k'uaì yaò k'aī le, ch'inǵ nimen k'uaìk'uārhte shanǵ-ch'ē pa.

11. Ch'inǵ nimen pūyaò chaǹ tsaì chèrh!

12. Chanǵ hsiensheng, ch'inǵ ni haŏhaŏrhte chaǹch'ilai!

WRITTEN EXERCISES

A. Transcribe Section B, above, in Chinese.

B. Render the following into English:

1. 請 你 不 要 一 頭 兒 叫 我 進 來, 一 頭 兒 叫 我 出 去.

2. 還 有 十 五 分 鐘 火 車 就 開 了, 你 們 還 不 快 快 兒 的 到 火 車 站 去 麼 ?

3. 張 先 生 昨 天 告 訴 我 們 這 是 一 本 沒 有 用 的 舊 書.

4. 這 條 路 不 好 走, 請 你 叫 他 們
不 要 來.

5. 錢 舖 跟 書 舖 都 是 白 先 生, 白
太 太 開 的, 你 不 知 道 麼?

6. 今 天 晚 上 快 車 開 了, 我 就 回
來 寫 信 給 他.

7. 中 國 人 用 筷 子 吃 飯; 美 國 人
用 刀 叉 吃 飯.

8. 張 太 太 還 有 一 個 鐘 頭 就 要
回 來 了, 請 你 坐 在 這 裏 等 他 一 等.

9. 你 們 會 開 汽 車 麼? 我 會 開
一 點 兒.

10. 他 站 在 外 頭 跟 我 説 話 説 了
十 幾 分 鐘.

C. Render the following into Chinese:

1. There are two roads outside; one is short and one is long.
2. The Chinese characters written by me with a brush are not very well written.
3. How many hours did you wait for him last night?
4. What time is it now? It is 5:49 p.m.
5. Recently there have been many people going to the city by train.
6. I don't know why your new automobile is very difficult to drive.
7. After fifteen minutes he came out to tell me that he didn't speak Russian.
8. China is very far from America, but very near Russia.
9. When he came to see me this morning I was reading the newspaper.
10. When you are driving an automobile, don't talk.

Lesson TWENTY

A Review Lesson

CHARACTERS

Number of Strokes	Characters	Pronunciation and Tone	Meaning	Lesson Reference
Three	久	Chiŭ	A long time	19
Four	比	Pĭ	To compare	17
	友	Yŭ	Friend, companion	18
	文	Weń	Written language, writing, literature	18
	分	Feñ	To divide, to distinguish; tenth of an inch, etc.	19
		Feǹ	Part, share	19
Five	以	Ĭ	By, with, by means of	16
	句	Chǜ	Sentence, phrase, etc.	16
	用	Yunǵ	To use, to employ; use	19
	半	Paǹ	Half	19
Six	因	Yiñ	Reason, cause	16
Seven	完	Wań	To finish, to complete, etc.	16
	快	K'uaì	Fast, quick; happy	17
	低	Tĭ	Low, base	17
	更	Kenǵ	(The comparative sign)	17
Eight	長	Ch'anǵ	Long	17
	兒	Erh́	Son, child	17
		Erh	(noun suffix)	17
	朋	P'enǵ	Friend, companion	18
	法	Fá	Method, device	18
		Fà	(For transliterating similar sounds)	18
	易	Ì	Easy	18

Number of Strokes	Characters	Pronunciation and Tone	Meaning	Lesson Reference
Eight	刻	K'ò	Time; quarter of an hour	19
	近	Chìn	Near; recent	19
Nine	為	Wèi	For, on account of; for the sake of	16
	英	Yīng	(For transliterating similar sounds); heroic	18
	俄	Ó or Ò	(For transliterating similar sounds)	18
Ten	起	Ch'ĭ	To rise, to raise; to begin, to start	16
	高	Kaō	Tall, high, lofty	17
	容	Junǵ	Easy; (a surname)	18
	站	Chàn	To stand; station	19
Eleven	教	{Chiaō	To teach, to instruct	16
		{Chiaò	Teaching, religion	16
	現	Hsièn	Now; to appear, to manifest	16
	條	T'iaó	(Classifier for long and narrow things)	19
Twelve	就	Chiù	Then, thereupon, etc.	16
	短	Tuăn	Short	17
	最	Tsuì	(Sign of the superlative)	17
	等	Tenǧ	To wait; class, grade	19
	着	Che	(Progressive suffix)	19
	開	K'aī	To open; to start or drive a vehicle; to begin; to run (as a store)	19
Thirteen	新	Hsiñ	New	17
	跟	Keñ	To follow, to accompany; and; with	18
	路	Lù	Road, path	19
Fourteen	對	Tuì	To correspond; to face, etc.	16

Number of Strokes	Characters	Pronunciation and Tone	Meaning	Lesson Reference
Fourteen	慢	Maǹ	Slow	17
	認	Jeǹ	To recognize; to admit	18
	像	Hsiang̀	To resemble; like; similar	18
	遠	Yüan̆	Far, distant	19
Fifteen	樣	Yang̀	Manner, appearance; sort, etc.	18
	舖	P'ù	Shop, store	19
Sixteen	學	Hsüeh́	To learn, to study; learning	16
	錯	Ts'ò	Wrong; error, mistake	16
Seventeen	點	Tien̆	Dot, speck, point; a little; to light	17
	還	Haí	Still, yet	17
Eighteen	舊	Chiù	Old	17
Nineteen	識	Shih́ or Shih̀	To know, to recognize, etc.	18
	難	Nań	Difficult	18
	離	Lí	To be distant from; to leave	19
Twenty	鐘	Chunḡ	Bell; clock	19

ORAL DRILL

A. Say the following in Chinese:

1. house	money	to tell	to wait
writing brush	meat	before (time)	to ask
letter	tea	a little	hog
ink pen	hand	France	cow
difficult	to see	train	cup
clock	to hear	again	bowl
bread	red	long	Russian (people)
vegetable	knife	tall	friend
to give	to eat	far	fast
to buy	to drink	shop	slow

newspaper   chopsticks   road   desk
chair   good   wrong   easy
               to go in   to come out

2. a road   a sentence   an hour
   a house   a desk   half an hour
   a chair   a minute   a fork
   a knife   a quarter-hour   a word (character)
   a store   a hog   a bowl
   a dish   a letter   an envelope
   a clock   a railway station   a man
   an automobile   a friend   a book
   a glass of water a cup of tea   a bowl of rice (cooked)
   a sheet of paper a table   a pair of chopsticks

3. Please come in!   Don't speak!
   Please sit down!   Don't speak French!
   Please drink tea!   Give me some water!
   Please come back!   Go home quickly!
   Please go in!   Give him some bread!
   Go up!   Walk slowly!
   Come down!   Is it right?
   Come up!   Is it wrong?
   Go down!   Is it far?
   Have you eaten enough?   Is it near?
   Has he drunk enough?   How much?
   How much money?   What day [of the month] is today?
   Please stand up!   Tell them not to stand there!
   Make a comparison!   Can [it] stand a comparison?
   What day of the week was   Yesterday was Monday.
     yesterday?   Tomorrow will be Wednesday.
   What time is it [by the clock]? Now!
   I have finished eating.   He has finished writing.
   Have you finished speaking? Is it finished?
   A little larger.   A little shorter.
   A little nearer.   Are you going?
   What do you want?   What does he want to buy?
   Is it early?   Isn't it late yet?
   Neither fast nor slow.   Not bad!
   Too long!   Too difficult!
   Not the same.   Who is he?
   Whose automobile is that?   Is he like me?
   See you again!   Where is the railway station?

B. Render the following in English:

1. Wŭshihsañ   Liùshihchiŭ
   Erhshihszù   Pāshihī
   Chiŭshih   Chiŭyüeh
   Shiherhyüeh   Ch'īyüeh szùhaò

Sañyüeh erhshihchiŭhaò

Liangˇko lǐpaì

Lǐpaìt'ien

Shang-lǐpaì

Tà-ch'ieńt'ien

Tà-hoùt'ien

Shang-pant'ien

Sañtień wŭshihfeñ

Wŭko chungt'oú

Sañk'ò chung

Szùshiherhfeñ chung

Wŭ nień

Liùko yüeh ich'ień

Ts'ungch'ień

Hsiehhsieh

Paí hsiensheng

Chang hsiensheng Chang t'aìt'ai

Hungch'á

Tsò waìkuo-faǹ

Īko lǐpaì ich'ień

Lǐpaìliù

Hsià-lǐpaì

Chiñt'ien

Hoùt'ien

Hsià-pant'ien

Ītień chung

Shangwŭ ch'ītieň-paǹ chung

Liangˇko-paǹ chungt'oú

Shihch'ifeñ chung

Paǹ nień

Paǹko yüeh

Sañko-paǹ yüeh ihoù

Hsieǹtsaì

Ch'ŭnien chiùyüeh shihpāhaò

Ch'ień t'aìt'ai

Niújoù

Tsò ch'ìch'ē

Meĭkuo-ch'ień

2. Shuí chiaò ni ch'ǜ te?

Chang t'aìt'ai chiaò wo ch'ǜ te.

Ch'ü tsò sheñma?

Ch'ü maǐ paò.

Maǐ paò keī shuí k'aǹ?

Keī Chang hsiensheng k'aǹ.

Chang t'aìt'ai shiň-tzù ma?

Wŏ meí weǹkuo t'a, sóī pū chihtao.

Nǐ taò nǎrh maǐ paò ch'ǜ te?

Taò huŏch'ē-chaǹ maǐ paò ch'ü te.

Nǐ tsaì nàrh k'aǹchienle sheñma jeń?

K'aǹchienle hsieh waìkuo-jeń.

Shiň nǎi kuóte jeń? Shiň Fàkuo-jeń pushiň?

Pū shiň, shiň Ókuo-jeń.

Ní tseñma chihtao shiň Ókuo-jeń?

T'āmen shuō Ókuo-huà, sóī wŏ chihtao.

Nǐ huì shuō Ókuo-huà ma?

Huì shuō ītiǎrh.

Sheñma shihhou hsüeh te?

Wŭ nień ich'ień hsüeh te.

Tsaì nǎrh hsüeh te?

Tsaì Ókuo hsüeh te.

Shuí keñ ni taò Ókuo ch'ǜ te?

Paō hsiensheng keñ wo ch'ǜ te.

Nǐmen tsaì Ókuo chùle chīko yüeh le?

Liangˇko-tō yüeh le.

Ókuo-huà junǵi hsüeh ma?

Pū heň junǵi, yeȟ pū heň nań.
Ókuote jeń tō puto?
Tōteheň.
Yǔ meiyu Meïkuo nèma tō?
Wǒ k'aň pí Meïkuo haí yaò tō.
Pǐ Chunḡkuo tō haíshih pǐ Chunḡkuo shaǒ?
Pǐ Chunḡkuo shaǒ ïtiǎrh.
Nǐmen sheńma shiȟhou huí Yinḡkuo lai te?
Ch'ǔnien erȟyüeh huílai te.

Nǐ shuō wǔ nień ïch'ień taò Ókuo ch'ü te, tsaì nàrh chùle lianǧko-tō yüeȟ, tseńma k'ói shiȟ ch'ǔnien huílai te?

Nǐ pū minǵpai le, lík'aile Ó-kuo ïhoù, wǒmen chiù taò Fàkuo ch'ü, tsaì nàrh chùle sañ nień-tō, chùwańle chiù huí Yinḡkuo lai. Hsieǹtsaì nǐ minǵpai le ma?

Minǵpai le, hsieȟhsieh! Hsieǹtsaì chítieň chunḡ le?

K'uaì yaò taò hsiàwǔ sañtieň ïk'ò le. Tuìpuch'ï, wǒ yaò k'uaìk'uārhte huích'ü le.

Shiȟ te, nǐ k'uaì ïtiǎrh huích'ü pa.

WRITING DRILL

A.   Write out the items in Section A of Oral Drill, above, in Chinese.

B.   Transcribe Section B of Oral Drill, above, in Chinese.

READING DRILL

After reading the following, render it into English.

1.　一個月很快就過去了。我們在最近的一個月裏頭，看見過很多的外國人，有從英國來的，有從法國來的，有從俄國來的，都有。這些外國人，有的會說中國話，有的不會說。會說中國話的美國人，說他們美國可以……會說法國話，會說甚麼話，請……怎麼……有些外國人沒知道有些不說的……從前都有……他報……他家國跟美國……

們報很國人人

朋一的天的訴上了是回是

他國國話美國國國在他他去告要下半車可

麼美的跟美英了美他住以裏他們是多汽有

甚看說們跟以白個是頭所城有他可們開也

有會人他人所明一可裏遠到也多快他就人

說請國以國的就有大子很見車很了車的

們也英所英樣看前分房不得慢人得走火去

他候們的易一一從十的站看有的走的了家

給時他說容是報生高低車都也車都兒下回

人的訴人很字國先分很火裏車火候慢慢的路

的白告國話文美白十小離家快坐時慢車走了

話明人美說的看

2.人很子在車們的就汽去少

國不的像人用要友,所房天火我車車有家很

VOCABULARY CHARACTERS

(Kunḡ)
Work, worker [*]; time [*]

(Fū)
Man [*]; husband [*]; laborer [*]

(Tsŏ)
The left side; (a surname)

(Yù)
The right side

(Fanḡ)
Square; direction [*]; region [*]; method [*]; device [*]; (a surname)

(Pieǹ)
Convenient [*]

(Manǵ)
To be in haste; busy

(Shih̀)
Affair, thing, event

(K'uaì)
Lump, piece, clod; (unit of measure for money, land, etc.)

(Hsĭ)
To be pleased with [*]; to be glad [*]

(Huañ)
To be joyous [*]

(Hsianğ)
To think, to call to mind; to like to, to desire

(Chí)
Extremely, exceedingly, very

(Kuañ)
Establishment [*]; private dwelling [*]
Also written 舘.

(Tieǹ)
Electricity; electric [*]

(Ne)
(Interrogative particle)

COMPOUNDS

工 夫 (Kunḡfu) Time, leisure

喜 歡 (Hsĭhuan) Glad, delighted, pleased with

方 便 (Fanḡpieǹ) Convenient

左 右 (Tsŏyù) Left and right; approximately, about

123

不 過 (Pūkuò) Not exceeding, only, merely, just; however

有 事 (Yǔ-shih) To have business to attend to, occupied, busy

飯館子 (Faǹkuaňtzu) Restaurant

電 車 (Tieǹch'ē) Electric cars, trams, streetcars

一塊兒 (Īk'uàrh) Together

汽車房 (Ch'ìch'ē-fang) Garage

READING MATERIAL

1. 高先生今天忙不忙？

2. 不很忙,白先生有甚麼事？

3. 沒有甚麼事,不過很想知道高先生今天下午有沒有工夫跟我到城裏去.

4. 有工夫,我很喜歡跟白先生一塊兒去.請問到城裏去做甚麼呢？

5. 吃中國飯去.

6. 那好極了.我五六天沒吃中國飯了,很想吃吃.我們幾點鐘去呢？

7. 三點鐘左右去好不好？

8. 很好,怎麼去呢？開汽車去呢,還是坐火車去呢？

9. 三點十五分有火車開到城裏去,我們就坐火車去罷.

10. 坐火車不很方便.為甚麼不開汽車去呢？

11. 怎麼不方便呢？

12. 我可以告訴你．城裏的火車站離中國飯館子很遠．火車到了，我們不走路，就要坐電車．電車走得很慢．坐電車的人很多．上車下車都很不方便．我想還是開汽車去罷．

13. 那麼我們就開汽車去罷．高先生的汽車在這兒麼？

14. 不在這兒，在汽車房裏頭．

15. 汽車房在那兒？

16. 在房子後頭．今天晚上我們可以九點半在這兒走麼？我有一點兒事．

17. 可以可以．我先回家去，走一走，九點鐘以前就回來．

18. 好，我就在這兒等白先生回來罷．再見！

19. 再見再見！

ROMANIZED TEXT OF READING MATERIAL

1. Kaō hsiensheng chiñt'ien mań pumang?
2. Pū heň mań, Paí hsiensheng yǔ sheḿma shiȟ?
3. Meí yǔ shemma shiȟ, pūkuò heń hsianǧ chiñtao Kaō hsiensheng chiñt'ien hsiàwú yǔ meiyu kungfu keñ wo taò ch'eńgli ch'ü.
4. Yǔ kungfu, wó heń hsīhuan keñ Paí hsiensheng īk'uàrh ch'ü. Ch'iń weǹ taò ch'eńgli ch'ü tsò sheḿma ne?
5. Ch'iȟ Chungkuo-faǹ ch'ü.

6. Nà haŏchí le. Wó wŭ-liù t'ieñ meí ch'iĥ Chuñḡkuo-faǹ le, heń hsiaṅg ch'iĥch'ih. Wŏmen chítieñ chuñḡ ch'ù ne?

7. Sañtieň chuñḡ tsŏyù ch'ù haŏ puhao?

8. Heń haŏ, tseḿma ch'ü ne? K'aī ch'ìch'ē ch'ü ne, haíshih tsò huŏch'ē ch'ü ne?

9. Sañtieň shiĥwŭfeñ yú huŏch'ē k'aītaò ch'eńgli ch'ü, wŏmen chiù tsò huŏch'ē ch'ü pa.

10. Tsò huŏch'ē pū heň fañḡpieň. Weìsheḿma pū k'aī ch'ìch'ē ch'ü ne?

11. Tseḿma pū fañḡpieň ne?

12. Wó k'ói kaòsu ni. Ch'eńgli te huŏch'ē-chaǹ lí Chuñḡkuo faǹkuaňtzu heń yüaň. Huŏch'ē taòle, wŏmen pū tsoŭ-lù, chiù yaò tsò tieňch'ē. Tieňch'ē tsoūte heň maǹ. Tsò tieňch'ē te jeń heň tō. Shaṅḡ-ch'ē hsià-ch'ē toū heň pū fañḡpieň. Wó hsiaň haíshih k'aī ch'ìch'ē ch'ü haŏ.

13. Nèma wŏmen chiù k'aī ch'ìch'ē ch'ü pa. Kaō hsienshengte ch'ìch'ē tsaì chèrh ma?

14. Pū tsaì chèrh, tsaì ch'ìch'ē-fañ lit'ou.

15. Ch'ìch'ē-fañ tsaì nărh?

16. Tsaì fañgtzu hoùt'ou. Chiñt'ien waňshang chiútieň-paǹ wó yŭ ītiărh shiĥ. Wŏmen k'ói tsaì chiútieň īk'ò ich'ień huílai ma?

17. K'ói k'oi. Wŏ hsieñ huí-chiā ch'ü tsoŭitsou, sañtieň chuñḡ ich'ień chiù huílai.

18. Haŏ, wŏ chiù tsaì chèrh teṅg Paí hsiensheng huílai pa. Tsaì chieǹ tsai chien!

19. Tsaì chieǹ tsai chien!

NOTES

1. 有事, literally "to have business," can be taken to mean either "to have business to attend to, to be engaged in business, busy" or "to have something happen," depending on the context, of course. Sentence 2 in the Reading Material above should be taken in the former connotation and rendered into English something like "What business do you have [in mind], Mr. Paí" or "What business is on your mind, Mr. Paí?" Similarly, 今天晚上九點半我有一點兒事 of sentence 16 means "I have a little business at 9:30 to attend to this evening." However, in the latter connotation, 有甚麼事 may be asked as a question roughly equivalent to "What is the matter, what is happening?"

2. 極, like 很, is an intensive, but unlike 很 it usually follows the adjective or adverb it intensifies, as 大極, 好極, etc. Since 很 is often used to round out monosyllabic predicate adjectives (see Note 1, Lesson Eight), it is a weaker intensive than 極.

3. When 想 is followed by a noun clause or a complete sentence serving as its object, it means "to think that" and somewhat resembles 看 in meaning and usage, except that the opinion expressed after 看 is probably formed as a result of observation, casual or otherwise, whereas that expressed after 想 represents the outcome of cogitation. 想 is often used with the meaning of "to like, to desire." The English expression "to like very much" is to

be rendered into Chinese simply as 很想. Note the absence of "much" and the different position of "very" in the Chinese construction.

4. 左右, literally "left and right," means "in the neighborhood of, approximately, about." Note the postpositional use of the compound.

5. The adverbial compound 不過, "not exceeding, merely, only, just, however," is to be placed before the words it qualifies. For example: 不過兩天, "not exceeding two days, not more than two days, merely two days," etc.; 不過三塊錢, "not exceeding three dollars, not more than three dollars, merely three dollars," etc. 不過 is often used as a conjunction to show a mild contradiction to the idea or situation stated in the clause or sentence immediately before it, as 我要買那本書, 不過現在沒錢買, "I want to buy that book, only now I don't have the money to buy it"; 他快要走了, 不過現在還沒走, "He will leave soon, but at present he hasn't left yet." For this purpose 不過 may be used interchangeably with 可是, although the latter seems to be somewhat stronger in effect.

6. 還是 in sentence 12 of the Reading Material above is to be taken in the sense of "after all" or "it still is."

7. The difference between 麼 and 呢 as interrogative particles is that whereas the former is used only for asking questions anticipating either a positive or negative answer, the latter may be used for asking questions for a number of purposes. Most commonly, 呢 is used for asking a question involving a choice of alternatives presented. In such cases it may be, though not necessarily, used in pairs, as 昨天沒來的人是你(呢)還是他呢, "Is the person who didn't come yesterday you or he?"; 我去好(呢)還是不去好呢, "Is it better for me to go or not?"; etc. 呢 is sometimes used for questioning without the necessity of repeating the essential elements of the question which have already been clearly understood or stated previously. For example, see sentence 9 in the Reading Material of Lesson Twenty-three.

Furthermore, 呢 may be added to already completed questions to express doubt, surprise, or curiosity, as 他說今天早上要來, 為甚麼他還沒來呢, "He said that he would come this morning; why is it that he hasn't come yet?; 我也知道了, 你怎麼不知道呢, "Even I know [about it]; how is it that you don't know [anything about it]?"

ORAL EXERCISES

A. Say the following in Chinese:

1. Do you have any leisure, Mr. Chang?
2. Is Mrs. Tsŏ busy now?
3. I am very sorry. I have no leisure this evening.
4. Is it convenient to go to the city by train?
5. Are the Chinese restaurants here big?
6. There is no streetcar in this town.
7. Do you like to read American newspapers?
8. I will come back around half-past five this afternoon.
9. I am delighted that you and I are going together.
10. I think he is not the person who came last week.

B. Render the following into English:

1. T'ā heń hsiang maì īsó yŭ ch'ìch'ē-fang te fangťzu.
2. Weìsheḿma nĭmen tsóťien yŭ kunḡfu yeḣ meí ch'ù ne?
3. Chanḡ t'aìt'ai tsaì Yinḡkuo te shiḣhou, tsòkuo tieṅch'ē meiyu?
4. Wŏ chiñťien meí yŭ shemma shiḣ, heń hsianǧ huí-chiā k'aṅk'an t'amen.
5. T'ā heń hsǐhuan ni tsò t'ate p'enǵyu.
6. Wŏ chiñťien t'aì mang le, ch'inǵ ni minǵťien tsaì laí pa.
7. Kaō t'aìt'ai heń hsiang maḣ īchanḡ chōtzu, pūkuò meí ch'ień maì.
8. T'āmen tsaì Meĭkuo chù, sheḿma toū fanḡpieṅteheǹ.
9. T'ā shuō nimen pūyaò tsò tsaì īk'uàrh.
10. Tieṅch'ē meí yú huōch'ē haŏtsò, ní hsianǧ tuì putui?

WRITTEN EXERCISES

A. Transcribe Section B, above, in Chinese.

B. Render the following into English:

1. 我們住在那所舊房子裏頭,
甚麼都沒有, 很不方便.

2. 你要到那兒去, 我沒有工夫
跟你一塊兒去了.

3. 那個飯館子裏頭, 有很多美
國人吃中國飯.

4. 到他的家裏去的電車今天
不開了, 你走路去罷.

5. 今天晚上九點三十五分鐘
左右我就可以回來了.

6. 我明天下午不很忙, 你要我
來, 我就很喜歡來.

7. 他們昨天有甚麼事, 你可以
告訴我麼?

8. 你 明 天 可 以 跟 他 一 塊 兒 去
就 好 極 了.

9. 我 明 天 晚 上 很 想 吃 中 國 飯,
不 過 這 兒 沒 有 中 國 飯 館 子.

10. 請 問 電 車 甚 麼 時 候 開 ?

C. Render the following into Chinese:

1. You came together; why don't you go together?
2. We didn't come together, so we are not going together.
3. Where is the restaurant which you told us about night before last?
4. It is quite far from here, but you can go [there] by streetcar.
5. Is it convenient for you to come again day after tomorrow morning?
6. There is nothing inconvenient, only there is a friend coming to see me day after tomorrow morning.
7. On which day will you have the time [leisure] to come again?
8. I won't have anything to attend to next Wednesday morning. I can come again.
9. Are you coming by automobile or by streetcar?
10. By streetcar. I have no automobile.

VOCABULARY CHARACTERS

(Paī)
Hundred

(Ch'ień)
Thousand [*]

(Waǹ)
Ten thousand [*]

(Kueì)
Expensive; (honorific for "your")

(Maì)
To sell

(Chià)
Price [*]

(Í)
Proper [*], fit [*]; suitable [*]

(Shiň)
Solid, not hollow [*]

(Kunǵ)
Together [*], all [*], the whole [*]; to share [*]

(Suaǹ)
To calculate, to reckon; to consider as, to regard as

(Hsinǵ)
To walk [*]; will do, all right

(P'ień)
Cheap [*]; advantageous [*]

(Linǵ)
Fragment [*], fraction [*]; zero

(Tunḡ)
East [*]

(Hsī)
West [*]

(Pieh́)
To distinguish [*]; to part [*]; another [*]; do not!

(Huań)
To return; ... back to [*]

COMPOUNDS

別的 (Pieh́te) Other, another

別人 (Piehjen) Other people

老實 (Laŏshih) Honest, frank

東西 (Tunḡhsi) Thing, article

一共 (Īkuǹg) Altogether

做人 (Tsò-jeń) To be a man or person

價錢 (Chiàch'ien) Price

便宜 (P'ień) Cheap, reasonable

一百 (Īpaǐ) One hundred

一千 (Īch'ień) One thousand

一萬 (Īwaǹ) Ten thousand

一塊錢 (Īk'uaì ch'ień) One dollar

一毛錢 (Īmaó ch'ień) One 'ime, ten cents

一分錢 (Īfeñ ch'ien) One penny, one cent

半塊錢 (Paǹk'uaì ch'ień) Half a dollar

一百萬 (Īpaǐwaǹ) One million

一千萬 (Īch'ieñwaǹ) Ten million

一萬萬 (Īwaǹwaǹ) One hundred million

還價 (Huań-chià) To bargain

行不行 (Hsiń puhsing) Will it do? Will it be all right?

行了 (Hsiń le) It will do. It will be all right.

不行 (Pū hsiń) It will not do.

READING MATERIAL

1. 先生今天要買甚麼？

2. 我要買些中國筆．你們有好的中國筆賣沒有？

3. 有，我去拿些來給先生看看好不好？

4. 很好，請快一點兒拿來．

5. 這些筆都是寫大字用的，那些都是寫小字用的．請先生看看．

6. 很好，謝謝這些寫大字用的賣多少錢一枝？

7. 賣半塊錢一枝.

8. 價錢太貴罷? 便宜一點兒可以麼?

9. 對不起,我們的舖子是不還價的.

10. 四毛五一枝也不行麼?

11. 不行,很對不起.

12. 那麼我就買六枝罷.

13. 寫小字用的先生還要買不要?

14. 賣幾毛錢一枝?

15. 賣三毛五一枝.

16. 請你給我八枝好的罷.

17. 請先生看看,這八枝行不行?

18. 行了,請算算一共多少錢罷.

19. 好,寫大字用的六枝是三塊錢,寫小字用的八枝是兩塊八毛,那麼一共就是五塊八毛了.請先生再算算.

20. 不用再算了.這就是五塊八毛.你們有中國信紙賣沒有?

21. 有,我們賣的中國信紙很不錯.

22. 價錢便宜麼?

23. 便宜得很.

24. 兩 千 張 賣 多 少 錢？

25. 賣 兩 塊 二 毛 五, 五 千 張 賣 五
塊 半, 一 萬 張 賣 十 塊 錢.

26. 請 你 給 我 五 千 張 罷. 這 是 五
塊 半 錢.

27. 謝 謝, 這 是 五 千 張 信 紙. 先 生
還 有 別 的 東 西 要 買 沒 有？

28. 沒 有 了, 謝 謝. 再 見.

29. 再 見.

ROMANIZED TEXT OF READING MATERIAL

1. Hsieñsheng chiñt'ien yaò maï sheḿma?
2. Wŏ yaò maï hsieĥ Chungkuo-pĭ. Nĭmen yú haŏ te Chungkuo-pĭ maì meiyu?
3. Yŭ, wŏ ch'ü ná hsieĥ lai keĭ hsieñsheng k'aǹk'an haŏ puhao?
4. Heń haŏ, ch'ing k'uaì ītiǎrh nálai.
5. Chèhsieh pĭ toū shiĥ hsieĥ tà tzù yunǵ te, nàhsieh toū shiĥ hsieĥ hsiaŏ tzù yunǵ te. Ch'ing hsieñsheng k'aǹk'an.
6. Heń haŏ, hsieĥhsieh. Chèhsieh hsieĥ tà tzù yunǵ te maì tōshaŏ ch'ień īchiĥ?
7. Maì paǹk'uaì ch'ień īchiĥ.
8. Chiàch'ien t'aì kueì pa? P'ieńi ītiǎrh k'ŏi ma?
9. Tuìpuch'ĭ, wŏmente p'ùtzu shiĥ pū huań-chià te.
10. Szùmaó-wŭ īchiĥ yeĥ pū hsinǵ ma?
11. Pū hsinǵ, heň tuìpuch'ĭ.
12. Nèma wŏ chiù maì liùchiĥ pa.
13. Hsieĥ hsiaŏ tzù yunǵ te hsieñsheng haí yaò maï puyao?
14. Maì chĭmaó ch'ień īchiĥ?
15. Maì sañmaó-wŭ īchiĥ.
16. Ch'inǵ ni keí wo pāchiĥ haŏ te pa.
17. Ch'ing hsieñsheng k'aǹk'an, chè pāchiĥ hsinǵ puhsing?
18. Hsinǵ le, ch'ing suaǹsuan īkung tōshaŏ ch'ień pa.
19. Haŏ, hsieĥ tà tzù yunǵ te liùchiĥ shiĥ sañk'uaì ch'ień, hsieĥ hsiaŏ tzù yunǵ te pāchiĥ shiĥ liangk'uaì pāmaó, nèma īkung chiù shiĥ wŭk'uaì pāmaó le. Ch'ing hsieñsheng tsaì suaǹsuan.
20. Pū yunǵ tsaì suaǹ le. Chè chiù shiĥ wŭk'uaì pāmaó. Nĭmen yŭ Chungkuo hsiǹchiĥ maì meiyu?

21. Yū, wǒmen maì te Chungkuo hsińchih heň pūts'ò.
22. Chiàch'ien p'ieńi ma?
23. P'ieńite heň.
24. Liangǧch'ieñchang maì tōshaǒ ch'ień?
25. Maì liangǧk'uaì erhmaó-wǔ, wǔch'ieñchang maì wǔk'uaì-paǹ, iwaǹchang maì shihk'uaì ch'ień.
26. Ch'ińǵ ni keí wo wǔch'ieñchang pa. Chè shih wǔk'uaì-paǹ ch'ień.
27. Hsiehhsieh, chè shih wǔch'ieñchang hsińchih. Hsieñsheng haí yū piehte tungǧhsi yaò maì meiyu?
28. Meí yū le, hsiehhsieh. Tsaì chieǹ.
29. Tsaì chieǹ.

NOTES

1. The measure words 塊, 毛, 分 are used with 錢 to indicate the various denominations of money, as 一塊錢, "one dollar," 一毛錢, "one dime," 一分錢, "one penny, one cent." When more than one denomination is used in a given amount, and if the implication is clear, one generally omits not only 錢 at the end of the amount, but sometimes even the smallest denomination involved, as 一塊九毛五, rather than the full form 一塊九毛五分錢, "$1.95," for conversational purposes. Compare "one dollar and ninety-five cents" and "a dollar ninety-five." However, there is nothing compulsory about these omissions.

2. 不用 literally means "not to use," hence, "it is unnecessary, there is no need."

3. In rendering numbers in excess of 9,999 into Chinese, 萬, "ten thousand," the largest common unit of calculation without its counterpart in English, must be used, as 一萬 (never 十千), "10,000," 二十五萬 (never 二百五十千), "250,000." The best way, therefore, to handle such large numbers is to divide them into groups of four instead of three digits and use 萬 with every digit immediately before a dividing comma; thus 123,456,-789 becomes in Chinese 一萬(萬)二千三百四十五萬六千七百八十九. The 萬 in parentheses may be omitted; its use is required only if the "1" in this case is followed by four or more zeros; thus "1,0000,0000" (100,000,000), becomes 一萬萬, and "1,0000,2345" (100,002,345), becomes 一萬萬零二千三百四十五. 一萬萬 is also known as 一億 (ì). Therefore, "one billion" is either 十萬萬 or 十億.

4. Since the basic meaning of 零 is "fragment, fraction," it is often used to represent a medial zero in any number, as 一百零一, "101," 一千零六十九, "1,069," 一萬零四百五十七, "10,457," etc. When a number has more than one medial zero running consecutively together, one 零 ordinarily will suffice. 零 may also be used to indicate a fractional excess, as 一塊零八分(錢), "one dollar and eight cents," 一年零三天, "one year and three days," 一個月零三天, "one month and three days," 兩個禮拜零兩天, "two weeks and two days," etc. In this latter use of 零, it is quite different from 多. 零 is quite specific about the extent of excess, whereas 多 is vague about it. See Note 5 below.

5. 多 "many, much" is used often to indicate vaguely an excess, as 十多, "ten plus a few more, ten-odd," implying of course that the excess may range anywhere from eleven to and including nineteen, 三百多, "three hundred-odd, more than three hundred," the excess ranging from 301 to 399. In the expressions 一年多, 七塊多錢, the excesses range from one year and one day to one day short of two years, and from seven dollars and one cent to one cent short of eight dollars, respectively.

6. Either 二 or 兩 may be used with 百, 千, or 萬 to form numbers involving "two hundred," "two thousand," or "twenty thousand," respectively. But in the case of 萬, 兩 is used only when the number does not exceed five digits; otherwise, only 二 is used, even if the number contains in it "twenty thousand," as "224,321" is 二十二萬四千三百二十一.

7. 別 as an auxiliary verb used, in negative imperative sentences is a fusion of 不要 and may therefore be used interchangeably with the latter expression.

8. In order to pronounce properly compounds such as "p'ieṅi," 便宜, "yüaṅi," 願意 [see Lesson Twenty-nine], etc., the final consonant "n" of the first syllable must not be carried over to the following syllable, "i," which should be pronounced with a "y" effect. See Note 10, Lesson Sixteen, above.

ORAL EXERCISES

A. Say the following in Chinese:

1. 102, 204, 306, 408, 300, 500.
2. 5,000, 7,000, 8,000, 1,035, 2,081, 9,635, 3,269.
3. 10,000, 20,000, 42,000, 26,012, 57,704.
4. 123,456, 234,567, 345,678, 456,789.
5. 9,876,543, 8,765,432, 7,654,321, 6,543,210.
6. 55,678,879, 23,456,789, 111,443,221.
7. Five cents, fifteen cents, twenty-five cents, ninety cents, ninety-four cents, ninety-nine cents.
8. $1.44, $6.05, $15.27, $33.69, $100.00, $2,500.00.
9. 250-odd, 3,480-odd, 4,800-odd, 60,500-odd.
10. More than two months, more than 800 dollars, one week and four days, two years and three months.

B. Render the following into English:

1. Chèpaō tunḡhsi shih pushih nǐ tsót'ien maǐ te?
2. Nàpeň shū maì tōshaǒ ch'ień?
3. Ní yú chǐk'uaì ch'ien?
4. Nǐ chiāli īkunḡ yú chǐko jeń?
5. Chiñt'ien mieṅpaōte chiàch'ien p'ieṅi ma?
6. Pieň shuō-huà! Pieň ch'ūch'ü!
7. Nǐmen pieň shuō pieňjen pū haǒ!
8. T'ā yaò nimen keǐ t'a liangǩ'uaì-tō Meǐkuo-ch'ień.
9. Wǒmente chiù fanḡtzu maìle chiùch'ieñ linǵ pāshihwǔk'uaì ch'ień.
10. T'ā tsò-jeń heń laǒshih, shuō-huà yeň heń laǒshih.

WRITTEN EXERCISES

A. Transcribe Section B, above, in Chinese.

B. Render the following into English:

1.他們都説白先生做人很老
實, 你想對不對?

2.你們看書也行, 寫字也行, 可
是説話就不行了.

3.錢太太, 請你再算一算, 一共
七塊錢對不對?

4.這本書的價錢便宜一點兒,
他就可以買了.

5.那句話是很難對別人説的.

6.那些東西都是沒有用的, 我
不要了.

7.不還價的舖子, 中國跟美國
都有.

8.這三本書是我的; 別的都是
你們的.

9.我在這兒等了他一個多鐘
頭, 可是他還沒回來.

10.外頭有兩個外國人要進來
買東西.

C. Render the following into Chinese:

1. The price of those new houses is very reasonable.

2. He knows when I am coming back; there is no need of your telling
him again.

3. There are altogether fifteen desks and fifteen chairs in this house.

4. When other people see it, it doesn't look nice.

5. There isn't even a single one-price store in this city.

6. Now, one hundred and six dollars of American money can buy 5,300,000 dollars of Chinese money.

7. Then how many dollars of Chinese money can one American dollar buy?

8. I have lived here for five weeks and six days.

9. Have you any other slightly better rice bowls?

10. He has finished selling his old books, of which there were 2,000-odd volumes.

VOCABULARY CHARACTERS

(Chì)
Season

(Tunḡ)
Winter [*]

(Yeh)
Night [*]

(Ch'ì)
Air [*]

(Yŭ)
Rain

(Lenḡ)
Cold

(Fenḡ)
Wind; custom

(Jè)
Hot

(Ch'uñ)
Spring (season) [*]

(Chaó) Also written 著.
To attain [*]; to reach
by effort [*]

(Hsià)
Summer [*]; (a surname)

(Shuì)
To sleep

(Ch'iū)
Autumn [*]

(Chiaò)
Sleep, nap

COMPOUNDS

白天　(Paít'ien) Daytime

夜裏　(Yehli) At night

下雨　(Hsià-yŭ) To rain

風雨　(Fenḡyŭ) Wind and rain

春天　(Ch'uñt'ien) ⎱
　　　　　　　　　　 ⎰ The spring
春季　(Ch'uñchì) ⎰ season

138

夏 天	(Hsiàt'ien)	⎫ The summer	秋 天	(Ch'iūt'ien)	⎫ The autumn
夏 季	(Hsiàchì)	⎭ season	秋 季	(Ch'iūchì)	⎭ season

四 季 (Szù-chì) The four seasons

冬 天 (Tungt'ien) ⎫ The winter
冬 季 (Tungchì) ⎭ season

睡 覺 (Shuì-chiaò) To sleep

天 氣 (T'iench'i) Weather

睡不着 (Shuìpuchaó) Not capable of falling asleep

睡得着 (Shuìtechaó) Capable of falling asleep

睡 着 (Shuìchaó) To fall asleep

READING MATERIAL

1. 一 年 有 幾 季？

2. 一 年 有 四 季.

3. 四 季 叫 甚 麼？

4. 叫 春, 夏, 秋, 冬.

5. 一 季 有 幾 個 月？

6. 有 三 個 月. 四 季 一 共 有 十 二 個 月.

7. 春 天 的 三 個 月 是 那 三 個 月？

8. 是 三 月, 四 月, 五 月.

9. 夏 天 的 三 個 月 呢？

10. 是 六 月, 七 月, 八 月.

11. 秋 天 的 三 個 月 是 不 是 九 月, 十 月, 十 一 月？

12. 是, 冬 天 的 三 個 月 是 十 二 月, 一 月, 二 月.

13. 這 裏 的 天 氣 是 怎 麼 樣 的？

14. 是 冬 天 冷, 夏 天 熱, 春 天 秋 天 不 冷 不 熱 的.

15. 春 天 下 雨 多, 還 是 冬 天 下 雨 多 呢?

16. 冬 天 下 雨 多.

17. 昨 天 風 大 不 大?

18. 不 很 大, 今 天 風 比 昨 天 大.

19. 他 們 天 天 白 天 做 甚 麼?

20. 在 家 裏 看 書, 看 完 了 書 就 寫 字.

21. 他 們 夜 裏 還 寫 字 不 寫?

22. 不 寫 了, 他 們 夜 裏 睡 覺.

ROMANIZED TEXT OF READING MATERIAL

1. Ī nień yú chī chì?
2. Ī nień yŭ szù chì.
3. Szù-chì chiaò sheḿma?
4. Chiaò ch'uñ, hsià, ch'iū, tuñg.
5. Ī chì yú chīko yüeh̀?
6. Yū sañko yüeh̀. Szù-chì īkuñg yŭ shih̀erh̀ko yüeh̀.
7. Ch'uñt'ien te sañko yüeh̀ shih̀ nǎ sañko yüeh̀?
8. Shih̀ sañyüeh, szùyüeh, wŭyüeh.
9. Hsiàt'ien te sañko yüeh̀ ne?
10. Shih̀ liùyüeh, ch'īyüeh, pāyüeh.
11. Ch'iūt'ien te sañko yüeh̀ shih̀ pushih chiùyüeh, shih̀yüeh, shih̀īyüeh?
12. Shih̀, tuñgt'ien te sañko yüeh̀ shih̀ shih̀erh̀yüeh, īyüeh, erh̀yüeh.
13. Chèli te t'ieñch'i shih̀ tseḿmayañg te?
14. Shih̀ tuñgt'ien leñg, hsiàt'ien jè, ch'uñt'ien ch'iūt'ien pū leñg pū jè te.
15. Ch'uñt'ien hsià-yǔ tō, haíshih tuñgt'ien hsià-yǔ tō ne?
16. Tuñgt'ien hsià-yǔ tō.
17. Tsót'ien feñg tà puta?
18. Pū heǹ tà, chiñt'ien feñg pǐ tsót'ien tà.
19. T'āmen t'ieñt'ieñ paít'ien tsò sheḿma?
20. Tsaì chiāli k'aǹ-shū, k'aǹwáñle shū chiù hsieh̀-tzù.

21. T'āmen yeh̀li haí hsieh̀-tzù puhsieh?
22. Pū hsieǔ le, t'āmen yeh̀li shuì-chiaò.

NOTES

1. 不•••不, "not . . . not," perform the same function of negating the words after them as "neither . . . nor" in English. 不冷不熱 may indeed be rendered into English as "neither cold nor hot."

2. Note that the compound 睡覺, "to sleep," literally means "to sleep a sleep." It is formed by a transitive verb plus its cognate object. Sometimes 覺 is used as a classifier for sleep, as 我睡了一覺了, "I have slept a sleep."

3. 着 (chaó) is used with action verbs to form resultative compounds to indicate attainment of an aim and should be differentiated from the progressive suffix 着 (che), which is similarly written. 睡着了 means "to have fallen asleep"; 睡得着, "capable of falling asleep"; 睡不着, "incapable of falling asleep"; 買着了, "to have bought"; 找 (chaǒ, "to look for, to seek"; see Lesson 24) 着了, "to have found"; etc.

4. Except when the four seasons of a year are being named, do not use 春, 夏, 秋, 冬 as though they were free forms. Use 春天 or 春季 for "spring," 夏天 or 夏季 for "summer," etc.

ORAL EXERCISES

A. Say the following in Chinese:

1. We don't sleep in the daytime.
2. At night the weather here is very cold.
3. In autumn the days are neither long nor short.
4. May has thirty-one days.
5. It will rain soon today.
6. Was it hot yesterday?
7. It was very hot in the afternoon.
8. Is it he or you who spoke?
9. Are they asleep yet?
10. No, they say they can't fall asleep.

B. Render the following into English:

1. Nǐmen shuìtechaó shuipuchao?
2. T'āmen weìshem̀ma haí meí ch'ù shuì-chiaò ne?
3. Tsót'ien t'aì jè le, ìtiǎrh fēng yeǔ meí yǔ.
4. Chāng t'aìt'ai shuō Tsǒ hsiensheng míngnien ch'uñt'ien chiù k'ói huílai le.
5. Ī nień te szù-chì Chūngkuo-huà chiaò shem̀ma, nǐ chih̀tao puchihtao?
6. Hsiàchì t'ieñch'ì jè, tūngchì t'ieñch'ì lěng.
7. T'ā tsem̀ma haí meí kaòsu ni ne?
8. Nàko waìkuo-jeń shih̀ Meǐkuo-jeń ne haíshih Yīngkuo-jeń ne?
9. Ch'iǔng kaòsu t'amen pūyaò tsaì chèrh shuì-chiaò pa.
10. Wǒ paít'ien k'aǹ-shū, yeh̀li pū k'aǹ-shū.

WRITTEN EXERCISES

A. Transcribe Section B, above, in Chinese.

B. Render the following into English:

1. 為 甚 麼 你 睡 了 兩 個 鐘 頭 也 沒 睡 着 呢？

2. 今 年 春 天 的 天 氣 很 好, 沒 有 風, 也 沒 有 雨.

3. 雨 下 完 了, 你 回 家 去 就 要 快 快 兒 的 去.

4. 秋 季 冷 呢 還 是 冬 季 冷 呢？

5. 夏 天 天 長 夜 短; 冬 天 天 短 夜 長.

6. 這 杯 牛 奶 太 熱; 我 不 喝 了.

7. 近 來 天 天 下 大 雨; 我 們 甚 麼 也 沒 做.

8. 你 說 今 年 風 雨 多, 還 是 去 年 風 雨 多 呢？

9. 白 先 生 到 中 國 去 了, 明 年 冬 天 就 要 回 來.

10. 外 頭 很 冷, 叫 他 們 別 出 去.

C. Render the following into Chinese:

1. We have read for a whole day and now we want to go to sleep.
2. It is too hot in the little room; don't sleep there.
3. Are those foreigners who can't speak Chinese Russians or Frenchmen?
4. Who is it that tells you we will come back to China next summer?
5. It rained in the daytime yesterday, so we didn't go to see them.
6. Recently he has been reading too much; at night he can't fall asleep.
7. This cup of tea is too cold; please don't drink it.
8. How is it that the weather here is so warm in September?
9. I came here last fall; I will go back next spring.
10. The rain is not yet over; please tell him that he and I can't go together.

VOCABULARY CHARACTERS

(Neng)
To be able, can

(Tzù)
Self [*]; from [*]

(Chì)
Self [*]

(Ĭ)
To come to an end [*]; already [*]

(Chīng)
To pass through [*]; to manage [*]; warp; a classic

(Tì)
Earth, land; place [*]

(Chiŕ)
Site, location [*]

(Chieh)
To receive; to join

(Chaŏ)
To look for, to seek; to make up the balance

(Sung)
To escort; to send; to present as a gift

(Wang)
To forget

(Chì)
To remember [*]; to record; sign, mark [*]

(Tì)
(The ordinal prefix)

(Hsŭ)
Perhaps [*]; to allow; to promise; very; (a surname)

(Kaň)
To dare

COMPOUNDS

自己 (Tzùchĭ) Self

我自己 (Wŏ-tzùchĭ) Myself

他自己 (T'ā-tzùchĭ) Himself, herself

你自己 (Nĭ-tzùchĭ) Yourself

143

我們自己　(Wŏmen-tzŭchī) Ourselves

你們自己　(Nĭmen-tzŭchī) Yourselves

他們自己　(T'āmen-tzŭchī) Themselves

自　從　(Tzùts'ung) Ever since

地　址　(Tìchiĥ) ⎫
住　址　(Chùchiĥ) ⎬ Address

記　住　(Chìchu) ⎫
記　得　(Chìte) ⎬ To remember

記不得　(Chìpute) ⎫
記不住　(Chìpuchù) ⎬ Unable to remember

記得住　(Chìtechù) Able to remember

找來找去　(Chaŏlaí-chaŏch'ừ) To look for here and there, to look for high and low

已　經　(Ĭching) Already

電車站　(Tieñch'ē-chañ) Street-car station

也　許　(Yeĥhsŭ) Perhaps, possibly, probably

找　着　(Chaŏchaó) ⎫
找　到　(Chaŏtaò) ⎬ To find

找得着　(Chaŏtechaó) ⎫
找得到　(Chaŏtetaò) ⎬ Able to find

找不着　(Chaŏpuchaó) ⎫
找不到　(Chaŏputaò) ⎬ Unable to find

接　到　(Chieñtaò) To receive

想來想去　(Hsiangŏlaí-hsiangŏch'ừ) To turn something over and over in the mind

想　起　(Hsiangch'ỉ) To recall to mind

想起來　(Hsiangch'ilai) To think or recall

READING MATERIAL

1. 張　太　太, 你　好　麼?

2. 很　好, 謝　謝. 白　先　生, 你　也　好　罷?

3. 也　很　好, 謝　謝. 張　太　太　昨　天　下　午　要　找　的　書　舖, 已　經　找　到　了　沒　有?

4. 還　沒　找　到.

5. 怎　麼　還　沒　找　到　呢? 那　書　舖　不　是　在　城　裏　的　麼?

6. 是　的, 可　是　我　把　地　址　忘　了, 想找來找去也想不起來,所以找不着.

7. 你還記得地址是誰告訴你的麼?

8. 記得,是左太太告訴我的.

9. 那麼你可以去見左太太,再問他一問,把地址寫下來就行了.

10. 你能跟我一塊兒去見左太太麼?

11. 能,不過我現在沒有工夫去,因為我先要到火車站去接朋友,接了還要送他回家.

12. 你送了朋友回家,還有別的事沒有?

13. 沒有了,你喜歡我到那兒去呢?

14. 請你到我家裏去好不好?

15. 很好,請你把住址寫下來給我罷.你有鉛筆沒有?

16. 有,我可以給你寫.你知道怎麼去的?

17. 不很知道.是不是坐第九號電車去的?

18. 不 是, 不 要 坐 第 九 號 的 電 車.
那 是 到 火 車 站 去 的. 你 要 坐 第 二
號 的 電 車, 不 坐 第 二 號 的, 坐 第 五
號 的 也 行.

19. 好, 可 是 下 了 電 車, 我 還 要 走
路 不 要?

20. 還 要 走 一 點 兒. 現 在 上 午 十
一 點 鐘 了. 你 十 一 點 三 刻 能 到 我
家 裏 去 不 能?

21. 那 我 不 敢 説; 也 許 能, 也 許 不 能.

22. 為 甚 麼 呢?

23. 電 車 走 得 快 就 能, 走 得 慢 就
不 能.

24. 我 要 在 家 裏 等 你 多 久 呢?

25. 那 我 也 不 敢 説. 我 看 不 會 太
久 罷.

26. 那 麼 我 就 在 家 裏 等 你 罷.

ROMANIZED TEXT OF READING MATERIAL

1. Chăng t'aìt'ai, ní haŏ ma?
2. Heń haŏ, hsiehhsieh. Paí hsiensheng, ní yeń haŏ pa?
3. Yeń heń haŏ, hsiehhsieh. Chăng t'aìt'ai tsót'ien hsiàwŭ yaò chaŏ te shūp'ù, ĭching chaŏtaòle meiyu?
4. Haí meí chaŏtaò.
5. Tsĕmma haí meí chaŏtaò ne? Nà shūp'ù pū shiĥ tsaì ch'enǵli te ma?
6. Shiĥ te, k'ŏshih wó pă tìchiĥ wang le, hsiangǎi-hsiangǎch'ù yeń hsiangǎpuch'ilai, sóí chaŏlaí-chaŏch'ù yeń chaŏpuchaó.
7. Nĭ haí chìte tìchiĥ shiĥ shuí kaòsu ni te ma?
8. Chìte, shiĥ Tsŏ t'aìt'ai kaòsu wo te.

9. Nèma nǐ k'ói ch'ü chieǹ Tsŏ t'aìt'ai, tsaì weǹ t'a iwen, pǎ tìchiň hsieňhsialai chiù hsiǵ le.

10. Nǐ neǵ keň wo īk'uàrh ch'ü chieǹ Tsŏ t'aìt'ai ma?

11. Neǵ pūkuò wŏ hsieǹtsaì meí yǔ kunǵfu ch'ü, yiňweì wŏ hsieň yaò taò huŏch'ē-chaǹ ch'ü chieň p'enǵyu, chieňle haí yaò sunǵ t'a huí-chiā.

12. Nǐ sunǵle p'enǵyu huí-chiā, haí yǔ pieňte shiň meiyu?

13. Meí yǔ le, ní hsǐhuan wo taò nǎrh ch'ü huì ni ne?

14. Ch'iǵ ni taò wo chiāli ch'ü haǒ puhao?

15. Heň haǒ, ch'iǵ ni pǎ chùchiň hsieňhsialai keí wo pa. Ní yǔ ch'ieňpī meiyu?

16. Yū, wŏ k'ói keí ni hsieň. Nǐ chiňtao tseňma ch'ü ma?

17. Pū heň chiňtao. Shiň pushih tsò tìchiŭhaò te tieňch'ē ch'ü te?

18. Pū shiň, pūyaò tsò tìchiŭhaò te tieňch'ē. Nà shiň taò huŏch'ē-chaǹ ch'ü te. Nǐ yaò tsò tìerňhaò te tieňch'ē, pū tsò tìerňhaò te, tsò tìwūhaò tᴇ yeň hsiǵ.

19. Haǒ, k'ŏshih hsiàle tieňch'ē, wŏ haí yaò tsoŭ-lù puyao?

20. Haí yaò tsoŭ ītiǎrh. Hsieǹtsaì shanǵwū shiňtieň chunḡ le. Nǐ shiňtieň sañk'ò neǵ taò wo chiāli ch'ü puneǵ?

21. Nà wŏ pū kaň shuō; yeňhsǔ neǵ, yeňhsǔ pū neǵ.

22. Weìsheňma ne?

23. Tieňch'ē tsoŭtek'uaì chiù neǵ, tsoŭtemaǹ chiù pū neǵ.

24. Wŏ yaò tsaì chiāli teǵ ni tó chiŭ ne?

25. Nà wó yeň pū kaň shuō. Wŏ k'aǹ pū huì t'aì chiŭ pa.

26. Nèma wŏ chiù tsaì chiāli teǵ ni pa.

NOTES

1. The adverb 已經, like any other adverb of time in Chinese, is to be placed before the principal verb of the sentence.

2. Since 找着 and 找到 mean the same thing, they may be used interchangeably, although for the sake of consistency in usage it is expected that whichever form is used in the question will also be used in the answer.

3. 來, "to come," and 去, "to go," are often used with a verb to form the equivalent of adverbial phrases such as "to and fro, back and forth," etc. When so used, 來 immediately follows the verb, which is usually monosyllabic, while 去 immediately follows the repeated form of the same verb. Thus, 看來看去 means "to look back and forth"; 走來走去, "to walk back and forth, to walk to and fro"; 想來想去, "to turn over and over in the mind"; 做來做去, "to do this way and that way."

4. 會, as used in sentence 13 above, carries the meaning of "to meet" (in the sense of coming into the presence of"; see Vocabulary, Lesson Four), and should not be confused with 接 of sentence 11 above, which means "to receive" (but in the sense of "meeting"). 接 may also be used in compounds, such as 接船 (ch'uań), "to meet a boat," 接火車, "to meet a train," etc.

5. 會, as used in sentence 25 above, is an "auxiliary" verb and carries the meaning of "being likely," indicating an action which is expected or

probable. Hence, it is quite similar to "would" in English when the latter is used to indicate expected or probable action.

6. Note that 不很知道 should be taken to mean "not to know very well."

7. The ordinals are formed in Chinese by placing the ordinal prefix 第 immediately before the cardinals. In forming the ordinal "second," use the cardinal 二.

8. The reflexive pronouns in Chinese are formed by using the nominative forms plus 自己. Thus, we have 我自己, 你自己, 他自己, 我們自己, etc.

9. 自從, "ever since," may be intensified by 以後, "afterward," to bring out in clearer terms the duration of time involved, but in translating such an idea into English, 以後 should be dropped to avoid redundancy: 自從你去了以後, 他就沒再來過了, "Ever since you left he has not come again."

10. Although 能, 會, and 可以 may sometimes be rendered into English by "can," their connotations should be distinguished. 能 implies "ability or physical power"; 會 means "to know how to, to possess the skill or technique"; 可以 denotes "permissibility or possibility."

ORAL EXERCISES

A. Say the following in Chinese:

1. Mr. Ch'ień, I haven't seen you for a long time.
2. I can't remember who the man was that came yesterday.
3. I still haven't forgotten what this is called in Chinese.
4. Perhaps he is right, perhaps he is not right.
5. Mr. Hsŭ has already finished writing the fifth letter for you.
6. He says he doesn't dare go in himself.
7. I can't find the book which he bought yesterday.
8. He doesn't have my address. Do you have it?
9. Are you capable of finding the railway station?
10. He would not come back so soon today.

B. Render the following into English:

1. Wŏ-tzùchĭ ch'ǔ chiù haŏ le, nĭ pūyaò ch'ǔ.
2. T'ā keí ni k'àn te shū wó ĭching maĭtaò le.
3. Weìsheńma chè chĭ t'ień nĭ toū meí huílai k'àn-shū ne?
4. Wŏ hsièntsaì chìpute t'a chiaò shuí ch'ü chaŏ Chāng t'aìt'ai le.
5. T'ā shàng-lĭpaì chiaò wo chaŏ te fángtzu ĭching chaŏtaò le.
6. Nàko tzù wó hsiehlaí-hsiehch'ǔ yeh hsiehts'ò le.
7. Yeńhsŭ t'āmen mingt'ien wǎnshang yaò laí k'àn-paò.
8. Wŏ pū kaň kaòsu nimen huŏch'ē-chàn tsaì nǎrh.
9. Tsót'ien t'āmen pǎ sheńma sùng keī Chāng hsiensheng?
10. Wŏ tsót'ien kaòsu ni te huà nĭ haí chìtechù chipuchu?
11. Tìiko tzù wŏ huì hsieh, tierhko pū huì.
12. Tzùts'ung nĭ ch'ùle ĭhoù, t'ā chiù meí shuōkuo Chūngkuo-huà le.

WRITTEN EXERCISES

A. Transcribe Section B, above, in Chinese.

B. Render the following into English:

1. 第 一 所 房 子 是 我 的, 第 二 所 不 是 我 的.

2. 我 知 道 他 的 住 址; 我 能 給 你 寫 下 來.

3. 錢 太 太 記 不 得 你 是 誰 了.

4. 我 現 在 到 中 國 去, 不 久 就 可 以 回 來.

5. 昨 天 的 報, 我 今 天 找 來 找 去 也 找 不 着.

6. 我 不 敢 説 他 做 人 老 實 不 老 實.

7. 電 車 站 離 飯 館 子 不 遠, 我 一 找 就 找 到 了.

8. 他 們 自 己 也 不 買, 為 甚 麼 要 你 們 買?

9. 我 昨 天 告 訴 你 的 事, 你 忘 了 沒 有?

10. 我 送 你 去, 他 接 你 回 來 好 不 好?

11. 自 從 我 到 了 美 國, 你 就 沒 有 寫 過 信 給 我 了.

12. 自 從 他 買 了 那 輛 汽 車 以 後, 就 天 天 開 汽 車 上 學 了.

C. Render the following into Chinese:

1. He has already been in America for five days, but I haven't seen him yet.

2. All these new books here are not our own.

3. Perhaps they speak Chinese, perhaps not.

4. I have waited for you for a long time. Where have you been?

5. He told me yesterday that he would meet you here, but I had forgotten about it.

6. On the morning of the third day they all left for home.

7. Have you received the letter which I wrote you last week?

8. I don't know why they are walking to and fro in that house.

9. I didn't dare ask him yesterday what your address was.

10. He has already left. Please ask him not to come back again tomorrow.

11. He has not read any newspaper ever since you came back.

12. Ever since he bought that book, he has been reading it every day.

CHARACTERS

Number of Strokes	Characters	Pronunciation and Tone	Meaning	Lesson Reference
Three	工	Kunḡ	Work, worker; time	21
	千	Ch'ień	Thousand	22
	己	Chǐ	Self	24
	已	Ǐ	To come to an end; already	24
Four	夫	Fū	Man; husband; laborer	21
	方	Fanḡ	Square; direction; region; method, device; (a surname)	21
Five	左	Tsǒ	The left side; (a surname)	21
	右	Yù	The right side	21
	冬	Tunḡ	Winter	23
Six	忙	Manǵ	To be in haste; busy	21
	百	Paǐ	Hundred	22
	共	Kung̀	Together, all, the whole; to share	22
	行	Hsinǵ	To walk; will do, all right	22
	西	Hsī	West	22
	自	Tzù	Self; from	24
	地	Tì	Earth, land; place	24
Seven	別	Pień	To distinguish; to part; another; do not!	22
	冷	Lenǧ	Cold	23
	址	Chiǐ	Site, location	24

151

Number of Strokes	Characters	Pronunciation and Tone	Meaning	Lesson Reference
Seven	忘	Wang̀	To forget	24
	找	Chaǒ	To look for, to seek; to make up the balance	24
Eight	事	Shih̀	Affair, thing, event	21
	宜	Í	Proper, fit; suitable	22
	東	Tunḡ	East	22
	呢	Ne	(Interrogative particle)	21
	季	Chì	Season	23
	夜	Yeh̀	Night	23
	雨	Yǔ	Rain	23
Nine	便	Pieǹ	Convenient	21
	便	P'ień	Cheap; advantageous	22
	風	Fenḡ	Wind; custom	23
	春	Ch'un̄	Spring (season)	23
	秋	Ch'iū	Autumn	23
Ten	夏	Hsià	Summer; (a surname)	23
	氣	Ch'ì	Air	23
	能	Nenǵ	To be able, can	24
	送	Sung̀	To escort; to send; to present as a gift	24
	記	Chì	To remember; to record; sign, mark	24
Eleven	接	Chieh̄	To receive; to join	24
	第	Tì	(The ordinal sign)	24
	許	Hsǔ	Perhaps; to allow; to promise; very; (a surname)	24

Number of Strokes	Characters	Pronunciation and Tone	Meaning	Lesson Reference
Twelve	喜	Hsǐ	To be pleased with; to be glad	21
	貴	Kueì	Expensive; (honorific for "your")	22
	着	Chaó	To attain; to reach by effort	23
	敢	Kǎn	To dare	24
Thirteen	想	Hsiǎng	To think, to call to mind; to like to, to desire	21
	極	Chí	Extremely, exceedingly, very	21
	塊	K'uaì	Lump, piece, clod; (unit of measure for money, etc.)	21
	電	Tieǹ	Electricity; electric	21
	萬	Waǹ	Ten thousand	22
	零	Líng	Fragment, fraction; zero	22
	經	Chīng	To pass through; to manage; warp; a classic	24
Fourteen	算	Suaǹ	To calculate, to reckon; to consider as, to regard as	22
	實	Shíh	Solid, not hollow	22
	睡	Shuì	To sleep	23
Fifteen	賣	Maì	To sell	22
	價	Chià	Price	22
	熱	Jè	Hot	23
Sixteen	館	Kuǎn	Establishment; private dwelling	21
Seventeen	還	Huań	To return; ... back to	22
Twenty	覺	Chiaò	Sleep, nap	23
Twenty-two	歡	Huañ	To be joyous	21

ORAL DRILL

A. Say the following in Chinese:

1. busy | perhaps
   streetcar | to rain
   convenient | autumn
   price | weather
   cheap | to sleep
   honest | daytime
   other | summer
   address | glad
   already | restaurant
   railway station | garage

2. thirty | 12,031
   thirty-five | 22,404
   eighty | 48,765
   ninety-nine | 104,001
   fourteen | 202,963
   eleven | 4,168,507
   twenty-four | 9,942,610
   one hundred | 10,631,097
   three hundred and one | 67,045,700
   two thousand books | 89,046,720

3. No. 4 | 50 cents
   No. 69 | $1.00
   No. 470 | $4.02
   No. 2,001 | $35.67
   1:30 p.m. | $225.04
   4:07 p.m. | $1,035.00
   9:45 a.m. | one year and seven months
   11:37 a.m. | nine weeks and three days
   20-odd | eight months and thirteen days
   1,400-odd | two hours and nine minutes

B. Render the following into English:

1. ĭk'uàrh | tunḡhsi
   shuìpuchaó | piehjen
   pū huań-chià te p'ùtzu | hsinǵ puhsing?
   shanḡwǔ ch'ītieň-pań chunḡ | hsiàwú chiútieň sañk'ò chunḡ
   hsiàwǔ pātieň ling liùfeň | ch'ùnien tunḡt'ien
   mingnien ch'uñt'ien | maĭlaí-maĭch'ù
   tsoŭlaí-tsoŭch'ù | īching
   nĭmen-tzùchĭ | wŏmen-tzùchĭ
   wŏmen-tzùchĭte | t'āmen-tzùchĭ

2. Nĭ wang̀le meiyu?
   Wŏ haí meí wang̀.
   Nĭ chìtechù ma?

Wŏ chìpuchù.
Chèma tsò hsinǵ puhsinǵ?
Hsinǵ, nèma tsò yeǐ hsinǵ.
Chèma shuō ní hsiangǔ tuì putui?
Wó hsiangǔ pū heǐ tuì.
Chèko maì tōshaŏ ch'ień?
Maì liùk'uaì ch'ień.
Shiǐ Chungǔkuo-ch'ień pushih?
Pū shiǐ Chungǔkuo-ch'ień, shiǐ Meīkuo-ch'ień.
Ní hsǐhuan keǐ wo ch'ü ma?
Wó heń hsǐhuan keǐ ni ch'ü.
Chù tsaì chèrh fangǔpieǐ pufangpien?
Fangǔpieǐchí le.
T'ā chiñt'ien yǔ-shiǐ meiyu?
Yǔ ītiǎrh shiǐ!
Ĭkungǔ chǐk'uaì ch'ień?
Ĭkungǔ sañshihliùk'uaì ch'ień.
Chiàch'ien kueì pukuei?
Pū kueì, p'ieńiteheǐ.
T'āmen tsò-jeń laŏshih ma?
Heń laŏshih.
Tsót'ien hsiàle yǔ meiyu?
Hsiàle wǔko chungǔt'oú yǔ.
Yǔ tà puta?
Heǐ tà, k'ōshih meí yǔ fengǔ.
T'ā shuì-chiaò shuìle tó chiŭ le?
T'ā shuìle liangǔko chungǔt'oú le.
Shuìchaóle meiyu?
Haí meí shuìchaó.

WRITING DRILL

A. Write out the items in Section A of Oral Drill, above, in Chinese.
B. Transcribe Section B of Oral Drill, above, in Chinese.

READING DRILL

After reading the following, render it into English:

1. 上禮拜三下午兩點十分鐘,
我接到我的朋友從中國寫來給
我的信. 我看見了那封信就很喜
歡, 因為我的朋友很久沒有寫信

很家．頭便．錢塊錢萬張人的錢錢，了．要就
來回外方價千塊四一多用國．國塊就天
近上．到不的幾萬三賣以要美中萬他秋
他．晚上．很東西用三賣買以天塊的春明
說事，晚路，茶用兩也錢所天一多幾年月．
頭．做他走麼茶用塊了．們右，一塊到年月
裏去以要甚紅奶的千極他左三買明個．
信出所就在杯奶的千宜買以我幾
在上．車現一牛好五便去以不可訴住
他．早有汽電國．喝杯很四算錢年到在告來．去．
了．天有坐中貴一不用就有十買現後國．國
我天沒不說很枝錢子沒西以是最美中
給忙，他去．他都錢．一塊椊都東可可他到回

2. 一年有四季．四季就是春，夏，秋，冬．一季有三個月．一季就是三個月．春季夏季秋季冬季．春季有正月，二月，三月．夏季有四月，五月，六月．秋季有七月，八月，九月．冬季有十月，十一月，十二月，一月，二月．一年的三個月的第一個月．一年的三三的的季

春不秋多，冷天不

長長春雨天的冷。

天不熱風冬熱不

夜不氣天歡天天。

短也天冬喜夏秋

季短季熱人歡跟多。

冬不夏不些喜天最

短，長冷冷有人春人

夜不氣不少些歡的。

長天季天風氣，是天

天季天氣雨有喜氣。

季兩冬季天天可的。

夏秋短。兩夏的。氣。熱

VOCABULARY CHARACTERS

(Pień)
Side, border [*]

(Nań)
South [*]

(Peǐ)
North [*]

(Ts'unḡ)
Clever, astute [*]

(Tanḡ)
Ought, should [*]; to assume the role; just at [*]

(Ts'aí) Also written 纔. Just now [*]; then, before, until

(Tunǧ)
To understand, to comprehend

(Ì)
Meaning, idea, will, intention [*]

(Ā)
Ah!
(A)
(Particle of interrogation and direct address)

(Szū)
To think [*]

(Meń)
Door, gate

(Chień, chień)
Space, interval; between, among [*]; (classifier for rooms and buildings)

(Hsiang̀)
To face; toward, to

(Kanḡ)
Just, exactly; just now

(T'ań)
To chat, to converse, to discuss

(K'ò)
Guest, visitor [*]

COMPOUNDS

邊 兒 (Piērh) Side, border

東邊兒 (Tunḡpierh) The east

南邊兒 (Nańpierh) The south

西邊兒 (Hsīpierh) The west

北邊兒 (Peǐpierh) The north

東 南 (Tunḡnań) Southeast

東 北 (Tungpeï) Northeast

西 南 (Hsïnań) Southwest

西 北 (Hsīpeï) Northwest

四 方 (Szù-fang) The four directions

八 方 (Pā-fang) The eight directions

方 向 (Fanghsiang) Direction

地 方 (Tìfang) Place, spot, region

客 人 (K'òjen) Guest

客 氣 (K'òch'i) To assume an air of formality, to stand on ceremony

請 客 (Ch'ing-k'ò) To invite or entertain guests

時 間 (Shińchieñ) Time

左 邊 兒 (Tsŏpierh) The left (side)

右 邊 兒 (Yùpierh) The right (side)

意 思 (Ìszu) Meaning

後 門 (Hoùmeń) The back door

大 門 (Tàmeń) }
前 門 (Ch'ieńmeń) } The front door, the main door

剛 剛 (Kangkang) Just now, just, exactly

剛 才 (Kangts'aí) Just now, a moment ago

當 時 (Tangshiń) At the time

談 話 (T'ań-huà) To talk, to chat, to converse

談 談 (T'ańt'an) To talk, chat or converse a little

有 意 思 (Yǔ-ìszu) To have a meaning, meaningful, interesting

不 好 意 思 (Pūhaǒ-ìszu) Not to have the nerve, to be embarrassed.

中 間 兒 (Chungchièrh) The space in the middle, among

聰 明 (Ts'ungming) Clever, keen, astute

一 看 (Īk'aǹ) As soon as [a person] looks at

不 敢 當 (Pūkaǹtang) Thank you

READING MATERIAL

1. 你今天甚麼時候回來的？

2. 我剛才回來的.沒有人告訴你麼？

3. 沒有,現在你有工夫沒有啊？我很想問你一句話.

4. 我有工夫,你要問我甚麼話啊？

5. 我 要 問 問 你, 昨 天 許 先 生 對
我 們 説 的 話 的 意 思, 你 懂 不 懂 啊?

6. 我 懂, 你 不 懂 麼?

7. 當 時 我 懂 一 點 兒.

8. 現 在 你 有 甚 麼 不 懂 啊?

9. 他 説 "四 方" 的 意 思, 我 現 在 不
很 懂.

10. 你 昨 天 為 甚 麼 沒 問 許 先 生 呢?

11. 昨 天 人 太 多, 我 不 好 意 思 問 他.

12. 那 麼 我 就 告 訴 你 罷. "四 方"
的 "方" 字, 就 是 "方 向" 的 意 思. "四 方"
就 不 過 是 四 個 方 向 罷. 四 方 就 是
東, 南, 西, 北. 現 在 你 懂 了 麼?

13. 啊, 懂 了, 謝 謝.

14. 還 有 甚 麼 你 不 懂 的 沒 有 啊?

15. 還 有 "八 方" 的 意 思 我 不 很 懂.

16. "八 方" 就 是 東, 南, 西, 北, 東 南,
東 北, 西 南, 西 北 八 個 方 向.

17. 東 南 在 那 兒?

18. 在 東 邊 兒 跟 南 邊 兒 的 中 間
兒. 那 個 方 向 我 們 叫 "東 南."

19. 那 麼 東 北 就 是 在 東 邊 兒 跟
北 邊 兒 的 中 間 兒 的 麼?

20. 是 的, 你 説 得 很 對.

21. 西 南 在 那 兒？

22. 在 西 邊 兒 跟 南 邊 兒 的 中 間 兒. 你 知 道 西 北 在 那 裏 麼？

23. 知 道 了, 在 西 邊 兒 跟 東 邊 兒 的 中 間 兒, 對 不 對？

24. 不 對, 你 要 説 在 西 邊 兒 跟 北 邊 兒 的 中 間 兒 才 對. 我 們 房 子 的 前 門 是 向 東 的, 那 麼, 請 你 告 訴 我, 房 子 的 後 門 是 向 那 一 個 方 向 的 呢？

25. 是 向 西 的, 對 麼？

26. 對 了, 你 很 聰 明.

27. 不 敢 當. 現 在 "四 方" 跟 "八 方" 的 意 思, 我 都 懂 了. 謝 謝.

28. 別 客 氣. 現 在 客 人 到 了. 我 們 明 天 再 談 好 不 好？

29. 很 好, 我 們 明 天 有 時 間 就 再 談 罷.

ROMANIZED TEXT OF READING MATERIAL

1. Nǐ chiñt'ien sheḿma shiḣhou huílai te?
2. Wǒ kaṅgts'aí huílai te. Meí yǔ jeń kaòsu ni ma?
3. Meí yǔ, hsieǹtsaì ní yǔ kuṅgfu meiyu a? Wó heń hsiaṅg weǹ ni īchǔ huà.
4. Wó yǔ kuṅgfu, nǐ yaò weǹ wo sheḿma huà a?
5. Wǒ yaò weǹwen ni, tsót'ien Hsǔ hsiensheng tuì women shuō te huàte ìszu, ní tuṅg putung a?
6. Wó tuṅg, nǐ pū tuṅg ma?

7. Tanḡshih wó tunḡ ītiǎrh.

8. Hsieǹtsai ní yǔ sheḿma pū tunǧ a?

9. T'ā shuō "szù-fanḡ"-te ìszu, wǒ hsieǹtsai pū heń tunǧ.

10. Nǐ tsót'ien weìsheḿma meí weǹ Hsǔ hsiensheng ne?

11. Tsòt'ien jeń t'aì tō, wǒ pūhaǒ-ìszu weǹ t'a.

12. Nèma wǒ chiù kaòsu ni pa. "Szù-fanḡ"-te "fanḡ" tzù, chiù shih "fanḡhsianǧ" te ìszu. "Szù-fanḡ" chiù pūkuò shih szùko fanḡhsianǧ pa. "Szù-fanḡ" chiù shih tunḡ, nań, hsī, peī. Hsieǹtsai ní tunǧ le ma?

13. Ā, tunǧ le, hsiehhsieh.

14. Haí yǔ sheḿma nǐ pū tunǧ te meiyu a?

15. Haí yǔ "pā-fanḡ"-te ìszu wǒ pū heń tunǧ.

16. "Pā-fanḡ" chiù shih tunḡ, nań, hsī, peī, tunḡnań, tunḡpeī, hsīnań, hsīpeī, pāko fanḡhsianǧ.

17. Tunḡnań tsaì nǎrh?

18. Tsaì tunḡpierh keñ nańpierhte chunḡchièrh. Nàko fanḡhsianǧ wǒ-men chiaò "tunḡnań."

19. Nèma tunḡpeī chiù shih tsaì tunḡpierh keñ peīpierhte chunḡchièrhte ma?

20. Shih te, nǐ shuōte heń tuì.

21. Hsīnań tsaì nǎrh?

22. Tsaì hsīpierh keñ nańpierhte chunḡchièrh. Nǐ chihtao hsīpeī tsaì nǎli ma?

23. Chihtao le, tsaì hsīpierh keñ tunḡpierhte chunḡchièrh, tuì putuì?

24. Pū tuì, nǐ yaò shuō tsaì hsīpierh keñ peīpierhte chunḡchièrh ts'aí tuì. Wǒmen fanǵtzute ch'ieńmeń shih hsianǧ tunḡ te, nèma, ch'ínǧ ni kaòsu wo, fanǵtzute hoùmeń shih hsianǧ nǎiko fanḡhsianǧ te ne?

25. Shih hsianǧ hsī te, tuì ma?

26. Tuì le, ní heń ts'uńgming.

27. Pūkaňtanḡ. Hsieǹtsai "szù-fanḡ" keñ "pā-fanḡ"-te ìszu, wǒ toū tunḡ le. Hsiehhsieh.

28. Pień k'òch'i. Hsieǹtsai k'òjen taò le. Wǒmen mínǵt'ien tsaì t'ań haǒ puhao?

29. Heń haǒ, wǒmen mínǵt'ien yǔ shihchieñ chiù tsaì t'ań pa.

NOTES

1. 四方 and 八方, "the four cardinal points of the compass, the four directions" and "the eight points of the compass, the eight directions," are literary Chinese compounds and are used only as proper nouns. Therefore the student should not confuse 四方 and 四個方向 in usage though they mean precisely the same things. Use 方向 for translating the common noun "direction," and say 一個方向 for "one direction" instead of 一方, which is literary.

2. 東, 南, 西, and 北 are only used for identifying the four directions or for forming compounds with other elements, such as 東方 or 東邊兒, "the east side," hence, "the eastern direction or region." Use either of the

latter for "east" when that is the intended connotation and use 南方 or 南邊兒 for "south," etc. The suffix 兒 is often joined with 邊 to form the dissyllabic compound 邊兒.

3. The intermediate points of the compass are formed in Chinese as in English by the use of the four cardinal points. But unlike English, which gives preference to the magnetic poles in forming these intermediate points, Chinese gives preference to the directions of sunrise and sunset. Hence, we have 東北 for "northeast," 西北 for "northwest," 東南 for "southeast," and 西南 for "southwest."

4. Note the postpositional use of 中間兒, "the space in the middle, between, among." Cf. Note 1, Lesson Six above.

5. 才 is often used to show how an action or state following it is entirely dependent upon the fulfillment of the only possible condition preceding it. When so used it may be rendered into English by "then, before, until" or even "in order to," depending on how the sentence is to be worded. For example, 你要有錢才可以買書 may be expressed in English as "You have to have money [and] then you can buy books; you have to have money before you can buy books; you have to have money in order to be able to buy books"; etc. In a way, 才 somewhat resembles 就, but the latter is different from the former in that the condition preceding it is not necessarily the only possible condition the fulfillment of which can alone produce the resultant action or state following it. For example, 你去我就去, "[If] you go, then I [will] go," does not rule out any other possible condition which may produce the same result, namely "going on my part." It is therefore not impossible for the same person who has made that statement to say afterward, 你不去我也去, "Even [if] you don't go, I still [will] go." However, if that person had said 你去我才去, "You [have to] go before I [will] go; I won't go until you go," then it would simply be impossible for him to say anything else that would bring about "my going." In other words, going on your part is the sole condition which must be fulfilled before the resultant action, going on my part, can become a possibility.

6. 有意思 means "to have a meaning, meaningful, interesting" and is adjectival in function. 有 may often be used with nouns in Chinese to form compounds that are adjectival in function. Cf. 有用, "useful," 有錢, "rich," etc. So, 沒有意思 connotes "meaningless, insignificant, uninteresting." Note also that 不好意思, "not to have the nerve," conveys the meaning of "being embarrassing." 我不好意思説 means "It is embarrassing for me to say; I find it embarrassing to say."

7. 不敢當, "[I] dare not assume or venture," is to be said in reply to highly complimentary remarks in order to show one's humbleness. It may of course be rendered into English as "thank you," but the student should note the difference in implication between this particular use of that remark and the use of the same expression to show gratitude, which in Chinese is 謝謝.

8. 客氣, literally "to assume the air of a guest," hence means "to assume an air of formality, to stand on ceremony," etc. The negative form of

this in an imperative sentence is 不要客氣, or 別客氣. See sentence 28 in the Reading Material above for an example. It may be rendered into English as "Don't insist on formality; don't stand on ceremony," etc. Sometimes the expression may be repeated for greater effect or for lessening the abruptness of the command.

9.   — may be used as an adverb with the meaning of "as soon as" and joined to verbs to form compounds such as 一看, "as soon as [a person] looks at"; 一來, "as soon as [a person] comes "; 一去, "as soon as [a person] goes"; 一出來, "as soon as [a person] comes out"; 一進去, "as soon as [a person] comes in"; etc. When such compounds are used, they are usually intensified by 就. Examples: 你一來我就去, "As soon as you come, I will go"; 他一出去你就進來, "As soon as he goes out, you will come in."

10.   啊 as an interrogative particle is placed at the end of a question which is already adequately stated without it.   Unlike 呢, it is casual and not confined to questions about a subject already under consideration. Whether it is used as a particle of interrogation or direct address, 啊 is to be freely linked to the preceding consonants or vowels.   When it is linked to "a," "e," "i," and "o," it sounds like "ya," but when it is linked to "u," it sounds like "wa."   If a neutral "e" precedes it, it causes the former to be elided.   Thus, 大啊 is to be pronounced "tà ya"; 熱啊, "jè ya"; 雞啊, "chī ya"; 走啊, "tsoŭ wa"; 吃了啊, "ch'iň la."   When it is pronounced "ya," it is written 呀; when it is pronounced "wa," it is written 哇; when it is pronounced "la," it is written 啦.   However, in this book only the basic forms "a" and 啊 are used.

ORAL EXERCISES

A.   Say the following in Chinese:

1.   I am between you and him.
2.   Who is the man that just came?
3.   I don't quite understand the meaning of those three words.
4.   That new Chinese book is quite interesting.
5.   Our house has a front door, but not a back door.
6.   He is going east tomorrow.
7.   You are the guests; he and I are not guests.
8.   A clever man can comprehend what they say.
9.   You are too polite [ceremonious], Mr. Hsü.
10.   The new restaurant faces south; the old one faces north.

B.   Render the following into English:

1.   Wŏmente fanǵtzu tsaì tunḡpierh, nǐmente tsaì hsīpierh.

2.   T'āmen chù tsaì Meǐkuote hsīpeípierh, wŏmen chù tsaì Chunḡkuote tunḡnańpierh.

3.   Wŏ ts'unǵ ch'ieńmeń chin̄ch'ü, t'ā ts'unǵ hoùmeń ch'ūlai.

4.   Nàhsieh shū toū shih meí ìszu te.   Ch'inǵ nimen pūyaò k'àn.

5.   Hsü t'aìt'ai kanḡts'aí shuōkuo Hsü hsiensheng chiñt'ien waňshang chiù huílai le.

6.   Nà liangˇchù huàte ìszu, t'āmen toū pū heń tungˇ.

7. Fanḡhsianḡ t'ā ītiǎrh toū pū tunḡ. Ch'inǵ ni kaòsu t'a pa.
8. Nǐ īk'aǹ chiù k'ói chin̂tao t'ā shih heň ts'unḡming te jeń le.
9. Chanḡ hsiensheng t'aì k'òch'i le. Wó heň pū kaň tanḡ.
10. T'āte shū tsaì tsŏpierh, nǐte pǐ tsaì yùpierh, wŏte chiĥ tsaì chunḡ-chièrh.

WRITTEN EXERCISES

A. Transcribe Section B, above, in Chinese.

B. Render the following into English:

1. 我想不到錢先生剛剛出去了你就不看書, 也不寫字.

2. 許太太是中國北方的人, 可是他剛才說的不是中國北方的話.

3. 我昨天接到你寫給我的信了, 可是我看來看去也看不懂.

4. 我們要識字才會看書; 不識字就有書也不會看.

5. 聽說他們今天晚上要請些外國客人吃飯. 你知道那些客人是誰麼?

6. 五年以前張先生, 張太太就回到中國的西北邊兒去了. 那兒的字太難寫了; 你可以給我寫寫麼?

7. 這個句子我寫

8. 你說他是一個聰明的人, 怎麼他方向也不懂呢?

9. 咋天他向我們說了一個鐘頭的法國話. 我一句也聽不懂.

10. 左 先 生, 左 太 太, 我 們 都 是 好
朋 友, 說 話 可 以 老 實 一 點 兒, 不 要
客 氣.

C.　Render the following into Chinese:

1.　I heard that Mr. and Mrs. Hsŭ had in their home guests who had come from the east.

2.　The house that faces southeast is not theirs; it is mine. Theirs faces north.

3.　They told me that it rained more in China in the southeast than in the northeast. Is that correct?

4.　You are a very clever man. You know yourself that that is correct.

5.　Is the front door or the back door of that house larger?

6.　He has just gone to the city by train to buy the books which you said were very good.

7.　I know the direction his house faces, but I don't know where it is.

8.　There are guests in front of the main door. Please go out and ask them to come in.

9.　Now I can understand the meaning of the word[1] "clever."

10.　The desk in front is new and so is the one in back. But the one in the middle is old.

---

[1] Say "two words" in Chinese because "clever" is a two-character compound.

VOCABULARY CHARACTERS

(Haĭ)
Sea

(Yang̊)
Ocean; foreign [*]

(Tin̊g)
To fix, to decide; certain, steady

(P'in̊g)
Even, level; tranquil [*]; tranquillity [*]

(Chin̊g)
Capital, metropolis [*]

(Tū) Printed form: 都.
Metropolis [*]

(Pù)
Section, part, division, department [*]

(Huang̊) Printed form: 黃.
Yellow; (a surname)

(Hó)
River; stream

(Chiang̊)
A large river [*] (see Note 8); (a surname)

(Feĭ)
To fly

(Chī)
Machine [*]; opportune [*]

(Lĭ)
Length measure roughly equivalent to one-third of a mile; li

(Ch'uań) Also written 舩, 船.
Boat

(Cheñ) Printed form: 眞.
True, real, genuine

(Chià)
(Classifier of machines and airplanes); frame, rack, stand [*]

COMPOUNDS

中部 (Chung̊pù) The central part

東部 (Tung̊pù) The eastern part

南部 (Nańpù) The southern part

西部 (Hsīpù) The western part

北部 (Peĭpù) The northern part

上海 (Shang̊haĭ) Shanghai

北 平　(Peĭp' inǵ) Peiping

北 京　(Peĭchinḡ) Peking

南 京　(Nańchinḡ) Nanking

長 江　(Ch'anǵchianḡ) The Yangtze River

黄 河　(Huanǵhó) The Yellow River

京 城　(Chinḡch'enǵ)

京 都　(Chinḡtū) } National capital

國 都　(Kuótū)

洋 車　(Yanǵch'ē) Rickshaw

洋 錢　(Yanǵch'ień) Foreign money or currency

洋 房　(Yanǵfang) Foreign-styled building

西 洋　(Hsīyanǵ) The Occident

西 洋 人　(Hsīyanǵ-jeń) An Occidental

經 過　(Chinḡkuò) To pass through; experience, what has happened

部 分　(Pùfen) Part, division, section

坐 飛 機　(Tsò feīchī) To ride in an airplane, by airplane

東 洋　(Tunḡyanǵ) Japan

東 洋 人　(Tunḡyanǵ-jeń) The Japanese people; a Japanese

遠 東　(Yüañtunḡ) The Far East

近 東　(Chiǹtunḡ) The Near East

坐 船　(Tsò-ch'uań) To ride in a boat, by boat

英 里　(Yinḡlĭ) A mile

飛 機　(Feīchī) Airplane

不 到　(Pūtaò) Not reaching, not quite, under

洋 火　(Yanǵhuŏ) Matches

一 定　(Ītinġ) Certainly, positively, necessarily

説 定　(Shuōtinġ) To say definitely or positively

説 得 定　(Shuōtetinġ) Capable of saying positively or definitely

説 不 定　(Shuōputinġ) Incapable of saying positively or definitely

太 平 洋　(T'aìp'inǵ-yanǵ) The Pacific Ocean

大 西 洋　(Tàhsī-yanǵ) The Atlantic Ocean

萬 里 長 城　(Waǹlĭ-ch'anǵ-ch'enǵ) The Great Wall of China

READING MATERIAL

1. 我聽説江先生江太太明天
就要離開我們了．是真的不是？
是真的．我們明天上
2. 許先生，生，是真的．我們明天上
午就要走了．

3. 要 到 甚 麼 地 方 去?

4. 我 們 在 美 國 住 了 好 幾 個 月 了, 明 天 要 回 中 國 去.

5. 坐 船 回 去 還 是 坐 飛 機 回 去 呢?

6. 坐 船 回 去.

7. 飛 機 不 好 坐 麼?

8. 好 坐 得 很, 可 是 我 們 最 喜 歡 坐 船.

9. 坐 那 一 國 的 船? 中 國 船 還 是 美 國 船?

10. 明 天 沒 有 中 國 船 開, 我 們 坐 美 國 船 回 去.

11. 坐 船 到 上 海 去 要 用 多 少 天 的 工 夫?

12. 以 前 要 用 十 八 九 天, 可 是 現 在 的 船 走 得 快, 十 五 六 天 就 可 以 到 上 海 了.

13. 上 海 是 不 是 在 中 國 北 部 的?

14. 不 是, 上 海 是 在 中 國 東 部 的.

15. 中 國 北 部 有 甚 麼 大 城?

16. 有 北 平, 地 方 很 大, 人 也 很 多.

17. 江 先 生 江 太 太 都 是 北 平 人 不 是?

18. 都 不 是, 我 們 是 上 海 人.

19. 江 先 生 江 太 太 到 北 平 去 過 沒 有?

20. 五 年 以 前 去 過 一 回.

21. 怎 麼 去 的?

22. 坐 火 車 去 的.

23. 北 平 是 中 國 現 在 的 國 都 不 是?

24. 不 是, 北 平 是 中 國 從 前 的 國 都, 叫 北 京. 中 國 現 在 的 國 都 是 南 京.

25. 南 京 在 中 國 甚 麼 地 方?

26. 也 是 在 中 國 的 東 部 的, 在 上 海 的 西 北.

27. 從 上 海 到 北 平 去 要 經 過 南 京 不 要?

28. 不 一 定 要 經 過; 坐 火 車 就 經 過, 坐 船 就 不 經 過.

29. 南 京 離 上 海 多 遠 呢?

30. 還 不 到 二 百 英 里.

31. 江 先 生 江 太 太 甚 麼 時 候 可 以 再 到 美 國 來 住 呢?

32. 也 許 明 年, 也 許 後 年, 現 在 說 不 定 了. 許 先 生 今 年 夏 天 有 工 夫 到 中 國 去 沒 有?

33. 今 年 夏 天 沒 有 工 夫 去 了, 可
是 明 年 春 天 我 一 定 可 以 去.

34. 那 好 極 了, 我 們 明 年 在 中 國
再 見 罷.

ROMANIZED TEXT OF READING MATERIAL

1. Wǒ t'ingshuō Chiang hsiensheng Chiang t'aìt'ai mingt'ien chiù yaò lík'ai women le. Shih chen te pushih?

2. Hsü hsiensheng, shih chen te. Wǒmen mingt'ien shangwu chiù yaò tsoū le.

3. Yaò taò shemma tìfang ch'ü?

4. Wǒmen tsaì Meīkuo chùle haó chiko yüeh le, mingt'ien yaò huí Chungkuo ch'ü.

5. Tsò-ch'uan huích'ü haíshih tsò feīchī huích'ü ne?

6. Tsò-ch'uan huích'ü.

7. Feīchī pū haòtsò ma?

8. Haòtsòtehen, k'ǒshih wǒmen tsuì hsīhuan tsò-ch'uan.

9. Tsò nǎi kuóte ch'uan? Chungkuo-ch'uan haíshih Meīkuo-ch'uan?

10. Mingt'ien meí yǔ Chungkuo-ch'uan k'aī, wǒmen tsò Meīkuo-ch'uan huích'ü.

11. Tsò-ch'uan taò Shanghaī ch'ü yaò yung tōshaǒ t'iente kungfu?

12. Ich'ien yaò yung shihpā-chiù t'ien, k'ǒshih hsientsaì te ch'uan tsoūtek'uaì, shihwǔ-liù t'ien chiù k'ói taò Shanghaī le.

13. Shanghaī shih pushih tsaì Chungkuo peīpù te?

14. Pū shih, Shanghaī shih tsaì Chungkuo tungpù te.

15. Chungkuo peīpù yǔ shemma tà ch'eng?

16. Yú Peīp'ing, tìfang hen tà, jen yeh hen tō.

17. Chiang hsiensheng Chiang t'aìt'ai toū shih Peīp'ing-jen pushih?

18. Toū pū shih, wǒmen shih Shanghaī-jen.

19. Chiang hsiensheng Chiang t'aìt'ai taò Peīp'ing ch'ükuo meiyu?

20. Wǔ nien ich'ien ch'ükuo ī huí.

21. Tsemma ch'ü te.

22. Tsò huǒch'ē ch'ü te.

23. Peīp'ing shih Chungkuo hsientsaì te kuótū pushih?

24. Pū shih, Peīp'ing shih Chungkuo ts'ungch'ien te kuótū, chiaò Peīching. Chungkuo hsientsaì te kuótū shih Nanching.

25. Nanching tsaì Chungkuo shemma tìfang?

26. Yeh shih tsaì Chungkuote tungpù te, tsaì Shanghaīte hsīpeī.

27. Ts'ung Shanghaī taò Peīp'ing ch'ü yaò chingkuò Nanching puyao?

28. Pū itìng yaò chingkuò, tsò huǒch'ē chiù chingkuò, tsò-ch'uan chiù pū chingkuò.

29. Nanching lí Shanghaī tó yüan ne?

30. Haí pū taò erhpaí yinḡlǐ.

31. Chianḡ hsiensheng Chianḡ t'aìt'ai sheṁma shiḣhou k'ói tsaì taò Meǐkuo lai chù ne?

32. Yeḣhsǔ minǵnien, yeḣhsǔ hoùnien, hsieǹtsaì shuōputinḡ le. Hsǔ hsiensheng chiñnien hsiàt'ien yǔ kunḡfu taò Chunḡkuo ch'ü meiyu?

33. Chiñnien hsiàt'ien meí yǔ kunḡfu ch'ü le, k'ōshih minǵnien ch'uñ- t'ien wǒ ǐtinḡ k'ói ch'ǔ.

34. Nà haǒchí le, wǒmen minǵnien tsaì Chunḡkuo tsaì chieǹ pa.

NOTES

1. 人 is frequently used as a suffix and joined to a place name to form a compound meaning a native of such a place. Thus, 北平人 means "a native of Peiping," 南京人, "a native of Nanking," 上海人, "a native of Shanghai," etc. Compare this particular usage of 人 with the different suffixes currently employed in similar words in English such as "New York*er*, Boston*ian*," etc.

2. Note that the pronunciation of 都, "metropolis, capital," is "tū," slightly different from that of 都, "all, invariably," which is "toū."

3. When 里 is used as a measure word of distance or length, it does not require a classifier for itself. So, "one li" is simply 一里, "one hundred li," 一百里, etc. When so used it frequently precedes 路, "road," to indicate distance in terms of a land journey, and 長, "long," to indicate length: 走一里路, "to walk one li [of road]," 十里長, "ten li long." But to indicate sheer distance, 里 alone is adequate. See sentence 30 of the Reading Material above. Note also that distance may be expressed with or without the help of 有 after it: 火車站離書舖有四英里 or 火車站離書舖四英里, "The railway station is four miles away from the bookstore."

4. Since the Pacific Ocean has for so long isolated China, the Chinese have come to use 洋, "ocean," to refer to anything which is not of indigenous origin, more or less in the sense of "foreign, alien." Thus, 洋車, which is the shortened form of 東洋車, "eastern ocean [hence, Japan] vehicle," means a rickshaw; 洋錢, "foreign money"; 洋房, "foreign-styled building"; etc. The "Occident" is 西洋, literally "the western ocean."

5. 英里, like 里, does not require a classifier for itself.

6. The classifier for boats is 隻, although it is also possible to use 條 for them. Examples: 兩隻船 or 兩條船, "two boats."

7. The way to form the equivalent in Chinese of such an expression as "east of," "west of," etc., is to use 以 immediately before the direction involved. Thus, 以東 is "east of," 以西, "west of," etc. Note that these expressions designate directions and as such are used postpositively. Examples: "east of China" is 中國以東, "west of America" is 美國以西, etc.

8. 江, "river," is not used freely in Chinese except for the formation of compounds, such as 江河, "rivers" (in general), 江頭, "river bank," etc., or as the abbreviation of 長江, "the Yangtze River." Use 河 for translating "river."

ORAL EXERCISES

A. Say the following in Chinese:

1. Where is the Pacific Ocean? Where is the Atlantic Ocean?
2. I have ridden in boats, but I have never ridden in an airplane.
3. The Yellow River is in China; the Yangtze River is also in China.
4. The matches are mine; they are not theirs.
5. He said that trains are not necessarily faster than boats.
6. Do they like to go to the Far East by airplane?
7. The Pacific Ocean is west of America; the Atlantic Ocean is east of America.
8. We pass through very many places when we go from Shanghai to Peiping.
9. Where is the Great Wall of China? Is it very far from Peiping?
10. I can't say for sure whether he is Chinese or Japanese.

B. Render the following into English:

1. Ts'uṅg Meǐkuo taò Chuṅgkuo ch'ü te ch'uaṅ chiṅgkuò T'aìp'iṅg-yang, pū chiṅgkuò Tàhsī-yang.
2. Ch'aṅgchiaṅg pī Huaṅghó ch'aṅg wúpaǐ yiṅglǐ.
3. Nǐ chiaò t'a miṅgt'ien laí, t'ā miṅgt'ien chiù ītiṅg laí.
4. Chuṅgkuo chuṅgpùte tà hó chiaò sheṁma hó?
5. Hsieǹtsaì te feīchī cheň k'uaì, ts'uṅg Shaṅghaǐ taò Peǐp'iṅg yaò yuṅg pūkuò szùko chuṅgt'oú.
6. Meǐkuote tà ch'eṅg toū yú heň kaō te faṅgtzu, yeḣ yú heň tō te ch'ìch'ē.
7. T'ā shaṅgyüeh taò Yiṅgkuo ch'ü shiḣ tsò-ch'uaṅ ch'ü te ne, haíshih tsò feīchī ch'ü te ne?
8. Nǐ ts'uṅgch'ieṅ tsaì Peǐp'iṅg chù te shiḣhou, tsòkuo yaṅgch'ē meiyu?
9. Chèrh shiḣ Chuṅgkuote tìfang, wǒmen yaò yuṅg Chuṅgkuo-ch'ieṅ, pūyaò yuṅg yaṅgch'ieṅ.
10. T'aìp'iṅg-yaṅg shiḣ īko heň tà te yaṅg, Tàhsī-yang yeḣ shiḣ īko heň tà te yaṅg.

WRITTEN EXERCISES

A. Transcribe Section B, above, in Chinese.

B. Render the following into English:

1. 黃先生, 黃太太昨天晚上對我們説, 他們在北平住得太久了, 所以下禮拜一早上就要回上海去.

2. 為甚麼呢？ 北平地方很好

住，天氣也不錯。他們在北平住了不過幾個月，算甚麼久呢？

他們三個月就可以到上海，對，兩三個月就可以到上海。他三個月就可以到上海以後，黃先生他們去上海一塊兒。他甚麼也不多，七個人的話以後，黃先生、黃太太回到北平。我平年三個……

3. 昨天他們坐火車到……的時候，坐火車完了，聽甚麼？請等的兒說，等到……時候坐火車。

4. 聽完了甚麼沒有？你有？

5. 他說他有一個好朋友，下禮拜坐飛機到美國，一定要到上海。他要從上海坐飛機到美國去，他以前跟黃太太回到上海，所以禮拜三去，禮拜三就要從上海坐飛機到美國。

6. 他們送了朋友坐飛機到美國去以後，還要到甚麼地方去不要？

7. 還要到南京去。坐飛機去還是坐火車去？坐飛機快，可是飛機說不定；現在坐火車也不慢。飛機真好。

8. 黃先生、黃太太好，跟他們談過的話，都是今年還會再到北平來。我對你看怎麼？跟他們說……

9. 他許會，也許不會，很難說得定。

10. 他 們 再 來, 我 一 定 再 跟 他 們 談 話.

C. Render the following into Chinese:

1. I have heard that you have been to China. Is that true?

2. That is true, but I was in China for only several months.

3. Were you in north China[1] or south China?[1]

4. I was neither in north China nor south China. I was in southeastern China.

5. Have you been to Nanking, the national capital of China?

6. Yes, I have; it is truly a big city. I like Nanking more than I do Shanghai.

7. Do you know that Peiping was formerly called Peking?

8. Yes, I do. Peking means "the northern capital."

9. How did you come back to America?

10. I came back to America by boat. I didn't like to fly,[2] hence I came back by boat.

11. I have finished reading a part of your long letter to me.

12. There are three sections in this book: one section is very short; two sections are quite long.

[1] Render into Chinese by "northern section" and "southern section" of China, respectively.

[2] Say "to ride in airplanes."

VOCABULARY CHARACTERS

普 (P'ŭ)
General, universal [*]

通 (T'ung)
All; universal [*]; to go through [*]; to communicate [*]

箱 (Hsiang)
Box, chest, trunk [*]

寄 (Chì)
To send; to mail

郵 (Yú)
Post, mail [*]

政 (Cheng)
Political affairs [*]

局 (Chú)
Office, bureau [*]

票 (P'iaò)
Warrant, ticket, bill, note

掛 (Kuà)
To suspend, to hang up; to show anxiety [*]

件 (Chien)
(Classifier of affairs, upper garments, documents, etc.)

片 (P'ien)
Slice, flake, strip, slip (often used as a measure word for appropriate nouns); photographic film [*]

貼 (T'ieh)
To stick on, to paste on

差 (Ch'à)
To differ by; to lack
(Ch'aī)
Servant of an official [*]

擱 (Kō)
To place, to put

費 (Feì)
Expenditure [*], fee [*]; to waste, to expend

屋 (Wū)
Room, house [*]

COMPOUNDS

郵 政 (Yúcheng) Postal administration

郵 票 (Yúp'iaò) Postage stamp

郵政局 (Yúcheng-chú) Post office

郵 差 (Yúch'aī) Postman

郵 費 (Yúfeì) Postage

郵 件 (Yúchien) Mail

普 通　(P'ŭt'unḡ)　Ordinary, usual, general

平 信　(P'inḡhsiǹ) Ordinary letter

寄 信　(Chì-hsiǹ) To mail letters

掛 號　(Kuà-haò) To register

快 信　(K'uaìhsiǹ) Express letter, special delivery letter

掛 號 信　(Kuàhaò-hsiǹ) Registered letter

明 信 片 兒　(Mínghsiǹ-p'ièrh) Post card

信 箱　(Hsiǹhsianḡ) Mailbox

箱 子　(Hsianḡtzu) Box, trunk, chest

差 得 多　(Ch'àtetō) Quite different, quite unlike

差 不 多　(Ch'àputō) Not much different, almost, nearly

屋 子　(Wūtzu) Room, house

READING MATERIAL

1. 請 問 中 國 郵 政 局 在 甚 麼 地 方?

2. 在 城 裏 的 西 北 邊 兒.

3. 離 這 兒 多 遠 啊?

4. 還 不 到 兩 英 里.

5. 請 問 怎 麼 去 最 好 啊?

6. 坐 電 車 去 最 好.

7. 坐 第 幾 號 的 電 車 啊?

8. 坐 第 三 號 的 就 行 了. 你 看, 前 頭 剛 有 第 三 號 的 電 車 來. 請 你 在 這 兒 上 車 罷.

9. 請 問 這 是 中 國 郵 政 局 不 是?

10. 是, 這 是 中 國 郵 政 局. 先 生 要 寄 信 麼?

11. 我 有 兩 封 信 要 寄, 一 封 是 寄 北 平 的, 一 封 是 寄 美 國 的.

12. 兩封都是平信麼？

13. 不是,寄北平的是平信,寄美國的是掛號信.請問要用多少郵費？

14. 寄北平的平信要用一塊錢,寄美國的掛號信要用四塊七毛五.

15. 那麼兩封信一共要用的郵費,是五塊七毛五,對不對？

16. 對了.

17. 這就是五塊七毛五.請把郵票給我罷.

18. 很好,這是五個一塊錢的跟一個七毛五的郵票.你貼上了郵票就請你把信擱進信箱裏頭就行了.

19. 請問寄北平的信要用幾天的工夫才到？

20. 我看要用三四天的工夫就到了.

21. 寄美國的呢？

22. 那最少要用三個禮拜的工夫才到.

23. 我差不多忘了.我還要買些明信片兒.你可以給我十張麼？

24. 可以，十張一共三塊錢．

25. 這就是三塊錢．明信片兒真
方便．

26. 是的，現在有很多人喜歡用
明信片兒．先生還有別的東西要
買沒有？

27. 沒有了，謝謝，再見再見！

28. 再見再見！

ROMANIZED TEXT OF READING MATERIAL

1. Ch'ĭng weǹ Chunḡkuo-yúchenġ-chú tsaì sheṁma tìfang?

2. Tsaì ch'enǵli te hsīpeīpierh.

3. Lí chèrh tó yüäñ a?

4. Haí pū taò liangˇ yinḡlī.

5. Ch'ĭng weǹ tseṁma ch'ü tsuì haǒ a?

6. Tsò tiench̄'ē ch'ü tsuì haǒ.

7. Tsò tìchīhaò te tiench̄'ē a?

8. Tsò tìsañhaò te chiù hsing le. Nĭ k'aǹ, ch'ieńt'ou kanḡ yü tìsañhaò
te tiench̄'ē laí. Ch'ing ni tsaì chèrh shanġ-ch'ē pa.

9. Ch'ĭng weǹ chè shih̄ Chunḡkuo-yúchenġ-chú pushih?

10. Shih̄, chè shih̄ Chunḡkuo-yúchenġ-chú. Hsieñsheng yaò chì-hsiǹ ma?

11. Wó yú liangˇfenḡ hsiǹ yaò chì, īfenḡ shih̄ chì Peīp'ing te, īfenḡ
shih̄ chì Meīkuo te.

12. Liangˇfenḡ toū shih̄ p'inǵhsiǹ ma?

13. Pū shih̄, chì Peīp'ing te shih̄ p'inǵhsiǹ, chì Meīkuo te shih̄ kuàhaò-
hsiǹ. Ch'ĭng weǹ yaò yungˋ tōshaǒ yúfeì?

14. Chì Peīp'ing te p'inǵhsiǹ yaò yungˋ īk'uaì ch'ień, chì Meīkuo te
kuàhaò-hsiǹ yaò yungˋ szùk'uaì ch'īmaó-wŭ.

15. Nèma liangˇfenḡ hsiǹ īkungˋ yaò yungˋ te yúfeì, shih̄ wŭk'uaì ch'īmaó-
wŭ, tuì putui?

16. Tuì le.

17. Chè chiù shih̄ wŭk'uaì ch'īmaó-wŭ. Ch'ĭng pā yúp'iaò keí wo pa.

18. Heń haǒ, chè shih̄ wŭko īk'uaì ch'ień te keñ īko ch'īmaó-wŭ te yú-
p'iaò. Nĭ t'ieh̄shangle yúp'iaò chiù ch'ing ni pă hsiǹ kōchin hsiǹhsiang
lit'ou chiù hsing le.

19. Ch'ĭng weǹ chì Peīp'ing te hsiǹ yaò yungˋ chī t'ieñte kunḡfu ts'aí
taò?

20. Wŏ k'aǹ yaò yungˋ sañ-szù t'ieñte kunḡfu chiù taò le.

21. Chì Meĭkuo te ne?

22. Nà tsuì shaŏ yaò yunğ sañko lĭpaìte kunğfu ts'aí taò.

23. Wŏ ch'àputō wanğ le. Wŏ haí yaò maĭ hsieň minğhsìn-p'ièrh. Ní k'ói keí wo shihchanğ ma?

24. K'ói, shihchanğ īkunğ sañ-k'uaì ch'ień.

25. Chè chiù shìh sañk'uaì ch'ień. Minğhsìn-p'ièrh cheň fanğpień.

26. Shìh te, hsieǹtsaì heň tō jeń hsĭhuan yunğ minğhsìn-p'ièrh. Hsieñ-sheng haí yŭ pieňte tunğhsi yaò maĭ meiyu?

27. Meí yŭ le, hsiehhsieh, tsaì chień tsai chien!

28. Tsaì chień tsai chien!

NOTES

1. 不到 in sentence 4 in the Reading Material above literally means "not reaching," hence, "not quite." 不到一英里 is "not quite a mile"; 不到一塊錢, "not quite a dollar"; 不到一個鐘頭, "not quite an hour"; etc.

2. Use the verb 給, "to give," after 寄 when the latter takes an indirect object: 我的朋友寄了一封信給我, "My friend mailed a letter to me"; 我已經把很多書寄給他們了, "I have already mailed them very many books" (see Note 4, Lesson Eight). But when an adverb of place instead of an indirect object follows 寄, serving as the goal of the action indicated by it, 給 should be left out. Use 寄 alone or 寄 plus the verb 到, "to reach," in its prepositional function of "to" before the destination.

3. 屋 usually means "room" in northern China and "house" in southern China. For our purpose, let us use 屋子 in the former sense. The classifier for 屋子 is 間 or 個.

ORAL EXERCISES

A. Say the following in Chinese:

1. This is an ordinary letter; that is a registered letter.
2. When the postman comes, please tell me.
3. Please stick the postage stamp on this envelope.
4. To whom are you mailing this letter by special delivery?
5. Is there a post office in this town?
6. There is not much mail today.
7. These postage stamps are all new.
8. Some people like post cards; some people don't.
9. I have waited almost an hour for him.
10. He has put your new book on my desk.

B. Render the following into English:

1. Chèhsieh yúchień toū shìh chì Nańchinğ te.
2. Wŏ tsót'ien chìle liangğfenğ k'uaìhsìn keí wote p'enğyu.
3. Yúch'āi kanğts'aí laí le, k'ŏshih meí keī t'amen sunğ yúchień lai.
4. Ch'ień't'ou te tà fanğtzu shìh Meĭkuo-yúchenğ-chú pushih?
5. Ch'inğ ni pūyaò tsoŭ, nĭ haí meí pă yúfeì keí wo ne.

6. Nàhsieh Chunḡkuo-shū toū shiĥ heń p'ŭt'unḡ te.
7. Nǐ k'aǹchienle t'a pǎ hsiǹ kōchin hsiǹhsianḡ lit'ou ma?
8. Wó ïching pǎ t'āte chùchiĥ chìle keí ni le.
9. Nà shiĥ shūp'ù, pū shiĥ yúcheng̀-chú.
10. Ní hsieǐ te tzù keñ t'a hsieǐ te ch'àputō īyang̀ haǒ.

WRITTEN EXERCISES

A. Transcribe Section B, above, in Chinese.

B. Render the following into English:

1. 郵差今天早上來了沒有？

2. 來了,他把很多郵件送來,可是沒有一件是你的.

3. 你怎麼知道沒有一件是我的呢？

4. 我把他送來的郵件,一件一件的看過,所以我知道.

5. 今天下午他還會再來不會？

6. 今天是禮拜五,下午他一定再來的.今天上午我接到朋友從上海寄給我的快信了.

7. 從上海寄快信到這裏要用多少郵票？

8. 要用三塊二毛五.

9. 那不算多,還不到四塊錢,跟掛號信差不多一樣.

10. 是的,可是掛號信比快信就慢得多了.

C. Render the following into Chinese:

1. This is an American post office, Mr. Chang. You said you had some letters you wanted to mail. Is that correct?

2. It is. I have three letters which I want to mail. One is to be mailed to the western part of the United States; two are to be mailed to China.

3. Are they all ordinary letters?

4. Yes, they all are. How much postage does it take to mail an ordinary letter to the western part of the United States?

5. It takes four cents. The postage for mailing a registered letter there is thirteen cents.

6. How about the postage for an ordinary letter to be mailed to China?

7. The postage is eight cents.

8. How many days does it take an ordinary letter to reach Shanghai?

9. That cannot be said for sure. Sometimes it takes three weeks, sometimes it takes four weeks.

10. Now I am going in to mail these three letters. Please wait awhile for me here.

VOCABULARY CHARACTERS

每 (Meĭ)
Each, every [*]

馬 (Mǎ)
Horse; (a surname)

科 (K'ō)
Course; department

校 (Hsiaò)
School [*]

員 (Yüań)
Official [*]

課 (K'ò)
Lesson; class; (classifier for lessons)

室 (Shìh)
Room [*]

男 (Nań)
Male [*]

願 (Yüaǹ)
To be willing [*]

應 (Yinḡ)
Ought, should, must [*]

該 (Kaī)
Ought, should, must [*]

初 (Ch'ū)
First; beginning [*]

級 (Chí)
Step, grade, rank

女 (Nŭ)
Female [*]

念 (Nieǹ)
To read aloud; to think of [*]; to study

處 (Ch'ù) Also written 處.
Place; point [*]

COMPOUNDS

馬 路 (Mǎlù) Modern paved road, avenue

馬 車 (Mǎch'ē) Carriage

有 課 (Yŭ-k'ò) To have classes

學 費 (Hsüeńfeì) Tuition

教 員 (Chiaòyüań) Teacher

應該	(Yīngkāi)	⎱ Should, ought, it is proper to
應當	(Yīngtāng)	⎰
開學	(K'āi-hsüeh)	To begin school, to start school
學校	(Hsüehhsiaò)	School
學生	(Hsüehsheng)	Student, pupil
小學	(Hsiaŏhsüeh)	Elementary school, grammar school
中學	(Chūnghsüeh)	Middle school, high school
大學	(Tàhsüeh)	College, university
上學	(Shang-hsüeh)	To go to school
上課	(Shang-k'ò)	To go to classes, to begin classes
下課	(Hsià-k'ò)	To get through with classes
初級	(Ch'ūchí)	Elementary grade
高級	(Kaōchí)	Advanced grade
初級中學	(Ch'ūchí chūng-hsüeh)	Junior high school
初級大學	(Ch'ūchí tàhsüeh)	Junior college
高級中學	(Kaōchí chūng-hsüeh)	Senior high school
男人	(Nańjen)	Man, a male person
女人	(Nǔjen)	Woman
男學校	(Nań-hsüehhsiaò)	School for boys or men
女學校	(Nǔ-hsüehhsiaò)	School for girls or women
教科書	(Chiaòk'ō-shū)	⎱ Text-book
課本子	(K'òpeńtzu)	⎰
課室	(K'òshih)	Classroom
願意	(Yüàni)	Willing
念書	(Nień-shu)	To study (books)
本來	(Peńlaí)	Originally, at first; as a matter of fact
好處	(Haŏch'u)	Merit; advantages
長處	(Ch'ańgch'u)	Excellence, merit
短處	(Tuańch'u)	Shortcoming, defect
用處	(Yungch'u)	Use, usefulness
南京大學	(Nańchīng-tàhsüeh)	The University of Nanking
北京大學	(Peīchīng-tàhsüeh)	The University of Peking
中國文學	(Chūngkuo weń-hsüeh)	Chinese literature
英國文學	(Yīngkuo weń-hsüeh)	English literature
男教員	(Nań-chiaòyüań)	Male or man teacher
女教員	(Nǔ-chiaòyüań)	Female or woman teacher
男學生	(Nań-hsüehsheng)	Male or man student
女學生	(Nǔ-hsüehsheng)	Female or woman (or girl) student
男朋友	(Nań-p'eńgyu)	Male or boy friend
女朋友	(Nǔ-p'eńgyu)	Lady or girl friend

READING MATERIAL

1. 黃先生到了美國多久了？
2. 馬先生，我到了美國三天了. 我前天坐船到的.
3. 請問黃先生從前到美國來過沒有？
4. 沒有，這是第一回.
5. 黃先生從前在中國那一個學校念書的？
6. 在上海大學¹念書的.
7. 上海有沒有初級中學跟高級中學？
8. 有，可是沒有初級大學.
9. 上海大學在上海甚麼地方？是男學校不是？
10. 是男學校，在上海三馬路. 地址是中國上海三馬路三千五百四十七號.
11. 黃先生甚麼時候念完的？
12. 今年六月念完的.
13. 念甚麼的？
14. 念英國文學的.

¹ This "University of Shanghai" is only a fictitious institution, and should not, therefore, be confused with Shanghai College, which is a real school in Shanghai and which is known in Chinese as 滬江大學 (hùchianḡ tàhsüeh).

15. 上海大學的學生跟教員多不多?

16. 很多,去年一共有三千七百多個學生,二百多個教員.

17. 你們念英國文學的教科書是英國人寫的不是?

18. 不是,是美國人寫的,寫得很不錯.

19. 黃先生喜歡甚麼時候到我們的大學來念書啊?

20. 我現在還不知道應該甚麼時候來.你們的大學開了學沒有?

21. 還沒有,今天不過九月三號,要等到九月十五號才開學.

22. 那麼我就等到開學那一天才來罷.你們大學的學費貴不貴?

23. 不很貴,每年不過三百塊錢.

24. 每天早上幾點鐘上課,下午幾點鐘下課呢?

25. 每天早上八點鐘上課,下午四點鐘下課.

26. 課室都是很大的麼?

27. 不都是,有些大,有些小.你願意跟我去看看麼?

28. 願 意 得 很, 可 是 今 天 我 沒 有
很 多 工 夫 去 看 了. 馬 先 生, 我 們 明
天 去 看 行 不 行?

29. 行, 那 麼 我 們 明 天 去 看 罷.

30. 馬 先 生, 謝 謝, 明 天 再 見.

ROMANIZED TEXT OF READING MATERIAL

1. Huanǵ hsiensheng taòle Meǐkuo tó chiŭ le?

2. Mǎ hsiensheng, wŏ taòle Meǐkuo san t'ieñ le. Wŏ ch'ieńt'ien tsò-ch'uań taò te.

3. Ch'iñǵ weǹ Huanǵ hsiensheng ts'unǵch'ień taò Meǐkuo laikuo meiyu?

4. Meǐ yŭ, chè shiȟ tíi huí.

5. Huanǵ hsiensheng ts'unǵch'ień tsaì Chunḡkuo nǎiko hsüeȟhsiaò nieǹ-shū te?

6. Tsaì Shanǵhaǐ-tàhsüeȟ nieǹ-shū te.

7. Shanǵhaǐ yŭ meiyu ch'ūchí chunḡhsüeȟ keñ kaōchí chunḡhsüeȟ?

8. Yŭ, k'ōshih meí yŭ ch'ūchí tàhsüeȟ.

9. Shanǵhaǐ-tàhsüeȟ tsaì Shanǵhaǐ sheḿma tìfang? Shiȟ nań-hsüeȟhsiaò pushiȟ?

10. Shiȟ nań-hsüeȟhsiaò, tsaì Shanǵhaǐ Sañ-mǎlù. Tìchiȟ shiȟ Chunḡkuo Shanǵhaǐ Sañ-mǎlù sañch'ieñ wúpaǐ szùshihch'íhaò.

11. Huanǵ hsiensheng sheḿma shiȟhou nieǹwań te?

12. Chiññien liùyüeh nieǹwań te.

13. Nieǹ sheḿma te?

14. Nieǹ Yinḡkuo weńhsüeȟ te.

15. Shanǵhaǐ-tàhsüeȟte hsüeȟsheng keñ chiaòyüań tō puto?

16. Heñ tō, ch'ùnien ikunǵ yŭ sañch'ieñ ch'īpaǐ-tōko hsüeȟsheng, erȟpaǐ-tōko chiaòyüań.

17. Nimen nieǹ Yinḡkuo weńhsüeȟ te chiaòk'ō-shū shiȟ Yinḡkuo-jeń hsieȟ te pushih?

18. Pū shiȟ, shiȟ Meǐkuo-jeń hsieȟ te, hsieȟte heñ pūts'ò.

19. Huanǵ hsiensheng hsīhuan sheḿma shiȟhou taò womente tàhsüeȟ lai nieǹ-shū a?

20. Wŏ hsieǹtsaì haí pū chiȟtao yinḡkaī sheḿma shiȟhou laí. Nimente tàhsüeȟ k'aīle hsüeȟ meiyu?

21. Haí meí yŭ, chiǹt'ien pūkuò chiūyüeh sānhaò, yaò tenḡtaò chiūyüeh shihwūhaò ts'aí k'aī-hsüeȟ.

22. Nèma wŏ chiù tenḡtaò k'aī-hsüeȟ nàì t'ieñ ts'aí laí pa. Nimen tà-hsüeȟte hsüeȟfeì kueì pukuei?

23. Pū heñ kueì, meǐ nień pūkuò sañpaǐk'uaì ch'ień.

24. Meǐ t'ieñ tsaōshang chítieñ chunḡ shanǵ-k'ò, hsiàwú chítieñ chunḡ hsià-k'ò ne?

25. Meĭ t'ieñ tsaŏshang pātieň chunḡ shang̊-k'ò, hsiàwŭ szùtieň chunḡ hsià-k'ò.
26. K'òshiȟ toū shiȟ heň tà te ma?
27. Pū toū shiȟ, yŭhsieȟ tà, yŭhsieȟ hsiaŏ. Nĭ yüàni keň wo ch'ü k'aň-k'an ma?
28. Yüàniteheň, k'òshih chiñt'ien wŏ meí yú heň tō kunḡfu ch'ü k'aň le. Mǎ hsiensheng, wŏmen minḡt'ien ch'ü k'aň hsinḡ puhsing?
29. Hsinḡ, nèma wŏmen minḡt'ien ch'ü k'aň pa.
30. Mǎ hsiensheng, hsieȟhsieh, minḡt'ien tsaì chieň.

NOTES

1. 初級中學, "junior high school," and 高級中學, "senior high school," are frequently abbreviated into 初中 and 高中, respectively.

2. Note that the way to give an address in Chinese is just opposite to the process of doing it in English. It begins with the name of the country; then comes the province (or state), if any, then the city, then the street, and finally the house number. In addressing an envelope, the name of the addressee is always written after the house number, on a separate line, of course.

3. 處, "place; point," is frequently joined to adjectives or nouns to form abstract nouns, such as 好處, "merit, advantage"; 長處, "merit, excellence"; 短處, "shortcoming, defect"; 用處, "use, usefulness"; etc. Note the neutral tone of 處 in such compounds.

4. 馬路, "modern paved road," may be rendered into English as "avenue" when it is used as part of an address. Note that the ordinal sign 第 is usually dropped before any number which forms part of an address.

5. Though 課 means "lesson" in addition to being a classifier for lessons in a school text, we do not say 一課課, but 一課書, for "one lesson." Of course, in conversation, when the context so justifies it, we may say 一課 for 一課書, "one lesson," as in 我們天天都念一課書. 前天念了一課, 昨天念了一課, 今天念了一課, "We study a lesson a day. We studied one lesson day before yesterday, one yesterday, and one today." 課 in its meaning of "lesson" is usually used to indicate the various "units" of a textbook. For example, 第一課, "Lesson One," 第五十六課, "Lesson Fifty-six," etc.

6. Note the falling tone of 教 (chiaò) in the compound 教員, "teacher," in which 教 is not used as a verb, but as a noun, "instruction." 教員 literally means "an official in charge of instruction," a vestige of the old China wherein education and politics were identical and education was merely a means to an end.

7. 初 is frequently prefixed to the first ten days of the month; when 初 is so used, 號, which follows the number, should be dropped. Note, however, that from 十一 on, 初 cannot be used. Thus, we may say 初一, 初十, or 一號, 十號, but we have to say 十一號, 二十號, 三十號, and so forth.

ORAL EXERCISES

A. Say the following in Chinese:

1. Are you willing to come tomorrow, Mr. Chanḡ?
2. Have you brought your textbooks here today?
3. What do you think are his shortcomings as a man [being a man]?
4. Should I ask him to come again next week?
5. What is that elementary school for girls called?
6. Do you know in which high school she is studying?
7. What does your [man] teacher, Mr. Hsŭ, teach in school?
8. Can you tell me whose classroom that is?
9. Are they junior college girl students?
10. Are all those Chinese books textbooks?

B. Render the following into English:

1. Wŏ tsót'ien nièn̄le lianḡk'ò shū, chiñt'ien yeȟ nièn̄le lianḡk'ò shū.
2. T'āmen tsót'ien shanḡwŭ shiȟtieň chunḡ yŭ-k'ò, chiñt'ien shanḡwŭ shiȟtieň chunḡ yeȟ yŭ-k'ò.
3. Nīmen k'ói tsò tieňch'ē ch'ü, tsò măch'ē huílai.
4. Chèhsieh chiaòk'ò-shū yú heň tō tuaňch'u, nimen pū chiȟtao ma?
5. Nàhsieh chiù te paò toū meí yū shemma yunḡch'u le.
6. Mă hsiensheng meȉ t'ieň toū tsaì chèko k'òshiȟ lit'ou shang̀-k'ò.
7. Nī yüaǹi ch'ụ̀, wŏ ts'aí chiaò ni ch'ụ̀, nī pū yüaǹi ch'ụ̀, wŏ chiù chiaò pieȟjen ch'ụ̀ pa.
8. T'ā chiaò nimen laí, nīmen chiù yīnḡkaī k'uaìk'uārhte laí.
9. Wŏte hsüeȟhsiaǒ shiȟ chunḡhsüeȟ, pū shiȟ tàhsüeȟ, yeȟ pū shiȟ hsiaŏhsüeȟ.
10. Chianḡ t'aìt'ai ts'unḡch'ień tsaì Nańchinḡ-tàhsüeȟ nièǹkuo lianḡ-sañ nień Fàweń, t'ā hsieǹtsaì haí huì k'aǹ Fàkuo-shū.

WRITTEN EXERCISES

A. Transcribe Section B, above, in Chinese.

B. Render the following into English:

五船通晚飛機二十五
十了文江下了坐飛機
三點九午上海了下江吃完晚
上午九點到上海了
拜三上到我男朋友江文
禮的船就到上海了
上我坐的船就到上

覺友。學四去學完都來。中美話，了
睡朋來。的有兒國。談們方看從國。聽了錯，沒的。到
頭女學好還那外話，他地會是中們。不秋你天明年
裏的大很少。到個兒人麼不我兒。他很平不你來。
機你京個不我多點國。甚會們點書。氣。北好。
飛機北一也天十一美國。話，他一國。天說要天。
在飛到是員昨了。了是美國。訴說中的聽還就
平。下送大多，學看我道是說我的。點雨，的好
北好。就京很開回，跟知我會來來一歡。有在最
到很太。北京生要一們都道不後部看喜現沒
就得太。學就了他就知會書。東會很也比來，
分睡謝校。天走生。了想的。國國。也都有風，氣平天北

C. Render the following into Chinese:

When you came to see me last evening it happened that I was writing a letter to my girl friend, and so I didn't have any time to chat with you. I am very sorry. The textbook in Chinese literature which you brought me has very many merits. It is written by a woman teacher at Nanking University. I am quite willing to ask my students to buy it. Can you buy twelve copies for us?

Tomorrow morning I have something to attend to and cannot go back to school to attend classes. Please ask my students to study by themselves.

I have almost forgotten to tell you that I received a long letter this afternoon from Mr. Huang's son. He is now studying in a senior high school in Shanghai. He has many new friends; some are boy friends, others are girl friends. He likes the school very much, but he dislikes the hot summer weather in Shanghai. His father will go to Shanghai by airplane next Thursday to see him.

I will be at home tomorrow afternoon. Please come to my home for a chat if you have time after classes.[2]

[2] Say "getting through with classes."

Lesson THIRTY

A Review Lesson

CHARACTERS

Number of Strokes	Characters	Pronunciation and Tone	Meaning	Lesson Reference
Three	才	Ts'aí	Just now, then, before, until	26
	女	Nŭ	Female	29
Five	北	Peï	North	26
	平	P'inǵ	Even, level, tranquil, etc.	27
	片	P'ieǹ	Slice, flake, strip, etc.	28
Six	向	Hsianǵ	To face; toward, to	26
	江	Chianḡ	A large river; (a surname)	27
	件	Chieǹ	(Classifier for affairs, upper garments, etc.)	28
Seven	里	Lĭ	Length measure roughly equivalent to one-third of a mile; li	27
	局	Chú	Office, bureau	28
	初	Ch'ū	First; beginning	29
	男	Nań	Male	29
	每	Meĭ	Each, every	29
Eight	門	Meń	Door, gate	26
	定	Tinǵ	To fix, to decide; certain, steady	27
	京	Chinḡ	Capital, metropolis	27
	河	Hó	River, stream	27
	念	Nieǹ	To read aloud; to think of; to study	29
Nine	南	Nań	South	26

Number of Strokes	Characters	Pronunciation and Tone	Meaning	Lesson Reference
Nine	思	Szū	To think	26
	客	K'ò	Guest, visitor	26
	洋	Yang	Ocean; foreign	27
	架	Chià	(Classifier for machines and airplanes); frame, rack, stand	27
	屋	Wū	Room, house	28
	政	Chenĝ	Political affairs	28
	科	K'ō	Course; department	29
	室	Shih	Room	29
Ten	剛	Kang	Just, exactly; just now	26
	海	Haï	Sea	27
	飛	Feï	To fly	27
	真	Cheñ	True, real, genuine	27
	差	Ch'à	To differ, to mistake, to err	28
		Ch'aï	Servant of an official	28
	校	Hsiaò	School	29
	員	Yüań	Official	29
	馬	Mă	Horse; (a surname)	29
	級	Chí	Step, grade, rank	29
Eleven	啊	Ā	Ah!	26
		A	(Particle of interrogation and direct address)	26
	都	Tū	Metropolis	27
	部	Pù	Section, division, department	27
	黃	Huang	Yellow; (a surname)	27
	船	Ch'uań	Boat	27

Number of Strokes	Characters	Pronunciation and Tone	Meaning	Lesson Reference
Eleven	通	T'unḡ	All; universal; to go through; to communicate	28
	寄	Chì	To send, to mail	28
	票	P'iaò	Warrant, ticket, bill, note	28
	掛	Kuà	To suspend, to hang up; to show anxiety	28
	處	Ch'ù	Place; point	29
Twelve	間	Chieñ / Chieǹ	Space, interval; between, among; (classifier for rooms and buildings)	26
	普	P'ǔ	General, universal	28
	郵	Yú	Post, mail	28
	貼	T'ieh̄	To stick on, to paste on	28
	費	Feì	Expenditure, fee; to waste, to expend	28
Thirteen	當	Tanḡ	Ought, should; to assume with confidence	26
	意	Ì	Meaning, idea, will, intention	26
	該	Kaī	Ought, should, must	29
Fifteen	談	T'ań	To chat, to converse, to discuss	26
	箱	Hsianḡ	Box, chest, trunk	28
	課	K'ò	Lesson; class; (classifier for lessons)	29
Sixteen	懂	Tunǧ	To understand, to comprehend	26
	機	Chī	Machine; opportune	27
Seventeen	聰	Ts'unḡ	Clever, astute	26
	擱	Kō	To place, to put	28
	應	Yinḡ	Ought, should, must	29
Nineteen	邊	Pieñ	Side, border	26

Number of Strokes	Charac- ters	Pronuncia- tion and Tone	Meaning	Lesson Reference
Nineteen	願	Yüaǹ	To be willing	29

ORAL DRILL

A. Say the following in Chinese:

1. guest   post card   tuition
   place   textbook   elementary school
   direction   junior college   meaning
   middle   merit   postage stamps
   airplane   usefulness   express letter
   positively   to study (books)   literature
   to comprehend   registered letter   to be willing
   clever   ordinary   to be formal
   mail   mailbox   should
   postage   mile   postman

2. forty thousand miles   two directions
   nine airplanes   fifty-five rickshaws
   seventeen hundred boats   ten classrooms
   twenty-nine rooms   three modern paved roads
   eight ordinary letters   eighteen textbooks
   sixty-four post cards   seven junior high schools
                    three hundred and five guests

3. the Pacific Ocean   the Atlantic Ocean
   the Yellow River   the Yangtze River
   the Far East   the Near East
   Peiping   Shanghai
   Nanking   the University of Peking
   the University of Nanking   the northwest
   the southeast   the southwest
                    the northeast

4. Where is the Great Wall?
   It is in the northern part of China.
   Is the Great Wall north or south of Peiping?
   It is north of Peiping.
   How far is it from Peiping?
   It is almost thirty miles.
   Where are you going to go tomorrow?
   It can't be said for sure, perhaps to Nanking, perhaps to Shanghai.
   How is it that it can't be said for sure?
   [If] there is any airplane leaving tomorrow we will go to Nanking;
   [if] we have to take the boat, we will then go to Shanghai.
   Why can't you go to Nanking by boat?
   Going to Nanking by boat is very inconvenient. So we will go to

Shanghai first and three or four days later we will go to Nanking from Shanghai by motor car.

Whom are you going to see in Shanghai?

We are going to see some American friends.

Who are they?

One is Mr. Marshall, one is Mr. White, one is Mr. Sheffield.

Have they all been in Shanghai long?

Yes, they have been in Shanghai for ten-odd years.

What do they do now?

Mr. Marshall and Mr. Sheffield are teaching in a college in Shanghai.

What do they teach?

Mr. Marshall teaches the English language [written] and Mr. Sheffield teaches English literature.

What about Mr. White?

He works [to perform affairs] in the Shanghai Chinese Post Office.

Can he speak the Shanghai dialect [hua]?

He can speak a little bit, but when he works in the post office he speaks English.

Have you written them any letter to tell them that you are going to see them in Shanghai?

We haven't written them any letter yet, but we shall send them an express letter this evening.

How long will it take an express letter to reach Shanghai? Three days or five days?

Not as long as that. I think it will reach there in two days. But I don't know how much postage an express letter will require [use].

I don't know either. I know that an ordinary letter to Shanghai requires one dollar.

That being the case, an express letter will perhaps require two dollars and fifty cents.

That probably is right. The postman will deliver the mail to us this afternoon. I can ask him.

What you said is quite meaningful. Please ask him for me. After he has told you, you can tell me.

B.   Render the following into English:

Ní pá womente chùchih kaòsule t'a meiyu?

Meí yŭ. Wŏ wanġ le, cheñ tuìpuch'ĭ.

T'ā chiñt'ien hsiàwŭ haí huì tsaì laí puhui?

Nà wŏ pū kăn shuō, yehhsŭ huì, yehhsŭ pū huì.

Weìshemma ne?

Chiñt'ien hsiàwú yú huŏch'ē k'aī, t'ā chiù huì tsaì laí, meí yú huŏch'ē k'aī, t'ā chiù pū huì tsaì laí le.

T'ā pū tsaì laí wŏmen chiù tsemma tsò haŏ a?

Wŏ k'àn tsuì haŏ haíshih hsieh k'uaìhsìn keī t'a.

Nèma chiù ch'ing ni hsieh pa.

Tuìpuch'ĭ, wŏ hsieñtsaì meí yú kunġfu le. Haí yú wŭfeñ chunġ wŏ chiù yaò k'aī ch'ìch'ē sunġ p'enġyu ch'ü tsò feīchī taò tunġpierh ch'ü le.

Ni sheḿma shiȟhou k'ói huílai a?

Chiñt'ien waňshang ts'aí huílai, yiñweì sunġwańle p'enġyu wŏ haí teĭ shanġ-hsüeḿ ne.

Ni hsiàwŭ chítieň chunġ hsià-k'ò a?

Szùtieň hsià-k'ò, k'ŏshih hsiàle k'ò wŏ haí yaò chiǹ-ch'enġ ch'ü.

Chiǹ-ch'enġ ch'ü tsò sheḿma?

Ch'ü maĭ tunġhsi.

Minġt'ien ch'ǜ pū hsinġ ma?

Pū hsinġ, wŏ chiāli ītiărh mieǹpaō toū meí yŭ le, niúnaí yeȟ hōwań le. Pū chiǹ-ch'enġ ch'ü maĭ, minġt'ien tsaŏshang chiù meí tunġhsi ch'iȟ le. Wŏ pū shiȟ pū yüaǹi hsieȟ nàfenġ hsiǹ, pūkuò meí kunġfu, sóĭ haíshih ch'inġ ni hsieȟ pa.

Haŏ, wó hsieȟ pa. Wŏ shuō hsieȟ sheḿma haŏ a?

Ni k'ói shuō Chanġ hsiensheng tà-hoùt'ien yaò ch'inġ hsieȟ waìkuo p'enġyu taò ch'enġli ch'ü ch'iȟ Chunġkuo-faǹ, waňshang pū tsaì chiā, ch'inġ t'a pūyaò taò Chanġ hsienshengte chiāli ch'ü. T'ā hsĭhuan chiù k'ói taò nīte chiāli lai t'ańt'an. Nà t'ieň waňshang wŏ yeḿhsŭ nenġ laí.

Ni laí chiù haŏchí le. Nèma wŏ chiù chèyang kaòsu t'a pa.

WRITING DRILL

A.   Write out Section 4 of Oral Drill, above, in Chinese.

B.   Transcribe Section B of Oral Drill, above, in Chinese.

READING DRILL

After reading the following, render it into English:

十一月十五號

今天禮拜三，早上下雨下得很大。吃了早飯就開汽車到學校去上課。從八點到九點念英文，九點到十點念法文，十點到十一點念英國文學，十一點到十二點本來是念中國文學的，可是因為教員在家裏有事，沒回學校上課，所以就沒有課。

下午接到朋友從南京寄給

有些禮，每海。坐得家。近那每國，上天快回家最部的美回八天，坐船說西快到飛七坐船朋友頭國很飛國。十比坐到朋裏美大海美用天，就頭信到很上從要三完在飛新，從六去過了。下個他海很四拜美國。不多兩信上是拜美用得上了覺。快從都禮三，到要便晚的機機一，拜船機方我飛飛拜禮坐飛多，裏十十

號冷半城新都英文去就不了到多本的英局了就好，看車很三我些政完很課。火見了。書看郵買氣下坐看買科。到郵天就友舖，就教想到兒。四鐘朋書很文飯信拜點跟家得英以午明六禮九就一宜的，所十天上書，到便用好，月今早頭先錢中很書。一熱鐘去。價高不科十不個裏書，是文教買回

晚上寫了三封短信，一封是寄北平的，一封是寄南京的，一封是寄上海的．寫完了信就看報．十點一刻睡覺．

VOCABULARY CHARACTERS

姓 (Hsiǹg)
Surname; to have the surname of

名 (Miń)
Name [*]

敝 (Pì)
My, our (in speaking of one's name or country, etc.)

街 (Chieh̄)
Street

牌 (P'aí)
Signboard; cards, mahjongg piece, a game of cards, etc.

 (Fŭ)
Mansion [*]

舍 (Shè)
Residence [*]

理 (Lì)
Reason, principle [*]; to regulate, to set in order [*]; to pay attention to, to mind

 (Chieh̀)
To introduce [*]

 (Shaò)
To connect [*]

 (Paǹ)
To manage, to transact, to carry out

 (T'uń)
Same; together, with [*]

 (Piaŏ) Also written 表.
Watch

 (Chiň)
Tight; important, urgent [*]

 (Huaì)
Bad; to be out of order

 (Shù)
Number [*]
(Shŭ)
To count

 (Hsiū)
To repair

COMPOUNDS

貴 姓 (Kueìhsinǵ) [What is] your surname?

貴 國 (Kueìkuó) [What is] your country?

儆 姓 (Pìhsinǵ) My surname

儆 國 (Pìkuó) My country

府 上 (Fūshang) Your home

舍 下 (Shèhsià) My home

介 紹 (Chieňshaò) To introduce

大 街 (Tàchieň) Main street

分 別 (Feňpieh) To distinguish; difference

辦 事 (Paǹ-shiň) To transact business, to work

道 理 (Taòli) Reason, principle

有 道 理 (Yǔ taòli) Right, sound, correct

同 學 (T'unǵhsüeň) Schoolmate

同 時 (T'unǵshiň) At the same time, simultaneously

名 字 (Minǵtzu) Name

要 緊 (Yaòchiň) Important, urgent; importance

門 牌 (Meńp'aí) Doorplate

號 數 (Haòshu) A register number

街 道 (Chieňtaò) Streets (collectively)

數 學 (Shùhsüeň) Mathematics

介 紹 信 (Chieňshaò-hsiǹ) Letter of introduction

修 理 (Hsiūli) To repair

同 事 (T'unǵshiǹ) Colleague

手 錶 (Shoúpiaǒ) Wrist watch

READING MATERIAL

1. 請 問 先 生 貴 姓 ?
2. 儆 姓 高.
3. 貴 國 是 那 一 國 ?
4. 儆 國 是 中 國. 先 生 貴 姓 ? 是 美 國 人 不 是 ?
5. 儆 姓 馬, 是 美 國 人.
6. 府 上 在 那 裏 ?
7. 舍 下 在 城 裏.

8. 請問在城裏甚麼地方？
9. 三馬路.
10. 三馬路幾號門牌？
11. 七十五號.
12. 馬先生在那裏住了多久了？
13. 一年多了.
14. 我有一個美國朋友,他是姓白的,是我從前的同學.馬先生認識他麼?
15. 不認識.高先生能把我介紹給白先生麼?
16. 能,明天下午馬先生有工夫我就同馬先生看白先生去.
17. 明天下午我有工夫.白先生住在甚麼地方?
18. 他住在青河大街,可是門牌數目我記不得了.怎麼辦好啊?
19. 那麼我還有一個美國朋友,跟白先生在上海同學,他就可以知道白先生家的門牌號數了.
20. 我現在就問他.他姓謝,跟白先生一塊兒在上海教數學,他就可以知道白先生家的門牌號數了.

21. 謝先生，他是不是兩年以前從美國東部來的？

22. 是的，人很好，說話說得很慢的。馬先生從前在美國跟他認識麼？

23. 認識，他是我的老同學。念書的時候，我們差不多每天都在一塊兒的。他現在的住址先生知道麼？

24. 知道，就是江西路一千五百六十五號。

25. 高先生，我們現在去看看謝先生好不好？

26. 好，現在幾點鐘了？我的手錶壞了，還沒有修理好。馬先生有沒有？

27. 有，現在十點四十八分了，也不要緊。我們走罷，請高先生去把我的汽車開到汽車房去。

28. 我快去還是汽車等一等，我開過來？

29. 等車開一開好，也許路上兒汽……

30. 好，馬先生，我就在這兒等罷。

ROMANIZED TEXT OF READING MATERIAL

1. Ch'ing̊ weṅ hsieñsheng kueìhsinġ?
2. Pìhsinġ Kaō.
3. Kueìkuó shiḣ nǎi kuó?
4. Pìkuó shiḣ Chung̊kuo. Hsieñsheng kueìhsinġ? Shiḣ Meïkuo-jeń pushih?
5. Pìhsinġ Mǎ, shiḣ Meïkuo-jeń.
6. Fǔshang tsaì nǎli?
7. Shèhsià tsaì ch'eng̊li.
8. Ch'ing̊ weṅ tsaì ch'eng̊li sheṁma tìfang?
9. Sañ mǎlù.
10. Sañ mǎlù chĭhaò meńp'aí?
11. Ch'īshihwǔhaò.
12. Mǎ hsiensheng tsaì nàli chùle tó chiŭ le?
13. Ī nień-tō le.
14. Wó yŭ īko Meïkuo p'eng̊yu, t'ā shiḣ hsinġ-Paí te, shiḣ wǒ ts'ung̊-ch'ień te t'ung̊hsüeṅ. Mǎ hsiensheng jeṅshih t'a ma?
15. Pū jeṅshih. Kaō hsiensheng neng̊ pá wo chieḣshaò keï Paí hsiensheng ma?
16. Neng̊, ming̊t'ien hsiàwú Mǎ hsiensheng yŭ kung̊fu meiyu? Yŭ kung̊fu wǒ chiù t'ung̊ Mǎ hsiensheng k'aṅ Paí hsiensheng ch'ü.
17. Ming̊t'ien hsiàwú wó yŭ kung̊fu. Paí hsiensheng chù tsaì sheṁma tìfang?
18. T'ā chù tsaì Ch'ing̊hó-tàchieṅ, k'ŏshih meńp'aí haòshu wǒ hsieṅtsaì chìpute le.
19. Nèma wǒmen tseṁma paṅ haǒ a?
20. Wǒ haí yŭ īko Meïkuo p'eng̊yu, keñ Paí hsiensheng īk'uàrh tsaì Shangḣaī-chung̊hsüeṅ chiaō shùhsüeṅ te. T'ā hsinġ-Hsieḣ. Wǒ weṅwen t'a chiù k'óï chiḣtao Paí hsiensheng chiāte meńp'aí haòshu le.
21. Hsieḣ hsiensheng ma? T'ā shiḣ pushih liang̊ nień ich'ień ts'ung̊ Meïkuo tung̊pù lai te?
22. Shiḣ te, jeń heṅ haǒ, shuō-huà shuōte heṅ maṅ te. Mǎ hsiensheng ts'ung̊ch'ień tsaì Meïkuo keñ t'a jeṅshih ma?
23. Jeṅshih, t'ā shiḣ wŏte laǒ t'ung̊hsüeṅ. Tsaì tàhsüeṅ nieṅ-shū te shiḣhou, wǒmen ch'àputō meǐ t'ień toū tsaì īk'uàrh te. T'ā hsieṅtsaì te chùchiḣ Kaō hsiensheng chiḣtao ma?
24. Chiḣtao, chiù shiḣ Chiang̊hsī-lù ich'ień wúpaï liùshihwǔhaò.
25. Kaō hsiensheng, wǒmen hsieṅtsaì ch'ü k'aṅk'an Hsieḣ hsiensheng haǒ puhao?
26. Haǒ, hsieṅtsaì chítieṅ chung̊ le? Wǒte shoúpiaǒ huaì le, haí meí yŭ hsiūlíhaǒ. Mǎ hsiensheng yú piaǒ meiyu?
27. Yŭ, hsieṅtsaì shihtieṅ szùshihpāfeñ le, yeḣhsú wóte piaǒ k'uaì ītiǎrh.
28. K'uaì ītiǎrh yeḣ pū yaòchiṅ. Wǒmen tsoŭ-lù ch'ü, haíshih k'aī ch'ìch'ē ch'ü a?
29. K'aī ch'ìch'ē ch'ü pa. Ch'ing̊ Kaō hsiensheng tsaì chèrh teng̊iteng, wǒ taò ch'ìch'ē-fang ch'ü pá wote ch'ìch'ē k'aīkuolai.

30. Haŏ, Mǎ hsiensheng, wŏ chiù tsaì chèrh tenǧ pa.

NOTES

1. In polite or formal conversation, 貴, "expensive, precious, honorable," and 敝, "humble, mean," are used to refer to the things either possessed by or connected with the person addressed and the person doing the speaking, respectively.   So for practical purposes 貴 means "your" and 敝, "my." Note, however, that "your home" is not 貴家, but 府上, and "my home" is not 敝家, either, but 舍下. Note also the grammatical formlessness of the question 先生貴姓, "Sir, [what is] your surname?" This decidedly is idiomatic usage which the student should learn by heart. But the question 貴國是那一國, "Your country is which one country?" structurally does not present any departure from the normally accepted interrogative pattern involving the use of an interrogative adjective. Anything connected with the third person in the conversation, if any, is not affected by this polite usage.

2. 姓, "surname," may be often used as a verb, "to be surnamed, to have the surname of." Thus, one may say 先生姓甚麼, "Sir, what are you surnamed? Sir, what surname do you have?" and 敝姓馬, "My surname is Mǎ. I have the humble surname, Mǎ."

3. When one wants to find out about a house number, even though the number anticipated in the answer may be greater than ten—and it frequently is—one should still use 幾 instead of 多少. 幾, used for this purpose, simply means "which registered number?" Hence, 多少 will not fit.

4. A Chinese name is composed of a surname or family name, 姓, and a personal name, 名. The 姓, which is always written first, usually consists of one syllable, although there are a few common dissyllabic surnames in use, such as 歐陽 (Oūyáng), 司徒 (Szūt'ú), etc. The 名, given shortly after a person's birth, is to be used only by the person himself and his parents or other elderly or close members of his family in their mutual dealings. Besides the 名, a person is given or may choose for himself later in life a 字, "style," which is meant for use by him and his friends in their mutual dealings. The 名 usually is dissyllabic, but monosyllabic ones are not uncommon. The 字 is usually dissyllabic. Both the 名 and the 字 are written after the 姓. This is unlike western practices and should be noted. There are people in China who do not have any 字; their 名 in such cases has to perform a double duty.

ORAL EXERCISES

A. Say the following in Chinese:
1. Mr. Chanǧ, can you drive your automobile over here now?
2. Is your home [polite term] far from the University of Nanking?
3. I live at 1201, Chunǧt'ieñ [middle heaven] Road.
4. Is your country [polite term] China?
5. I know where he lives, but I don't know him.

6. He introduced me last night to his schoolmates.
7. I am surnamed Hsià [summer] and am a native of Shanghai, China.
8. Have you written the letter of introduction for him?
9. Who told you this morning that my automobile was out of order?
10. We study mathematics and English in school.

B. Render the following into English:

1. Ch'inǧ weǹ Mǎ t'aìt'ai fūshang tsaì Shanǧhaǐ Chianǧhsī-lù chǐhaò ménp'aí?
2. Nǐ chiȟtao t'ā hsinǧ-sheḿma, minǧtzu chiaò sheḿma puchihtao?
3. Wǒmen tsót'ien k'aǹchien Hsǔ hsiensheng te shiȟhou, t'ā shuō t'a yǔ hsieȟ heǐ yaòchiǐ te shiȟ.
4. Minǧnien wǒ t'unǵ ni taò Meǐkuo nieǹ-shū ch'ü haǒ puhao?
5. Kueìkuó shiȟ Yinǧkuo ne, haíshih Meǐkuo ne?
6. Ch'inǧ weǹ ch'ieńt'ou naǹt'iaó tàchieȟ chiaò sheḿma chieȟ?
7. Nǐ k'aǹ te shū keǐ t'a k'aǹ te shū yǔ sheḿma feǹpieh meiyu?
8. Cheȟrh te Meǐkuo-jeń wǒ īko yeȟ pū jeǹshih.
9. Shiȟ-tzù te jeń toū huì k'aǹ-shū, toū huì k'aǹ paò.
10. Chanǧ hsiensheng hsieǹtsai haí tsaì Chunǧkuo-yúchenǧ-chǔ paǹ-shiȟ ma?
11. T'ā shuō te huà t'aì meí yū taòli le, pieȟ lǐ t'a pa.
12. Tsǒ hsiensheng tsót'ien pá wǒte chiù ch'ìch'ē hsiūlíhaǒ le.

WRITTEN EXERCISES

A. Transcribe Section B, above, in Chinese.
B. Render the following into English:

1. 這兒的中國書多得很,你可以給我數數一共有多少本麼?

2. 我的朋友馬文通先生,從前在這兒辦事的時候,我差不多每天都來看他.

3. 現在謝太太在南京中學教英文,同時也在南京大學念數學.

4. 敝姓高,名字叫國英,中國北平人,從前在北京大學念過書,現在很想到美國去.

　5. 我們在上海河南路五百零九號住了好幾年了.

　6. 你能告訴我許先生寫的字,跟別人寫的字,有甚麼分別麼?

　7. 那件事是很要緊的,你們不要自己辦,請黃念初先生給你們辦就好了.

　8. 他昨天晚上給你寫的介紹信擱在棹子上頭,你可以自己拿來看看.

　9. 府上離火車站遠不遠? 在甚麼街? 幾號門牌?

　10. 我們都是初到北平的,所以街道不很認識.

　11. 他的汽車今天早上已經修理好了,他可以開車去了.

　12. 別告訴他我是誰,看看他還認識我不認識.

C.　Render the following into Chinese:

1.　Mr. Tsŏ was a former schoolmate of mine; we studied in the University of Peking twenty-one years ago.

2.　That is a very important matter; you should write him a letter to tell him [about it].

3.　Mr. Ch'ień, I have already mailed the letter of introduction to your home [polite].

4.　Who told you that his automobile was out of order?　He drove it to town just half an hour ago.

5. Can you tell me again what surname the friend had who came to see you last Friday?

6. I have never met [seen] him before; hence I don't know him.

7. Night before last as I was about to come home, he introduced me to an Englishman who could speak Chinese very well.

8. Mr. Huang, will you be at home [polite] this evening at nine o'clock?

9. I didn't come to your country [polite] until yesterday and so I don't know any of these people here.

10. Please write down your house number on this piece of paper. I shall tell him [about it] when he returns tomorrow afternoon.

11. [Since] other people can go, why can't I go?

12. That principle is very easy to understand. After you have finished reading this book, you will understand it, too.

VOCABULARY CHARACTERS

(Huò)
Goods, wares [*]

(P'iň)
Manufactured articles [*]; grade [*]; character [*]

(Kunḡ)
Public [*]; just, fair [*]

•(Szū)
To control, to be in charge of [*]; department [*]

(P'iaò)
Smart, elegant, handsome [*]

(Liang̀)
Bright, clear

(Szū)
Silk

(Taì)
To put on, to wear (as hats, eyeglasses, etc.); (a surname)

(Maò)
Hat [*]

(Ch'uañ)
To pierce, to go through; to wear, to put on (as clothes, socks, shoes)

(Ī)
Clothes [*]

(Shanḡ)
Clothes [*]

(Hsień)
Shoe

(Wà) Also written 袜.
Socks, stockings [*]

(Chaī)
To pick (as fruits, flowers); to take off (as hats, eyeglasses)

(T'ō)
To get away from [*]; to take off (as clothes, socks, shoes, etc.)

(Tiṅg)
Top; (sign of the superlative); to withstand; (classifier for hats)

(T'aò)
Covering, sheath [*]; set (as of books, implements); suit (as of clothes); to sheathe

209

COMPOUNDS

摘下來	(Chaīhsialai) To take off (as hats)
公司	(Kungszū) Business firm or company
百貨公司	(Paīhuò-kungszū) Department store
漂亮	(P'iaòliang) Smart, elegant, handsome
月亮子	(Yüeh̀liang) Moon
帽子	(Maòtzu) Hat, cap
衣裳子	(Īshang) Clothes
襪子	(Wàtzu) Socks, stockings
大衣	(Tài) Overcoat
毛衣	(Maói) Woolen jacket, woolen sweater
毛襪子	(Maó-wàtzu) Woolen socks, woolen stockings
絲襪子	(Szū-wàtzu) Silk socks, silk stockings
穿上	(Ch'uañshang) To put on (as clothes)

戴上	(Taìshang) To put on (as hats, etc.)
手套	(Shoùt'aò) Gloves
貨品	(Huòp'iň) Goods, wares
洋貨	(Yanghuò) } Foreign goods
外國貨	(Waíkuo-huò) }
中國貨	(Chungkuo-huò) Chinese goods
上等	(Shangtenǧ) First class, top grade
中等	(Chungtenǧ) Middle class, medium grade
下等	(Hsiàtenǧ) Low class, low grade
不見了	(Pūchieňle) Disappeared; lost
字號	(Tzùhaò) Shop name, shop sign
買到	(Maītaò) To have purchased or bought
買得到	(Maītetaò) To be able to buy
買不到	(Maīputaò) To be unable to buy

READING MATERIAL

我見看看點了.我看來四點
了.極頭上要到
好鐘早你點
來多天我兩
回個今午告下
在一我訴
現你麼沒天？
你了怎你今有
英,等初,候,你沒
國兒念時？課
1. 這的啊有
在你我鐘

3. 沒有,所以我很想跟你去買些東西.

4. 你自己去不行麼?

5. 行,可是沒有你同我去好.我到了上海不過兩個禮拜,那一個舖子好,那一個舖子不好,我都不很知道.你願意同我去麼?

6. 願意得很.我下午沒有課.你要買些甚麼?

7. 我要買的東西多極了,可是最要緊的就是一件大衣,一頂帽子跟幾雙襪子.

8. 我自己也想買一雙鞋.你看,我穿着的這一雙很舊了.我們到新新百貨公司去看看好不好?

9. 很好,我沒到上海來以前,在家裏就聽見過新新百貨公司的字號了.那裏東西的價錢貴不貴?

10. 不貴,我看比別的百貨公司的價錢還要便宜一點兒.我們去罷.

11. 國英,新新百貨公司的地方真大,人真多,貨品也不少,都是上等的.你看,我買了這件大衣,這頂帽子跟這六雙毛襪子,都是中國貨.

12. 念初,中國貨比洋貨便宜.請你把大衣穿上,把帽子戴上給我看看好不好?

13. 好,大衣穿上了,帽子也戴上了.你說漂亮不漂亮?

14. 漂亮極了,再好沒有了.

15. 你買了鞋了麼?

16. 沒買,買不到.

17. 怎麼了?是不是因為價錢太貴啊?

18. 不是,因為沒有七號的,六號太小,我穿不上,七號半的太大,穿不上,可是七號的太難看,所以我沒買.別的地方去買一套衣裳跟兩雙毛襪子.明天我買到,就給你看.電車到了,我回到家裏,我們上車罷.

19. 好,可是上了電車我要把帽子摘下來不要?

20. 不一定要.有些人摘,有些人不摘.

21. 那麼我就不摘了.請你先上車罷.

ROMANIZED TEXT OF READING MATERIAL

1. Kuóyinḡ, nǐ hsièntsaì huílai haǒchí le. Wǒ tsaì chèrh tenǧle ni īko-tō chunḡt'oú le.

2. Nieǹch'ū, tseḿma wǒ chiñt'ien tsaǒshang k'aǹchien ni te shiȟhou, nǐ meí kaòsu wo nǐ yaò lai k'aǹ wo a? Nǐ chiñt'ien hsiàwú lianǵtieň taò szùtieň chunḡ yǔ-k'ò meiyu?

3. Meí yǔ, sóí wó heń hsianǧ keñ ni ch'ü maǐ hsieȟ tunḡhsi.

4. Nǐ-tzùchǐ ch'ǔ pū hsinǵ ma?

5. Hsinǵ, k'ǒshih meí yú nǐ t'unǵ wo ch'ü haǒ. Wǒ taòle Shanǧhaǐ pūkuò lianǧko lipaì, nǎiko p'ùtzu haǒ, nǎiko p'ùtzu pū haǒ, wǒ toū pū heň chiȟtao. Nǐ yüaǹi t'unǵ wo ch'ü ma?

6. Yüaǹiteheň. Wǒ hsiàwǔ meí yǔ k'ò. Nǐ yaò maǐ hsieȟ sheḿma?

7. Wǒ yaò maǐ te tunḡhsi tōchí le, k'ǒshih tsuì yaòchiň te chiù shiȟ īchieǹ tàǐ, ītinǧ maòtzu keñ chīshuanǧ wàtzu.

8. Wǒ-tzùchí yeȟ hsianǧ maǐ īshuanǧ hsieȟ. Nǐ k'aǹ, wǒ ch'uañche te chèishuanǧ heň chiù le. Wǒmen taò Hsiñhsiñ-paǐhuò-kunḡszū ch'ü k'aǹk'an haǒ puhao?

9. Heń haǒ, wǒ meí taò Shanǧhaǐ lai īch'ien, tsaì chiāli chiù t'inḡ-chienkuo Hsiñhsiñ-paǐhuò-kunḡszūte tzùhaò le. Nàli tunḡhsite chiàch'ien kueì pukuei?

10. Pū kueì, wǒ k'aǹ pǐ pieȟte paǐhuò-kunḡszūte chiàch'ien haí yaò p'ieńi ītiǎrh. Wǒmen ch'ǔ pa.

11. Kuóyinḡ, Hsiñhsiñ-paǐhuò-kunḡszūte tìfang cheñ tà, jeń cheñ tō, huóp'iń yeȟ pū shaǒ, toū shiȟ shanǧtenǧ te. Nǐ k'aǹ, wó maǐle chèchieǹ tàǐ, chètinǧ maòtzu keñ chè liùshuanǧ maó-wàtzu, toū shiȟ Chunḡkuo-huò.

12. Nieǹch'ū, Chunḡkuo-huò pǐ yanǵhuò p'ieńi. Ch'inǵ ni pǎ tàǐ ch'uañ-shang, pǎ maòtzu taìshang keí wo k'aǹk'an haǒ puhao?

13. Haǒ, tàǐ ch'uañshangle, maòtzu yeȟ taìshangle, nǐ k'aǹk'an pa. Nǐ shuō p'iaòliang pup'iaoliang?

14. P'iaòliangchí le, tsaì haǒ te meí yǔ le.

15. Ní maǐle hsieȟ le ma?

16. Meí maǐ, maǐputaò.

17. Tseḿma le? Shiȟ pushih yiñweì chiàch'ien t'aì kueì a?

18. Pū shiȟ, yiñweì meí yǔ ch'īhaò te, liùhaò-pañ te t'aì hsiaǒ, wǒ ch'uañpushanǧ, ch'īhaò-pañ te t'aì tà, ch'uañshangle t'aì nan̆k'aǹ, sóí wǒ meí maǐ. Minǵt'ien wǒ k'óì taò pieȟte tìfang ch'ü maǐ. K'ǒshih wó maǐle īt'aò īshang keñ lianǧshuanǧ maó-wàtzu. Huítaò chiāli wǒ chiù keí ni k'aǹ. Tieǹch'ē taò le, wǒmen shanǧ-ch'ē pa.

19. Haǒ, k'ǒshih shanǧle tieǹch'ē wǒ yaò pǎ maòtzu chaīhsialai puyao?

20. Pū ītinǧ yaò. Yǔhsieȟ jeń chaī, yǔshieȟ jeń pū chaī.

21. Nèma wǒ chiù pū chaī le. Chínǵ ni hsieň shanǧ-ch'ē pa.

NOTES

1. 百貨公司, literally meaning "hundred wares company," is the Chinese term for "department store." Another term is 百貨店 (tieǹ), which means "hundred wares store."

2. 穿 and 戴 may both be used so that they can be rendered into English as "to wear, to put on," but they are used quite differently in Chinese. 穿, which basically means "to pierce, to go through," is used in connection with clothes (which have either sleeves or trousers for the limbs to go through), socks, shoes, etc. 戴, which originally meant "to wear on the head," is now used in connection with hats, eyeglasses, wrist watches, jewelry, gloves, flowers, decorations, etc.

3. 脫 and 摘, both meaning "to take off," like 穿 and 戴, are used differently. 脫 is the antonym of 穿, and 摘 of 戴.

4. 字號 should not be confused with 名字. The former is used exclusively for a shop, whereas the latter can be used for both a person and a shop.

5. 號 may be used to mean the arbitrary numbers which indicate the various gradations of size, length, thickness, etc., of articles. For example, 七號 in sentence 18 of the Reading Material above means "Size 7"; 六號半, "Size 6½."

6. 套 as a measure word is used for things that belong together to form a series, collection, group, or set. For practical purposes it may be rendered into English as "set," except when it is used in connection with clothes, in which case "suit" seems to be more idiomatic.

7. The verb 到, "to arrive, to reach," is often used with another verb to form a resultative compound to indicate contact with the object of the first verb of the compound. Thus, 買到 means "to have purchased or bought [the thing in question]"; 找到, "to have found [the thing being sought for]"; 想到, "to have thought of [the thing in question]"; etc.

ORAL EXERCISES

A. Say the following in Chinese:

1. Americans wear American clothes; Chinese wear Chinese clothes.
2. Do you know whose hat this is?
3. I like to wear Chinese shoes; he likes to wear foreign shoes.
4. When you go out you should wear a hat.
5. The price of this set of Chinese books is very expensive.
6. Chinese shops sell Chinese goods; they also sell foreign goods.
7. It is not very cold today. Don't wear your overcoat.
8. It is too hot here. Please take off your hat.
9. There are many goods in the department stores in the city.
10. Did you hear what he said the name of that shop was?

B. Render the following into English:

1. Wǒ t'ingshuō ni tsót'ien maǐle ichieñ tàì, wó heń hsiang̃ k'an̆k'an.
2. Chèchieñ p'ùtzu maì te huòp'iñ toū shih Chung̃kuo-huò.
3. Chè szùshuang̃ maó-wàtzu shih nǐte pushih?
4. Nǐ chèshuang̃ hsiñ te hsieh̆ heñ p'iaòliang. Tsaì ñarh maì te?
5. Wǒ chiñt'ien meí taì shoúpiaò, sóì pū chiĥtao hsieǹtsaì chítieñ chung.
6. T'ā taìshangle maòtzu chiù tsoŭch'uch'ü le.

7. Wǒ yīngtang maǐ īchieǹ maóī, k'ǒshih meí ch'ień maǐ.
8. Nǐ tsót'ien maǐ te shoūt'aò hsieǹtsaì pūchieǹ le. Shuí nále ch'ü le?
9. Hsiǎng chèyang̀ haǒ te szū-wàtzu, wǒmen maǐtetaò maiputao?
10. Nàhsieh toū shih̀ hsiàteng te huòp'iň, nǐmen pūyaò maǐ.

WRITTEN EXERCISES

A. Transcribe Section B, above, in Chinese.

B. Render the following into English:

1. 請你在外頭等一等,我穿好了衣裳就出來同你在一塊兒出去.

2. 去年冬天天氣很冷,我在北平住的時候,天氣我在家裏也要穿大衣.

3. 我們賣的等下的毛衣都是上等的,中等跟下等的我們都不賣.

4. 你這頂帽子太舊了,下禮拜你有錢就應當買一頂新的.

5. 我們在美國買美國貨很便宜,買中國貨就貴極了.

6. 我剛把鞋脫了下來,可是現在不見了,找來找去也找不到.

7. 他叫我給他去買一套四十八號的衣裳,可是我買來買去也買不到.

8. 穿絲襪子的人不一定比穿毛襪子的人漂亮.

9. 上海有好幾個百貨公司,賣

的 貨 品, 中 國 貨 也 有, 洋 貨 也 有, 可
是 都 是 不 還 價 的.
　　10. 我 們 到 外 頭 去 應 該 戴 帽 子,
回 到 家 裏 就 要 把 帽 子 摘 下 來.

C.　Translate the following into Chinese:

Dear Friend:

　　I received your special-delivery letter day before yesterday. I shall be very glad to buy for you a new hat, eight pairs of socks, two pairs of gloves, and a wrist watch. When I get through with my classes this afternoon, I shall go to the city by automobile to buy them for you. But I have to wait until next Saturday before I can mail them to you.

　　How have you been lately? Have you seen my American friend Mr. White [Pái]? He asked me last week to buy for him four or five sets of Chinese books to present to his old schoolmates. He hasn't the time to go to buy them himself. I know there is a very huge bookstore not far from the Chinese post office, but I don't know very many Chinese characters and so I can't buy them for him. Will it be possible for you to buy them for him? After buying the books, you may tell him how much money you have spent. He will certainly reimburse [give back the money to] you.

　　When you have time, please write me.

Your friend,

VOCABULARY CHARACTERS

(Tǎ)
To strike, to beat, etc.
(See Note 1)

(Shū)
To relax [*]; comfortable
[*]; (a surname)

(Fú)
Garment [*]; to submit;
to take (as medicine)

(Ch'ú)
To deduct; to divide;
except, besides

(Fù)
Father [*]; male rela-
tives of one's parents'
generation [*]

(Mǔ)
Mother [*]; female rela-
tives of one's parents'
generation

Ch'iñ)
Close relatives [*]; intimate [*]; to caress, to
kiss [*]

(Kō)
Elder brother [*]

(Tì)
Younger brother [*]

(Chieȟ) Also written 姊.
Elder sister [*]; unmar-
ried young lady [*]

(Mei)
Younger sister [*]

(Feī)
Not to be [*]

(Ch'ánǧ)
Often, frequently; con-
stant, regular [*]

(Yù)
Again

(Chüeȟ)
To feel, to perceive, to
be aware of [*]

(Hsinǧ)
Interest [*]

(Ch'ù)
Interest [*]

(Hsiunǧ)
Elder brother [*]

217

COMPOUNDS

舒 服 (Shūfu) Comfortable

衣 服 (Īfu) Clothes

父 母 (Fùmŭ) Parents

父 親 (Fùch'in) Father

母 親 (Mŭch'in) Mother

兄 弟 (Hsiungtì) ⎫
弟 兄 (Tìhsiung) ⎬ Brothers

哥 哥 (Kōko) Elder brother

弟 弟 (Tìti) Younger brother

姐 妹 (Chiehmeì) Sisters

姐 姐 (Chiehchieh) Elder sister

妹 妹 (Meìmei) Younger sister

常 常 (Ch'angch'ang) ⎫
常 時 (Ch'angshih) ⎬ Frequently, often

平 時 (P'ingshih) Usually, ordinarily

做 事 (Tsò-shih) To work, to be employed in an occupation

興 趣 (Hsingch'ü) Interest

小 姐 (Hsiaóchieh) Young lady (unmarried), Miss

打 字 (Tă-tzù) To typewrite

打字機 (Tătzù-chī) Typewriter

打 水 (Tá-shui) To fetch water

打 牌 (Tă-p'aí) To play mahjongg or cards

電 話 (Tienhuà) Telephone

打電話 (Tă tienhuà) To telephone, to make a telephone call

電 報 (Tienpaò) Telegram, telegraph

打電報 (Tă tienpaò) To send a telegram, to cable

電話局 (Tienhuà-chú) Telephone Bureau

覺 得 (Chüehte) To feel, to be aware of

打 聽 (Tăt'ing) To make inquiries

平 常 (P'ingch'ang) Usually, ordinarily; common, usual, ordinary

非 常 (Feich'ang) Unusually, extraordinarily, exceptionally, extremely; unusual, exceptional

READING MATERIAL

我有一個同學姓張，名字叫
定國，人很好，很喜歡念書。他常常
到我家裏來，跟我一塊兒學英文。
可是上禮拜三早上，他打電話給

我天坐他號，很．除親．跟是話樣．了兒，知完一今文去在

報．那就了．六得人．母弟可海一．住點就念事姐．英弟還

國．歡課，到十服個親，弟人上海一聽經做姐他弟妹．

外喜了．就九舒幾個父個平以海上說一已頭他說的妹

看常下鐘百大好的一北所上會人都頭事聽他個

去非我分三又有他姐．是書跟人也別了．哥局做學好兩

裏得鐘多路高頭有姐親過平話好人哥話頭大很的

家覺刻十東又裏還個父念不北海很海個電裏了．他

他就一了京房，家外，一他海差是上不上兩在局進念．

到話點坐北洋的以哥妹上好也年，得是的個政剛都初書．

我電三去．在所他國哥妹在很親一說不他一郵天學了念

請了午車家一定個個前得母過是他學，在秋數進學

我．接下電的是了兩兩從說他不可道．大個年跟年小

那天我在定國家裏看報,看
了一個多鐘頭,覺得很有興趣.看
完了就坐電車回家了.

ROMANIZED TEXT OF READING MATERIAL

Wó yŭ īko t'unǵhsüeń hsin̊g-Chanḡ, minǵtzu chiaò Tin̊gkuó, jeń heń haŏ, heń hsīhuan nieǹ-shū. T'ā ch'anǵch'anǵ taò wo chiāli lai, keń wo īk'uàrh hsüeń Yin̄gweń. K'ŏshih shanǵ-līpaìsañ tsaŏshang, t'ā tă tieǹhuà keí wo, ch'inǵ wo taò t'a chiāli ch'ü k'añ waìkuo-paò. Wŏ chieńle tieǹhuà chiù chüeńte feīch'anǵ hsīhuan. Nà t'ieñ hsiàwŭ sañtieň īk'ò chunḡ wŏ hsiàle k'ò, chiù tsò tieǹch'ē ch'ü. Tsòle shih̄-tōfeñ chunḡ chiù taò le. T'āte chiā tsai Peīchinḡ-tunḡlù sañpaí chiŭshihliùhaò, shiḣ īsŏ yanǵfanǵ, yù kaō yù tà, shūfuteheň.

T'āte chiā lit'ou yú haó chīko jeń. Ch'úle Tin̊gkuó īwaì, haí yŭ t'āte fùch'in, mŭch'in, liangǩo kōko, īko chieḣchieh, īko tìti keń liangǩo meìmei. T'ā fùch'in shiḣ Peīp'inǵ-jeń, k'ŏshih ts'unǵch'ień tsaì Shanḡhaī nieǹkuo shū, sói Shanḡhaī-huà shuōte heń haŏ, ch'àputō keń Shanḡhaī-jeń īyanǵ. T'ā mŭch'in yeḣ shiḣ Peīp'inǵ-jeń, tsaì Shanḡhaī chùle pūkuò ī nień, Shanḡ-haī-huà yeḣ huì shuō ītiărh, k'ŏshih shuōte pū heń haŏ. Pieḣjen īt'inḡ chiù chiḣtao t'a pū shiḣ Shanḡhaī-jeń le.

T'āte liangǩo kōko toū īching nieǹwań tàhsüeń, īko tsaì tieǹhuà-chú lit'ou tsò-shiḣ, īko tsaì yúcheng̊-chú lit'ou tsò-shiḣ. T'ā chieḣchieh chiññien ch'iūt'ien kanḡ chìnle tàhsüeń, t'inḡshuō t'a Yin̄gweń keń shùhsüeń toū nieǹte heń haŏ. T'āte tìti ch'ùnien chìnle ch'ūchunḡ. T'āte liangǩo meìmei haí tsaì hsiaŏhsüeń nieǹ-shū.

Nà t'ieñ wŏ tsaì Tin̊gkuó chiāli k'añ-paò, k'aǹle īko-tō chunḡt'oú, chüeńte heń yŭ hsin̊gch'ü. K'aǹwańle chiù tsò tieǹch'ē huí-chiā le.

NOTES

1. The verb 打, "to beat, to strike," may be used to mean "to make, to do, to get," etc., depending on its object. Thus, 打電話 means "to telephone, to make a telephone call"; 打電報, "to send a telegram, to telegraph"; 打字, "to typewrite"; 打水, "to draw water, to fetch water"; 打牌, "to play mah-jongg, to play cards"; etc.

2. 北京東路 means "East Peking Road." Note how the position of 東 in Chinese differs from that of "East" in English.

3. The correlative conjunctions 又...又 mean "both...and." They are followed only by predicates. Do not use them to correlate nouns or pronouns.

4. 又 and 再 both mean "again," but they are used differently. In connection with an actual action, use 又; in connection with an action yet to take place or contemplated, use 再. For example, 你已經說過今天不再

看書, 可是你現在又看了, "You have already said that you would not read again, but now you are reading again."

　　5. 除了 ... 以外 means "besides, with the exception of ... "

　　6. 一 is often used adverbially to mean "once, as soon as." Thus, 別人一聽就知道他不是上海人了 may be rendered into English as "As soon as people hear [her speak the Shanghai dialect] they will know she is not a native of Shanghai."

　　7. Do not use 姊 in place of 姐 in the compound 小姐, "Miss, unmarried young lady." It is pronounced "hsiaóchieh."

　　8. 非 is primarily a literary word which means the same as 不是, but it should not be used in place of the latter in modern colloquial Chinese. It is introduced here for the sake of forming compounds such as 非常, etc. Used in this limited way, 非 resembles such negative prefixes in English as "un-, in-, im-".

ORAL EXERCISES

A.　Say the following in Chinese ;

1. Did you telephone him yesterday asking him not to go again?
2. No, I didn't, but I sent him a telegram.
3. I don't know why I frequently don't feel very well.
4. He ordinarily writes Chinese characters both fast and well.
5. His father is surnamed "Ch'ień" and his mother is surnamed "Chang."
6. She is my elder sister, not my younger sister.
7. His parents are both natives of Nanking.
8. My younger brother's colleagues all live in the city.
9. I haven't seen them for almost two years and three months.
10. The new houses on Nanking Road are not very comfortable.

B.　Render the following into English :

1. Chèchià tǎtzù-chī shih t'āte fùch'in tsót'ien maǐ te.
2. Huáng hsiensheng chiaò ni hsieh te chiehshaò-hsìn, ní hsiehhaǒle meiyu?
3. Nǐ p'ingshih hsieh te Chungkuo-tzù ken t'a hsieh te ch'àputō iyang.
4. Ch'úle shoǔt'aò iwaì, wǒ chiñt'ien tsaì paǐhuò-kungszū maǐ te tunghsi toū pū shih yanghuò.
5. T'āmen hsüeh Yingweń ch'angch'ang chüehte hen yǔ hsingch'ü.
6. Wǒ chiaò ni pūyaò tsaì tǎ-p'aí, k'ǒshih nǐ hsientsaì yù tā le.
7. Maó hsienhengte meìmei shih wǒmen hsüehhsiaò tsuì p'iaòliang te nǔ-hsüehsheng.
8. T'ā kang tsoǔ le, weishemma nǐ pū tsaǒ itiǎrh laí?
9. Wǒ meí ch'uañ taì, k'ǒshih wǒ hsientsaì pū chüehte leng.
10. Ní yú chǐko hsiungtì, chǐko chiehmeì ne?

WRITTEN EXERCISES

A.　Transcribe Section B, above, in Chinese.

B. Render the following into English:

1. 我母親今天不大舒服,所以沒有跟我來看你們.

2. 他明天要請你們弟兄三個人到他家裏去打牌.

3. 你不常常打字,可是打得又快又好,我真比不上你.

4. 我們的同學常常給他們的朋友打電話,每天最少打一回.

5. 黃先生昨天打給我的電報,怎麼不見了? 你拿去看了沒有?

6. 我去年九月在他家裏住了好幾天,很舒服.

7. 你剛看完了他的信,不要再看了.

8. 你們學中國話,覺得有興趣沒有?

9. 這裏的水,我們已經用完了. 叫他們到外頭去打一點兒回來.

10. 他的父親剛從美國回來. 聽說他兩個月以後,就要再到美國去.

C. Render the following into Chinese:

1. Mr. Chang, may I ask whom you are now telephoning?
2. Who is it that has sent you this lengthy telegram?
3. He has two brothers and four sisters; they all are my schoolmates.

4. I have heard that their parents are natives of Shanghai, but that they cannot speak the Shanghai dialect very well.

5. In the evening I like to read newspapers; I don't like to play cards.

6. What is he doing there? He is typewriting there.

7. With the exception of my younger brother and my younger sister, we all are interested [have interest] in reading.

8. Are your new shoes comfortable? Are they size $7\frac{1}{2}$?

9. I have almost forgotten your name. Is it "Hsieh Tin̆gkuó"?

10. I feel that he was somewhat wrong in what he said last night.

VOCABULARY CHARACTERS

(Yeń)
Countenance [*]; color [*]; (a surname)

(Sè or Shaĩ)
Color [*]

(Lań)
Blue [*]

(Heĩ)
Black [*]; dark [*]

(Lǜ)
Green [*]

(Sheń)
Deep, profound

(Ch'ieň)
Shallow; light (as of color)

(Huã)
Flower [*]; to spend (as money, time)

(Hsĩ)
To hope [*]

(Wanġ)
To hope [*]; to look toward [*]

(Ts'aŏ)
Grass

(Yeh)
Leaf [*]; (a surname)

(K'õ)
(Classifier for trees)

(Tŏ) Also written 朵.
(Classifier for flowers)

(P'ińg) Also written 瓶.
Vase [*]; bottle, jar [*]

(Mò)
Ink stick; (a surname)

(Shù)
Tree

COMPOUNDS

花 兒 (Huārh) Flower

顏 色 (Yeńse, yeńshai) Color

草 地 (Ts'aŏti) Lawn

茶 葉 (Ch'áyeh) Tea leaves

樹 葉 子 (Shùyehtzu) Leaves of trees

瓶 子 (P'ingtzu) Bottle, jar

花 瓶 (Huāp'ing) Vase

記 得 起 (Chìtech'ĭ) Able to recall or remember

自 來 水 筆 (Tzùlaíshuí-pĭ) Fountain pen

開 花 兒 (K'aī-huārh) To bloom

深 淺 (Sheńch'ieň) Deep or shallow; depth; shade (of colors)

希 望 (Hsīwanǵ) To hope; hope

馬 上 (Mǎshanǵ) At once; immediately

吃 墨 紙 (Ch'iħmò-chiħ) Blotting paper

記 不 起 (Chìpuch'ĭ) Unable to recall or remember

墨 水 (Mòshuǐ) Ink (in liquid form)

READING MATERIAL

1. 你 們 學 校 前 頭 的 大 樹, 現 在 開 了 花 兒 沒 有?

2. 已 經 開 了 四 五 天 了, 你 沒 看 見 麼?

3. 還 沒 有, 我 希 望 明 天 能 去 看 看.

4. 甚 麼 顏 色 的 花 兒 都 有. 紅 的 也 有, 黃 的 也 有, 白 的 也 有. 我 也 希 望 你 明 天 能 去 看 看.

5. 開 紅 花 兒 的 樹 一 共 有 幾 棵?

6. 一 共 有 六 棵.

7. 開 黃 花 兒 的 呢?

8. 一 共 有 三 棵.

9. 開白花兒的呢?

10. 那我不知道了.我看最少也有三四棵罷.

11. 你們近來下了課,還坐在草地上頭談話麼?

12. 我們近來很忙,下了課就馬上回家看書,沒有工夫再坐在草地上頭談話了.

13. 我聽説張太太大前天下午買了一輛新的汽車,你看見過沒有?

14. 沒有,是甚麼顏色的?

15. 是綠的.

16. 是深綠的還是淺綠的?

17. 綠色的深淺,我不能告訴你,那輛汽車我自己還沒看見過,因為我昨天回來,已經進城去買了那些東西了.

18. 我前天早上進城去,買了一枝自來水筆,一瓶藍墨水,跟兩張自來水紙.

19. 你已經有一枝新的自來水筆了,為甚麼又買的呢?

20. 我那枝新的自來水筆前天給誰拿了去了,我就不知道;舊的不見了,所以不能不買一枝新的.

21. 那個黑的花瓶很好看,是誰賣給你的?

22. 是白太太賣給我的,五塊錢你說貴不貴?

23. 這樣好的花瓶,五塊錢一點兒也不貴.

24. 你明天下午要再進城麼?

25. 也許要進,也許不要.你要我給你買東西麼?

26. 是的,我的茶葉昨天給高先生用完了.我很想請你給我買一點兒.

27. 那麼我進城就給你買罷.

ROMANIZED TEXT OF READING MATERIAL

1. Nĭmen hsüéhhsiaò ch'ieńt'ou te tà shù, hsieǹtsaì k'aīle huārh meiyu?
2. Ĭching k'aīle szù-wŭ t'ieñ le, nĭ meí k'aǹchien ma?
3. Haí meí yŭ, wŏ hsīwanġ mínġt'ien nenġ ch'ü k'aǹk'an.
4. Sheńma yeńse te huārh toū yŭ. Hunġ-te yeń yŭ, huanġ-te yeń yŭ, paíte yeń yŭ. Wó yeń hsīwanġ ni mínġt'ien nenġ ch'ü k'aǹk'an.
5. K'aī hunġ-huārh te shù īkunġ yú chīk'ō?
6. Īkunġ yŭ liùk'ō.
7. K'aī huanġ-huārh te ne?
8. Īkunġ yŭ sañk'ō.
9. K'aī paí-huārh te ne?
10. Nà wŏ pū chiñtao le. Wŏ k'aǹ tsuì shaó yeń yŭ sañ-szùk'ō pa.
11. Nĭmen chiǹlaí hsiàle k'ò, haí tsò tsaì ts'aŏtì shanġt'ou t'añ-huà ma?
12. Wŏmen chiǹlaí heń manġ, hsiàle k'ò chiù mǎshanġ huí-chiā k'aǹ-shū, meí yŭ kunġfu tsaì tsò tsaì ts'aŏtì shanġt'ou t'añ-huà le.
13. Wŏ t'inġshuō Chanġ t'aìt'ai tà-ch'ieńt'ien hsiàwú maīle īlianġ hsiñ te ch'ìch'ē, nĭ k'aǹchienkuo meiyu?
14. Meí yŭ, shiḥ sheńma yeńse te?
15. Shiḥ lǜ-te.
16. Shiḥ sheñ lǜ-te haíshih ch'ieñ lǜ-te?

17. Lùsete sheñch'ieñ, wǒ pū neng kaòsu ni le, yīnweì wǒ-tzùchǐ haí meí k'àñchienkuo nàliang ch'ìch'ē ne. Tsót'ien nǐ chiñ-ch'eng ch'ü maǐle hsieh sheñma tunḡhsi huilai le?

18. Maǐle īchih tzùlaíshuí-pǐ, īp'ing lan-mòshui keñ liangchang ch'iḥmò-chih.

19. Ní īching yūle tzùlaíshuí-pǐ le, weìsheñma yù maǐ hsiñ te?

20. Wǒte chiù te tzùlaíshuí-pǐ ch'ieñt'ien tsaǒshang chiù pūchieñle, pū chiñtao keǐ shuí nále ch'ü le, sóǐ pū neng pū maǐ īchih hsiñ te.

21. Nàko heī-te huāp'ing heñ haǒk'añ, shih shuí maì keí ni te?

22. Shih Paí t'aìt'ai maì keí wo te. Wǔk'uaì ch'ień nǐ shuō kueì pukueì?

23. Chèyang haǒ te huāp'ing, wǔk'uaì ch'ień ītiǎrh yeḥ pū kueì.

24. Nǐ mingt'ien hsiàwǔ yaò tsaì chiñ-ch'eng ma?

25. Yeḥhsǔ yaò chiñ, yeḥhsǔ pū yaò. Nǐ yaò wo keí ni maǐ tunḡhsi ma?

26. Shih te, wǒte ch'áyeh tsót'ien keǐ Kaō hsiensheng yunḡwaǹ le. Wó heñ hsiang ch'ing ni keí wo maǐ ītiǎrh.

27. Nèma wǒ chiñ-ch'eng chiù keí ni maǐ pa.

NOTES

1. The fact that the active construction is preferred in Chinese to the passive has already been pointed out above (Note 7, Lesson Eight). The truth of the matter is that there is no real passive construction in Chinese. However, there are various ways of expressing the effect peculiar to the passive construction in English, depending on how it is constructed. One way, as has been pointed out in Lesson Eight, is to use a transitive verb in such a way as to leave out its object, so that the subject of the verb can only be sensibly regarded as having been acted upon by the action expressed by the verb. This way is generally resorted to when the agent is not mentioned. Examples: 我的錢已經用完了, "My money was already used up"; 門開了, "The door was opened"; 大衣已經買到了, "The overcoat has already been bought."

When the agent is mentioned along with the recipient or object of the action, and if the predicate nominative is included, one can use the copula 是 plus the relative clause: 這些字是他寫的, "These words were written by him"; 那些房子是張先生買的, "Those houses have been bought by Mr. Chang"; 那句話是我説的, "That statement was made by me." If the sentence does not take a predicate nominative, one can use certain other verbs if the subject does not equate the predicate, then one can use certain verbs to indicate the passive effect. One must bear in mind, however, that such a construction is actually active. One such commonly used verb is 給, "to give"; another is 被 (peì), "to suffer"; a third is 叫, "to call, to cause," etc. There are others: 受 (shoù), "to receive, to suffer, to bear"; 挨 (aí), "to suffer." When these verbs are used, they and their objects (that is, the agents) come before the main or action verb. Thus, "He was beaten by me" becomes 他給我打了; "Your books were sold by him," 你的書給他賣了; "I was seen by him," 我叫他看見了. Whenever possible, try to arrange the thoughts of a sentence in such a way that the subject can actually be the agent of the action asserted by the verb.

2. 呢 as a final assertive particle is used to reinforce the fact stated

in a statement, and when so used it should not be confused with the inter-rogative particle similarly written and pronounced. Example: 我現在才知道他不是你的朋友呢, "Now I know he is not your friend!" or "I didn't know he was not your friend until now!"

3. The double negative 不能不' means "cannot but" or "cannot help but."

ORAL EXERCISES

A. Say the following in Chinese:
1. What color is this? What is this color called in Chinese?
2. By whom was he beaten? He was beaten by me.
3. Do you see the lawn in front of their new house?
4. I want a pen; I don't want a fountain pen.
5. I have no red ink; it was used up by them.
6. We have two jars of tea leaves here: one is good; one is not good.
7. This tree is very old. I hope it will bloom again.
8. He likes to write with green ink; I like to write with blue ink.
9. Please take this bottle of water out to Mr. Huáng.
10. I don't know by whom his old books were sold.

B. Render the following into English:
1. Shùyehtzu shih sheńma yeńse te t'ā yeḣ shuōpuch'ulai.
2. Wŏmen hsieǹtsaì yunġ ch'ieñpí hsieḣ-tzù, sói pū yaò ch'iḣmò-chiḣ.
3. Chèp'inǵ mòshuǐ shiḣ t'āmen-tzùchǐ ch'ieńt'ien maǐ te, pū shiḣ nǐ nálai te.
4. Mǎ t'aìt'ai kanġ tāle tieǹhuà lai chiaò nimen mǎshanġ huích'ü.
5. Wŏmente fanġtzu ch'ieńt'ou yú lianġk'ō laŏ shù.
6. T'ā yú heń tà te hsīwanġ. T'ā kaòsule ni meiyu?
7. Nàchiḣ tzùlaíshuí-pī shiḣ wŏte t'unǵshihte, pū shiḣ nǐ t'aìt'ai sunġ keí wo te.
8. Nǐmen tsaì hsüeḣhsiaò yunġ te mòshuǐ shiḣ sheńma yeńse te?
9. Wŏ tsót'ien maǐ te maòtzu keí t'a taìhui chiāli ch'ü le.
10. T'āte shoúli yǔ sañtŏ huārh, lianġtŏ hunġ-te, ītŏ paí-te.

WRITTEN EXERCISES

A. Transcribe Section B, above, in Chinese.

B. Render the following into English:

1. 桌子上頭的花瓶,你説是甚麼顏色的呢?

2. 那真難説.看起來有一點兒像深紅的,也有一點兒像淺藍的,你説對不對?

3. 對了.花瓶裏頭一共有幾朵花兒?

4. 有八朵,是我姐姐今天早上買回來的.你喜歡花兒不喜歡?

5. 很喜歡,可是現在花兒的價錢很貴.像你姐姐買回來的,一朵錢最少賣兩毛錢.我的錢快要用完了,不能買花兒了.

6. 坐在外頭草地上頭看中國報的人是誰?是你的同事麼?

7. 沒戴帽子的都是我的同事;戴黑帽子的都是在百貨公司做事的.

8. 那兩瓶墨水是甚麼顏色的?是誰買給你的?

9. 一瓶是淺綠的,一瓶是深紅的.淺綠的是我自己買的,深紅的是左先生買給我的.

10. 現在時候不早了,我要馬上開汽車回家去.我們明天再見.

C. Render the following into Chinese:

1. Please tell him that I hope very much he will buy a bottle of blue ink for my schoolmate.

2. This blotting paper was sold to him two days ago by Mr. Chang of the department store.

3. When I came to see you this morning I saw a lot of [tree] leaves on your lawn.

4. He told me what tree this was, but now I have forgotten about it.

5. I don't know by whom my fountain pen was taken away.

6. Have the old trees at the back of your house bloomed?

7. This package of tea [leaves] was bought by him in Shanghai last spring.

8. The color of the hat bought by Mrs. Paí last week is quite elegant. Do you like it?

9. He is leaving quite soon. I have to go back at once to tell him not to write the letter of introduction for me.

10. The water here is very shallow. Is the water there deep?

CHARACTERS

Number of Strokes	Characters	Pronunciation and Tone	Meaning	Lesson Reference
Two	又	Yù	Again	33
Four	介	Chieh̀	To introduce	31
	公	Kunḡ	Public; just, fair	32
	父	Fù	Father; male relative of one's parents' generation	33
Five	司	Szū	To control, to be in charge of; department	32
	打	Tă	To strike, to beat, etc.	33
	母	Mŭ	Mother; female relatives of one's parents' generation	33
	兄	Hsiunḡ	Elder brother	33
Six	名	Miń	Name	31
	同	T'uń	Same; together, with	31
	衣	Ī	Clothes	32
	色	Sè Shaì }	Color	34
	朵	Tŏ	(Classifier for flowers)	34
Seven	弟	Tì	Younger brother	33
	希	Hsī	To hope	34
Eight	姓	Hsiǹ	Surname; to have the surname of	31
	府	Fŭ	Mansion	31
	舍	Shè	Residence	31
	服	Fú	Garment; to submit; to take (as medicine)	33

Number of Strokes	Characters	Pronunciation and Tone	Meaning	Lesson Reference
Eight	姐	Chieh	Elder sister; unmarried young lady	33
	妹	Mei	Younger sister	33
	非	Feī	Not to be	33
	花	Huā	Flower; to spend (as money, time)	34
Nine	品	P'iň	Manufactured articles; grade; character	32
	亮	Liang	Bright, clear	32
	穿	Ch'uañ	To pierce, to go through; to wear, to put on	32
Ten	修	Hsiū	To repair	31
	套	T'aò	Covering, sheath; set (as of books, implements); suit (as of clothes)	32
	除	Ch'ú	To deduct; to divide; except, besides	33
	哥	Kō	Elder brother	33
	草	Ts'aŏ	Grass	34
Eleven	理	Lǐ	Reason, principle; to regulate, etc.	31
	紹	Shaò	To connect	31
	貨	Huò	Goods, wares	32
	脫	T'ō	To get away from; to take off (as clothes, socks)	32
	頂	Tiň	Top; (superlative sign); to withstand; (unit of measure for hats)	32
	常	Ch'ang	Often, frequently; constant, regular	33
	深	Sheň	Deep, profound	34
	淺	Ch'ieň	Shallow, light (as of color)	34
	望	Wang	To hope; to look toward	34
Twelve	敝	Pì	My, our	31

Number of Strokes	Characters	Pronunciation and Tone	Meaning	Lesson Reference
Twelve	街	Chieh̄	Street	31
	絲	Szū	Silk	32
	帽	Maò	Hat	32
	舒	Shū	To relax; comfortable; (a surname)	33
	黑	Heī	Black; dark	34
	棵	K'ō	(Classifier for trees)	34
Thirteen	牌	P'aí	Signboard; cards, mah-jongg piece, a game of cards	31
	葉	Yeh̀	Leaf; (a surname)	34
	瓶	P'ínǵ	Vase; bottle, jar	34
Fourteen	緊	Chiň	Tight; urgent	31
	漂	P'iaò	Smart, elegant, handsome	32
	裳	Shan̄g	Clothes	32
	摘	Chaī	To pick (as flowers, fruits); to take off (as hats, etc.)	32
	綠	Lǜ	Green	34
Fifteen	數	Shù / Shū	Number / To count	31 / 31
	鞋	Hsieh́	Shoe	32
	趣	Ch'ǜ	Interest	33
	墨	Mò	Ink stick; (a surname)	34
Sixteen	辦	Paǹ	To manage, to transact, to carry out	31
	錶	Piaǒ	Watch	31
	親	Ch'in̄	Close relatives; intimate; to caress, to kiss	33
	興	Hsiǹg	Interest	33

Number of Strokes	Characters	Pronunciation and Tone	Meaning	Lesson Reference
Sixteen	樹	Shù	Tree	34
Seventeen	戴	Tài	To put on, to wear (as hats, eyeglasses, etc.); (a surname)	32
Eighteen	顏	Yén	Countenance; color; (a surname)	34
	藍	Lán	Blue	34
Nineteen	壞	Huài	Bad; to be out of order	31
Twenty	襪	Wà	Sock, stocking	32
	覺	Chüeh	To feel, to perceive, to be aware of	33

ORAL DRILL

A. Say the following in Chinese:

1. department store
    vase
    to typewrite
    to telephone
    wrist watch
    gloves
    overcoat
    simultaneously
    mathematics
    letter of introduction

    colleagues
    schoolmates
    smart
    foreign goods
    father
    mother
    elder sister
    elder brother
    younger sister
    younger brother

    comfortable
    frequently
    almost
    usually
    interest
    hat
    important
    streets
    clothes
    immediately

2. a hat
    two sets of books
    five suits of clothes
    nine pairs of socks
    an overcoat
    four leaves
    seven trees
    twenty bottles
    two typewriters

    a pair of shoes
    three letters of introduction
    two woolen jackets
    three wrist watches
    a department store
    eight vases
    six flowers
    fifteen bottles of ink
    two telegrams

3. to play cards
    just now
    to put on a hat
    to take off a hat
    to send a telegram

    to make inquiries
    to fetch water
    to put on shoes
    to take off shoes
    exceptionally large

4. almost two years

    to feel comfortable

both tall and big   with the exception of houses
to have the surname of Yeh   unable to have purchased
to return at once   to go simultaneously
to work [transact business] here   to have lost his gloves

5. Those are all low-grade foreign goods.
    What is the [shop] name of that bookstore [called]?
    Of what country, Sir, are you a citizen?
    What is he surnamed?
    Where is your home [polite]?
    Mr. Yeh, this is my father, this is my mother.
    How many sisters does Mr. Tsŏ have?
    Do you feel cold here?
    My elder sister has quite an interest in learning English.
    He has already bought a hat.
    Can you wear my clothes?
    His shoes are too small; I can't wear them.
    My wrist watch was lost yesterday.
    By whom were you hit last night?
    By whom were these big characters written?
    Do you know where he lives?
    Does your younger sister know Mr. Ch'ien?
    This is a very important letter.
    After you have finished reading this book, you may go home.
    He is illiterate; he can't write that letter for them.
    The water here is very deep; the water there is very shallow.
    There isn't even a single tree in front of our house.
    The dark blue automobile is very smart.
    I hope we can come again next spring.
    He hasn't finished speaking French yet.

B. Render the following into English:

1. Ichang ch'ihmò-chih
    Sañtŏ huang-te huãrh
    Szùp'ing lan-mòshui
    Ishuang szū-wàtzu
    Liangt'aò Chungkuo-shū
    Sañko chiehmei
    Iko hsiaóchieh
    Ik'uai ts'aŏtì
    Liangt'iaó tàchieh
    Iko hsīwang

2. Chiehshaò-hsin ní hsiehhaŏle meiyu?
    Kaō hsiensheng shih pushih nite t'ungshih?
    T'ā chiāte menp'ai haòshu ni chitech'i chipuch'i?
    Shèhsià lí huŏch'ē-chan hen yüan.
    Chang hsiaóchiehte míngtzu chiaò sheńma?
    Shih-tzù te jen hui k'an-shū, pū shih-tzù te jen pū hui k'an-shū.

Nàhsieh Meĭkuo-jeń nĭmen toū jeǹshih ma?

Chèyang̊ te shoŭt'aò nĭmen tsaì chèrh maĭtetaò maiputao?

T'āmen chiāli yú tătzù-chī meiyu?

Huang̊ t'aìt'ai chiñt'ien chüeńte pū heň shūfu.

Shang̊haĭ-huà t'ā shuōte heň p'iaòliang.

Ch'úle ch'áyeh̊ īwaì, nĭmen haí yaò maĭ hsieh̊ sheńma?

Wŏ chiaòle ni pūyaò tsaì laí, hsieǹtsaì nĭ yù laí le.

Chung̊kuo-tzù t'ā hsieh̊te yù k'uaì yù haŏ.

K'aǹ Meĭkuo-paò t'āmen yŭ hsing̊ch'ü meiyu?

Chèrh shang̊teng̊ te yang̊huò chiàch'ien kueì pukuei?

T'āmen p'ing̊shih toū heň pū hsīhuan tă-p'aí te.

Tzùlaíshuí-pĭ t'ā kang̊ yŭ sañchih̊.

Kaō hsiaóchieh kang̊ ch'ūch'ü le, heň k'uaì chiù yaò huílai.

Nĭmente īshang ch'àputō meí yŭ īchieǹ shih haŏ te.

Nàhsieh hsüeh̊sheng tă-tzù tăte feĭch'ang̊ haŏ.

Wŏte piaò huaì le, ní yú piaŏ meiyu?

T'ā meìmeite t'ung̊hsüeh̊ hsing̊-Huang̊, ming̊tzu chiaò "Ting̊kuó."

Wŏ t'ung̊shih̊te chùchih̊ shih Shang̊haĭ Nańching̊-lù wúpaì liùshih-pāhaò meńp'aí.

T'āmen heň hsīwang̊ ni neng̊ măshang̊ k'aī ch'ìch'ē huich'ü.

WRITING DRILL

A. Write out the items in Section A of Oral Drill, above, in Chinese.

B. Transcribe Section B of Oral Drill in Chinese.

C. Render the following into Chinese:

1. I can't recall on what street in Shanghai he lives and what the number of the doorplate is.

2. That thing is exceptionally difficult to do; if you don't know how to do it, you may ask him to do it for you.

3. I haven't seen Miss Mă for almost a month. When I write her tomorrow, I can tell her your friend's name.

4. I feel that what he said last night was quite wrong. How do you feel about it?

5. I truly wouldn't have thought that he would have bought a typewriter so soon!

6. The goods sold in the department stores here are all low-grade foreign goods.

7. His hope is to go to China next spring, but he doesn't know whether his parents will go with him.

8. They like very much to play cards at night. Do you like to play cards, too?

9. The Chinese he speaks is very ordinary; however, he speaks it exceptionally fast.

10. I know that there are very many old books here, but I have never counted them, and so I can't tell you how many there are altogether.

READING DRILL

After reading the following, render it into English:

1. "到甚麼地方說甚麼話."

2. 有希望的人才能做大事;沒有希望的人小事也不能做.

3. 那些外國人都是我的好朋友,我很喜歡把他們介紹給你.

4. 昨天晚上除了看書以外,我還給我的姐姐打了一個電報到北平去給張太太.

5. 謝文英小姐坐的火車下午幾點鐘到,你能給我到火車站去打聽打聽麼?

6. 他們的同學昨天買的新汽車,顏色太深,我不很喜歡.

7. 黃先生告訴我們說,我們應該先摘帽子,再脫大衣.

8. 你前天買的毛襪子都是九號半的,太小了,我真的穿不上呢!

9. 這幾套中國書都是他去年在上海買的.

10. 你上禮拜叫我給你買的毛衣,我買來買去也買不到三十八號的.

VOCABULARY CHARACTERS

(Chiǎ)
False
(Chià)
Holiday, vacation [*]

(Fanġ)
To let go, to let out; to put, to place

(Shǔ) Its printed form is 暑·
Summer heat [*]

(Hań)
Cold [*]; in poor circumstances [*]

(Ch'í)
Period of time [*]; to hope [*]

(Jań)
So, thus [*]

(Chiȟ)
Only, merely [*]

(Pei)
Times, -fold

(Yǘ)
At, in; in regard to [*]

(K'unǧ)
To fear, to be afraid [*]

(P'à)
To fear, to be afraid

(Fǎ)
Method [*]; law [*]

(Ch'inǵ)
Emotion, feeling [*]; facts of a case [*]

(Chieȟ)
To borrow; to lend [*]

(T'í)
Subject, theme, title [*]

(Chunǵ)
Heavy; weighty, serious [*]

(Kuañ)
To shut, to close; a mountain pass [*]; a guardhouse [*]; to concern [*]; (a surname)

COMPOUNDS

然後 (Jańhoù) Then, afterward

當然 (Tanḡjań) Of course; ex officio

長短 (Ch'anǵtuań) Long and short, length; merits and shortcomings

自然 (Tzùjań) Naturally, of course; Nature

對於 (Tuìyű) As to ..., relative to ..., in relation to ...

壞處 (Huaìch'u) Bad points, bad features

地理 (Tìlĭ) Geography

同意 (T'unǵì) To agree, to consent; consent

打算 (Tǎsuan) To plan, to figure

車費 (Ch'ēfeì) Train fare

船費 (Ch'uańfeì) Boat fare, passage money

費用 (Feìyung) Expenses

機關 (Chīkuań) Organ, organization

關於 (Kuańyű) Concerning, respecting, in connection with

小説 (Hsiaŏshuō) Small talk; fiction

放假 (Fanǵ-chià) To have a holiday or vacation

假期 (Chiàch'í) Vacation period

春假 (Ch'uńchià) Spring vacation

暑假 (Shǔchià) Summer vacation

意見 (Ìchien) Idea, opinion

得到 (Tétaò) To get, to obtain

冬假 (Tunḡchià) | Winter vacation
寒假 (Hańchià) |

請假 (Ch'inǵ-chià) | To ask for a leave of absence
告假 (Kaò-chià) |

學年 (Hsüeńnień) School year

學期 (Hsüeńch'í) Semester, quarter

重要 (Chunḡyaò) | Weighty, serious,
重大 (Chunḡtà) | important

事情 (Shihch'ing) Thing, affair, event

問題 (Weǹt'í) Question, problem

願望 (Yüaǹwanǵ) To hope, to desire; hope, desire

期間 (Ch'íchieñ) Specified period of time

方法 (Fanḡfǎ) | Method, device, way
法子 (Fátzu) |

辦法 (Paǹfǎ) Method of transaction, way of management

政府 (Chenǵfǔ) Government

中國政府 (Chunḡkuo-chenǵfǔ) The Chinese government

美國政府 (Meǐkuo-chenǵfǔ) The American government

送還 (Sunǵhuań) To send back (to original owner)

分做 (Feñtso) To divide into

想得出 (Hsianḡtech'ū) Capable of thinking out

想不出　(Hsiăngpuch'ū) Incapable of thinking out　　恐怕　(K'ŭngp'à) To be afraid, to fear

READING MATERIAL

1. 國亮啊，我聽説你們學校還有三個禮拜就要放暑假了。那是真的還是假的？

2. 文英，那是真的，可是你在那兒聽見的？是誰告訴你的？

3. 是你的英文教員黃先生告訴我的。怎麼你們學校今年春季學期這麼不早就要放暑假呢？是太短了麼？

4. 也許是我們春季學期開學就開得早一點兒罷。我們學校一個學年分做兩個學期，一個是春季學期，一個是秋季學期。每個學期都有二十一個禮拜。今年的春季學期跟秋季學期，所以暑假也把兩個學期的長短一樣。

5. 你們學校的假期是怎麼樣的，你能告訴我不能？

6. 我當然能告訴你。我們一年

有兩個假期,一個叫寒假,也叫冬假,一個叫暑假。秋季學期完了就放寒假,春季學期完了就放暑假。

7. 寒假的假期長呢,還是暑假的假期長呢?

8. 暑假的長得多。寒假只有兩個禮拜,暑假有十個禮拜,比寒假長五倍。你們學校的假期,是不是跟我們的一樣?

9. 差不多一樣。不同的地方,就是我們的寒假比你們的長兩個禮拜,暑假比你們的短兩個禮拜。

10. 文英,關於假期長短的問題,你們有甚麼意見?

11. 沒有甚麼意見。我覺得假期長,也有好處,也有壞處,因為放假放得太久,我們念書的時間就太短了。

11. …關於文學的書，我家裏想必有一點兒。是不費事的，在我這兒，可以給你找一本的看。你看過、看完了，你能借給我，馬上就送給你。沒看過的，你能借給我就馬上送去罷。

12. 你說的話很有道理，我也跟你同意。今年暑假你打算做些甚麼地方？你同麼？

13. 我打算回家的暑假，你也學恐怕看府你得好。我打算先自己把算去的辦書機喜很，然後地在看，我們我書在做。我大看子情，方，跟能書。

14. 我為太裏法事。

15. 喜歡有本我麼？

16. 我這本書甚麼的。

17. 這五天給你的，我這四還給你。

18. 能，你喜歡看就請你拿去罷。

ROMANIZED TEXT OF READING MATERIAL

1. Kuóliang a, wǒ t'ingshuō nimen hsüehhsiaò haí yū sanko lǐpaì chiù yaò fang shūchià le. Nà shih chen te haíshih chiă te?

2. Weńying, nà shih cheñ te, k'ŏshih nǐ tsaì nǎrh t'ingchien te? Shih shuí kaòsu ni te?

3. Shih nǐte Yingweń chiaòyüań Huang .hsiensheng kaòsu wo te. Tsemma nǐmen hsüehhsiaò chiññien chèma tsaŏ chiù yaŏ fang shūchià ne? Ch'uñchì hsüehch'í pū shih t'aì tuañ le ma?

4. Yehhsŭ shih wŏmen ch'uñchì hsüehch'í k'aī-hsüeh k'aīte tsaŏ ītiǎrh, sóí shūchià yeh chiù fangte tsaŏ ītiǎrh pa. Wŏmen hsüehhsiaò pǎ īko hsüehnień feñtso liangko hsüehch'í, īko shih ch'iūchì hsüehch'í, īko shih ch'uñchì hsüehch'í. Meǐiko hsüehch'í toū yǔ erhshihko lǐpaì. Chiññiente ch'uñchì hsüehch'í yeh yǔ erhshihko lǐpaì, keñ ch'iūchì hsüehch'íte ch'angtuañ iyang.

5. Nǐmen hsüehhsiaòte chiàch'í shih tsemma yang te, nǐ neng kaòsu wo puneng?

6. Wŏ tangjań neng kaòsu ni. Wŏmen ī nień yú liangko chiàch'í, īko chiaò hańchià, yeh chiaò tungchià, īko chiaò shūchià. Ch'iūchì hsüehch'í wańle chiù fang hańchià, ch'uñchì hsüehch'í wańle chiù fang shūchià.

7. Hańchiàte chiàch'í ch'ang ne, haíshih shūchiàte chiàch'í ch'ang ne?

8. Shūchiàte ch'angtetō. Hańchià chih yú liangko lǐpaì, shūchià yǔ shihko lǐpaì, pī hańchià ch'ang wǔ peì. Nǐmen hsüehhsiaòte chiàch'í, shih pushih keñ womente iyang?

9. Ch'àputō iyang. Pū t'ung te tìfang, chiù shih wŏmente hańchià pí nimente ch'ang liangko lǐpaì, shūchià pí nimente tuañ liangko lǐpaì.

10. Weńying, kuañyú shūchià hańchià chiàch'í ch'angtuañ te weńt'í, nǐ yǔ shemma ìchien meiyu?

11. Meí yǔ shemma chungyaò te ìchien, pūkuò wŏ chüehte women ī nień nień-shū, t'ieñt'ień mangchí le, yú heñ tō hsiang tsò te shihch'ing, toū meí yǔ kungfu ch'ü tsò. Taòle hańchià shūchià te shihhou, wŏmen hsiang tsò shemma, chiù k'ói tsò shemma le. Chè chiù shih fang-chià tuìyú women te haŏch'u. K'ŏshih chiàch'í t'aì ch'ang, yeh yǔ huaìch'u, yiñwei fang-chià fangte t'aì chiū, wŏmen nień-shū te shihchieñ chiù t'aì tuañ le.

12. Nǐ shuō te huà heń yǔ taòli, wó yeh keñ ni t'ungì. Chiññien shū- chià ní tăsuan tsò hsieh shemma?

13. Wó tăsuan hsieñ taò Peīp'ing ch'ü k'ank'an tìfang, jańhoù huí-chià tzùchī k'an hsieñ kuañyú weńhsüeh keñ tìli te shū. Wŏ tsuì tà te yüanwang, chiù shih neng tsaì shūchià lit'ou, pǎ shihpeñ-pāpeń haŏ te shū k'anwań. Ní tăsuan tsò hsieñ shemma?

14. Wó yeh hsiang ch'ü k'ank'an tìfang, k'ŏshih yiñwei wŏmen hsüeh- hsiaòte hsüehfeì keñ piehte feìyung t'aì tà, wó k'ungp'à panputaò le. Wŏ yaò tsaì chiāli k'an-shū, pū k'an-shū chiù ch'ing p'engyu keí wo hsiang fátzu tsaì chengfū chīkuañ lit'ou, chaŏ ītiǎrh shihch'ing tsò pa. Ní hsīhuan k'an hsiaŏshuō ma?

15. Hsīhuantehen, ní yú haŏ te meiyu?

16. Wó yú haó chípeń. Ch'ing ni k'ank'an.

17. Chèpeń wŏ meí k'ankuo, nǐ neng chieh keí wo szù-wǔ t'ieñ ma? Wŏ k'anwańle chiù măshang sunghuań keí ni te.

18. Neng, ní hsīhuan k'an chiù ch'ing ni nách'ü pa.

NOTES

1. Note that 法 of 法子 is to be pronounced as "fá". 沒有法子, literally "there is no way," means "there is no way out" or "it cannot be helped." It is quite a common expression.

2. While 怕 and 恐怕 may be loosely rendered into English as "to fear, to be afraid," they should not be used interchangeably. 怕 implies the display of fright or terror, mental or actual, whereas 恐怕 reveals anticipation of something unfavorable or contrary to one's wishes or expectations.

3. Although 借 is used to mean both "to borrow" and "to lend," the way in which it is used will ordinarily reveal which meaning of the two it is intended to have. When it is used to mean "to borrow," usually 向 or 跟 or 問 is used along with it but placed before the dative, while 借 itself precedes the accusative: 我向 (跟, 問) 他借了一件大衣, "I borrowed an overcoat from him." It is true that one can also say 我借了他一件大衣, but this latter way is more susceptible to misinterpretation. When 借 is used to mean "to lend," 給 is usually used before the dative, while 借 itself may come before or after the dative though before the accusative in either case. Thus, 我借給你中國錢 or 我借中國錢給你 means "I lend Chinese money to you."

ORAL EXERCISES

A. Say the following in Chinese:

1. Fifteen times [-fold]; fifteen times better; seven times shorter; twice as long; three times as many.

2. Concerning his school; in relation to your expenses; his opinion in relation to that question; to borrow money; to borrow books.

3. The Chinese government; the American government; government organs; Chinese government organs; American government organs.

4. Good and bad points; merits and shortcomings; the good and bad points of this book; his merits and shortcomings; other people's good and bad points.

5. To be afraid of difficulties; don't be afraid of him; there is no way out; I am afraid there is no way out.

6. The school declares a holiday. The school declares the summer vacation. I want to ask for a leave of absence.

7. That is not true, of course. Of course, what he says is right.

8. An important problem; a good method of transaction; an important affair.

9. The spring semester; the fall semester; geography books; literature books; a geographical question; a literary problem; a question relative to geography; a question concerning literature.

10. My consent; his consent. Do you agree? Do you agree with him?

11. Have you any device? What device do you have? Is this device good?

12. I have no method of transaction. Have you?

13. This book is too heavy. Don't ask her to bring it to me.

B. Render the following into English:

1. Wŏ ī nień te hsüeḣfeì; t'ā taò Meĭkuo ch'ü te ch'uańfeì; nǐmen taò Peǐp'ing ch'ü te ch'ēfeì.

2. Paǹ pupan? Tseṁma paǹ? Nàchieǹ shiḣch'ing t'ā tăsuan tseṁma paǹ?

3. Ní ch'inğle chià meiyu? Ní ch'inğle chī t'ień chià?

4. Wŏmen shanğ-hsüeḣch'í nieǹle Yinğkuo weńhsüeh, sóĭ chèko hsüeḣ-ch'í tăsuan pū tsaì nieǹ le.

5. T'āmen hsià-hsüeḣch'í yaò nień te tĭlĭ chiaòk'ō-shū yú heň tō ch'anğ-ch'u, k'ŏshih yeḣ yú heň tō tuaňch'u.

6. Huanǵ hsiensheng ch'ǜ, wŏ chiù tanḡjań yeň ch'ǜ; t'ā pū ch'ǜ, wŏ chiù yeḣhsŭ ch'ǜ, yeḣhsŭ pū ch'ǜ.

7. Wŏte piaŏ huaìle, wŏ k'óĭ chieḣ nite yunğyung ma?

8. T'ā ch'ùnien chieḣle wote ch'ień, taò hsieǹtsaì haí meí huań keí wo.

9. Wŏ minǵnien yaò taò chenğfŭ chīkuaň lit'ou ch'ü tsò-shiḣ, nĭ shuō haŏ puhao?

10. Nàko weǹt'í shiḣ feīch'anǵ chunğtà te, wŏ cheń pū kaň shuō wo yŭ shemma haŏ te paňfă.

WRITTEN EXERCISES

A. Transcribe Section B, above, into Chinese.

B. Render the following into English:

1. 我們不要說別人的長短, 也不要說我們自己的長短.

2. 謝先生家裏只有他父親, 母親跟他自己三個人, 可是他們一年的費用很大.

3. 從上海坐船到美國去要用多麼? 十六天, 坐飛機只用三四天, 那麼飛機比船不是快四倍有多麼?

4. 張太太昨天說過他今天下午要來看你的, 可是他弟弟明天就要到南京去, 我恐怕他今天不能來了.

5. 你前天借給我的小說太長，我恐怕四五天裏頭我看不完，到下禮拜五才還給你行不行？

6. 我聽說左先生還沒得到他父親的同意，就自己一個人去辦那件很重要的事情了。

7. 我們學校上學年的春假假期，比寒假假期短三倍，可是寒假假期比暑假假期短四倍。

8. 這個學期我念地理，下學期也許不念了，因為我一定要念中國文學呢！

9. 你昨天告訴我那件事情，我自己真的想不出辦法來。

10. 你叫我來，我當然很喜歡來，可是我對於那個重大的問題，一點兒意見也沒有。

C. Render the following into Chinese:

1. How is it that you don't even know that your tuition is three times as much as mine?

2. I am planning to go to America to study geography as soon as I get my father's consent.

3. May I ask what organ of the Chinese government this is?

4. Relative to the question of what you should study in college, you, of course, have your own opinion.

5. The question which he asked me last night was what difference there was between Chinese and English fiction.

6. Mr. Chang, my colleague, didn't feel very well this morning. He has asked for a leave of absence and gone home.

7. The train fare to Peiping is quite high. Probably I won't be able to go there to see you during the summer vacation of this year.

8. With regard to Chinese literature, my younger brother has studied it for three years in college and is exceptionally interested in it.

9. I am afraid that the method of learning how to speak Chinese which he told us [about] last night is not very good.

10. This overcoat is too heavy. I am not going to wear it today. I can lend it to you to wear.

VOCABULARY CHARACTERS

(Erh)
Ear [*]

(Pí)
Nose [*]

(Tsuǐ)
Mouth

(Meí)
Eyebrows [*]

(Fǎ)
Hair (on the head)

(Shé)
Tongue [*]

(Ch'uń)
Lip [*]

(Yá)
Tooth

(Fù)
A set; secondary, vice-
[*]

(Mieǹ)
Surface, face [*]; (classifier for mirrors, flags,
etc.)

(Hsiñ)
Heart, mind

(Yüeh)
To pass over, to exceed
[*]

(Yeň)
Eye [*]

(Chiñg)
Pupil of the eye [*]

(K'unǧ)
Hole; (a surname)

(Lieň)
Face

(Chinǧ)
Mirror [*]

(Kuñg)
Accomplishment, merit
[*]

(Pù)
Step, pace; a land
measure of five Chi-
nese feet

(P'ań)
Side [*]

COMPOUNDS

耳朶子 (Eřhto) The ear

鼻子 (Pítzu) The nose

鼻孔 (Pík'unǧ) The nostril

嘴唇 (Tsuǐch'uń) The lips

眉毛 (Meímao) The eyebrows

頭髮 (T'oúfǎ) Hair on the head

舌頭 (Shét'ou) The tongue

眼睛 (Yeňching) The eyes

眼鏡兒 (Yeňchinǧerh) Eyeglasses

鏡子 (Chinǧtzu) Mirror; speculum

心地 (Hsiñtì) Moral nature

關心 (Kuañ-hsiñ) To be concerned with, to give attention to

進步 (Chiǹ-pù) Progress; to progress

用功 (Yunǧkunḡ) Diligent; diligently

功用 (Kunḡyunǵ) Function

旁邊兒 (P'anǵpierh) By the side of; side

以上 (Ǐshanǧ) Above

以下 (Ǐhsià) Below, beneath

小心 (Hsiaǒhsin) }
當心 (Tanḡhsiñ) } Careful, cautious; carefully, cautiously

一步一步 (Īpùipu) Step by step, gradually

READING MATERIAL

1. 教員: 我們今天再學説中國話好不好啊?

2. 學生: 很好, 我好幾天沒説過中國話了.

3. 教員: 這個中國話叫甚麼?

4. 學生: 這個叫"臉"罷? 對不對?

5. 教員: 對了, 那就是你的臉, 這就是我的臉. 我們臉上有甚麼?

6. 學生: 有一雙眉毛, 眉毛底下有一雙眼睛. 臉的中間兒有一個

鼻子,鼻子的下部有兩個鼻孔.鼻
孔底下有一張嘴.嘴有兩個嘴唇.
在上頭的叫上唇,在底下的叫下唇.

7. 教員:你説中國話,近來很有
進步,我想一定是因為這兩個月
裏頭很用功學,所以進步得這麼
快.我要問問你,我們的嘴裏頭有
甚麼,你知道麼?

8. 學生:知道,嘴裏頭有牙,還有
一個舌頭.

9. 教員:我們的耳朵在那兒?

10. 學生:在臉的兩旁.

11. 教員:你的頭髮是甚麼顏色的?

12. 學生:是黑的.

13. 教員:你剛才看的報,是你的
麼? 裏頭的字非常小,我的眼睛
不很好,戴了眼鏡兒也看不見.

14. 學生:報不是我的,是同學借
給我的.裏頭的字,真是太小,可是
我的眼睛還好,所以用不着戴眼
鏡兒也看得見.

15. 教員:你的眼睛比我的好,我
早已經知道了,不過你也要當心.

字太小的，書也好，報也好，都不要多看。多看了眼睛很快就壞了。眼睛壞了就要戴眼鏡兒，像我一樣，你說多麼不方便呢！

16. 學生：我明白了，以後字太小的書報，我就少看一點兒罷。

17. 教員：越少看越好，這一點你最要記在心裏頭。

18. 學生：是的，那我一定不敢忘的。謝謝你對我這麼關心。

ROMANIZED TEXT OF READING MATERIAL

1. Chiaòyüań: Wǒmen chiñt'ien tsaì hsüeñ shuō Chunḡkuo-huà haǒ puhao a?

2. Hsüeñsheng: Heń haǒ, wó haó chǐ t'ieñ meí shuōkuo Chunḡkuo-huà le.

3. Chiaòyüań: Chèko Chunḡkuo-huà chiaò sheḿma?

4. Hsüeñsheng: Chèko chiaò "lieñ" pa? Tuì putui?

5. Chiaòyüań: Tuì le, nà chiù shiñ nīte lieñ, chè chiù shiñ wǒte lieñ. Wǒmen lieñshang yǔ sheḿma?

6. Hsüeñsheng: Yǔ īshuanḡ meímao, meímao tīhsia yǔ īshuanḡ yeñching. Lieñte chunḡchièrh yǔ iko pítzu, pítzute hsiàpù yú lianǧko pík'unḡ. Pík'unḡ tīhsia yǔ ichanḡ tsuǐ. Tsuí yú lianǧko tsuǐch'uń, tsaì shanḡt'ou te chiaò shanḡch'uń, tsaì tīhsia te chiaò hsiàch'uń.

7. Chiaòyüań: Nǐ shuō Chunḡkuo-huà, chiǹlai heń yǔ chiǹ-pù, wó hsianǧ ītinḡ shiñ yiñweì chè lianǧko yüeñ lit'ou heñ yunǧkunḡ hsüeñ, sóí chiǹ-pùte chèma k'uaì. Wǒ yaò wenwen ni, wǒmente tsuí lit'ou yǔ sheḿma, nǐ chiñtao ma?

8. Hsüeñsheng: Chiñtao, tsuí lit'ou yǔ yá, haí yǔ iko shét'ou.

9. Chiaòyüań: Wǒmente erḥto tsaì nǎrh?

10. Hsüeñsheng: Tsaì lieñte lianǧ-p'anḡ.

11. Chiaòyüań: Nīte t'oúfǎ shiñ sheḿma yeńse te?

12. Hsüeñsheng: Shiñ heī-te.

13. Chiaòyüań: Nǐ kanḡts'aí k'aǹ te paò, shiñ nīte ma? Lǐt'ou te tzù feích'ang hsiaǒ, wǒte yeñching pū heń haǒ, taìle yeñchinḡerh yeñ k'aǹpuchieǹ.

14. Hsüehsheng: Paò pū shih wote, shih t'unghsüeh chieh kei wo te. Lit'ou te tzù chen shih t'ai hsiaŏ, k'oshih wŏte yenching haí haŏ, sói yungpuchaó taì yenchingerh yeh k'antechien.

15. Chiaòyüan: Nite yenching pí wote haŏ, wó tsaó iching chihtao le, pūkuò ní yeh yaò tanghsiñ. Tzù t'aì hsiaŏ te shū yeh haŏ, paò yeh haŏ, toū pūyaò tō k'an, tō k'anle yenching heñ k'uaì chiù huaì le. Yenching huaìle chiù yaò taì yenchingerh, hsiang wo iyang le. Ni shuō tóma pū fangpien ne!

16. Hsüehsheng: Wŏ mingpai le, ihoù tzù t'aì hsiaŏ te shū-paò, wŏ chiù shaŏ k'añ itiărh pa.

17. Chiaòyüan: Yüeh shaŏ k'añ yüeh haŏ, chèi tień nĭ tsuì yaò chì tsaì hsiñ lit'ou.

18. Hsüehsheng: Shih te, nà wŏ itíng pū kañ wang te. Hsiehhsieh ni tuì wo chèma kuañ-hsiñ.

NOTES

1. 越 has an adverbial use in certain statements of comparison and performs a function similar to "the" in English, as "the more the better," 越多越好; "the newer the more expensive," 越新越貴; etc. Note that the adverbs or adjectives qualified by 越 are all positive in form though comparative in implication.

2. 有進步 literally means "to have progress," hence, "to make progress" or "to make headway." Thus, 你説中國話，近來很有進步 may be rendered into English as "Recently you have shown quite a good deal of progress in speaking Chinese." Note that 很 actually qualifies 有 (cf. 很有錢, "quite wealthy," 很想, "to want very much," etc.).

3. The classifier for 鏡子, "mirrors," is 面. 副 is used for "pair" with 眼鏡兒.

4. The classifier for 臉 is 張.

5. The vowel "o" in a neutral tone position after dentals becomes "ou," as in the case of 耳朵 (ěrhto).

ORAL EXERCISES

A. Say the following in Chinese:

1. A pair of eyeglasses; a pair of ears; a lip; the upper lip; the lower lip; the tongue; the eyebrows.

2. To study hard; to work hard; to learn assiduously; beside me; above the eyes; below the eyes.

3. The earlier the better; the slower the better; the fewer the more expensive.

4. Are your eyes good? Can you see the words I have just written?

5. I stand beside you; you stand beside him.

6. His hair is white, but his eyebrows are black.

7. My ears cannot compare with yours; yours are better by far.

8. He progresses very swiftly; you progress quite slowly.

9. Everyone has a face, a nose, and a mouth.

10. He walks a step toward the front; I walk a step toward the rear.

B. Render the following into English:

1. Īk'uaì ch'ień īshang̀; shiḣk'uaì ch'ień īhsià; sañ t'ień īshang̀; ch'ī t'ień ihsià; īmień ching̀tzu.

2. T'ā heń yŭ chiṅ-pù; nĭ meí yŭ chiṅ-pù; t'ā yŭ sañfù yeńching̀erh.

3. T'ā nieṅ-shū pí ni yung̀kunḡ, sóī chiṅ-pù yeḣ pí ni k'uaì.

4. Wŏmen tsoŭ-lù īting̀ yaò īpùipu tsoŭ.

5. Huŏch'ē-chaṅ p'anǵpierh te p'ùtzu toū shiḣ heń chiù te.

6. Chunḡkuo-jeńte t'oúfā toū shiḣ heī-te.

7. Wŏmen ch'iḣ tunḡhsi īting̀ yaò yung̀ yá, sóī meí yŭ yá, wŏmen chiù pū neng ch'iḣ tunḡhsi le.

8. Wŏ tuì t'a heń kuañ-hsiñ.

9. Chanḡ hsiaóchiehte hsiñtì feīch'anǵ haŏ, sóī wŏmen toū heń hsīhuan t'a.

10. Shét'ou tuaň te jeń shuō-huà nań shuōtehaŏ.

WRITTEN EXERCISES

A. Transcribe Section B, above, in Chinese.

B. Render the following into English:

1. 心地不好的人, 沒有人喜歡跟他做朋友的.

2. 近來左先生的耳朵沒有從前那麼好, 我們說話, 他不很容易聽得見.

3. 眼睛好的人用不着戴眼鏡兒, 眼睛壞的人非戴眼鏡兒不可.

4. 我們做事要非常小心, 不小心就會做錯了.

5. 嘴的功用是吃東西跟說話; 眼睛的功用是看東西.

6. 我們學甚麼都要一步一步學, 不可太快.

7. 有十個人以上願意跟我到城裏去,我就去,沒有,我就不去了.

8. 這些自來水筆每枝賣五塊錢以下,我們就也許買,賣五塊錢以上,我們就一定不買了.

9. 那面鏡子上頭的字,都是他寫的;這面鏡子上頭的字,都是你寫的.

10. 他不聽我的話,所以我心裏頭不大喜歡.

C. Render the following into Chinese:

1. I have forgotten to bring my eyeglasses, so I cannot see the words written by you.

2. Who lives in the little house by the side of the post office, do you know?

3. When you learn to speak Chinese, you ought to learn it step by step.

4. The more you write, the more words you know.

5. When you come here tomorrow, the earlier the better.

6. When we speak we cannot afford not to use our tongue, teeth, and lips.

7. You don't study conscientiously; hence, you are not making any progress.

8. Please take a look. What is there on my face?

9. My hair is much thinner [fewer] than yours; yours is much thinner than his.

10. To whom have you lent the mirror you bought last Wednesday?

VOCABULARY CHARACTERS

 (Kuā)
To blow (as the wind)

 (Chèn)
A spell, a gust; dis-
position of troops

 (Ch'ǎng) Also written
場.
Field [*]

 (Yún)
Cloud [*]

 (Ts'aï)
Color [*]; prize (in lot-
tery, etc.)

 (Hsieñ)
Fresh [*]

 (Hsüeh)
Snow

 (Ch'íng)
Clear (of weather); to
clear up

 (K'ung)
Empty, hollow

 (Liáng)
Cool [*]

 (Yáng)
The male principle

 (Yiñ) Also written 陰.
The female principle;
cloudy, shady

 (Kuang)
Light; smooth, bare

 (Nuǎn)
Warm [*]

 (Hó) (Huó)
Harmonious [*]; mild,
affable [*]; with, and

 (T'íng)
To stop, to cease

 (Weí)
To be, to act, to do;
as [*]

COMPOUNDS

下雪 (Hsià-hsüeh) To snow

颳風 (Kuā-fenḡ) To blow (as the wind)

雲彩 (Yünts'ai) Clouds

晴天 (Ch'ingt'ien) A clear sunny day

大風 (Tà fenḡ) Strong wind

大雨 (Tà yǔ) Heavy rain

大雪 (Tà hsüeh) Heavy snow

陰天 (Yint'ien) Cloudy day

太陽 (T'aìyang) The sun

太陽光 (T'aìyang-kuaḡ) Sunlight

以來 (Ǐlaí) From . . . till now; for the last . . .

天上 (T'ienshang) In the sky

出門 (Ch'ū-men) To go out (of the house); to be married (said of a girl)

前邊兒 (Ch'ienpierh) Front

後邊兒 (Hoùpierh) Rear, back

飛機場 (Feīchī-ch'aṇg) Airfield

空氣 (K'ungch'ì) Air, atmosphere

暖和 (Nuanho) Warm

涼快 (Liangk'uai) Cool (of weather)

雨衣 (Yǔi) Raincoat

雨帽 (Yǔmaò) Rain hat

套鞋 (T'aòsien) Rubber overshoes

暖氣 (Nuanch'ì) Warm air, steam heat

談天 (T'an·t'ien) To chat

新鮮 (Hsiṇhsien) Fresh

接着 (Chiehche) To succeed, to follow immediately; connectedly

了事 (Liaǒ-shih) To finish or be through with something

說到 (Shuōtaò) To speak of, to mention

難過 (Naṇkuò) Sad; to feel bad; difficult to live through

以為 (Ǐweí) To take it that, to think that

READING MATERIAL

1. 裏個以常先生家三十的時候，家江這兒近五六兒的時候，我在最這兒東邊兒晚上他說氣，是在天的天拜的壞的。我昨天談天禮來

天，我江先生很得，記得時候得冷，不沒大晴，也又你氣，下算候十雪，

的上天不記的，記天來，天天是氣着完。天天，時是下

兒早十兒一到點，還火你說，"今以前一為天接下

邊一到點，還車還你火三大了以了，道才？八兩時不到

西拜不一呢？我拜大了以道才？

們禮還有？下麼對禮雪颳們陽知上壞壞，十颳邊出也，到下

你上天的白，你大頭上下，禮大是我太誰晚不太下風東想到下

說的今真，明上，麼裏從是雪，完看兒昨氣不下天們也事的

友好到我，不早多站自，就下颳以點到天還天八，我門了

朋麼兒，麼一得車？雨，沒颳可一下的

2. 怎拜下火麼？大也天了，和雨，這樣看八天麼？到就

上禮雨在了"下雨，前到暖大這

候，你極是下風，天會下說

3. 我天十甚冷，天十下得氣八

冷雪不天天

下只的多所算們下差陽。夏冬天許生起帽兒套來

常了天最的不我過天太跟說夏也先下雨這雙用車鞋。

常完兩天光還見五有天以和，快江又有我一用汽套

就下一冬陽氣，不看十是冬可暖涼雪，在又有

下的有的太天對少六都有還的的下現也

一完只年有的很百天也們兒了看衣去雨借我雨

麼，下天每是在得人三晴然我邊邊見你雨家頂以謝衣

有拜的下八們說的年是當是東東看罷有回一可謝雨

甚才晴了天現話兒一都氣可比近壞沒能衣就了

沒禮天再天你的邊裏天天別，也最氣你怎雨我要沒

還個兩又十說你西這天到分天氣為天了鞋件要不以

下三一陽過我呢。4. 在的多說的的天因說來套一你

不兩有太不以壞住雪不的天天的是就雨跟有鞋

5. 的，所

6. 你的汽車停在甚麼地方？
離我這兒遠不遠？

7. 停在你家的前邊兒, 所以下
大雨我也不怕了.

8. 那就好極了. 我們就在這兒
吃中飯. 吃完了一塊兒到飛機場去.

9. 好, 就這麼辦罷.

ROMANIZED TEXT OF READING MATERIAL

1. Tsót'ien wǎnshang wǒ tsaì Chiāng hsiensheng chiāli t'ań-t'ien te shiḣhou, t'ā shuō tsuì chiṅ chè lianǧ-sañko līpaìte t'ieñch'i, shiḣ chèrh wǔ-liùshiḣ nień īlaí tsuì huaì te. Wǒ tsaì tunḡpierh te shiḣhou, ch'ángch'ang t'inḡchien p'engyu shuō nimen hsīpierhte t'ieñch'i shiḣ tóma haǒ te. Shang̀-līpaiī tsaǒshang wǒ ts'aí taò chèrh, taò chiñt'ien haí pū taò shiḣ t'ieñ. Chiāng hsienshengte huà, wǒ cheñte yǔ ītiǎrh pū heṅ míngpai.

2. Tsem̌ma pū míngpai ne? Nǐ haí chìte shang̀·līpaiī tsaǒshang, nǐ hsiàle huǒch'ē te shiḣhou, yǔ hsiàte tóma tà ma? Nǐ haí chìte ni tsaì huǒch'ē-chaṅ lit'ou tuì wo shuō, "Chiñt'ien lenǧchí le" ma? Tzùts'unḡ shang̀-līpaìsañ īlaí, pū shiḣ hsià tà yǔ, chiù shiḣ hsià tà hsüeh. Tà-ch'ieńt'ien meí hsià-yǔ, yeḣ meí hsià-hsüeh, k'ǒshih kuāle ī t'ieñ tà fenḡ. Ch'ieńt'ien fenḡ kuāwańle, wǒmen īweí shiḣ ch'ingt'ien taò le, k'ói k'aṅchien t'aìyang le, t'ieñch'i yeḣ huì nuaṅho ītiǎrh le. Shuí chiḣtao chieñche yù hsià tà yǔ, hsiàtaò tsót'ien wǎnshang ts'aí hsiàwań. Nǐ shuō chèyanǧ te t'ieñch'i huaì puhuai?

3. Wǒ k'aṅ haí pū suaṅ t'aì huaì pa? T'ieñch'i lenǧ shiḣ t'ieñ pā t'ieñ, hsiàyǔ hsià shiḣ t'ieñ pā t'ieñ, hsià-hsüeh hsià shiḣ t'ieñ pā t'ieñ, kuā-fenḡ kuā ī-lianǧ t'ieñ, suaṅpute shemma. Wǒmen tsaì tunḡpierh, yǔ shiḣhou t'ieñch'i lenǧtaò meń yeḣ pūhsianǧ ch'ū, yeḣ pū shiḣ shiḣ t'ieñ pā t'ieñ chiù liaǒ-shiḣ te. Shuōtaò hsià-yǔ hsià-hsüeh, pū hsià haí meí yǔ shemma, īhsià chiù ch'angch'ang hsià lianǧsañko līpaì ts'aí hsiàwań te. Hsiàwańle chiḣ yǔ ī-lianǧ t'ieñte ch'ingt'ien, chiḣ yǔ ī-lianǧ t'ieñte t'aìyang, yù tsaì hsià le. Meǐ nieńte tunḡt'ien, tsuì tō pūkuò shiḣ t'ieñ pā t'ieñ shiḣ yǔ t'aìyang-kuanḡ te. Sóí wǒ shuō nimen hsieṅtsaì te t'ieñch'i, haí pū suaṅ huaì ne.

4. Nīte huà shuōte heṅ tuì, pūkuò wǒmen chù tsaì hsīpierh te jeń, heṅ shaǒ k'aṅchienkuo hsià-hsüeh te. Chèli ī nień sañpaì liùshihwǔ t'ieñ, ch'àputō t'ieñt'ieñ toū shiḣ ch'ingt'ien, toū shiḣ yǔ t'aìyang te. Shuōtaò t'ieñch'i, tanḡjań yeḣ yǔ tunḡt'ien keñ hsiàt'ien te feñpieh, k'ǒshih wǒmen haí k'ói shuō tunḡt'iente t'ieñch'i, pǐ tunḡpierhte nuaṅho, hsiàt'iente t'ieñch'i, yeḣ pǐ tunḡpierhte lianǧk'uai. Yeḣhsü shiḣ yiñweì tsuì chiṅ k'aṅchienle hsià-

hsüeh, Chianḡ hsiensheng chiù shuō t'iench'i huaì pa. Nǐ k'an, hsientsaì
yù hsiàch'i yǔ lai le. Nǐ meí yú yǔī, yeh meí yú yǔmaò ken t'aòhsieh,
tsem neng huí-chiā ch'ü ne? Wǒ chèrh yǔ ichien yǔī, ītiṅg yǔmaò ken ī-
shuanḡ t'aòhsieh. Nǐ yaò wǒ chiù k'óí chieh keí ni yunḡyung.

5. Pū yaò le, hsiehhsieh. Wǒ shih k'aī ch'ìch'ē lai te, sóí meí ná yǔī,
yǔmaò ken t'aòhsieh.

6. Nite ch'ìch'ē t'ing tsaì shemma tìfang? Lí wǒ chèrh yüan puyüan?

7. T'ing tsaì nī chiāte ch'ienpierh, sóí hsià tà yǔ wó yeh pū p'à le.

8. Nà chiù haǒchí le. Wǒmen chiù tsaì chèrh ch'ih chunḡfan. Ch'ih-
wanle ik'uàrh taò feīchi-ch'ang ch'ü.

9. Haǒ, chiù chèma pan pa.

NOTES

1. 以來, a compound for indicating duration of time, implies "from a
given time in the past coming up to the present" and is often used to
intensify 自, 從, or 自從. When so used it may be left out in the English
translation for the avoidance of redundancy (cf. Note 9 on 以前 and 以後,
Lesson Twenty-four). But when it is used alone, it may be rendered into
English as "for the [duration of the] last . . ." Thus, 十年以來 becomes
"for the last ten years." In this latter usage it may be shortened to 來
alone, so that 十年以來 becomes simply 十年來.

2. 不是···就是 "[If it] is not . . . then [it] is" are correlative conjunctions used to show a conditional or hypothetical relationship. 昨天沒去的
人不是你就是他 means "[If] the person who did not go yesterday is not
you, then [it] is he."

3. It is true that "rain" and "snow" can be used both as nouns and verbs
in English and literary Chinese; in modern Chinese, however, the same
thing cannot be done. For "to rain" and "to snow" we have to use the
compounds 下雨 and 下雪, respectively. Remember that when the pronoun
"it" is used in English as an indeterminate subject of an impersonal sentence
to refer to conditions of the weather, it is either left out or replaced by
the noun for which it stands in Chinese. Thus, "It will rain soon" becomes
either 快要下雨了 or 天快要下雨了, and "It is very cold today," 今天很冷
or 今天天氣很冷.

4. 算不得甚麼, literally "not capable of being regarded as anything,"
may be taken to mean "to be of no special account," "to be nothing of
consequence."

5. When 到 is used as a co-verb joined to a verb of action, it performs
a function comparable to that of the preposition "until" in English and can
be translated as such. 我看書看到下午三點鐘 means "I read until 3:00
p.m." But when 到 is used as a modifier of adjectives or adverbs, it has
the effect of "so . . . that" or "to such an extent that . . ." 這本書的價錢
貴到甚麼人也買不起 means "The price of this book is so high that anyone
cannot afford to buy it," and 他走路走得快到好像火車一樣, "He walks so
fast that he is like a train."

6. 和, like 跟, may be used to join nouns or pronouns together.

7. 誰知道 means "Who knows but that" and is used to express surprise on the part of the speaker.

8. 為 is a literary word meaning "to be" (cf. 是) and "to act as, to do" (cf. 做). It is introduced here merely for the sake of the compound 以為. Do not try to use it in conversation as the equivalent of 是 or 做.

ORAL EXERCISES

A. Say the following in Chinese:

1. The air in the room; the warm air in the room; not quite an hour; not quite a week.

2. Is it warm here? Is it cool here?

3. Beautiful clouds; the warm sunshine; the cool wind.

4. Has the rain stopped? Has the wind stopped?

5. Today the weather is quite warm. It was a lot cooler yesterday.

6. Was yesterday a cloudy day? Is today a clear day?

7. To rain; to snow; to rain heavily; to snow heavily.

8. There is a sun in the sky. There is also a moon in the sky.

9. Yesterday the wind was quite strong, but it didn't snow.

10. Can you lend me your raincoat and rubber overshoes?

B. Render the following into English:

1. Kuā-fenḡ le; kuāle fenḡ; meí kuā-fenḡ; kuāch'i fenḡ lai; kuāle fenḡ meiyu? Kuāwańle fenḡ meiyu?

2. Hsiàle yǔ; hsià-yǔ le; meí hsià-yǔ; hsiàle ī t'ieñ yǔ; yǔ tà puta? Yǔ tà haíshih hsüeň tà? Yǔ hsiàwańle meiyu?

3. T'ieñ yiñ; yiñt'ieñ; t'ieñ ch'ing le; t'ieñ ch'inǵle meiyu? T'ieñ haí meí ch'ing.

4. Ītǒ yüńts'ai; ichen̄ lenḡ fenḡ; ichen̄ tà yǔ; hsiñhsien te k'unḡch'ì.

5. T'āte fanḡtzu ch'ieńpierh yú ts'aǒtì, hoùpierh yeň yú ts'aǒtì.

6. T'aìyang ch'ū le; t'aìyang ch'ūlai le. Yüeňliang ch'ūlai le meiyu? Yüeňliang haí meí ch'ūlai.

7. T'ā chiaò ni tsót'ien laí, nǐ meí laí, sói t'ā hsiñ lit'ou chüeňte heň nańkuò.

8. Yiñt'ieñ meí yǔ t'aìyang, ch'inǵt'ieñ ts'aí yǔ t'aìyang.

9. T'ieñshang te yüńts'ai chen̄ meǐ, nǐ k'ańtechien̄ k'anpuchien?

10. Ch'uñt'iente t'ieñch'i nuaňho, ch'iūt'iente t'ieñch'i lianǵk'uai.

WRITTEN EXERCISES

A. Transcribe Section B, above, in Chinese.

B. Render the following into English:

1. 天晴了我就出去買一件新的雨衣跟一頂新的雨帽.

2. 這所房子裏頭很冷,我看一定沒有暖氣了.

3. 風颳完了,雨也下完了,天快要晴了;天晴了太陽就要出來.

4. 雪下得這麼大,為甚麼你還要說天氣好?為甚麼你還要出門?

5. 昨天熱極了;今天比昨天涼快得多呢!

6. 火車停了不到三分鐘,你就下了車了.

7. 今天早上下了一陣大雨,下完了雨就接着颳了一陣風,風颳完了天就晴了.

8. 夏天熱起來的時候,沒有冷氣,這所房子就很不舒服了.

9. 我在這兒看書看了好幾個鐘頭,不知道甚麼時候下起雨來了.

10. 自從我到了美國以來,一雙套鞋也沒買過.

C. Render the following into Chinese:

1. I can tell you that [if] it rains this afternoon, I won't go out because I don't have any raincoat.

2. Do you know by whom my rain hat has been brought here?

3. It is quite hot today. Do you think it will be windy this evening?

4. Look, the moon is coming out quite slowly behind the clouds in the sky.

5. His son has just come back; ask him not to feel bad any more.

6. These houses here have all been empty for the last two weeks. Do you know to whom they belong?

7. The colder the weather is, the heavier it will snow.

8. The clearer the day, the fewer the clouds in the sky.

9. Tomorrow I will return to you the rubber overshoes and raincoat which you lent me last week.

10. The air here is not very fresh. Don't sit here to read.

VOCABULARY CHARACTERS

金 (Chiñ)
Gold (element); gold (metal) [*]; metal [*]; (a surname)

銀 (Yiń)
Silver (element); silver (metal) [*]

銅 (T'uń)
Brass, copper, bronze

鐵 (T'ieȟ) Often abbreviated as 鉄.
Iron

錫 (Hsí)
Pewter; tin [*]

玻 (Pō)
Glass [*]

璃 (Lí)
Glass [*]

輕 (Ch'iñg)
Light

厚 (Hoù)
Thick

薄 (Paó) Literary pronunciation: (Pó)
Thin

木 (Mù)
Wood [*]; trees [*]; numb [*]

石 (Shiȟ)
Stone, rock [*]; (a surname)

器 (Ch'ì)
Vessel, tool, implement [*]

瓷 (Tz'ú)
Porcelain, china

硬 (Yiǹg)
Hard, firm

軟 (Juaȟ) Also written 輭.
Soft, weak, yielding

賤 (Chieǹ)
Cheap, mean, low, worthless

265

COMPOUNDS

五金 金子 (Wŭ-chiñ) The five basic metals

金子 子 (Chiñtzu) Gold (the metal)

銀子 子 (Yińtzu) Silver (the metal)

石頭 頭 (Shiĥt'ou) Stone, rock

木頭 頭 (Mùt'ou) Wood

玻璃 璃 (Pōli) Glass

鐵器 器 (T'ieĥch'i) Ironware

木器 (Mùch'i) Woodenware

銀器 (Yińch'i) Silverware

瓷器 (Tz'úch'i) Porcelain, china

石器 (Shiĥch'i) Stone implements

錫器 (Hsích'i) Pewterware

機器 (Chīch'i) Machine, machinery

銅器 (T'ungch'i) Copperware, bronzeware, brassware

瓷瓶 (Tz'úp'ing) Porcelain vase

READING MATERIAL

1. 五 金 叫 甚 麼 ?
2. 五 金 叫 金, 銀, 銅, 鐵, 錫.
3. 五 金 價 錢 最 貴 的 是 甚 麼 ?
4. 價 錢 最 貴 的 是 金.
5. 價 錢 最 賤 的 是 甚 麼 ?
6. 價 錢 最 賤 的 是 鐵.
7. 最 有 用 處 的 呢 ?
8. 最 有 用 處 的 也 是 鐵.
9. 這 個 中 國 話 叫 甚 麼 ?
10. 這 個 中 國 話 叫 玻 璃.
11. 那 個 中 國 話 叫 甚 麼 ?
12. 那 個 中 國 話 叫 木 頭.
13. 木 頭 重 還 是 石 頭 重 ?

14. 石頭重,木頭比石頭輕.

15. 石頭硬還是木頭硬?

16. 石頭硬,木頭比石頭軟.

17. 用木頭做的東西叫甚麼?

18. 用木頭做的東西叫木器.

19. 那麼用鐵做的東西叫鐵器麼?

20. 是的,用銅做的東西叫銅器,用瓷做的叫瓷器,用石頭做的叫石器.

21. 這個玻璃杯是誰的,是你的麼?

22. 不是我的,是我的朋友的.我的在那兒,比這個厚一點兒.

23. 玻璃杯你說厚的好還是薄的好?

24. 我說厚的有厚的好處,薄的有薄的好處.我自己喜歡厚的.

25. 我不喜歡厚的,因為厚的太重了.

26. 我聽說江太太最近在城裏買了一套中國瓷器.你看見過沒有?

27. 看見過了,有很多碟子,飯碗跟茶杯,顏色非常好看,價錢也十分便宜.

28. 沒 有 瓷 瓶 麼？

29. 沒 有, 他 説 江 先 生 不 喜 歡 瓷
瓶, 所 以 他 沒 買.

30. 你 今 天 下 午 要 到 江 太 太 家
裏 去 麼？ 這 些 玻 璃 杯 是 他 上 禮
拜 借 給 我 的, 我 已 經 用 完 了. 我 很
想 請 你 給 我 送 回 去.

31. 今 天 下 午 我 沒 有 工 夫 去, 我
明 天 早 上 去 的 時 候, 給 你 送 回 去
就 好 了.

32. 那 麼 我 就 請 你 明 天 早 上 給
我 送 回 去 罷.

ROMANIZED TEXT OF READING MATERIAL

1. Wŭ-chiñ chiaò sheḿma?
2. Wŭ-chiñ chiaò chiñ, yiń, t'uńg, t'ieḣ, hsí.
3. Wŭ-chiñ chiàch'ien tsuì kueì te shiḣ sheḿma?
4. Chiàch'ien tsuì kueì te shiḣ chiñ.
5. Chiàch'ien tsuì chieǹ te shiḣ sheḿma?
6. Chiàch'ien tsuì chieǹ te shiḣ t'ieḣ.
7. Tsuì yŭ yunġch'u te ne?
8. Tsuì yŭ yunġch'u te yeḣ shiḣ t'ieḣ.
9. Chèko Chunḡkuo-huà chiaò sheḿma?
10. Chèko Chunḡkuo-huà chiaò pōli.
11. Nàko Chunḡkuo-huà chiaò sheḿma?
12. Nàko Chunḡkuo-huà chiaò mùt'ou.
13. Mùt'ou chunġ haíshih shiḣt'ou chunġ?
14. Shiḣt'ou chunġ, mùt'ou pī shiḣt'ou ch'inḡ.
15. Shiḣt'ou yinġ haíshih mùt'ou yinġ?
16. Shiḣt'ou yinġ, mùt'ou pī shiḣt'ou juañ.
17. Yunġ mùt'ou tsò te tunḡhsi chiaò sheḿma?
18. Yunġ mùt'ou tsò te tunḡhsi chiaò mùch'i.
19. Nèma yunġ t'ieḣ tsò te tunḡhsi chiaò t'ieḣch'i ma?

20. Shih̀ te, yunǵ t'unǵ tsò te tunḡhsi chiaò t'unǵch'i, yunǵ tz'ú tsò te chiaò tz'úch'i, yunǵ shih̀t'ou tsò te chiaò shih̀ch'i.

21. Chèko pōli-peī shih̀ shuíte, shih̀ nīte ma?

22. Pū shih̀ wŏte, shih̀ wŏte p'enǵyute. Wŏte tsaì nàrh, pī chèko hoù ītiărh.

23. Pōli-peī nī shuō hoù te haŏ haíshih paó te haŏ?

24. Wŏ shuō hoù te yŭ hoùte haŏch'u, paó te yŭ paóte haŏch'u. Wŏtzùchí hsīhuan hoù te.

25. Wŏ pū hsīhuan hoù te, yiñweì hoù te t'aì chunǵ le.

26. Wŏ t'inḡshuō Chianḡ t'aìt'ai tsuì chiǹ tsaì ch'enǵli maīle īt'aò Chunḡkuo tz'úch'i, nī k'aǹchienkuo meiyu?

27. K'aǹchienkuo le, yú heñ tō tiehtzu, faǹwañ keñ ch'ápeī, yeńse feīch'ang haŏk'aǹ, chiàch'ien yeñ shih̀feñ p'ieńi.

28. Meí yŭ tz'úp'inǵ ma?

29. Meí yŭ, t'ā shuō Chianḡ hsiensheng pū hsīhuan tz'úp'inǵ, sóī t'ā meí maī.

30. Nī chiñt'ien hsiàwŭ yaò taò Chianḡ t'aìt'ai chiǎli ch'ü ma? Chèhsieh pōli-peī shih̀ t'ā shanǵ-līpaì chieh̀ keí wo te, wó īching yunǵwañ le. Wó heñ hsianǵ ch'inǵ ni keí wo sunǵhuich'ü.

31. Chiñt'ien hsiàwú wŏ meí yŭ kunḡfu ch'ü, wŏ minǵt'ien tsaŏshang ch'ù te shih̀hou, keí ni sunǵhuich'ü chiù haŏ le.

32. Nèma wŏ chiù ch'inǵ ni minǵt'ien tsaŏshang keí wo sunǵhuich'ü pa.

NOTES

1. 用···做, "to use ... to make," when used as a participial adjective followed by the attributive 的, may be rendered into English as "to be made of ..." Thus, 用木頭做的東西 is to be understood as "the things [which are] made of wood"; 用鐵做的東西, as "the things [which are] made of iron"; 書是用紙做的, as "Books are made of paper"; etc.

2. Both 便宜 and 賤 may be used to mean "cheap," but their difference in implication should be noted. 便宜 means cheapness in the sense of buying or selling at a low price; it is quite similar to the French phrase *à bon marché*, whereas 賤 carries with it the implication of little or low worth.

3. Note the peculiarly Chinese construction in sentence 24 in the Reading Material: 厚的有厚的好處, etc., which means "Thick ones have their good points, etc." The subject is here repeated after the main verb to take the place of the genitival pronoun which is generally used in English. Such a construction is often used in Chinese to present a contrast or make a comparison.

ORAL EXERCISES

A. Say the following in Chinese:

1. Glass, wood, rock, a piece of glass, a piece of wood, a piece of rock.

2. Chinaware, ironware, copperware, glass bowls, copper dishes, porcelain vases.

3. A package of gold, a package of silver.

4. Gold is more expensive than silver; silver is more expensive than copper.

5. Wood is very useful; iron is more useful.

6. This pewterware is all made in China.

7. Which is softer, iron or steel?

8. Steel is made of iron; pewter is not made of copper.

9. Do you know what the five basic metals are?

10. I don't, but I know what the four seasons are.

B. Render the following into English:

1. Chèhsieh shiȟ Chungkuo tz'úch'i pushih?

2. T'iehch'ite yungch'u tà, haíshih mùch'ite yungch'u tà?

3. Chèk'uaì shih̀t'ou t'aì chung, wŏ īko jeń nápuch'ǐ.

4. Nǐ k'aǹchienkuo t'ā tsót'ien maǐ te tz'úp'ing meiyu?

5. Nàpeň hoù te shū shiȟ nīte, nàpeň paó te shū yeȟ shiȟ nīte.

6. Chèhsieh pōli-peī toū shiȟ Meīkuo tsò te, maì wūmaó ch'ień īko.

7. Hsích'i heň chung̀, k'ŏshih Chungkuo-jeń toū heń hsīhuan yung̀ hsích'i.

8. Yingkuo tsò te tz'úch'i heň haŏ, k'ŏshih heň chung̀ heň hoù.

9. Wŏte shoúpiaŏ shiȟ yung̀ yińtzu tsò te, t'āte shiȟ yung̀ chiñtzu tsò te.

10. Chèchià chīch'i shiȟ t'āte fùch'in ts'uń Meīkuo maīhuilai te.

WRITTEN EXERCISES

A. Transcribe Section B, above, in Chinese.

B. Render the following into English:

1. 這兒有三包金子，一包很大，兩包很小，大的比小的重五倍到六倍．

2. 中美兩國都有錫器，可是中國錫器的價錢比美國的賤兩倍到三倍．

3. 我昨天到百貨公司去買了一件大衣，不太厚，也不太薄，穿起來又漂亮又舒服．

4. 我 不 知 道 我 們 昨 天 晚 上 在 張 先 生 家 裏 看 見 的 銀 器,都 是 中 國 做 的.

5. 這 兩 個 玻 璃 瓶 子,一 個 是 紅 的, 一 個 是 藍 的;那 一 個 是 你 的,那 一 個 是 他 的 ?

6. 東 西 有 輕 有 重,事 情 有 大 有 小.

7. 中 國 瓷 器 有 中 國 瓷 器 的 好 處,英 國 瓷 器 也 有 英 國 瓷 器 的 好 處.

8. 鐵 是 非 常 有 用 處 的,沒 有 鐵 我 們 就 有 很 多 東 西 不 能 做 了.

9. 鋼 是 用 鐵 做 的,可 是 比 鐵 硬 得 多.

10. 銀 子 太 軟,不 能 用 來 做 機 器 的. 做 機 器 一 定 要 用 鋼 才 行. 你 看, 這 三 架 機 器 都 是 用 鋼 做 的.

C. Render the following into Chinese:

1. These four machines are all made in America. To whom do they belong?

2. All these bowls and dishes are made of glass; their prices are quite reasonable.

3. Mr. Chiang, this registered letter of yours is too heavy. Please stick more postage stamps on it.

4. The porcelainware which Mr. Ch'ien bought last year was both pretty and light.

5. The Chinese call gold, silver, copper, iron, and tin the five basic metals.

6. I have seen many houses built of wood, but I have never seen any built of stone.

7. All your silverware is very well made. Is it made here or abroad [foreign countries]?

8. My desk is made of wood; yours is made of steel. Mine has its good points and yours has its good points, too.

9. Is your wrist watch made of gold or is it made of silver?

10. This piece of gold I want to sell for one hundred forty-three dollars American money.

Lesson *FORTY*

A Review Lesson

CHARACTERS

Number of Strokes	Characters	Pronunciation and Tone	Meaning	Lesson Reference
Four	牙	Yá	Tooth	37
	心	Hsiñ	Heart, mind	37
	孔	K'unǧ	Hole; (a surname)	37
	木	Mù	Wood; trees; numb	39
Five	只	Chiȟ	Only, merely	36
	功	Kunḡ	Accomplishment, merit	37
	石	Shiȟ	Stone, rock	39
Six	耳	Erȟ	Ear	37
	舌	Shé	Tongue	37
	光	Kuanḡ	Light; smooth, bare	38
Seven	步	Pù	Step, pace; land measure of five Chinese feet	37
Eight	放	Fang̀	To let go, to let out; to put, to place	36
	於	Yǘ	At, in; in regard to	36
	怕	P'à	To be afraid, to fear	36
	法	Fǎ	Method; law	36
	空	K'unḡ	Empty, hollow	38
	和	Hó, huó	Harmonious; mild, affable; with, and	38
	金	Chiñ	Gold; metal	39
Nine	重	Chung̀	Heavy; weighty, serious	36

273

Number of Strokes	Characters	Pronunciation and Tone	Meaning	Lesson Reference
Nine	眉	Meí	Eyebrows	37
	面	Mièn	Surface, face, (classifier for mirrors, flags, etc.)	37
	陣	Chèn	A spell, a gust; disposition of troops	38
	為	Weí	To be, to act, to do, etc.	38
	玻	Pō	Glass	39
	厚	Hoù	Thick	39
Ten	倍	Peì	Times, -fold	36
	恐	K'unǧ	To fear, to be afraid	36
	借	Chièh	To borrow; to lend	36
	唇	Ch'uń	Lip	37
	旁	P'ań	Side	37
	假	Chiǎ / Chià	False / Holiday, vacation	36 / 36
	情	Ch'iń	Emotion, feeling; facts of a case	36
	副	Fù	A set; secondary, vice-	37
	眼	Yeň	Eye	37
	彩	Ts'aī	Color; prlze (in lottery, etc.)	38
	雪	Hsüèh	Snow	38
	涼	Liań	Cool	38
	陰	Yiñ	The female principle; cloudy, shady	38
	停	T'iń	To stop, to cease	38
	瓷	Tz'ú	Porcelain, china	39
	軟	Juǎn	Soft, weak, yielding	39

Number of Strokes	Characters	Pronunciation and Tone	Meaning	Lesson Reference
Twelve	暑	Shŭ	Summer heat	36
	寒	Hań	Cold; in poor circumstances	36
	期	Ch'í	Period of time; to hope	36
	然	Jań	So, thus	36
	越	Yüeh̀	To pass over, to exceed	37
	場	Ch'ǎn	Field	38
	雲	Yüń	Cloud	38
	晴	Ch'iń	Clear (of weather); to clear up	38
	陽	Yań	The male principle	38
	硬	Yiǹ	Hard, firm	39
Thirteen	睛	Chinḡ	Pupil of the eye	37
	暖	Nuaň	Warm	38
Fourteen	鼻	Pí	Nose	37
	銀	Yiń	Silver	39
	銅	T'uń	Brass, copper, bronze	39
	輕	Ch'inḡ	Light	39
Fifteen	髮	Fă	Hair (on the head)	37
	颳	Kuā	To blow (as the wind)	38
	璃	Lí	Glass	39
	賤	Chień	Cheap, mean, low, worthless	39
Sixteen	嘴	Tsuĭ	Mouth	37
	錫	Hsí	Pewter	39

Number of Strokes	Characters	Pronuncia- tion and Tone	Meaning	Lesson Reference
Sixteen	器	Ch'ì	Vessel, tool, implement	39
Seventeen	臉	Liěn	Face	37
	鮮	Hsieñ	Fresh	38
	薄	Paó	Thin	39
Eighteen	題	T'í	Subject, theme, title	36
Nineteen	關	Kuañ	To shut, to close; a mountain pass; guardhouse; to concern	36
	鏡	Chìng	Mirror, speculum	37
Twenty	鐵	T'ieʰ	Iron	39

ORAL DRILL

A. Say the following in Chinese:

1.
consent	expenses	affair	semester	empty
government	geography	fiction	naturally	of course
method	train fare	ear	eye	nose
eyebrows	careful	tongue	mirror	eyeglasses
progress	diligent	side	air	sun
warm	cool	cloud	snow	raincoat
fresh	airfield	steel	wood	rock
soft	hard	heavy	light	glass
silverware	china	copperware	machine	iron
tin	thick	thin	hair (head)	tooth

2. a suit of clothes   a pair of eyeglasses
a set of books   a pair of eyes
a face   a school year
a semester   a mouth
a cloud   a gust of wind

3. to rain   to snow
to blow (as wind)   to be afraid
to have a holiday   to borrow money
to lend a book   to ask for leave of absence
to be concerned with   to chat

4. Please think of a method of transaction.
Have you any device?

Please lend him some books.
Don't lend them any money!
Is the affair important?
Is the vacation period long?
Walk step by step!
Above fifty-five cents.
Below one dollar and seventy-five cents.
Please stand beside me!
Don't sit beside him!
It is very warm here.
Is it cool there?
It is not quite two hours.
Is there any cloud in the sky?
There is a moon in the sky.
I am going to the airfield.
This glass of milk is not very fresh.
It rains again!
It snows again!
The clouds in the sky are quite pretty.
Do you like to come to my home to chat?
Where is the airfield?
Is the airfield far from here?
How far is the train station from the airfield?
His moral nature is truly good.
You have to study diligently.
The older a man is, the worse are his eyes.

B. Render the following into English:

K'aī ch'ìch'ē
T'ińg ch'ìch'ē
K'aī-meń
Feìyung tà puta?
Hsüehfeì kueì pukuei?
Fańgfá haŏ puhao?
Chiñt'ien yū t'aìyang meiyu?
Taò lianǧk'uaì ch'ień putao?
Pū taò wū t'ieñ.
Haí pū taò erȟshiȟko jeń.
Īko heñ ch'ańg te chiàch'í.
Nīmen fang̀ chǐ t'ieñ chià?
Wŏ haí meí kaò-chià.
T'ā yaò kaò sañ t'ieñ chià.
Chèhsieh t'unǵch'i shiȟ wŏte.
Nàfù chīch'i feīch'ańg tà, feīch'ańg haŏ.
Mùch'i chiàch'ien hsieǹtsaì heñ p'ień.
Shiȟch'i yù chung̀ yù pū haŏyung̀.
Wŏ k'aǹchien īpaō yińtzu tsaì chōtzu shangt'ou.

Chè shih yung shemma tsò te, nǐ chihtao ma?
Chihtao, nà shih yung kang tsò te.
Shū shih yung chih tsò te.
Tsót'ien feng tà puta?
Ch'ient'ien kuāle feng meiyu?
Hsientsai yù hsiàch'i yǔ lai le.
T'āte yenchingerh nǐ ná taò shemma tìfang ch'ü le?
Nǐmen toū yaò tanghsiñ ītiǎrh!
T'āte erhto pū heñ haǒ.
Wǒte pítzu kaō pukao, tà puta?
Chèk'uaì niújoù hsiñhsienteheñ.
Nǐ chiaò t'a laí, t'ā tangjañ laí.
Nǐ shuō t'ate huaìch'u, t'ā tangjañ pū hsīhuan ni.
Huì k'an-shū te jeñ, tzùjañ huì k'an-paò.
Chè shih Chungkuo-chengfū chīkuañ, pū shih Meǐkuo-chengfū chīkuañ.
Nà pū shih kuañyú nimente ch'uañfeì te weñt'í.
T'āte p'engyu tuì ni feìch'ang kuañ-hsiñ.
Ch'ien hsienshengte yá, chiñlaí ī t'ieñ pī ī t'ieñ huaì le.
Weìshemma t'āte tàī ch'uañle īko tà k'ung, t'ā-tzùchí yeh pū chihtao ne?
Nǐmen shuí yǔ īmieñ chingtzu? Wó hsiang k'ank'an lieñshang yǔ shemma.
Tsót'ien t'ieñch'i feìch'ang haǒ, yù yū t'aìyang, yù nuañho.
Tsuì chiñ shih t'ieñ īlaí, ch'àputō meí yū ī t'ieñ pū shih yiñt'ieñ.
Chèhsieh pōli-peī cheñ haǒ, chiàch'ien yù p'ieñi, yangtzu yù haǒk'añ.
Wǒ meí k'anchien t'a pūkuò wū nieñ, k'ǒshih t'āte t'oúfā toū paí le.
Nàpeñ hsiaǒshuō nǐ chiehle keī shuí k'añ a?
Shang-lǐpaì wǒ weñ Kuañ hsiensheng chiehle wǔk'uaì ch'ieñ.
Wǒ k'añle t'ate lieñ, chiù chihtao t'a hsiñ lit'ou chüehte feìch'ang nañkuò.
Feīchī-ch'ang p'angpierh yú liangsó hsiaǒ fangtzu, toū shih wǒte.
Nǐ chiñt'ien pū mang chiù ch'ing ni taò wote chiāli lai t'añt'an t'ieñ pa.

WRITING DRILL

1. Write out in Chinese the items in Section A of Oral Drill, above.

2. Transcribe Section B of Oral Drill, above, in Chinese.

READING DRILL

After reading the following, render it into English:

1. 不久以前有一個人,有一天
早上走路去看朋友.他出門的時
候,天氣很晴,沒有風,也沒有雨,所

1. 下雨天，出門要戴雨帽，穿雨衣，套雨鞋。有一個人，他要到百貨公司去買雨衣、雨帽、套鞋。他看見天上起了黑雲，快要下雨了，就到百貨公司去。到了百貨公司，雨衣買完了，雨帽也沒有了，套鞋也沒有了。他知道百貨公司從路上經過。他心裏想：已經不下雨了，天上的黑雲也沒有了，也不颳風了，太陽也出來了。他對自己說：「不要緊，明天還會下的。」他走半路，天黑了，雨又下起來了。他沒戴雨帽，沒穿雨衣，沒套雨鞋，跟來的時候一樣，雨下得很緊，今天也黑到時候了，以帽子上套上了，跟來的就......

2. 有一個姓孔的人，寫信給他的朋友，就拿到郵政局去寄。郵政局裏的人看，信過重了，對他說：「這封信郵票是不夠的，請多貼一個罷。」姓孔的人說：「怎麼？剛才說我的信過重，現在又想要我多貼一個三分的郵票，信不是更重了麼？多貼一個郵票，信多重了，你要問我郵局他郵分分了？」郵政局的人告訴他三分......

3. 哥哥、姐姐、弟弟、妹妹四個人，那一天，吃完了晚飯，就坐在一塊兒談天。弟弟問哥哥：「你說一個人的......」吃完了哥哥......

部分最重要?"弟弟說,"嘴是最重
要的.要是我們沒有嘴,就不能吃
東西了."姐姐說,"不對,不對,只有
嘴,沒有牙,也不能吃東西,所以我
說牙是最重要的."妹妹說,"姐姐
說的也不對,我們沒有手,用甚麼
去拿東西吃呢? 我們的手當然
是最重要的了."哥哥聽完了姐姐,
弟弟,妹妹的話,就接着說,"你們說
的都不對,我說眼睛是最重要的,
因為沒有眼睛,就是有了好吃的
東西,我們也看不見了."他們四個
人,你一句,我一句,說得很有興趣.
他們的父親聽見了就說,"你們說
得都很對.嘴,牙,手跟眼睛,本來都
是一樣重要的."

1 要是 here means "if, should" (cf. 如果 in Lesson Forty-two). It is used before the subject only.

VOCABULARY CHARACTERS

(Weì)
(Classifier for persons);
  seat, position [*]

(Chī) Also written 鷄.
Chicken

(Yā)
Duck [*]

(Yú)
Fish

(Tàn)
Egg

(T'ang)
Soup; (a surname)

(Chiŭ)
Wine, liquor

(Hsień)
Salty

(Yeń)
Salt

(Chiàng) Printed form is
  醬.
Thick sauce; jam

(K'ā) or (Chiā)
(For transliterating "cof"
  of "coffee")

(Yú)
Oil, fat, grease; paint;
  to paint

(Ch'oū)
To draw, to pull

(Hsiang)
Fragrant; to small good;
  incense

(Yeñ) Also written 烟,
  菸.
Smoke; tobacco

(Aì)
To love; to love to, to
  like to; love [*]

(Chiā)
To add; plus

(K'ŏ)
Thirsty

(T'ień)
Sweet

(Ch'íh)
Spoon [*]

(T'ań)
Sugar; candy

(Feī)
(For transliterating "fee"
  of "coffee")

(Tień)
Store, shop [*]

COMPOUNDS

鴨子	(Yātzu) Duck
雞蛋	(Chītàn) Chicken egg
鴨蛋	(Yātàn) Duck egg
黃酒	(Huangchiŭ) Yellow wine
紅酒	(Hungchiŭ) Red wine
醬油	(Chiàngyú) Soybean sauce
香煙	(Hsiangyeñ) Cigarettes
後來	(Hoùlaí) Afterward
走過去	(Tsoŭkuoch'ü) To go over
走過來	(Tsoŭkuolai) To come over

抽煙	(Ch'oū-yeñ)	To smoke
吃煙	(Ch'iñ-yeñ)	
白菜	(Paíts'aì) Cabbage	
點心	(Tieñhsiñ) Light refreshments, dessert	
飯店	(Faǹtieǹ) Modern-style hotel	
咖啡	(K'āfeī) Coffee	
匙子	(Ch'iñtzu) Spoon	
酒杯	(Chiŭpeī) Wine cup, wine glass	
涼開水	(Liang-k'aīshuĭ) Boiled water which has been cooled or chilled	
要事	(Yaòshiñ) Important affair or business	

READING MATERIAL

1. 文英，你昨天下午沒在家麼？可是五點半的時候我給你打過電話，到了五點你家已經看見你，知道你下午出去了。我四點三刻給你打過電話，打來打去也打不通。我己還是着回你，就還沒的。大門了，還是走光。我打來打去，我大出。

2. 國光，我昨天下午出去了，到晚上九點才回來。你下午四點來找我十分，才我罷？上麼九點要事。甚麼要事？

3. 沒有，我不過想跟你一塊兒

到外頭吃晚飯去，吃完晚飯就回來跟你談談天，沒有要事。你昨天到那兒去了？

4. 我跟朋友江平春吃晚飯去。他的哥哥剛從南京回來，所以他請了幾個好朋友，到六國飯店去吃飯。

5. 六國飯店麼？那是這兒最大最好的飯店了。我也在那兒吃過飯。你們昨天吃的是中國菜，還是外國菜？

6. 我們都是中國人，吃的當然是中國菜了，怎麼會吃外國菜呢？

7. 你們吃的中國菜好不好？

8. 非常好。我們六個人吃了一共十道菜，有雞，有鴨子，有魚，有牛肉，有豬肉，有雞蛋，有青菜，差不多甚麼都有。

9. 你們喝了些甚麼湯呢？

10. 喝了些白菜豬肉湯。

11. 喝了酒沒有？

12. 喝了黃酒跟紅酒。平春，他的哥哥跟一位姓馬的喝黃酒，我跟兩位姓石的朋友喝一點兒紅酒.

13. 你們吃完了菜還吃了點心沒有?

14. 還吃了兩碟點心. 也許是白菜猪肉湯太鹹, 也許是我吃菜的時候用了太多的醬油, 也許是我喝了酒, 回來了就覺得渴極了.

15. 你喝湯加了很多的鹽麼?

16. 沒有, 我不過加了一點兒. 後來我喝了好幾杯茶, 才覺得舒服一點兒.

17. 文英, 我告訴你, 喝茶喝得太多, 對於我們是沒有好處的. 我常常因為喝茶喝得太多, 晚上我也睡不好, 所以現在我不敢多喝了.

18. 國光, 我明白了, 以後我也不再多喝了. 你要抽煙麼? 我這兒有一包前門牌香煙, 是你最愛抽的.

19. 我剛抽了一枝, 現在不再抽了, 謝謝. 我想喝一點兒咖啡.

20. 好, 我也想喝. 我去做兩杯來. 喝咖啡你喜歡加糖跟牛奶麼?

21. 我 喜 歡 加 一 點 兒 糖, 不 喜 歡 加 牛 奶. 你 呢?

22. 我 糖 也 不 加, 牛 奶 也 不 加. 這 兒 有 今 天 的 報, 你 可 以 看 看. 咖 啡 很 快 就 得 了.

ROMANIZED TEXT OF READING MATERIAL

1. Wényiṅg, nǐ tsót'ien hsiàwǔ meǐ tsaì chiā ma? Wǒ szùtieň sañk'ò keí ni tākuo tieṅhuà, k'ǒshih tǎlaí-tǎch'ǜ yeň tǎput'uṅg. Taòle wútieňpaṅ wǒ-tzùchí tsoǔkuolai chaó ni, k'aṅchien ni chiāte tàmeň haí shiḣ kuaṅche te, chiù chiḣtao ni īching ch'úch'ü le, haí meí huílai.

2. Kuókuaṅg, wǒ tsót'ien hsiàwǔ ch'úch'ü le, taò waňshang chiútien szùshiḣfeň ts'aí huílai. Nǐ meí yǔ shemma yaòshiḣ lai chaó wo pa?

3. Meí yǔ, wǒ pūkuò hsiaṅg keň ni īk'uàrh taò waìt'ou ch'iḣ waňfaṅ ch'ü, ch'iḣwaň waňfaṅ chiù huílai keň ni t'aṅt'an t'ieň, meí yǔ yaòshiḣ. Nǐ tsót'ien taò nǎrh ch'ü le?

4. Wǒ keň p'eṅgyu Chiaṅg P'iṅgch'uň ch'iḣ waňfaṅ ch'ü. T'āte kōko kaṅg ts'uṅg Nańchiṅg huílai, sóǐ t'ā ch'iṅgle chǐko haǒ p'eṅgyu, taò Liùkuó-Faṅtieň ch'ü ch'iḣ-faṅ.

5. Liùkuó-Faṅtieň ma? Nà shiḣ chèrh tsuì tà tsuì haǒ te faṅtien le. Wǒ yeň tsaì nàrh ch'iḣkuo faṅ. Nīmen tsót'ien ch'iḣ te shiḣ Chuṅgkuo-ts'aì, haíshih waìkuo-ts'aì?

6. Wǒmen toū shiḣ Chuṅgkuo-jeń, ch'iḣ te taṅgjaň shiḣ Chuṅgkuo-ts'aì le, tseḿma huì ch'iḣ waìkuo-ts'aì ne?

7. Nīmen ch'iḣ te Chuṅgkuo-ts'aì haǒ puhao?

8. Feīch'aṅg haǒ. Wǒmen liùko jeń ch'iḣle īkuṅg shiḣtaò ts'aì, yǔ chī, yǔ yātzu, yǔ yǔ, yǔ niújoù, yǔ chūjoù, yǔ chītaṅ, yǔ ch'iṅgts'aì, ch'àputō sheḿma toū yǔ.

9. Nīmen hōle hsieň sheḿma t'aṅg ne?

10. Hōle hsieň paíts'aì-chūjoù t'aṅg.

11. Hōle chiǔ meiyu?

12. Hōle huaṅgchiǔ keň huṅgchiǔ. P'iṅgch'uň, t'āte kōko keň īweì hsiṅg-Mǎ te hō huaṅgchiǔ, wǒ keň liaṅgweì hsiṅg-Shiḣ te p'eṅgyu hō ītiǎrh huṅgchiǔ.

13. Nīmen ch'iḣwaňle ts'aì haí ch'iḣle tieňhsiň meiyu?

14. Haí ch'iḣle liaṅgtieň tieňhsiň. Yeḣhsǔ shiḣ paíts'aì-chūjoù t'aṅg t'aì hsieň, yeḣhsǔ shiḣ wǒ ch'iḣ-ts'aì te shiḣhou, yuṅgle t'aì tō te chiaṅgyú, yeḣhsǔ shiḣ wǒ hōle chiǔ, huílaile chiù chüeḣte k'ǒchí le.

15. Nǐ hō-t'aṅg chiāle heň tō te yeń ma?

16. Meí yǔ, wǒ pūkuò chiāle ītiǎrh. Hoùlaí wǒ hōle haó chīpeī ch'á, ts'aí chüeḣte shūfu ītiǎrh.

17. Weńyinḡ, wǒ kaòsu ni, hō-ch'á hōte t'aì tō, tuìyǔ women shiⓗ meí yú haŏch'u te. Wǒ ch'anǵch'anǵ yiñweì hōle t'aì tō ch'á, wǎnshang shuìchiaò chiù shuìte pū haŏ, sóǐ hsieṅtsaì wó yeⓗ pū kaň tō hō le.

18. Kuókuanḡ, wǒ mínḡpai le, ìhoù wó yeⓗ pū tsaì tō hō le. Nǐ yaò ch'oūyeń ma? Wǒ chèrh yǔ īpaō Ch'ieńmeń-p'aí hsianḡyeñ, shiⓗ nǐ tsuì aì ch'oū te.

19. Wǒ kanḡ ch'oūle īchiⓗ, hsieṅtsaì pū tsaì ch'oū le, hsiehhsieh. Wó hsianǧ hō ītiǎrh k'āfeī.

20. Haǒ, wó yeⓗ hsianǧ hō. Wǒ ch'ü tsò lianǧpeī lai. Hō k'āfeī ní hsīhuan chiā t'anǵ keñ niúnaī ma?

21. Wó hsīhuan chiā ītiǎrh t'anǵ, pū hsīhuan chiā niúnaī. Nǐ ne?

22. Wǒ t'anǵ yeⓗ pū chiā, niúnaí yeⓗ pū chiā. Chèrh yǔ chiñt'ien te paò, nǐ k'ói k'aṅk'an. K'āfeī heň k'uaì chiù té le.

NOTES

1. The negative resultative compound 打不通 in sentence 1 of the Reading Material above is to be understood in the sense of "not capable of putting [the telephone call] through." In a different context the compound may be translated differently into English, depending on the sense in which the verb 打 is to be taken and on the object with which it is used (cf. Note 1, Lesson Thirty-three).

2. 位 as a classifier for persons definitely shows more respect than 個 on the part of the person doing the speaking.

3. 點心 is a general term for light refreshments, such as pastry and cakes, which may or may not be part of a main meal. Its meaning as "dessert" is of course entirely Western in concept.

4. 前門牌香煙 in sentence 18 of the Reading Material above is a popular brand of Chinese cigarettes. Its package bears a picture of the imposing 前門 ("South Gate") of 北平. 牌 is here used in the sense of "brand."

5. Note that "to smoke" in Chinese is either 抽煙, "to draw smoke," or 吃煙, "to eat smoke." Another variant is 吸 (hsī) 煙, "to inhale smoke."

6. The classifier for individual cigarettes is 枝. 包 is used for a pack of them. The round tin of fifty is 罐 or 礶 (kuaṅ).

7. 飯店 is a modern-style hotel, usually one that operates its own dining room, which is open to the public. Do not confuse it with 飯館子, which is strictly a restaurant. The proper classifier for it is 家, although 個 is acceptable.

8. The proper classifier for 匙子 is 把, although one can also use 個.

9. 得 in sentence 22 of the Reading Material above is to be taken in the sense of "done, ready."

ORAL EXERCISES

A. Say the following in Chinese:

1. A cigarette; a wine cup; to smoke; to drink wine.
2. Do you smoke? Did he smoke? He loves to smoke.

   3. Chicken eggs; duck eggs; chicken eggs or duck eggs?

   4. A glass of wine; a glass of yellow wine; a bottle of wine; a bottle
of red wine.

   5. Salty; salt; sugar; sweet; not sweet; neither salty nor sweet.

   6. What do you love to eat? Do you love to eat chicken or duck?

   7. Have you any spoon? Have you any cigarette?

   8. What is this? This is soybean sauce.

   9. What vegetable is this? This is cabbage.

  10. What hotel is that? That is the Hotel Nanking.

B. Render the following into English:

   1. Wŏ yaò maï īchih̄ chī ken̆ lianğchih̄ yātzu.

   2. Nǐ aì ch'oū Chunḡkuo hsianḡyeñ, t'ā aì ch'oū Yinḡkuo hsianḡyeñ.

   3. Ch'inğ weǹ chè lianğweì hsieñsheng shih̀ shuí?

   4. Wŏ ch'iñkuo tieñhsiñ le, hsieh̀hsieh.

   5. Nǐmen hō-ch'á yeh̆ chiā t'anǵ ma? Wŏ hō k'āfeī ts'aí chiā t'anǵ.

   6. T'ā heñ aì ch'ih̄ chǐtàn, t'ieñt'ieñ ch'ih̄ wŭ-liùko.

   7. T'anǵ shih̀ t'ień te, yeń shih̀ hsień te, shuí toū chih̄tao.

   8. Hō-ch'á yung̀ ch'ápeī, hō-chiŭ yung̀ chiūpeī.

   9. Yú haŏch'ih̄, paíts'aì yeh̆ haŏch'ih̄.

  10. Wŏ pū huì hō-chiŭ, yeh̆ pū huì ch'oū-yeñ.

WRITTEN EXERCISES

A. Transcribe Section B, above, in Chinese.

B. Render the following into English:

1. 江先生很愛喝酒,黃酒也好,
紅酒也好,他都能喝十多杯.

2. 我有香煙,沒有洋火.你們那
一位有洋火,就可以抽我的煙.

3. 二加二是四;四加三是幾?
五加八是十三;九加六是多少?

4. 中國人都愛中國,美國人都
愛美國.

5. 他渴極了,你有涼開水就請
你給他一點兒喝罷.

6. 我 朋 友 的 妹 妹 很 愛 吃 糖, 所 以 天 天 都 不 想 吃 飯.

7. 請 你 去 拿 一 碟 醬 油 來 給 我, 我 不 喜 歡 用 鹽 吃 菜 的.

8. 他 在 西 北 飯 店 住 了 一 個 多 禮 拜 就 到 我 家 裏 來 住 了.

9. 你 們 城 裏 一 共 有 幾 家 上 等 的 飯 店? 那 一 家 是 離 火 車 站 最 近 的?

10. 這 兒 有 六 把 匙 子, 都 是 用 銀 子 做 的, 我 想 價 錢 一 定 是 很 貴 的 了.

C. Render the following into Chinese:

1. Don't drink coffee at night. You may drink a glass of wine.

2. There is no Chinese cigarette for sale in America. You have to smoke American cigarettes.

3. He drinks tea with sugar and milk; how about you?

4. In telephoning him, did you put the call through?

5. Every day at breakfast he eats chicken eggs and drinks coffee.

6. He likes to drink pork soup, but does not like to eat cabbage.

7. My salt was all used up by him, but I still have a bottle of soybean sauce.

8. Some people like to eat fish; some people like to eat chicken.

9. Which hotel do you think is larger, the Hotel Shanghai or the Hotel Peking?

10. These two gentlemen have just come from China. This is Mr. Hsieh. That is Mr. Shih.

VOCABULARY CHARACTERS

(Mù)
Eye [*]; item, minor heading [*]

(Jú)
As; if [*]

(Kuŏ) Also written 菓.
Fruit [*]; result, outcome [*]

(Taǹ)
But [*]

(Erh́)
And, and yet; but, nevertheless; in order to [*]

(Ch'ieh́)
Moreover [*]

(Hsiaò)
To laugh, to laugh at

(K'ū)
To cry, to weep

(Añ)
Peace, peaceful [*]

(Yiñ)
Sound [*]

(Shenḡ) Often abbreviated to 声.
Sound, noise [*]; voice [*]; tone (of syllables)

(Shih́)
To begin [*]

(K'aŏ) Also written 攷.
To examine; examination [*]

(Shih́)
To try, to test

(Weñ)
Warm; to warm; (a surname)

(Hsí) Printed form 習.
To practice [*]

(Tā, Tá)
To answer, to reply

(Yinǵ)
To respond, to answer [*]

(Lò)
Happiness, happy [*]
(Yüeh́)
Music [*]

289

COMPOUNDS

答 應 (Tāyìng) To answer; to promise, to agree to, to consent to

平 安 (P'ingān) To be well and peaceful

如 果 (Júkuŏ) If, in case

但 是 (Tànshih) But, however

快 樂 (K'uàilo) Happy, happiness

音 樂 (Yīnyüeh) Music

開 始 (K'aīshih) To begin, to commence

高 興 (Kaōhsìng) Elated, pleased, to be in high spirits, to be keen on

考 試 (K'aŏshih) Examination, test

大 考 (Tàk'aŏ) Final examination

小 考 (Hsiaók'aŏ) Mid-quarter or mid-semester examination

溫 習 (Wēnhsí) To review; review

題 目 (T'ímu) Subject; heading; question

功 課 (Kūngk'ò) Schoolwork, lesson

果 子 (Kuŏtzu) Fruit
水 果 (Shuíkuŏ)

放 心 (Fànghsiñ) To be mentally at ease, to be free from anxiety

回 答 (Huítá) To answer, to reply

聲 音 (Shēngyin) Sound, voice, noise

音樂會 (Yīnyüeh-huì) Concert

開 會 (K'aī-huì) To hold a meeting, to begin a meeting

好 笑 (Haŏhsiaò) Laughable

青 年 (Ch'ingnieñ) Youth, a youth

青年會 (Ch'ingnieñ-huì) Young People's Association

男青年會 (Nań-ch'ingnieñ-huì) YMCA

女青年會 (Nǚ-ch'ingnieñhuì) YWCA

而 且 (Erhch'ieh) Moreover, also

不但...而且 (Pūtàn...erhch'ieh) Not only ... but also

學生會 (Hsüehsheng-huì) Students' association

會 員 (Huìyüań) Member of an organization

試 試 (Shìhshih) To try a little

大 聲 (Tàshenḡ) Loud, loudly

天 文 (T'ieñweń) Astronomy

READING MATERIAL

1. 我 剛 才 看 見 湯 明 道 先 生, 他
很 高 興 的 告 訴 我, 今 天 晚 上 我 們

請聽，你想不想聽音樂會？他要開一個音樂會，他很想請我們兩個人跟他一塊兒去聽。

很想於音樂你有沒有興趣？

他聽課於你有一定要去，是去喜歡就你看看會，我男歡在開看看我。

會兒功的，我想早一午有湯已下，你夫可着你我去了。

樂一你，很天上沒訴自天會工的，不果課裏舖完。

音他道有甚麼？以明晚怕就明開有用，如了城書開。

個跟知沒會所，我天恐你是員，遠下到你。

一人很去樂趣，今好，請甚麼生年？我會去兒以書來。好極了。

開個不夫音興不考習起，那學青罷？夫的校你塊可新回。

要兩我工開有去小溫不好罷，男了工會學送一我的兒。

校們是有常兒理都對去的道，生離車你候好塊。

學我可忙，非塊地課很，他裏知學會汽等時麼一。

2. 非塊地課很，他裏知

3. 常兒理都對去的道

4. 生離車你候好塊，我的兒

5. 那就好極了。我明天下午三

點就下課了，下了課我就馬上過來。

6. 就那麼辦罷。你這個學期念的幾門功課，都考完了小考沒有？

7. 還有中國文學跟數學兩門沒考。聽說要在下禮拜三四兩天考。上教員說學期出的題很長，才八個，而且很難。數學題目大，少一個。一位答完他就去了，他覺得題目不難了。我們個個覺得難，考得很慢，再看那麼難的題，覺得小考比大考還要回。這考得很慢，我就要哭，心裏頭希望回家。

8. 你聽聽，在外頭大聲說話的人是誰？聲音很像是我們的新同學黃雲天。你說是不是？

9. 是他了。他是不是要來找你？

10. 是，他要來跟我借小說看。前天他問我有沒有三國，我告訴他我有。他就問我借給他看看。

11. 你答應了他沒有？

12. 答應了．也許他現在來要書
了．他是很喜歡看小說的．

13. 三國我也沒看過．他看完了，
你可以借給我看麼？

14. 可以，他看完了，你就拿回家
去看罷．

15. 謝謝，我先走罷．明天下午再見．

16. 明天下午再見．

ROMANIZED TEXT OF READING MATERIAL

1. Wŏ kanḡts'aí k'aǹchien T'anḡ Minḡtaò hsiensheng, t'ā heň kaōhsinḡte kaòsu wo, chin̄t'ien wǎnshang wŏmen hsüeh̀hsiaò yaò k'aī īko yiñyüeh̀-huì. T'ā heň hsianǵ ch'ing women lianḡko jeń keň t'a īk'uàrh ch'ü t'inḡt'ing, k'ŏshih wŏ pū heň chih̄tao nite kunḡk'ò manḡ pumang, yŭ kunḡfu ch'ü meiyu.

2. K'aī yiñyüeh̀-huì ma? Wŏ tuìyú yiñyüeh feìch'anḡ yŭ hsinḡch'ü, sóí heň hsianǎ keň nimen īk'uàrh ch'ü, pūkuò wŏ minḡt'ien tsaŏshang yŭ īko tìlǐ hsiaók'aŏ, chin̄t'ien wǎnshang ītinḡ yaò pǎ kunḡk'ò toū weñhsíhaŏ, k'unǎp'à meí yŭ kunḡfu ch'ü le. Heň tuìpuch'ǐ. Ch'inǵ ni kaòsu T'anḡ hsiensheng pa.

3. Haŏ, nèma wŏ chiù tzùchǐ īko jeń keň t'a ch'ü pa. Hsüeh̀sheng-huì minḡt'ien hsiàwǔ yaò tsaì ch'enǵli te nań-ch'inḡnieńhuì k'aī-huì, nǐ ītinḡ īching chih̄tao le pa? Ní yŭ kunḡfu ch'ü meiyu?

4. Kunḡfu wŏ shih yŭ te, k'ŏshih wŏ pū shih hsüeh̀sheng-huìte huìyüań, yunḡpuchaó ch'ǜ. Nań-ch'inḡnieńhuì lí hsüeh̀hsiaò heň yüaň. Júkuó ní hsī-huan wo k'aī ch'ìch'ē sunḡ ni ch'ü, hsiàle k'ò wŏ chiù tsaì chèrh tenḡ ni, īk'uàrh taò ch'enǵli ch'ü. Nī k'aī-huì te shih̀hou, wŏ k'ói taò shūp'ù ch'ü k'aǹk'an yŭ shemma haŏ te hsiñ shū, nǐ k'aīwańle huì, wŏmen chiù īk'uàrh huílai.

5. Nà chiù hǎochí le. Wŏ minḡt'ien hsiàwǔ sañtieň chiù hsià-k'ò le, hsiàle k'ò wŏ chiù mǎshanḡ kuòlai.

6. Chiù nèma paǹ pa. Nǐ chèko hsüeh̀ch'í nieň te chīmeń kunḡk'ò, toū k'aŏwańle hsiaók'aŏ meiyu?

7. Haí yŭ Chunḡkuo weńhsüeh̀ keñ shùhsüeh liaňmeń meí k'aŏ. T'inḡ-shuō yaò tsaì hsià-līpaìsañ-szù liaň t'ieň k'aŏ. Shanḡ-hsüeh̀ch'í wŏmen k'aŏ shùhsüeh̀ tàk'aŏ te shih̀hou, chiaòyüań ch'ūle shih̄ko t'ímu keí women. T'ímu pūtaǹ heň ch'anḡ, erh̀ch'ieh heň nań. Tsuì shaŏ yaò yunḡ paǹko

chungt'oú ts'aí k'ói táwań iko, sóí wó chiȟ tále pāko. Yǔ iweì hsinġ-Chanġ te t'unġhsüeȟ, hsieȟ-tzù pí wo mańtetō, t'ā tále sañko, chiù meí yǔ shiȟ-chieñ tsaì táhsiach'ü. T'ā ch'àputō yaò k'ūch'ilai. Wǒ k'ańchienle t'ate yanġtzu, hsiñ lit'ou yù chüeȟte nańkuò, yù chüeȟte haǒhsiaò. Wǒ hsīwanġ chè huí hsiaók'aǒte t'ímu, pū yaò hsianġ shanġhui tàk'aǒte nèma nań le.

8. Nī t'inġt'ing, tsaì waìt'ou tàshenġ shuō-huà te jeń shiȟ shuí? Shenġyin heň hsianġ shiȟ wǒmente hsiñ t'unġhsüeñ Huanġ Yüńt'ieñ. Nī shuō shiȟ pushih?

9. Shiȟ t'ā le. T'ā shiȟ pushih yaò lai chaó ni?

10. Shiȟ, t'ā yaò lai keñ wo chieȟ hsiaǒshuō k'añ. Ch'ieńt'ien t'ā weñ wo yǔ meiyu *Sañkuó*, wǒ kaòsu t'a wó yǔ. T'ā chiù weñ wo chieȟ keī t'a k'añk'an.

11. Nǐ tāyingle t'a meiyu?

12. Tāying le. Yeȟhsǔ t'ā hsieñtsaì lai yaò shū le. T'ā shiȟ heń hsī-huan k'añ hsiaǒshuō te.

13. *Sañkuó* wó yeȟ meí k'añkuo. T'ā k'añwańle, ní k'ói chieȟ keí wo k'añ ma?

14. K'ói, t'ā k'añwańle, nǐ chiù náhui chiā ch'ü k'añ pa.

15. Hsieȟhsieh, wǒ hsieñ tsoū pa. Minġt'ien hsiàwǔ tsaì chieñ.

16. Minġt'ien hsiàwǔ tsaì chieñ.

NOTES

1. 菓, a variant of 果, is applicable only to the meaning of "fruit," not to that of "result" or "outcome."

2. When 如果 is used in the subordinate clause of a conditional sentence, it is necessary to use 就 in the co-ordinate clause to show the consequence which is stated therein. "If he wants to be literate, he must necessarily study" may be rendered into Chinese as 如果他要識字, 就一定要念書; "If he wants to buy this book, I will sell it to him" as 如果他要買這本書, 我就賣給他, etc. Since one of the primary functions of 就 is to indicate a consequence, its presence in the co-ordinate clause will imply the existence of a condition in the subordinate clause of the same sentence, thus making it sometimes unnecessary to use 如果. Examples: [如果] 他去, 我就去, "[If] he goes, I will go"; [如果] 他喜歡看書, 就可以看書, "[If] he likes to read, [he] may read."

3. 青年, literally "green years," means "youth, a youth" (cf. Shakespeare's "salad days," *Antony and Cleopatra*, Act I, scene 5). 青年會, "young people's association," is usually used to refer to either the YMCA or YWCA without specifying which. When 男 or 女 is used in front of it, the sexual reference is of course brought out clearly. The full names of the YMCA and YWCA in Chinese are, respectively, 基督教 (chītū chiaò, "Christian religion") 男青年會 and 基督教女青年會.

4. The proper classifier for 功課 is 門.

5. 小考, literally "small examination," may be understood as "mid-quarter" or "mid-semester" or "mid-term examination" and 大考 as "final examination."

6. 而 is primarily a particle in literary Chinese which may be used in different ways with different meanings. Usually, when it is used as an adversative particle, it means "but, yet, still." As a conjunctive particle it means "and," and as a purposive particle it means "in order to." It is introduced here mainly for the sake of the compound 而且, "but also, moreover."

7. The correlative conjunctions 不但···而且 mean "not only...but also." 他的房子不但很大，而且很新 means "His house is not only very big, but also very new."

8. 三國 in paragraph 10 of the Reading Material above is an abbreviation of the title of one of the most popular Chinese novels, the 三國志演義 (yĕnì) or *Popular History of the Three Kingdoms*, written by 羅貫中 (Ló Kuànchung) around the middle of the fifteenth century. It is a pseudo-historical novel consisting of one hundred and twenty chapters dealing with the happenings of the Three Kingdoms, A.D. 221–265. Each chapter is divided into two sections, each of which bears a summarizing caption or topic sentence. C. H. Brewitt-Taylor has translated it into English under the title of *San Kuo or Romance of the Three Kingdoms* (2 vols.; Shanghai, Hongkong, Singapore: Kelly & Walsh, Ltd., 1925).

9. In paragraphs 8 and 9 of the Reading Material there occur the sentences 聲音很像是我們的新同學黃雲天 and 是他了, respectively. In both sentences a person is identified simply by his voice. In terms of English grammar it would be more correct to add 的 after 黃雲天 and 他, but it is not necessary to do so in Chinese.

ORAL EXERCISES

A. Say the following in Chinese:

1. To review; to review lessons; to review old lessons; to review my geography lessons.

2. An examination; an easy examination; an extremely difficult examination.

3. Students' Association; YMCA; YWCA; members of the Students' Association; members of the YMCA; members of the YWCA.

4. Laughable. Is it laughable? It is quite laughable. It is not very laughable.

5. Happy; not happy; not quite happy; quite unhappy. Is he happy? Is he quite happy?

6. To begin; to begin to read; to begin to write; to begin to speak; fruit; to eat fruit; to like to eat fruit.

7. To answer; to answer a question; to know how to answer a difficult question.

8. If you laugh, I will laugh; if you cry, I will cry.

9. A sound. What sound? A sound quite good to listen to. There is no sound.

10. Not only big but also tall; not only expensive but also good.

B. Render the following into English:

1. T'ā heň kaōhsinġ; t'ā pū heň kaōhsinġ; t'ā heň pū kaōhsinġ.
2. Yiñyüeh-huì hsieǹtsaì k'aīshih̀ le, wǒmen k'uaì hsieh̀ tsòhaǒ pa.
3. Wǒ shih̀ huìyüań, t'ā yeh̀ shih̀ huìyüań, k'ǒshih nǐ pū shih̀.
4. T'ā kanġts'aí weǹ ni te huà, nǐ tále t'a meiyu?
5. Mǎ t'aìt'ai chiñt'ien hsiñ lit'ou heň k'uaìlo.
6. Nimen tsót'ien hsiàwǔ k'aīle huì meiyu?
7. Sheḿma shih̀hou k'aǒ tàk'aǒ a? Sañko lǐpaì ihoù k'aǒ.
8. T'ā shuō-huà te shengȳin heň hsianġ ni.
9. Nimen hsiaò shuí? Nimen hsiaò sheḿma?
10. Nǐ tāyingle t'a ch'ù̀, tseḿma haí meí ch'ù̀?

WRITTEN EXERCISES

A. Transcribe Section B, above, in Chinese.

B. Render the following into English:

1. 我聽了他説的話,真的覺得又想笑,又想哭.

2. 請問城裏的女青年會離火車站遠,還是離飛機場遠?

3. 我好幾天沒看見他們了.聽說他們不久就要考大考,我想他們的功課一定很忙罷?

4. 這兩課書是我要他們温習的,可是我不知道他們已經温習好了沒有.

5. 一頭兒笑,一頭兒哭是很難做得到的,你們自己試試就知道了.

6. 上禮拜三晚上去聽音樂會的人多不多? 你去了沒有?

7. 中國有中國的青年,美國有美國的青年.

8. 我們昨天晚上在石先生家裏談天,談到念音樂有甚麼好處,他就高興極了.

9. 中國不但地方非常大,而且人也很多,你說是不是?

10. 他們學校的學生會會員不多,所以常常開會.

11. 我們在學校都很平安,請你放心.

C.   Render the following into Chinese:

1.   Don't laugh at others; if you do, they will also laugh at you.

2.   There is a YMCA in our city, but there is no YWCA.

3.   I am studying four courses [schoolwork] this semester: geography, English literature, astronomy, and music.

4.   That lesson is too long; I have studied it once; but I have no time to review it.

5.   In three more days our final examination will begin; hence, I have to start reviewing my lessons tomorrow.

6.   Can you tell him that when he speaks he should not speak too loudly?

7.   If I have time this afternoon I will consent to go to the city with you by train.

8.   He is studying music in our school, hence he is very happy.

9.   If he is not keen on reading fiction, you should not lend him any more fiction to read.

10.   Typewriters now are not only very high in price, but also quite difficult to get.

VOCABULARY CHARACTERS

(Kù)
Old [*]; cause [*]

(Ch'ī)
Wife [*]

(Ch'iú)
To beg, to beseech, to seek

(Kuañ)
An official; official, governmental [*]

(Hsieǹ)
District, *hsien*

(Ch'í)
Strange [*]

(Kuaì)
Queer, odd; to blame

(Pù)
Cloth; to notify, to publish, to spread out, to display [*]

(Shañ)
Hill, mountain

(Shih̀)
World [*]; generation; a lifetime

(Chieh̀)
Realm [*]; boundary [*]

(Tsò)
(Unit of measure for mountains, buildings, etc.); a stand

(Mǐ)
Rice (hulled but uncooked); grain

(Ch'ǐh)
A Chinese foot (measure); ruler

(Toǔ)
A Chinese peck; a peck measure

(Liańg)
To measure
(Liaǹg)
Volume, capacity

(Ts'uǹ)
A Chinese inch

(Chaǹg)
Ten Chinese feet; elderly male person [*]

(Tiaò)
To fall, to drop; off, away, up [*]

COMPOUNDS

做官 (Tsò-kuañ) To be a government official

萬事 (Wànshih) All things

故事 (Kùshih) Story, tale

妻子 (Ch'ītzu) Wife

不如 (Pūjú) Not as good as; had better

縣官 (Hsiènkuañ) District magistrate

奇怪 (Ch'íkuaì) Strange

萬能 (Wànnéng) Almighty, omnipotent

兒女 (Erhnǚ) Sons and daughters, children

女兒 (Nǚerh) Daughter, girl

大量 (Tàliang) Broadminded

人家 (Jénchia) Other people

走過 (Tsoŭkuò) To pass by

大話 (Tàhuà) A boast

説大話 (Shuō tàhuà) To boast, to brag

去掉 (Ch'ùtiao) To take away, to remove

萬一 (Wànì) If by any chance

本事 (Peňshih) Ability, skill

世界 (Shiňchieh) World

世界上 (Shiňchiehshang) In the world

只好 (Chiňhaŏ) The only thing to do

白米 (Paímī) Hulled, uncooked rice

丈夫 (Changfu) Husband

掉下來 (Tiaòhsialai) To fall down, to drop down

英尺 (Yīngch'iň) Foot (12 English inches)

READING MATERIAL

萬事不求人

我知道你們是很喜歡聽故事的．今天我要把一個很有興趣的故事，説給你們聽．這個故事叫"萬事不求人．"

很久以前中國有一個人，家裏是很有錢的，可是那個時候離現在太久，所以他是姓甚麼的，名沒他一快麼，可是大事他都知道，在常甚麼就他一枝要大大的。知道甚麼地方住，非要大大的。地只裏想甚麼，他們兒女，以為一個，想做真的。一子，所想做真的。一天，他在大門上頭寫了"萬能的人"五個大字，給人家看，是多麼大的本事。

縣官出門，走過那門前頭，看見了，覺得很奇怪。心裏想："世上有萬能的人麼？我的見人要叫人去見他。"不知道到官那兒今天萬事不求甚，縣看求。他就上頭對他說，"我寫了'萬……"

住起子很他們買那個人家的。妻子很他買那個人家。記得個高興，以為甚麼的人，他不知道的。不久，縣官的大字就真不定是他錢的，會有的。喜歡說大話的怎樣的人。有錢的人，馬上就他大門的。

叫人一很，因可做能，在求知的大上是一看，叫要看你。甚記個高為以甚的人道不的真不定看有見見家。

字有有所樂，就以萬筆，不們。錢個界看人，他去麼官見。

...人.五個大字,是你寫的不是?"有錢的人回答説,"是我寫的".縣官説,"你一定是個萬能的人.現在我有三件事要你給我做來.第一件,我要像大路那麼長的布.第二件,我要像海水那麼多的酒.第三件,我要像大山那麼高,那麼大的牛.要是做不到,就得快快兒的把大字去掉."

有錢的人聽了縣官的話,就回到家裏,看見了他的妻子,覺得難過.他知道自己做不到那三件事,差不多的那三件事,都做不來,他自己不快樂.他的妻子問他為甚麼做那三件事.妻子説,"做那三件事,見縣官,量一量有多麼難.做罷.縣官叫你看山有多麼高,好問你甚麼.我教你一個法子:縣官叫你量海水跟山一樣長,海水量完了,這樣就對了.縣官要你把那多大的難處告訴縣官,就把縣官難住了.馬上,心裏多要把你告訴他,沒有拿他路多去,你請大高,好問題."

第二天有錢的人一早起來，
就拿了尺跟斗去見縣官，把妻子
教了他的話，對縣官說．縣官聽了
就沒有話可以說，只好叫有錢的
人回家去．
故事說完了．

ROMANIZED TEXT OF READING MATERIAL

Wànshih̀ pū ch'iú jeń

Wǒ chiñtao nimen shih̀ heń hsīhuan t'ing kùshih te. Chiñt'ien wǒ yaò pǎ īko heń yǔ hsingch'ü te kùshih, shuō keí nimen t'ing. Chèko kùshih chiaò "Wànshih̀ pū ch'iú jeń."

Heń chiú īch'ień Chungkuo yǔ īko jeń, chiāli shih̀ heń yǔ-ch'ień te, k'ǒshih nàko shih̀hou lí hsientsaì t'aì chiù, sói t'ā shih̀ hsing-shemma te, mingtzu chiaò shemma, chù tsaì nǎiko tìfang, toū meí yǔ jeń chìtech'ilai le. Wǒmen chih̀ chiñtao t'a yǔ īko ch'ītzu keñ chǐko erhnǔ, chù tsaì īsó heń kaō heń tà te fangtzu lit'ou, feīch'ang k'uaìlo. Yīnweì t'āmen yǔ-ch'ień, sói hsiang yaò shemma, chiù k'ói maï shemma, hsiang tsò shemma, yeh chiù k'ói tsò shemma. Nàko jeń cheñte īweí t'a shih̀ wànneng te jeń. Yǔ ī t'ieñ, t'ā chiù yung īchih̀ tà pī, tsaì t'ā chiāte tàmeń shangt'ou hsiehle "Wànshih̀ pū ch'iú jeń" wǔko tà tzù, keī jeńchia k'aǹ, yaò t'amen chiñtao t'ate peñshih, shih̀ tóma tà te.

Pū chiǔ, hsièkuañ ch'ū-meń, tsoūkuò nàko yǔ-ch'ień te jeńte tàmeń ch'ieńt'ou, k'aǹchienle nà wǔko tà tzù, chiù chüehte heñ ch'íkuaì. Hsiñli hsiang: "Shih̀chiehshang cheñte huì yǔ wànneng te jeń ma? Wǒ k'aǹ shih̀ pū huì yǔ te. Hsieh̀ chè wǔko tà tzù te jeń, ītiñg shih̀ hsīhuan shuō tàhuà te. Wǒ yaò chieñ t'a, k'aǹk'an t'a shih̀ tsemyang te jeń." T'ā chiù chiaò jeń ch'ü chiaò yǔ-ch'ień te jeń ch'ü chieñ t'a.

Yǔ-ch'ień te jeń pū chiñtao hsièkuañ weìshemma yaò chieñ t'a, chiù māshang taò kuañ nàrh ch'ü. Hsièkuañ k'aǹchienle t'a chiù tuì t'a shuō, "Wǒ chiñt'ien k'aǹchien ni chiāte tàmeńshang hsiehle 'Wànshih̀ pū ch'iú jeń' wǔko tà tzù, shih̀ ni hsieh̀ te pushih?" Yǔ-ch'ień te jeń huítá shuō, "Shih̀ wó hsieh̀ te." Hsièkuañ shuō, "Nǐ ītiñg shih̀ ko wànneng te jeń. Hsientsaì wó yǔ sañchieñ shih̀ yaò ni keí wo tsòlai. Tìīchieñ, wǒ yaò hsiang tà lù nèma ch'ang te pù. Tìerh̀chieñ, wǒ yaò hsiang haí shuí nèma tō te chiǔ. Tìsañchieñ, wǒ yaò hsiang shañ nèma kaō, nèma tà te niú. Yaòshih nǐ tsòputaò, chiù teī k'uaìk'uārhte pǎ tàmeńshang te tà tzù ch'ùtiao."

Yǔ-ch'ień te jeń t'ingle hsièkuañte huà, chiù māshang chiñtao tzùchǐ tsòputaò nà sañchieǹ shih̀, hsiñ lit'ou heň pū k'uaìlo. Huítaò chiāli, ch'àputō yaò k'ūch'ilai. T'āte ch'ītzu k'aǹchienle t'ate yanǵtzu, chiù weǹ t'a weì-sheḿma chüeh́te nańkuò. T'ā pǎ hsieǹkuañ yaò t'a tsò te nà sañchieǹ shih̀, toū kaòsule ch'ītzu. Ch'ītzu shuō, "Tsò nà sañchieǹ shih̀, meí yū shemma nańch'u. Wǒ chiaō ni tseḿma tsò pa. Nǐ ná īpá ch'ih̀ keñ īko toū ch'ü chieǹ hsieǹkuañ, ch'iñǧ t'a yunǵ nà liaňgyaǹg tunḡhsi, hsiéñ ch'ü lianǵiliang tà lù yǔ tó ch'anǵ, haí shuí yǔ tōshaǒ, shañ yǔ tó kaō tó tà. T'ā lianǵwańle chiù kaòsu ni, chiaò ni haǒ ch'ü tsò. Nǐ chèyang tuì t'a shuō, wǒ k'aǹ shemma weǹt'í chiù toū meí yū le."

Tìerh̀ t'ieñ yǔ-ch'ieǹ te jeń ītsaó ch'ǐlai, chiù nále ch'ih̀ keñ toū ch'ü chieǹ hsieǹkuañ, pǎ ch'ītzu chiaōle t'a te huà, tuì hsieǹkuañ shuō. Hsieǹ-kuañ t'iǹgle chiù meí yū huà k'ói shuō, chih̀haǒ chiaò yūch'ieñ te jeń huí-chiā ch'ü.

Kùshih shuōwań le.

NOTES

1. 萬能, literally "ten thousand [ways] capable," comes very close to connoting the idea of "all powerful" or "omnipotent." Being the highest number in notation, 萬 is frequently used to form compounds to mean "a myriad" or "all": 萬事 (waǹshih̀), "all things"; 萬國 (waǹkuó), "all the nations or countries"; 萬民 (waǹmiń), "all the people"; 萬物 (waǹwù), "all things, all creation"; 萬世, "all generations"; etc.

2. 大話, literally "big words," means "a boast" (cf. "a tall story"). The verb meaning "to boast, to brag" is 説大話.

3. 掉 is often used as a co-verb with another verb to indicate the direction of the action expressed by the latter. When used as such it may be rendered into English by "away, off, up," etc. Thus: 去掉 means "to take off, to remove"; 吃掉, "to eat up"; 賣掉, "to sell out"; etc.

4. Note that the Chinese equivalent for "in the world" is 世界上.

5. 尺, or a Chinese foot, is a length measurement consisting of ten 寸, or Chinese inches, each of which consists of ten 分. One 尺 is equivalent to 14.1 inches or .3581 meters. Ten 尺 make one 丈 and 180 丈 make one 里 (cf. Lesson Twenty-seven). In measuring land, however, an additional unit, 步 (cf. Lesson Thirty-seven), consisting of five 尺, is used. The use of 尺 and 丈 whenever the number of 寸 and 尺, respectively, exceeds ten is compulsory. Thus, for "eighteen inches," for example, we should not say 十八寸, but 一尺八寸, and, similarly, for "thirty-four feet" we should not say 三十四尺, but 三丈四尺. Since 分, 寸, 尺, 步, 丈, 里 are all units of measure, they may be used immediately after cardinal numbers.

6. In indicating height, length, or weight in Chinese, 有 rather than 是 is the verb to use. Thus, "How tall is this mountain?" is 這座山有多高?; "This piece of cloth is five feet four inches long," 這塊布有五尺四寸長. But frequently the verb 有 is omitted; hence, one may very well say 這座山多高? 這塊布五尺四寸長, etc.

7. 斗 is a dry measure often referred to in English as a "Chinese peck." A standard 斗 contains 316 cubic inches. Ten 斗 make a 石 (tàn, also written 擔), which is a picul (133-1/3 pounds) and which should not be confused with 石, "rock, stone" (cf. Lesson Thirty-nine). One 斗 consists of ten 升 (sheng, "Chinese quart").

8. When 布 is used as a verb it may also be written 佈, which is similarly pronounced (pù).

ORAL EXERCISES

A. Say the following in Chinese:

1. A mountain; a big mountain; a high mountain; the mountain is higher than the sea.

2. A foot of cloth; six feet of cloth; ten feet of cloth; thirteen feet of cloth.

3. This is my daughter. His daughter is here. Have you any daughter?

4. There is no such thing in the world. There are very many people in the world.

5. A long story; a short story; I like to hear stories; he likes to tell stories.

6. Mr. Hsieh is a broad-minded person; you may ask him to go with you.

7. How much rice do you want to buy? I want to buy a [Chinese] peck of rice.

8. Isn't that strange? That is very strange. This is not very strange.

9. I thought they were your children. I thought these were your friends.

10. Have you a ruler? Give me that ruler, please.

B. Render the following into English:

1. Chèko shih wŏte shihchieh, yeh shih nimente shihchieh.

2. Chungkuo-ch'ih ch'ang, haíshih Yingch'ih ch'ang?

3. Ī lí yŭ īpaĭ pāshih chang, ī chang yŭ shih ch'ih, ī ch'ih yŭ shih ts'un.

4. Nimente hsienkuan shih hsing-shemma te?

5. T'ā chiaò wo ch'ǜ, wó chihhaŏ ch'ǜ, t'ā pū chiaò ni ch'ǜ, nĭ chiù chihhaŏ pū ch'ǜ.

6. Nĭ chiaò t'a laí, t'ā yeh shih pū yüani laí te le, pūjú chiù pūyaò chiaò t'a laí pa.

7. T'ā chen penshih, yù huì tǎ-tzù, yù huì k'aī ch'ìch'ē.

8. Wŏ chiaò t'a laí, t'ā meí laí, wŏ chiaò ni ch'ǜ, ní yeh meí ch'ǜ, nĭ shuō ch'íkuaì puch'íkuai?

9. T'ā hen aì shuō tàhuà te, sói t'ā yaò tuì ni shuō shemma, nĭ toū pūyaò t'īng.

10. Hsienkuañte ch'ītzu hsing-Chang, shih Shanghaĭ-jen, pū shih Peĭp'ing-jen.

WRITTEN EXERCISES

A. Transcribe Section B, above, in Chinese.

B. Render the following into English:

1. 中國有一句話說得好,"求人不如求己",就是做事求人家沒有求自己那麼好的意思.

2. 他的朋友張平山先生一共有五個兒女,三個兒子,兩個女兒.

3. 飛機場後頭有兩座山,山上沒有房子,只有很多的高樹.

4. 你說的中國話非常好,人家聽見了一定以為你是在中國念過大學的.

5. 我昨天不知道他是你的哥哥,我還以為他是你的父親呢!

6. 世界上有很多奇怪的東西,是我們沒看見過的.

7. 他不但很有本事,而且人很大量.

8. 你們已經看完了書,在這兒沒有甚麼別的事再可以做的了,不如回家去罷.

9. 石先生很想在城裏買一所

房子,可是找來找去也找不着好
的,現在只好在中國飯店住着.
　　10.有人告訴我他的丈夫去年
到美國去了,到現在還沒回來.

C. Render the following into Chinese:

1. This piece of cloth is longer than that piece by thirty-seven inches.

2. Have you written down the strange story which Mrs. Mǎ told us last night?

3. The new books which you saw in the bookstore have already been sold out.

4. How many countries are there altogether in the world? Which is the largest? Which is the smallest?

5. He is very busy; the only thing for him to do is to ask his daughter to escort you to the airfield.

6. Now that you know he cannot read newspapers, do you still think that he is literate?

7. Don't put the newspaper on his desk! If by any chance he sees his name there, he will be greatly displeased.

8. Don't brag! No one would like a braggart!

9. It is unlikely that he will see you this afternoon. You had better go!

10. A man of ability can do great things; a man without ability cannot do anything.

VOCABULARY CHARACTERS

(Pìng)
Sick, sickness; to be sick

(Shāng)
To injure, to wound; injury, wound

(T'eńg)
To pain, to hurt; to love fondly; pain, ache

(Fā)
To send out; to develop; to break out with (an illness); to become, to turn

(Shaō)
To burn, to roast; fever [*]

(Tù)
Standard, measure [*]; degree

(Shìh)
Market; municipality

(Lì)
To set up, to stand; instantly [*]

(Ī) Often abbreviated to 医.
Medicine; to heal

(Yüàn)
Court, institution, courtyard [*]; a principal branch of the Chinese government

(Hsiū)
To rest; rest [*]

(Hsí)
To rest; rest [*]; to put out (as fire or light); interest [*]

(Yaò)
Medicine, drug

(K'ŭ)
Bitter, miserable; hard, intensely [*]

(P'eì)
To match, to be fit to, to qualify

(Hańg)
Row, line; guild, profession [*]; business, firm [*]

(Chīh)
To pay, to draw money; to support [*]; branch, division [*]

(K'eň)
To be willing to

(Huàn)
To change, to exchange

(Pāng) Also written 帮, 帮.
To help

COMPOUNDS

病人 (Pìngjeń) Sick person, patient

病好 (Pìnghǎo) To get well, to recover from illness

傷風 (Shāngfeng) To catch cold

發燒 (Fā-shaō) To run a fever

頭疼 (T'oút'eng) Headache

熱度 (Jètù) Body temperature

市立 (Shìhlì) Operated by the city; municipal

國立 (Kuólì) Operated by the country; national

醫院 (Īyüàn) Hospital

醫生 (Īsheng) / 大夫 (Taìfu) } Doctor, physician

藥水 (Yaòshuǐ) Liquid medicine

中藥 (Chungyaò) Chinese medicine

西藥 (Hsīyaò) Western medicine

城市 (Ch'engshìh) Cities, municipalities

配藥 (P'eì-yaò) To compound medicines, to fill a prescription

藥房 (Yaòfang) Modern-style drugstore

藥舖 (Yaòp'ù) Chinese-style drug shop

方子 (Fangtzu) Prescription

開方子 (K'aī fangtzu) To write a prescription

現錢 (Hsieñch'ień) Ready cash

支票 (Chihp'iaò) A check

幫忙 (Pang-mang) To help, to assist

有名 (Yǔ-ming) / 出名 (Ch'ūming) } Famous, renowned

吃苦 (Ch'ih-k'ǔ) To endure hardship

苦心 (K'ǔhsiñ) To take great pains, hard

休息 (Hsiūhsi) Rest, to rest

銀行 (Yińhang) Bank

市政府 (Shìh-chengfǔ) Municipal government

吃藥 (Ch'ih-yaò) To take medicine

READING MATERIAL

1. 平山,老沒見了. 你近來好罷?
2. 國安,我還好,謝謝. 你也好罷?
3. 還沒有甚麼. 不過這四五天以來有一點兒忙.

4. 現在學校不是放着春假麼?怎麼在家裏忙啊?

5. 我妹妹自從上禮拜五就病了,到現在還沒有好呢!在家裏的病了,

6. 他有甚麼病啊?

7. 上禮拜五早起來就傷了風,同時又發燒,睡覺也睡得最不好,頭很不好;上禮拜五早上來就高,最想吃,到晚上高得一百零三度;後來熱度甚麼不好.

8. 你們請了大夫沒有?他們請一位大夫,大夫說疼休息再想一個;他們請了他頭疼息再,這說疼休息過你鐘他回吃,大國立大美市立醫院;大夫姓馬,名字叫定通,在西醫院病麼用會一定回西藥,每樣藥,一非常苦,四妹妹的,個妹妹的;國立妹沒有行天吃一是也水是,有普緊,着的是;他最是要不好呢?

9. 請我夫風休息去,是大傷裏醫院;的是大傷裏院的的家醫藥;

10. 我幾是吃頭告訴,了,頭訴難;

11. 是吃我吃.難吃.鐘告很

12. 你手裏拿着的是甚麼？是不是方子？
13. 是的,是馬定大夫剛才開的.我要到藥房裏去,配好了就拿回家給妹妹吃.
14. 藥房在甚麼地方？離這兒遠不遠？
15. 在市立銀行旁邊兒,離這兒不很遠,走路五分鐘就到了.
16. 那好極了,我也要到市立銀行去.我們一塊兒走好不好？
17. 很好.你要到市立銀行去做甚麼？
18. 你不知道了.我的現錢差不多用完了.我有兩張支票,一張是三十五塊的,一張是五塊的.可是我從禮拜六一個人到上海,市立銀行裏頭做事的他們我一個也不認識,不知道他們肯不肯給我把支票換現錢.那兒你認識誰呢？
19. 認識一位姓江的,名字叫秋光,在那兒做事做了十多年了.我……

可 以 把 你 介 紹 給 他. 你 請 他 幫 忙
就 行 了.

20. 好, 謝 謝, 再 過 兩 三 天, 你 妹 妹
病 好 了, 我 就 到 你 的 家 裏 去 看 你.
再 見 再 見!

21. 再 見 再 見!

ROMANIZED TEXT OF READING MATERIAL

1. P'ingshañ, laŏ meí chieǹ le. Nī chiǹlai haŏ pa?
2. Kuóañ, wŏ haí haŏ, hsiehhsieh. Ní yeĥ haŏ pa?
3. Haí meí yŭ shemma, pūkuò chè szù-wŭ t'ieñ ĩlaí yŭ ĩtiărh mang.
4. Hsieǹtsaì hsüeĥhsiaò pū shih fangche ch'uñchià ma? Tsemma mang a?
5. Wŏte meìmei tzùts'ung shang-līpaìwŭ chiù tsaì chiāli piǹg le, taò hsieǹtsaì haí meí yú haŏ ne!
6. T'ā yŭ shemma piǹg a?
7. Shang-līpaìwú tsaŏshang t'ā chiù shangle feñg, houlaí t'oú chiù t'engch'ilai le, t'uñgshiĥ yù fā-shaŏ, jètù heñ kaō, tsuì kaō kaōtaò ĩpaī ling sañ tù, shemma yeĥ pū hsiaňg ch'iĥ, waňshang shuìchiaò yeĥ shuìte pū haŏ.
8. Nĭmen ch'iňgle taìfu meiyu?
9. Ch'iňgle ĩweì Meĭkuo taìfu, hsiǹg-Mātiňg te, shih wŏmen chèrh Shiĥlì-īyüaǹ tsuì yŭ- míng te taìfu. T'ā shuō wo meìmeite piǹg shih pŭt'uñg te shangfeñg-t'oút'enā-piǹg, meí yŭ shemma yaòchiň, tsaì chiāli hsiūhsi-hsiuhsi chiù hsiǹg le, yuǹgpuchaó taò īyüaǹ ch'ü. Tsaì kuò sañ-szù t'ieñ chiù huì haŏ te le.
10. Wó hsiang ni meìmei ch'iĥ te ĩtiǹg shih hsīyaò le, chĩko chunḡt'oú ch'iĥ ĩ huí ne?
11. Shih te, t'ā ch'iĥ te shih hsīyaò, meĭ szùko chunḡt'oú ch'iĥ ĩ huí, waňshang yeĥ shih ĩyaǹg. Meìmei kaòsu wo t'ā ch'iĥ te yaòshui shih feīch'áng k'ŭ te, heň nańch'iĥ.
12. Ní shoúli náche te shih shemma? Shih fangtzu pushih?
13. Shih te, shih Mātiňg taìfu kanḡts'aí k'aī te. Wŏ yaò taò yaòfang p'eì-yaò ch'ü, p'eìhaŏle chiù náhui chiāli ch'ü keī meìmei ch'iĥ.
14. Yaòfang tsaì shemma tìfang? Lí chèrh yüaň puyüan?
15. Tsaì Shiĥlì-yińhang p'angpierh, lí chèrh pū heń yüaň, tsoŭ-lù wŭfeñ chunḡ chiù taò le.
16. Nà haŏchí le, wó yeĥ yaò taò Shiĥlì-yińhang ch'ü. Wŏmen ĩk'uàrh tsoú haŏ puhao?
17. Heń haŏ. Nī yaò taò Shiĥlì-yińhang ch'ü tsò shemma?
18. Nī pū chiĥtao le. Wŏte hsieňch'ień ch'àputō yuǹgwań le. Wó yú

lianǧchanḡ chiȟp'iaò, īchanḡ shiȟ wǔshiȟk'uaì ch'ień te, īchanḡ shiȟ sañshihwǔk'uaì te. Wǒ yaò taò nàrh ch'ü huaȟ hsiench'ień. K'ǒshih wǒ ts'unǵ Shanǧhaǐ taòle chèrh, pū kuò wǔ-liùko lǐpaì, tsaì Shiȟlì yińhang lit'ou tsò-shiȟ te jeń, īko yeȟ pū jeȟshih. Pū chiȟtao t'amen k'eȟ puk'en keí wo pǎ chiȟp'iaò huaȟ hsiench'ień. Nàrh nǐ jeȟshih shuí ne?

19. Jeȟshih īweǐ hsing̀-Chianḡ te, minǵtzu chiaò Ch'iūkuanǧ, tsaì nàrh tsò-shiȟ tsòle shiȟ-tō nień le. Wó k'ói pá ni chieȟshaò keǐ t'a. Ní ch'inǧ t'a panḡ-mań chiù hsing le.

20. Haǒ, hsieȟhsieh. Tsaì kuò lianǧ-sañ t'ień, nǐ meìmei ping̀haǒle, wǒ chiù taò nite chiāli ch'ü k'aȟ ni. Tsaì chień tsai chien!

21. Tsaì chień tsai chien!

NOTES

1. 老沒見 in sentence 1 of the Reading Material above is a more or less set expression, meaning "[I] have not seen [you] for a long while."

2. 傷風 is a verb-object compound meaning "to catch cold." Treat it in the same way as you do all other similar verb-object compounds.

3. Note that 病 may be used as a verb, 他病了, "He has fallen sick"; as a noun, 他的是甚麼病, "What is his sickness?" or 他有病, "He is sick [has sickness]"; and as an adjective, 病人多不多, "Are the patients [sick people] numerous?" Usually the usage will make it clear which is meant.

4. 發燒, "to run a fever," literally means "to develop fever" and is another verb-object compound.

5. 度, "standard, measure," is often used to mean a degree in astronomy or geography, and in thermometers, barometers, etc. 熱度, literally "heat degree," means "temperature." In sentence 7 of the Reading Material above, 熱度很高，最高高到一百零三度 may be rendered into English as "[His] temperature was very high, [at its] highest [being so] high [as to] reach 103 degrees." Regarding the use of 到, see Note 5, Lesson Thirty-eight.

6. Note that the pronunciation of 大 in the compound 大夫 is *taì*. Both 大夫 and 醫生 mean "physician, doctor," but the former is more popular than the latter, especially in North China. When 大夫 or 醫生 is used as a title, like 先生, it is placed immediately after a person's name. For instance, "Dr. Shih" becomes 石大夫 or 石醫生.

7. 馬定 in sentence 9 of the Reading Material above represents one of several possible ways in which the name "Martin" may be transliterated by the use of Chinese characters. So far there has been no standard for determining which Chinese character should be used for transliterating any given non-Chinese syllable. The principle to bear in mind is that whenever and wherever possible, try to use those Chinese characters which will transliterate most accurately the original syllables and which will, in the case of a personal name, bear greatest resemblance to a typical name in Chinese.

8. 幫忙 is a verb-object compound, literally "to help busy," hence, "to

help, to assist." It is an intransitive verb: 你要請誰幫忙, "Whom do you want to ask to help?"; 我要請他幫忙, "I want to ask him to help." But when it is used transitively, the general practice is to insert an object in its genitival rather than accusative form as is the practice in English. Thus, "I want to help him" becomes 我要幫他的忙; "He is very glad to help me," 他很喜歡幫我的忙; etc.

ORAL EXERCISES

A. Say the following in Chinese:

1. A hospital; a drugstore; a doctor; a bank; a check.
2. The patients in the hospital; the doctors who live in the hospital; the drugstores run by him.
3. A check for twenty dollars and fifty-five cents; a check for two hundred dollars and eighty-seven cents.
4. A bottle of liquid medicine; to buy a bottle of liquid medicine; to buy a bottle of liquid medicine with ready cash.
5. To qualify; not to qualify; to qualify to teach; to qualify to be a teacher; not to qualify to be a doctor.
6. Is this bitter? Not very bitter. Is he in distressing circumstances? He is in very distressing circumstances.
7. Please rest a little! Please rest here a little! Please rest at home a little.
8. I help you, you help him, and he helps me.
9. Three times; five times; at least four times; at most eight times.
10. Famous books; the most famous book; the most famous hospital in China; the most famous university in America.

B. Render the following into English:

1. Ní yŭ shemma pin̆g? Wŏ meí-yŭ shemma pin̆g.
2. T'ā shan̆g-lĭpaì fāle lianğ t'ieñ shaō, k'ŏshih jètù pū heñ kaō.
3. T'ā tsaì lìt'ou tsŏ shemma? T'ā tsaì lìt'ou keí wo shaō-shuĭ.
4. Ní hsĭhuan ch'iĥ Chūnğyaò, haíshih hsīyaò a?
5. T'ā tsaì Shanğhaĭ shiĥ-chen̆gfú lìt'ou tsŏ shemma shiĥ?
6. Chè shiĥ yaòp'ù, pū shiĥ yaòfanğ. Yaòp'ù shiĥ maì chūnğyaò te, yaòfanğ shiĥ maì hsīyaò te.
7. Wó chiĥ yŭ īchanğ chiĥp'iaò, meí-yŭ hsieñch'ieñ.
8. Ch'in̆g weñ nàweì taìfu hsinğ-shemma, shiĥ nǎi kuóte jeñ!
9. Wŏ tìti tsuì chiñ chè lianğko yüeĥ feīch'anğ k'ŭhsiñ hsüeĥ yīnyüeĥ.
10. Wŏmente tàhsüeĥ shiĥ kuólì te, pū shiĥ shihlì te.

WRITTEN EXERCISES

A. Transcribe Section B, above, in Chinese.

B. Render the following into English:

1. 中國有一句很有意思的話，就是"吃得苦中苦，方¹為人上人."

2. 張大夫，我今天沒有甚麼事，如果你要我在醫院裏頭幫你的忙，就請你告訴我，千萬不要客氣.

3. 中國北部有出名的國立大學，南部也有出名的國立大學.

4. 中國銀行是中國的國立銀行，不是上海的市立銀行.

5. 今天熱極了，我看報看了不過一個鐘頭，就覺得頭疼了.

6. 他是常常傷風的，這兒風太大，叫他不要坐在你旁邊兒寫信罷.

7. 這本小說太長，我不喜歡看，你可以給我換一本短一點兒的不可以？

8. 錢大夫開了方子就走了，他叫你在家裏休息，我可以給你到藥房去配藥.

9. 他昨天才發完燒，所以今天不肯跟我們一塊兒走路到銀行換錢去.

¹ Means the same as 才 (纔).

10. 如 果 他 真 的 不 知 道 太 平 洋
跟 大 西 洋 在 那 兒, 他 就 不 配 做 我
們 的 地 理 教 員 了.

C. Render the following into Chinese:

1. I haven't any ready cash to give you, but may I write you a check for five dollars?

2. I think that hospital has at least fifty patients and at most two doctors.

3. That drugstore is run by Mr. White; this drug shop is run by Mr. T'ang.

4. Dr. Martin, please tell me. Is my temperature high? Has it reached 102 degrees?

5. My head is aching. I had better rest here a little. I am afraid I cannot help you.

6. Has he taken his medicine yet? The doctor says he has to take it once every two hours.

7. These two patients are well again. They can leave the hospital and go home today.

8. The University of Peking is a Chinese national university. It is a very famous university.

9. Please tell him I am not a doctor; hence, I cannot write any prescription for him.

10. He has a lot of leisure. I don't know why he is not willing to help me.

Lesson FORTY-FIVE

A Review Lesson

CHARACTERS

Number of Strokes	Characters	Pronunciation and Tone	Meaning	Lesson Reference
Three	山	Shan̄	Hill, mountain	43
	寸	Ts'uǹ	A Chinese inch	43
	丈	Chang̀	Ten Chinese feet	43
Four	尺	Ch'ih̆	A Chinese foot; ruler	43
	斗	Toŭ	A Chinese peck; a peck measure	43
	支	Chih̄	To pay, to draw money; to support; branch, division	44
Five	加	Chiā	To add; plus	41
	目	Mù	Eye; item, minor heading	42
	且	Ch'ieh̆	Moreover	42
	世	Shih̀	World; generation, lifetime	43
	布	Pù	Cloth; to notify, to publish, to spread out, to display	43
	市	Shih̀	Market; municipality	44
	立	Lì	To set up, to stand; instantly	44
Six	如	Jú	As; if	42
	而	Erh́	And, and yet; but, nevertheless; in order to	42
	安	An̄	Peaceful, peace	42
	考	K'aŏ	To examine, examination	42
	米	Mǐ	Rice (hulled but uncooked); grain	43
	休	Hsiū	To rest, rest	44

316

Number of Strokes	Characters	Pronunciation and Tone	Meaning	Lesson Reference
Six	行	Hang̒	Row, line; guild, profession; business, firm	44
Seven	位	Weì	(Classifier for persons); seat, position	41
	但	Taǹ	But	42
	求	Ch'iú	To beg, to beseech, to seek	43
Eight	咖	K'ā / Chiā	(For transliterating "cof" of "coffee")	41
	油	Yú	Oil, fat, grease; paint, to paint	41
	店	Tieǹ	Store, shop	41
	抽	Ch'oū	To draw, to pull	41
	果	Kuǒ	Fruit; result, outcome	42
	始	Shiȟ	To begin	42
	妻	Ch'ī	Wife	43
	官	Kuañ	An official; official, governmental	43
	奇	Ch'í	Strange	43
	怪	Kuaì	Queer; to blame	43
	肯	K'eň	To be willing to	44
Nine	香	Hsianḡ	Fragrant, to smell good; incense	41
	音	Yiñ	Sound	42
	故	Kù	Old; cause	43
	界	Chieȟ	Realm; boundary	43
	度	Tù	Standard, measure; degree	44
	苦	K'ǔ	Bitter, miserable; hard, intensely	44
Ten	酒	Chiǔ	Wine, liquor	41

Number of Strokes	Characters	Pronunciation and Tone	Meaning	Lesson Reference
Ten	笑	Hsiaò	To laugh, to laugh at	42
	哭	K'ū	To cry, to weep	42
	座	Tsò	(Classifier for mountains, buildings, etc.); a stand	43
	病	Piǹ	Sick; sickness; to be sick	44
	疼	T'enǵ	To pain, to hurt; to love fondly; pain, ache	44
	院	Yüaǹ	Court, institution, courtyard; principal branch of Chinese government	44
	息	Hsí	To rest; rest; to put out (fire); interest	44
	配	P'eì	To match, to fit, to qualify	44
Eleven	啡	Feī	(For transliterating "fee" of "coffee")	41
	魚	Yǘ	Fish	41
	蛋	Taǹ	Egg	41
	甜	T'ień	Sweet	41
	匙	Ch'iħ	Spoon	41
	習	Hsí	To practice	42
	掉	Tiaò	To fall, to drop; off, away, up	43
Twelve	湯	T'anǵ	Soup; (a surname)	41
	渴	K'ŏ	Thirsty	41
	溫	Weñ	Warm; to warm; (a surname)	42
	答	Tā, Tá	To answer, to reply	42
	量	{Lianǵ / Liaǹ	To measure / Volume, capacity	43 / 43
	發	Fā	To send out; to develop; to break out with (illness); to become, to turn	44
	換	Huaǹ	To change, to exchange	44

Number of Strokes	Characters	Pronunciation and Tone	Meaning	Lesson Reference
Thirteen	煙	Yeñ	Smoke; tobacco	41
	愛	Aì	To love; to love to, to like to; love	41
	試	Shih̀	To try, to test	42
	傷	Shañg	To injure, to wound; injury, wound	44
Fifteen	樂	Lò / Yüeh̀	Happiness; happy / Music	42 / 42
Sixten	鴨	Yā	Duck	41
	糖	T'anǵ	Sugar; candy	41
	縣	Hsieǹ	District, *hsien*	43
	燒	Shaō	To burn, to roast; fever	44
Seventeen	聲	Sheñg	Sound, voice, noise; tone (of syllables)	42
	應	Yiǹg	To respond, to answer	42
	幫	Pañg	To help	44
Eighteen	雞	Chī	Chicken	41
	醬	Chiaǹg	Thick sauce; jam	41
	醫	Ī	Medicine; to heal	44
Nineteen	藥	Yaò	Medicine, drug	44
Twenty	鹹	Hsień	Salty	41
Twenty-four	鹽	Yeń	Salt	41

ORAL DRILL

A. Say the following in Chinese:

1. story   music   to review
husband   laughable   to answer
wife   cigarette   elated
daughter   wine   YMCA

doctor	coffee	YWCA
check	ruler	candy
concert	strange	rice (hulled but uncooked)
hotel	famous	to rest
spoon	drugstore	bitter
happy	cash	liquid medicine

2. a ruler   a mountain
    a pack of cigarettes   a check
    a peck of rice (uncooked)   a concert
    a piece of cloth   a hospital
    a foot of cloth   a doctor
    a bottle of soybean sauce   a bank
    a chicken egg   a prescription
    a hotel   a patient
    an examination   a glass of wine
    a world   a drugstore

3. at most   to tell lies
    at least   broad-minded
    to suffer hardship   to think that
    the only thing to do   had better
    to write a prescription   not only . . . but also

4. Please smoke!
    I don't smoke, thank you.
    I have just smoked a cigarette.
    Please have some candy.
    Does he drink wine?
    Did he drink wine last night?
    Does he love to eat Chinese food?
    He likes to drink tea, I like to drink coffee.
    Please give me a spoon.
    Did he put the telephone call through?
    Is this vegetable called cabbage?
    Do you have American cigarettes?
    Is this chicken or duck?
    Is this a chicken egg or a duck egg?
    This is soybean sauce. Do you want any?
    No, thank you. Please give me some salt.
    What soup is this?
    This is chicken soup.
    This is duck soup.
    This is vegetable soup.
    This is not beef soup.
    Don't laugh! Don't laugh aloud?
    Don't cry! Don't cry too loudly!
    Whom are you laughing at?

Please answer me.
Please don't answer him.
Please don't answer that question.
Where is the YMCA?
Where is the YWCA?
Are you a member of the Students' Association?
He is not very pleased.
Why is he not very pleased?
When does the concert begin?
Whose voice is that?
Are you happy? Why aren't you very happy?
Whose is this piece of cloth?
How long is this piece of cloth?
It is twenty-six inches long.
It is thirteen feet long.
What is the name of their district magistrate?
Please tell me a long story.
That story is quite interesting.
What did he beg you to do?
Please ask him to measure this.
How tall is this mountain?
What illness does he have?
Where is the municipal hospital?
Who is your doctor? What is his name?
Who wrote this prescription for you?
How far is the drugstore from the hospital?
Have you reviewed your lessons yet?
He is a man of unusual ability.
Of what nationality is that famous man?
What is the name of that famous school?
China is a country in the world.
America is also a country in the world.
I have promised him to go.

B. Render the following into English:

Wŏte kungk'ò toū iching wenhsíhaŏ le.
T'āmen mingt'ien yaò k'aŏ tàk'aŏ, pū neng laí le.
Júkuŏ t'ā shuō haŏ, wŏ chiù yeh shuō haŏ pa.
T'āmen chiñt'ien yaò k'aī shemma huì, nĭ chiĥtao ma?
K'uaìlo shiĥ ch'ien maíputaò te.
Nĭ tāyingle women laí, weìshemma meí laí?
Tienhuà wó tăt'unğle, k'ŏshih t'ā ch'ūch'üle, meí tsaì chiā.
T'ā tsuì aì tsò-kuañ, wŏ tsuì pū hsĭhuan tsò-kuañ.
Chè shiĥ Chunğkuo-yiñhang, nà shiĥ Fàkuo-yiñhang.
T'āte nŭerh weìshemma k'ū, nĭ chiĥtao puchihtao?
T'ā kanğ ts'unğ Chunğkuo lai te, t'āte ch'ītzu haí tsaì Shanğhaĭ.
Mă taìfu t'inğle ni shuō te huà, heñ pū kaōhsinğ.

Nenǵ ch'iȟ-k'ŭ te jeń, chiù nenǵ tsò tà shiȟ, pū nenǵ ch'iȟ-k'ŭ te jeń, hsiaŏ shiȟ yeȟ pū nenǵ tsò.

T'ā tsót'ien fā-shaŏ, sói meí laí keñ women īk'uàrh ch'iȟ waňfaǹ.

Nàwaň t'anḡ feīch'anǵ jè, nǐ hō te shiȟhou yaò tanḡhsiñ.

Chanḡ hsiensheng yaò ch'oū-yeñ, ní keī t'a ch'ü ná yanḡhuŏ lai.

Mǎtinǵ taìfu shiȟ Meīkuo-jeȟ, heñ aì hō hunǵchiū.

Ch'inǵ ni keī t'a ītiǎrh chianḡyú pa, t'ā pū hsīhuan yunǵ yeń te.

Cheñ tuìpuch'ǐ, wōte hsianḡyeñ kanḡ keī t'amen ch'oūwaň le.

Tsót'ien t'ā laíle lianḡ huí, k'ŏshih chiñt'ien ī huí yeȟ meí laíkuo.

Nǐ chiaò t'a tsoŭ, t'ā yeȟ shiȟ pū tsoŭ te, pūjú chiù chiaò t'a pūyaò tsoŭ pa.

Chèpeň shū t'ā t'ieñt'ieñ toū yaò k'aǹ te, pū nenǵ chieȟ keí ni, nǐ pūjú tzùchí maǐ īpeň pa.

Paími hsieǹtsaì pūtaǹ chiàch'ien heň kueì, erȟch'ieȟ pū junǵi maǐtetaò.

T'ā shuō te huà pūtaǹ meí yŭ taòli, erȟch'ieȟ feīch'anǵ haŏhsiaò.

Chiñt'ien júkuó wó yŭ kunḡfu, wŏ chiù ītinǵ lai panḡ nite manǵ.

Chèchieǹ shiȟ wŏ-tzùchí īko jeń ītinǵ paňpuliaŏ te, ch'inǵ ni panḡpang manǵ.

Ní ch'inǧ t'a panḡ-manǵ wŏ chiù pū laí le, nǐ yaò wo laí, chiù pūyaò ch'inǧ t'a panḡ-manǵ.

Wŏ meí yŭ ch'ień maǐ nàpeń hsiaŏshuō le, chiȟhaŏ chieȟ t'ate lai k'aǹk'an.

Taìfu chiaò ni īt'ień ch'iȟ sañ huí yaòshuǐ, chiù haŏhaŏrhte ch'iȟ pa, pūyaò tō shuō meí yunǵch'u te huà le.

WRITING DRILL

A.   Write out in Chinese all the items in Section 1 of Oral Drill above.

B.   Transcribe in Chinese all the items in Section 2 of Oral Drill above.

C.   Render the following into Chinese:

1.   This is the Second Municipal Hospital of Peiping. It is one of the most famous hospitals in North China. It has more than twenty doctors. Four are Americans, three are British, two are French, five are Russian, nine are Chinese. They are all quite capable doctors.

2.   Mr. and Mrs. White invited me to have dinner at their home night before last. They had invited six guests altogether. Besides me, there were Mr. and Mrs. Martin, Mr. and Mrs. Shiȟ, and Miss Huanǵ Ch'iū-yinḡ. Mr. and Mrs. Martin had just arrived from America. Miss Huanǵ was to leave for America very soon. We had a foreign meal. The food was exceptionally well prepared. Aside from chicken, there were fish, beef, vegetables, and dessert. After dinner, some of us drank coffee and some of us drank tea.

3.   I have just received a long letter from my younger brother. He is now studying in the National University of Peking. He is taking four courses this semester: Chinese literature, Chinese geography, mathematics, and music. He has had one mid-term examination in Chinese geography.

The teacher gave him five questions. They were not only very long, but also very difficult. But he had reviewed his lessons well, hence he could answer all the questions.

4. Last week our teacher told us a very interesting story. It was called "A Braggart." After I heard it, I told it to my friends. I knew that no one in the world would like a braggart, but almost every one of my friends liked to hear the story. In your opinion,[1] isn't that strange?

[1] 你説.

VOCABULARY CHARACTERS

(Ch'iung)
Poor, exhausted, destitute

(Chì)
Record; order; year [*]; (a surname)

(Suì)
Year, year of age [*]

(Szǔ)
To die; dead; death

(Suī)
Although [*]

(Shoū)
To receive, to collect

(Shih)
To pick up; ten

(Chenǧ)
Regular, in good order [*]; whole [*]; to adjust [*]

(Ch'í)
Even, uniform in length or height [*]; to make even [*]

(Nunǧ)
To toy with, to fix, to do something to

(Kañ)
Dry

(Chinǧ)
Clean [*]

(Hsinǧ)
Quality, nature, character [*]; sex [*]

(Hsieǹ)
To envy [*]

(Mù)
To admire [*]

(T'ì)
To substitute for, to take the place of

(Kò)
Each [*]; various [*]

(Sheñ)
To stretch, to extend [*]

(Chiñ, Chiň)
Finger [*]; to point at [*]

(Wú)
Not to have, without [*]

324

COMPOUNDS

世 紀	(Shiḣchì) Century
窮 苦	(Ch'iunǵk'ǔ) Poor and wretched
年 紀	(Nieńchi)
歲數兒	(Suìshurh) ⎫ Age
年 歲	(Nieńsui) ⎭
雖 然	(Suïjań) Although
收 拾	(Shoūshih) To tidy up
收 條	(Shoūt'iaó) Receipt
拾起來	(Shiḣch'ilai) To pick up
一 早	(Ītsaǒ) Very early
整 齊	(Chenǧch'i) Neat, in good working order
弄 壞	(Nunğhuaì) To put out of order
弄 好	(Nunğhaǒ) To put in working order
各 樣	(Kòyanğ) Each kind, each type; various kinds, various types
各 國	(Kòkuó) Each country; various countries

乾 淨	(Kańching) Clean, tidy
性 情	(Hsinğch'ing) Temperament, nature
羨 慕	(Hsieǹmu) To admire, to envy
指 頭	(Chiḣt'ou) Finger
大 指	(Tàchiḣ) Thumb
二 指	(Erḣchiḣ) Forefinger
中 指	(Chunǧchiḣ) ⎫ Middle finger
三 指	(Sańchiḣ) ⎭
無名指	(Wúmińg-chiḣ) Fourth finger
小 指	(Hsiaóchiḣ) Little finger
指 教	(Chiḣchiaò) To teach, to instruct; instruction
指出來	(Chiḣch'ulai) To point out
伸 長	(Sheńch'ang) To extend
伸出來	(Sheńch'ulai) ⎫ To stretch out
伸出去	(Sheńch'uch'ü) ⎭
各 人	(Kòjeń) Each person; various persons

READING MATERIAL

十 個 小 朋 友

從 前 有 一 個 窮 苦 的 學 生, 姓
張, 名 字 叫 文 英. 他 的 年 紀 跟 我 們
的 差 不 多 一 樣. 他 兩 歲 的 時 候, 母

文英沒有兄弟姐妹，也沒有父親母親，父親母親早就死了。他一個人住，家裏的東西都收拾得乾乾淨淨，整整齊齊的。他的性情很好，常常跟朋友去談事情。

有一天，有幾個同學到他家裏去，看見他家裏整整齊齊的，東西都收拾得很乾淨，就問他，"文先生，家裏沒有別人，你怎麼弄得這麼乾淨呢？"

他笑笑說，"我自己做的。別人替我做，我也不放心。這也是我一個人住的好處。"

他家裏的東西都是他自己收拾的，一跟舊家裏的都一樣。他舊家裏的事，從前都是他母親做的。母親死了以後，家裏的事就沒有人做了，所以他就自己做。他做家事做得很好，朋友到他家裏去，看見他家裏整整齊齊的，東西都收拾得乾乾淨淨，都很羨慕他。

他每天出去的時候，常常把家裏的東西收拾好，才出去；回來的時候，又把東西放在一定的地方。他說，"東西放在一定的地方，要用的時候就很容易找得著。"

他的同學裏頭，有的家裏有兄弟姐妹，家裏的事都有人做，自己不必做，所以他們都很羨慕他能自己做事。也有幾個同學家裏沒有人幫忙，常常把家裏弄得很亂。他們看見文英家裏整整齊齊的，都很羨慕他，就請他幫忙，把家裏收拾收拾。文英很喜歡幫朋友的忙，常常去幫他們的忙。

都 收 拾 得 這 麼 整 齊,地 方 弄 得 這
麼 乾 淨."

那 個 同 學 覺 得 很 奇 怪,就 説,
"你 説 你 有 十 個 小 朋 友,天 天 在 這
兒 替 你 做 事,我 是 常 常 到 這 兒 來
看 你 的,怎 麼 到 現 在 我 都 沒 有 看
見 過 這 些 小 朋 友 呢?"

文 英 一 頭 兒 笑,一 頭 兒 伸 出
兩 隻 手 來,把 十 個 指 頭 給 他 的 朋
友 看.他 説,"這 十 個 指 頭,就 是 天 天
在 這 兒 給 我 做 事 的 小 朋 友 了.現
在 我 要 把 他 們 介 紹 給 你 認 識 認 識."

那 個 同 學 看 了,就 馬 上 明 白 了.

ROMANIZED TEXT OF READING MATERIAL

Shihko hsiaŏ p'engyu

Ts'ungch'ień yŭ īko ch'iungk'ŭ te hsüehsheng, hsing-Chang, mingtzu chiaŏ Wenying. T'āte nienchi keñ womente ch'àputō īyang. T'ā liangŏ suì te shihhou, mŭch'in chiù īching szŭ le. T'ā meí yŭ hsiungtì, yeĥ meí yú chiehmeì, chiāli chiĥ yŭ fùch'in keñ t'a-tzùchí liangŏko jeń. T'ā fùch'in meí t'ieñ toū yaò taò waìt'ou ch'ü tsò-kung, ītsaŏ chiù ch'ūch'ü, taò wanshang ts'aí huí-chiā. Wenying keñ t'ate fùch'in chù te fangtzu, suījań shiĥ heň chiù heń hsiaŏ te, k'ŏshih līt'ou te tunghsi, toū shoūshihte feīch'ang chengch'i, tìfang yeĥ nungte shihfeñ kanching.

Wenyingte hsingch'ing heń haŏ, t'unghsüehmen toū hsīhuan keñ t'a tsò p'engyu. T'āmen hsiàle k'ò ch'angch'ang taò t'ate chiāli ch'ü t'ańt'ieñ. K'anchienle kòyang tunghsi toū shiĥ nèma chengch'i te, chiù toū heñ hsienmu Wenyingte penshih.

Yŭ ī t'ieñ, yŭ īko t'unghsüeĥ weñ t'a, "Wenying, nĭ meí yú mŭch'in, yeĥ meí yŭ hsiungtì chiehmeì, fùch'in t'ieñt'ieñ yaò taò waìt'ou ch'ü tsò-kung, tsaì chiā te shihhou heń shaŏ. Yŭ shuí t'ieñt'ieñ lai pang nite mang, pă chiāli te tunḡhsi, shoūshihte chèma chenǧch'i, pă tìfang nunǵte chèma kañching ne?"

Weńyinḡ t'inḡchienle chiù hsiaòhsiao shuö, "Wó yŭ shińko hsiaŏ p'enǵyu, t'ieñt'ieñ tsaì chèrh panḡ wote manǵ, keí wo tsò-shih. Tà te shih yeh t'ì wo tsò, hsiaŏ te shih yeh t'ì wo tsò, sói chiāli te tunḡhsi toū shoūshihte chèma chenǧch'i, tìfang nunǵte chèma kañching."

Nàko t'unǵhsüeń chüeńte heń ch'íkuaì, chiù shuō, "Nĭ shuō ni yŭ shińko hsiaŏ p'enǵyu, t'ieñt'ieñ tsaì chèrh t'ì ni tsò-shih, wŏ shih ch'anǵch'anḡ taò chèrh lai k'aǹ ni te, tseḿma taò hsieǹtsaì wŏ toū meí yŭ k'aǹchienkuo chèhsieh hsiaŏ p'enǵyu ne?"

Weńyinḡ it'oúrh hsiaò, it'oúrh sheńch'u lianǧchiń shoŭ lai, pă shińko chiǹt'ou keī t'ate p'enǵyu k'aǹ. T'ā shuō, "Chè shińko chiǹt'ou, chiù shih t'ieñt'ieñ tsaì chèrh keí wo tsò-shih te hsiaŏ p'enǵyu le. Hsieǹtsaì wŏ yaò pă t'amen chieńshaò keí ni jeǹshihjenshih."

Nàko t'unǵhsüeń k'aǹle, chiù māshanǧ minǵpai le.

NOTES

1. If 雖然 is used to head a subordinate clause it is customary to head the co-ordinate clause of the same sentence with the conjunction 可是 to bring out more clearly the relationship between the two clauses.

2. 弄, "to fix, to do something to, to toy with," may be rendered into English in various ways, depending on the noun which serves as its object: 弄飯, "to prepare a meal, to cook a meal"; 弄菜, "to prepare food, to cook food"; 弄火, "to light a fire, to play with fire"; 弄舌, "to tattle, to jabber"; 弄錢, "to make money"; etc. It is often used together with another verb to form a resultative compound: 弄壞, "to put out of order, to spoil, to ruin"; 弄好, "to put back in working order, to fix, to adjust"; 弄完, "to finish"; etc.

3. Note that 指 in the compound 指頭 is to be pronounced "chiń." In compounds such as 大指, 二指, 中指, etc., its basic pronunciation, "chiń," is retained.

4. 無 is a literary character introduced here for the sake of the compounds involving its use. The student is warned against using it as a free form in conversation in place of 沒有.

5. 替 may be used in the sense of "for," for 給: 我替你寫信 and 我給你寫信 mean the same thing—"I write the letter for you." 替 is used more often than 給 in central China.

6. In asking a person about his age, 老 is not used. Instead we say 年紀多大 or 年歲多大. In answering such a question, the proper number in terms of years of age is stated, but in doing so, 歲, not 年, is the word to use: 他年紀多大了? 他五十三歲了. 歲數兒 is used only with the age of children. Sometimes in asking about the age of a small child, it is also permissible to say 他今年幾歲了?, "How many years of age is he this year?"

7. The general practice in designating the centuries is to omit the ordinal sign. Thus, the "eighth century" becomes merely 八世紀, the "sixteenth century," 十六世紀, etc. The above will not be mistaken re-

spectively for "eight centuries" and "sixteen centuries" because the latter terms will have to have the classifier 個, making them 八個世紀 and 十六個世紀, respectively.

ORAL EXERCISES

A. Say the following in Chinese:

1. These are my fingers; there are altogether ten of them.
2. His hands are very clean; yours are not very clean.
3. My age is the same as yours; his age is also the same as yours.
4. His parents have already passed away. When did they pass away?
5. He got up very early this morning to tidy up the things there.
6. Mr. Huang's character is quite good; it is much better than yours.
7. He has already fixed my wrist watch.
8. Stretch out your left hand. I want to look at it.
9. How old is your friend? How many years are there in a century?
10. Please pick up the books and put them on the desk.

B. Render the following into English:

1. Chèko shih̀ wŏte tàchiȟ; nàko shih̀ nīte chunḡchiȟ.
2. Nĭ shuō wúmíng-chiȟ ch'ang, háishih hsiaóchiȟ ch'ang?
3. T'ā pă shuíte piaŏ nunghuaì le? T'ā pá nite piaŏ nunghuaì le.
4. Wŏ tsuì hsiaŏ te nŭerh chiññien pā suì le.
5. Nĭ chiñt'ien ītsaŏ chiù taò nărh ch'ü le?
6. Nàchanḡ shoūt'iaó shih̀ t'ā chiaò wo keí ni te.
7. Chèting̀ maòtzu t'aì pū kañching le, ch̀'íng ni pūyaò taì pa.
8. Nĭmen ch'engli te fang̀tzu toū feích'ang chenḡch'i.
9. Wŏmen tsò ch'ìch'ē te shih̀hou, pūyaò pá shoŭ sheñch'uch'ü.
10. T'ā tìtite hsing̀ch'ing cheñ haŏ, sói wŏmen toū heń hsīhuan keñ t'a tsò p'engyu.

WRITTEN EXERCISES

A. Transcribe Section B, above, in Chinese.

B. Render the following into English:

1. 他家裏雖然很窮苦，可是他穿的衣裳都是很乾淨的.

2. 你們羨慕他甚麼？ 我們羨慕他的學問好.

3. 這兒的書我們都已經收拾好了，地方也已經弄乾淨了.

4. 石先生, 我們到了中國不久, 有很多事情不很明白, 都請你指教指教.

5. 一隻手的五個指頭叫大指, 二指, 中指, 無名指, 小指.

6. 六十五年以前還是十九世紀, 可是現在是二十世紀了.

7. 他現在看的小說, 是一本十九世紀很出名的英國小說.

8. 他年紀太小, 不應該到外頭去做工.

9. 請你把地上的紙都拾起來, 擱進這個小箱子裏頭去.

10. 你今天不能去, 我就替你去, 可是你要我替你去, 就要先把收條給我.

C. Render the following into Chinese:

1. How old is Chang Wényíng? Is he a wealthy student?

2. He is about the same age as we [are]. He is not a wealthy student.

3. Where is his mother? Has he any brother? Has he any sister?

4. His mother is already dead. He has no brother. He has no sister either.

5. Who lives with him at home?

6. His father lives with him at home, but he has to go out to work every day.

7. Who are Wényíng's ten little friends?

8. His ten little friends are the ten fingers of his two hands.

9. Why do his friends admire him?

10. They admire him because his character is good and he keeps his home very clean.

VOCABULARY CHARACTERS

(Ch'ing)
Pure, clear; the Ch'ing (Manchu) Dynasty, 1644–1912 [*]

(Ch'ŭ)
Distinct, clear [*]

(Ch'uań)
To pass on, to transmit
(Chuaǹ)
Biography [*]

(Chaò)
To shine on; to take photographs [*]; according to

(Tì)
Supreme ruler, emperor [*]

(Chunğ)
Seed [*]; kind; race [*]
(Chunğ)
To plant

(P'aò)
To steep, to soak; bubble [*]

(Taì)
Belt, bandage, ribbon [*]; to carry along

(Ló)
Gauze, netting; (a surname)

(Jiì)
Sun, day [*]

(Junǵ)
Glory [*]

(Lì)
To pass through [*]; calendar [*]

(Shiĥ)
History [*]; (a surname)

(Yiǹ)
To print; an official seal [*]

(Shuā)
To brush; a brush [*]

(Cheñ)
Needle, hand (of a timepiece); stitch

(Chianḡ) Printed form is 將.
To take [*]; to be about to [*]
(Chianǵ)
A general

(Weĭ)
Great, heroic [*]

(Huà)
To transform, to melt

(Ch'aǹ)
To produce, to reproduce [*]; property [*]

COMPOUNDS

清楚 (Ch'ingch'u) Clear, distinct

傳說 (Ch'uanshuō) Tradition, traditional account

泡茶 (P'aò-ch'á) To steep tea, to make tea

長久 (Ch'angćhiǔ) Lengthy (in time), permanent

帝國 (Tìkuó) Empire

羅馬 (Lómǎ) Rome

日記 (Jiħchì) Diary

日本 (Jiħpeň) Japan

日本人 (Jiħpeň-jeń) Japanese people

日本話 (Jiħpeň-huà) Japanese spoken language

日文 (Jiħweń) Japanese written language

生日 (Shenḡjih) Birthday

出產 (Ch'ūch'aň) To produce, product

歷史 (Lìshiħ) History

歷史家 (Lìshiħchiā) Historian

印刷 (Yiňshuā) Printing

印刷所 (Yiňshuā-sǒ) Printing works

刷子 (Shuātzu) Brush

刷牙 (S̩huā-yá) To brush teeth

牙刷子 (Yáshuātzu) Toothbrush

各種 (Kòchunǧ) Each kind, each type; various kinds, various types

火藥 (Huǒyaò) Gun powder

指南針 (Chiħnań-cheň) Compass

發明 (Fāmiń) To invent, invention

發明家 (Fāmińchiā) Inventor

科學 (K'ōhsüeń) Science

科學家 (K'ōhsüeħchiā) Scientist

偉大 (Weǐtà) Great

文化 (Weńhuà) Culture

化學 (Huàhsüeń) Chemistry

將來 (Chianḡlaí) In the future, the future

帶子 (Taìtzu) Belt, bandage, ribbon

帶來 (Taìlai) To bring along

帶去 (Taìch'ü) To take along

帶回來 (Taìhuilai) To bring back

帶回去 (Taìhuich'ü) To take back

光榮 (Kuanḡjung) Glory

意大利 (Ìtàlì) Italy

清清楚楚的 (Ch'ingch'ingch'úch'ūte) Clearly and distinctly

開辦 (K'aīpaň) To start and operate (as a business, etc.)

上帝 (Shanḡtì) God

中國人的發明

四個同學，有一天坐在屋子裏頭談天。

馬國安說，"英國，法國跟美國的人真聰明，真本事，出了不少的發明家跟科學家，發明了不少的東西。可是中國人裏頭，一個發明家都沒有。"

錢文長說，"那是甚麼話？中國人也有不少的科學家跟發明家，他們也發明了不少的東西呢！"

張秋光說，"中國人的發明真是不少，最早的可以說是絲了。絲的發明已經是三四千年以前的是因為離現在太久，所以是誰發明的，我們照中國的傳說，黃帝的妻子是發明絲的用處的人。他發明很清楚。不發明可是怎麼樣都不的可以說是中國的第一位女發明家。"

謝雲山接着說，"除了絲的用處以外，我知道中國人還有一種發明，也是很早的，那就是茶。茶葉國們喝，是誰發現的。幾百年以後他們帶回來，用開水泡了，多道。是中國很奇怪，把茶葉的開年幾看見茶葉，下葉不覺得就把它去了。摘茶兩，不在得就說，"我要問問你們，都是甚麼？"

馬安說，"是的，絲是從中國傳到別的地方去，都告訴了我們。現在的外國人，他們從中國別跟山，甚麼時候把茶葉帶回自己的國家去，用不着我再說了。"

種了也，我們中國就喝，中國用學文。以前傳法雲，以前傳法。馬利產，在自己過的，羅大出人自。多從意絲國們。一明在我外茶了的。從發現的那些喝會自己茶，那年羅大。是人到明，有人學自己跟人。

兩千，再在現在的外國他，絲是在羅馬去的，很多，傳到日本，都已經，把茶葉帶回。

張秋光很高興的說，"國安，中國過去的長久的，光榮的歷史，偉大的文化，我們不可不知道一點兒！"

謝雲山說，"是的，中國人還發明了三件別的很有用處的東西，

就 是 印 刷, 火 藥, 指 南 針. 將 來 有 工
夫, 我 一 定 把 那 三 種 發 明 的 經 過,
告 訴 你 們."

ROMANIZED TEXT OF READING MATERIAL

Chunḡkuo-jeńte fāming

Szùko t'unǵhsüeń, yǔ ī t'ień tsò tsaì wūtzu lit'ou t'ań-t'ień.

Mǎ Kuóań shuō, "Yinḡkuo, Fàkuo keñ Meǐkuote jeń cheñ ts'unḡming, cheñ peñshih, ch'ūle pū shaǒ te fāmingćhiā keñ k'ōhsüeńchiā, famińǵle pū shaǒ te tunḡhsi. K'ōshih Chunḡkuo-jeń lit'ou, īko fāmiǵ-chiā toū meí yǔ.

Ch'ień Weńch'ang shuō, "Nà shiḣ sheḿma huà? Chunḡkuo-jeń yeḣ yǔ pū shaǒ te k'ōhsüeńchiā keñ fāmingćhiā, t'āmen yeḣ fāmiǵle pū shaǒ te tunḡhsi ne!"

Chanḡ Ch'iūkuanḡ shuō, "Chunḡkuo-jeńte fāming cheñ shiḣ pū shaǒ, tsuì tsaǒ te k'ói shuō shiḣ szū le. Szūte fāmiǵ īching shiḣ sañ-szùch'ień nień īch'ień te shiḣ, k'ōshih yiñweì lí hsieǹtsaì t'aì chiǔ, sói shiḣ tseḿmayanḡ fāmiǵ te, shiḣ shuí fāmiǵ te, wǒmen toū pū heñ ch'inḡch'u. Chaò Chunḡkuote ch'uańshuō, Huangtite ch'ītzu shiḣ fāmiǵ szū te yunḡch'u te jeń. T'ā k'ói shuō shiḣ Chunḡkuote tììweì nǔ-fāmiǵchiā."

Hsieḣ Yúńshañ chieḣche shuō, "Ch'úle szūte yunḡch'u īwaì, wǒ chiḣtao Chunḡkuo-jeń haí yǔ ī chungˇ fāmiǵ, yeḣ shih heń tsaǒ te, nà chiù shiḣ ch'á. Ch'áyeḣ shih ts'unǵ ī chungˇ shù chaīhsialai te yeḣtzu. Chunḡkuo-jeń fāmiǵle pǎ ch'áyeḣ yung k'aīshui p'aòle hō, taò hsieǹtsaì yeḣ yú liangch'ień-tō nień le. Shiḣ shuí fāmiǵ te, wǒmen yeḣ pū chiḣtao. Chípaī nień īch'ień, yǔ hsieḣ waìkuo-jeń tsaì Chunḡkuo k'añchienle Chunḡkuojeń hō-ch'á, chiù chüeḣte heñ ch'íkuaì. Hoùlaí t'āmen hsüeḣhuìle hō-ch'á, chiù pǎ ch'áyeḣ taìhui t'amen-tzùchīte kuóchiā ch'ü le."

Mǎ Kuóañ shuō, "Wǒ yaò weǹwen nimen, szū keñ ch'áte yunḡch'u, toū shiḣ waìkuo-jeń ts'unǵ Chunḡkuo-jeń nàrh hsüeḣlai te ma?"

Ch'ień Weńch'ang shuō, "Shiḣ te. Szū shiḣ tsaì liangch'ień-tō nień īch'ień ts'unǵ Chunḡkuo ch'uańtaò Lómǎ ch'ü, tsaì ts'unǵ Lómǎ ch'uańtaò pieḣte tìfang ch'ü te. Hsieǹtsaì Ìtàlì, Fàkuo keñ Jiḣpeñ, toū yú heñ tō te szū ch'úch'añ. Yúńshañ īching kaòsule women waìkuo-jeń tsaì sheḿma shiḣhou, pǎ ch'áyeḣ taìhui t'amen-tzùchīte kuóchiā ch'ü, yunḡpuchaó wo tsaì shuō le."

Chanḡ Ch'iūkuanḡ heñ kaōhsing̀te shuō, "Kuóañ, Chunḡkuo kuòch'ǔ te ch'anḡchiù te, kuangjung te lìshiḣ, weītà te weńhuà, wǒmen pū k'ǒ pū chiḣtao ītiārh!"

Hsieḣ Yúńshañ shuō, "Shiḣ te, Chunḡkuo-jeń haí fāmiǵle sañchieǹ pieḣte heń yǔ yunḡch'u te tunḡhsi, chiù shiḣ yiǹshuā, huǒyaò, chiḣnańcheñ. Chianglaí yǔ kungfu, wǒ ītiǹg pǎ nà sañ chungˇ fāmiǵte chinḡkuò, kaòsu nimen."

NOTES

1. 家, in the sense of "specialist, expert," is often used as a suffix comparable to "-ist, -er, -ian" in English for the forming of compounds. Thus, 科學家 is "scientist," 發明家 is "inventor," 歷史家 is "historian," etc.

2. 羅馬, "Rome," and 意大利, "Italy" are both Chinese transliterations. One can also say and write 意國 for "Italy."

3. 日 is primarily a literary character. Although it means "sun" and "day," the student is warned against using it in place of 太陽 and 天. One uses 日, however, in modern Chinese for dating purposes and for forming certain compounds. For instance, for "May 10," one can write 五月十日, although in speaking, 號 is definitely preferable to 日. For "diary" one says "jihchì" (日記); for "birthday," one says "shenḡjih" (生日); etc.

4. 黄帝, usually referred to as the "Yellow Emperor" in English, is one of China's legendary rulers whose supposed reign lasted from 2705 to 2595 B.C. He is also known in Chinese historical accounts as 軒轅 (Hsieñyüań). He has been credited with building roads, perfecting the writing system, regulating the calendar, inventing the oxcart, and various other cultural contributions. His wife 西陵氏 (Hsīliṅg-shih), "The Lady of Hsīliṅǵ" (in modern Hupeh province), known also under her title of 螺祖 (Leítsŭ), is said to have discovered the art of raising silkworms.

ORAL EXERCISES

A. Say the following in Chinese:

1. Chinese history; American history; English history; Roman history; French history.

2. Japan; the Japanese spoken language; Japanese people; Japanese literature; Japanese history.

3. Diary; my diary; the diary of a student; the diary of an inventor; the diary of a scientist; to keep [write] a diary.

4. Chinese culture; Japanese culture; American culture; the history of American culture; my toothbrush; their toothbrushes.

5. He studies chemistry; you study science; my friend studies history.

6. Do you know how to make [steep] tea? Make me a cup of tea. Please make us some black tea.

7. Japan was formerly an empire; China also was formerly an empire.

8. What has he invented? What has he carried away with him?

9. America produces very many automobiles every year.

10. He speaks very clearly. We all can understand what he says.

B. Render the following into English:

1. T'āte fùch'in shih īko fāmiṅǵchiā, fāmiṅǵle heň tō yü yunḡch'u te tunḡhsi.

2. Chiñt'ien shih t'āte shenḡjih. T'ā wŭshihpā suì le.

3. Chèko yiṅshuā-sŏ shih t'ā wŭ nień ich'ień k'aīpaǹ te, meĭ nień yiǹ heň tō te shū.

4. Nàko chiȟnań-cheń shiȟ wǒ tsót'ien keī t'a maī te, chèpǎ yáshuātzu yeȟ shiȟ wǒ tsót'ien keī t'a maī te.

5. Chèchieȟ tàī pū shiȟ wǒte, wǒte tàī hoùt'ou meí yǔ taìtzu te.

6. Wǒ meí yū hsüeȟkuo Jiȟpeȟ-huà, sóī pū chiȟtao "huǒyaò" tsemma shuō.

7. Nǐmen shuō shemma huà toū teī ch'iȟgch'iȟgch'úch'úte shuō.

8. T'ā heń yú peňshih, neng īt'oúrh nung̀-fan, īt'oúrh p'aò-ch'á.

9. T'āmen chianḡlaí yaò taò Ìtàlì hsüeh yiñyüeȟ ch'ü, nǐ shuō haǒ puhao?

10. Chunḡkuo meī nień ch'ūch'aň te szū keń ch'á toū heň tō.

WRITTEN EXERCISES

A. Transcribe Section B, above, in Chinese.

B. Render the following into English:

1. 人不是萬能的, 只有上帝是萬能的.

2. 中國有中國的光榮的歷史, 羅馬也有羅馬的光榮的歷史.

3. 這包茶葉是你從中國帶回來給我們的, 你回中國去的時候, 我想把一個指南針給你帶回去送給你的弟弟.

4. 你要他明天甚麼時候跟你到我家裏去, 你對他説清楚了沒有?

5. 中國的文化不但有很長久的歷史, 而且也有很多偉大的地方.

6. 你最喜歡看的那幾種小説, 我們的學校都有.

7. 照中國的傳説, 黃帝的妻子就是發明絲的用處的人.

8. 他 的 父 親 是 中 國 最 近 一 百
五 十 年 來 最 有 名 的 歷 史 家.

9. 我 聽 説 你 近 來 功 課 很 忙, 五
六 天 以 來 都 沒 有 工 夫 寫 日 記 了.

10. 那 些 日 本 人 在 美 國 住 了 很
久, 現 在 都 想 回 日 本 去.

C. Render the following into Chinese:

1. I would like to be a great scientist; he would like to be a great inventor.

2. Do you know by whom printing was invented and when it was invented?

3. Please don't ask me that question because I am not a historian.

4. I know what you have brought here with you. It is a compass, isn't it?

5. I want to learn [written] Japanese in the future because all my friends here can read Japanese books.

6. Can you make me a cup of green tea while I sit here writing [in] my diary?

7. Last Saturday was Mr. Ló's birthday. A year ago he was thirty-seven years old. Now he is thirty-eight.

8. If you had not told me, I certainly wouldn't know that printing and powder were invented by the Chinese.

9. Do you know by whom the airplane was invented?

10. I don't know by whom the airplane was invented, but I know it was invented by an American.

VOCABULARY CHARACTERS

巴 (Pā)
To hope [*];
(noun suffix)

韓 (Hań)
(A surname); (name of a
Chinese feudal state)

助 (Chù)
To help, to assist [*]

祖 (Tsŭ)
Ancestor [*]

漢 (Hàn)
Chinese [*]; brave man
[*]; (name of a Chinese
dynasty)

連 (Lień)
To join [*]; to include;
even; a company (of
soldiers); (a surname)

主 (Chŭ)
Master, chief [*]; to ad-
vocate [*]

恨 (Hèn)
To hate; hatred [*]

釣 (Tiaò)
To fish

爬 (P'á)
To crawl; to climb

鄉 (Hsianğ)
Country (opposite of city)
[*]

殺 (Shā)
To kill, to put to death

膽 (Tăn) Also written 胆.
Gall bladder

勇 (Yunğ)
Brave [*]

忍 (Jeň)
To endure

朝 (Chaō)
Morning [*]
(Ch'aó)
To face; dynasty [*]

滿 (Mǎn)
Full; Manchu [*]

感 (Kǎn)
To affect, to move, to
feel [*]

339

餓 (Ò) Hungry

憐 (Lień) Pity [*]

瘦 (Shoù) Thin, lean

胯 (K'uà) Thigh, leg [*]

洗 (Hsǐ) To wash

負 (Fù) To bear, to shoulder [*]; to lose; to turn one's back on [*]

欺 (Ch'ī) To deceive [*]; to take unfair advantage of [*]

志 (Chih̀) The will [*]

COMPOUNDS

好漢 (Haǒhaǹ) A good Chinese; a brave fellow

欺負 (Ch'īfu) To bully, to take unfair advantage of

祖父 (Tsǔfù) Paternal grandfather

祖母 (Tsúmǔ) Paternal grandmother

祖父母 (Tsǔ-fùmǔ) Paternal grandparents

外祖父 (Waì-tsǔfù) Maternal grandfather

外祖母 (Waì-tsúmǔ) Maternal grandmother

外祖父母 (Waì-tsǔfùmǔ) Maternal grandparents

可憐 (K'ǒlień) To pity; pitiable, pitiful

釣魚 (Tiaò-yú) To fish

爬過去 (P'ákuoch'ü) / 爬過來 (P'ákuolai) } To crawl over

平定 (P'ingtiǹg) To pacify

得志 (Té-chih̀) To attain one's purpose, to realize one's ambition

故鄉 (Kùhsiāng) Native village

鄉下 (Hsiāghsia) The country

胯巴當 (K'ǎpatāng) / 胯下 (K'uàhsià) } Space between spread legs of a person standing

忍氣 (Jeň-ch'ì) To restrain one's anger

忍住 (Jeňchu) To endure; to restrain

勇敢 (Yungkaň) Courageous, brave

膽子 (Taňtzu) / 膽兒 (Tǎrh) / 勇氣 (Yunǧch'ì) } Courage, bravery

漢朝 (Haǹch'ao) The Han dynasty

幫助 (Panḡchu) To help, to assist

報應 (Paòying) Retribution

一時 (Īshiń) A moment; for the moment; offhand

殺人 (Shā-jeń) To kill people

殺死 (Shāszu) To kill, to put to death

洗掉 (Hsǐtiao) To wash out, to wash away

漢文 (Haǹweń) Chinese written language

報答 (Paòtá) To requite; a requital

故意 (Kùi) Intentionally; deliberately

初年 (Ch'ūnień) The beginning years, the early years

主人 (Chǔjen) Master, host

感謝 (Kaǹhsieh̀) To be grateful; gratitude

洗乾淨 (Hsǐkaňching) To wash clean

天下 (T'ieńhsià) Under heaven, the world

READING MATERIAL

中國過去朝代的別的很故事，就吃釣衣裳就多，

韓信是漢朝初年的人。他小的時候，家裏很窮，常常沒有飯吃。有一天他在河邊釣魚，有一個洗衣裳的女人看見他很可憐，就把自己的飯給他吃，一連幾天都是這樣。韓信非常感謝她，要報答她。

漢高祖平定天下的故事很多，他都是非有的的信在，有得感謝。漢高祖不是沒家飯方，餓心滿地，韓信幫漢高祖平定天下，差不多都是因為有韓信的幫助。

韓信是中國很有名的一個人，他是漢朝初年的人，他小的時候家裏很窮，每天沒有飯吃。連人恨意，魚裳給。

他吃了飯，就對那個女人說："將來我得了志，一定要報答你的。"那個女人說："我看你又瘦，心裏頭很可憐你，不是希望你報答的。"

又有一天，韓信在淮陰的街上走着路，有一個人要欺負他，說："韓信，誰說你是好漢？你是個敢殺人的好漢，就把我殺了；你不是好漢，就請你從我的胯下爬過去！"

韓信看他們都很可憐他，心裏很恨，把他的錢過小……韓信前很可憐他，但他……他官……的是別。

韓信真不過，真勇氣，聽來到人，恨……他果然爬就旁，勇……沒後找女前兒，負個……就旁邊沒後，找的從點欺一，就欺一。

上對如了。當看去。就的從點欺一，就到一到了。

出說，"將來我得了志……你的。"

哭說答餓把答……要人報，又就報道："就你殺吧，一過沒句去，裳到一到了。"

還把小官給那個人做，他説，"你們不明白了。那個人可以算是膽子不小的。他欺負我的時候，我不敢把他殺了，不過只是因為殺了他，我也不算勇敢，所以我就忍住一時的氣，要等到今天，才叫他知道我不是一個平常的人呢！"

ROMANIZED TEXT OF READING MATERIAL

Hań Hsìnte kùshih

Hań Hsìn shìh panḡchu Hàn Kaōtsŭ p'ingtinġ Chungkuo te jeń. Chungkuo·jeń ch'àputō toū t'ingchienkuo t'ate mingtzu, toū chihtao t'a shìh īko Hanch'ao ch'ūnień tsuì ch'ūming te jeń.

T'ā hsiaŏ te shìhhou shìh feīch'ang ch'iungk'ŭ te, lień tzùchī īko chiā toū meí yŭ, yaò chù tsaì piehjente chiā lit'ou. Nài chiāte nú-chūjen heń heǹ t'a. Meĭ t'ień taòle ch'ih-faǹ te shìhhou, chiù kùi hsień pă faǹ ch'ihwaǹ, chiaò Hań Hsìn meí yŭ faǹ ch'ih.

Yŭ ī t'ień, Hań Hsìn tsò tsaì hópiērh tiaò-yŭ. Lí t'a pū yüań te tìfang, yŭ īko hsī īshang te nŭjen, k'anchien t'a òte t'aì k'ŏlień, chiù keī t'a faǹ ch'ih. Hań Hsìn mañhsiń kañhsień, ch'àputō yaò k'ūch'ulai. T'ā ch'ihle faǹ chiù tuì nàko nŭjen shuō, "Chiānglaí wŏ téle chih, ītinġ yaò tōtō paòtá ni te." Nako nŭjen shuō, "Wŏ k'anchien ni yù ò yù shoù, hsień lit'ou heń k'ŏlień ni, sóī chiù pă faǹ keí ni ch'ih, pū shìh hsīwanġ ni chiānglaí paòtá wo te."

Yù yŭ ī t'ień, Hań Hsìn tsaì Huaíyińte chiehtaòshang tsoŭche lù, yŭ īko jeń yaò ch'ifu t'a, chiù tuì t'a shuō, "Hań Hsìn, shuí shuō ni shìh haŏhaǹ? Nĭ júkuŏ cheń shìh ko haŏhaǹ, chiù ch'ińg ni pá wo shā le. Nĭ pū kań shā wo, chiù teĭ ts'unġ wote k'ăpatanḡ p'ákuoch'ü!" Hań Hsìn k'anle nàko jeń ik'an, chiù cheńte ts'unġ t'ate k'ăpatanḡ p'ále kuoch'ü. P'angpierh te jeń toū hsiaŏ Hań Hsìn, shuō t'a meí yú yungch'ì. K'ŏshih t'āmente huà, Hań Hsìn īchù yeh meí t'ingchien.

Hoùlaí Hań Hsìn téle chih, huítaò kùhsianḡ ch'ü, chiù chaŏtaò ts'ungch'ień keī t'a faǹ ch'ih te hsī īshang te nŭjen, pá heń tō ch'ień sunġ keī t'a, yù chaŏtaò ts'ungch'ień heǹ t'a te nú-chūjen, yeh sunġ keī t'a ītiărh ch'ień, k'ŏshih pū heń tō. Tsuì hoù t'ā chaŏtaò ch'ifukuo t'a te nàko nańjen, chiaò t'a tsòle īko hsiaŏ kuañ. Piehjen weǹ Hań Hsìn weìshemma haí pá hsiaŏ kuañ keī nàko jeń tsò, t'a shuō, "Nĭmen pū mingpai le. Nàko jeń k'ói suàn

shih tañtzu pū hsiaŏ te. T'ā ch'ïfu wo te shihhou, wŏ pū shih pū kań pă
t'a shā le, pūkuò chih shih yiṅwei shāle t'a, wó yeh pū suaṅ yunǵkań, sói
wŏ chiù jeňchu īshih te ch'ì, yaò tenǵtaò chiñt'ien, ts'aí chiaò t'a chiñtao
wo pū shih īko p'inǵch'anǵ te jeń ne!"

NOTES

1. 韓信, a native of Huaíyiñ (淮陰) in Kiangsu (江蘇, Chianḡsū)
province, came from a very poor and humble family and proved his great
generalship when he was in the service of Liú Panḡ (劉邦), first Emperor
of the Han (漢) Dynasty, 206 B.C.-A.D. 221. Before his death in 196 B.C.,
he was ennobled as Marquis of Huaíyiñ. He is ranked as one of the three
"heroes" of the Han Dynasty, the other two being Chanḡ Liang (張良 [Cf.
Note 1, Lesson Fifty-one]) and Ch'eń P'inǵ (陳平), or Hsiaō Hó (蕭何). For
fuller biographical information see No. 617 in Herbert A. Giles's *A Chinese
Biographical Dictionary* (古今姓氏族譜), pp. 246-49.

2. The Han Dynasty is divided into Former Han and Later Han by the
Hsiñ (新) Dynasty set up by the usurper Wanǵ Manǧ (王莽), A.D. 9–23.

3. 漢高祖 is the imperial title of Liù Panḡ (劉邦), founder of the Han
Dynasty, who reigned from 206 to 195 B.C. A native of P'eì (沛) in modern
Kiangsu province, he was born in 247 B.C. In 209 B.C. he was made Duke
of P'eì. A capable leader and general, Liú led his own forces successfully
against those of Ch'iń (秦) and entered the latter's capital of Hsieńyanǵ
(咸陽) before those of his archrival Hsianǵ Chí (項籍). After defeating
Hsianǵ Chí in the decisive battle of Kaīhsià (垓下) in modern Anhui (安徽,
Añhuī) province, Liú Panḡ proclaimed himself the first Emperor of the Han
Dynasty. He died in 195 B.C. See No. 1334 in Giles's *Biographical Dictionary*, pp. 543–45.

4. 淮陰 was a district created during the Ch'iń (秦) Dynasty, 221-206
B.C., and kept by the Han. Hań Hsiǹ was made Marquis of Huaíyiñ by
Liú Panǵ. The site of the old district is slightly to the southeast of the
present district of the same name which is located in northern Kiangsu
province, northwest of Huaíañ (淮安).

5. When 連 is used adverbially as an intensive particle in the sense of
"even" to indicate what might not be expected, it is itself often further
intensified by the use of 都 or 也: 你説他是一個好學生，可是他連書也不
看, "You say that he is a good student, but he does not even read books";
他是非常窮的，連自己一個家也沒有, "He is quite poor and wretched, not
having even his own home."

6. 幫助 means the same as 幫忙. In usage, however, they differ to
the extent that the latter, when used transitively, takes an object in its
genitival rather than accusative form, which splits up the compound [cf.
Note 8, Lesson Forty-four above], whereas the former takes an object in
the accusative form, which does not split up the compound. Examples: 他
幫我的忙 and 他幫助我.

7. 初 may be used as a prefix for any of the first ten days of a month.
So instead of saying 五月七號, one can also say 五月初七 for "May 7."

This usage has been taken over from the practice formerly confined to dating the first ten days of a month in terms of the lunar or old calendar.

8. 滿, "full," is frequently joined with a noun to convey the idea of "entire or whole . . . full of, all over." So 滿心 is to be understood to mean "the whole heart is full of" or "all over the heart"; 滿臉 as "the entire face is full of" or "all over the face"; 滿地 as "the whole place is full of" or "all over the place"; etc.

9. 祖父 and 祖母 are not to be used in direct address. The compounds to be used for that purpose are 爺爺 (yéhyeh) for "Grandpa" and 奶奶 (nainai) for "Grandma."

10. Note that 胯 of 胯巴當 is to be pronounced "k'ǎ." It is the colloquial equivalent of 胯下, which is a literary expression.

ORAL EXERCISES

A. Say the following in Chinese:

1. Whom do you hate? I hate him. I hate them. I hate myself.
2. To fish; to fish here; to fish there. I like to fish.
3. Whom did he kill? What did he kill?
4. He is our host; we are his guests.
5. My paternal grandfather; his paternal grandmother; your paternal grandparents.
6. His courage is very great. He is a very brave man.
7. Please wash this away. Please wash this piece of cloth clean.
8. A good reward; a bad reward; to reward him. Don't reward me.
9. The history of the Han Dynasty; to be born during the Han Dynasty; China at the time of the Han Dynasty.
10. Don't bully me. Don't bully him. Don't bully anybody.

B. Render the following into English:

1. Nǐ pan̄gchukuo t'a, sói t'ā man̆hsin̄ kan̄hsieh.
2. Chèrh mañtì toū shih shuī, nàrh mañtì toū shih chih.
3. T'ā ch'angćh'ang ch'ifu wo, wó jen̆le pū shaǒ te ch'ì.
4. Nǐ shuō t'a shih shih-tzù te, k'ǒshih t'ā lien̄ ītsò shañ te "shañ" tzù yeh̆ pū jeñshih.
5. T'āmente īshang hsieñtsaì toū hsīkan̄chingle meiyu?
6. Han̄ hsiensheng, nǐ chiñlaí shoùle hen̆ tō le.
7. T'ā shuōts'òle huà, tzùchǐ toū pū chihtao, nǐ shuō k'ǒlien ma?
8. Nǐte tan̄tzu t'aì hsiaǒ le, weìshem̄ma pū kan̆ tzùchǐ ch'ǜ?
9. Tsò haǒ shih chiù yú haǒ paòying, tsò pū haǒ te shih chiù yǔ pū haǒ te paòying.
10. T'ā ts'un̄g chōtzu tīhsia p'ákuoch'ü, nǐ ts'un̄g chōtzu tīhsia p'á-kuolai haǒ puhao?

WRITTEN EXERCISES

A. Transcribe Section B, above, in Chinese.

B. Render the following into English:

1. 韓信是漢朝一個很有名的人，可是他小的時候很窮，連飯也沒有得吃。

2. 他做人膽子是有的，不過他願意忍氣，不喜歡生氣。

3. 後來他得了志就叫人家知道他不是一個平常的、沒有勇氣的人。

4. 女主人非常喜歡他，別人恨他，可是別人不知道為了甚麼女主人喜歡他、別人恨他。

5. 欺負別人的、恨別人的人是沒有的；喜歡欺負別人、恨別人的人也是沒有的。

6. 我們幫助了別人，千萬不要希望人家報答。

7. 他在鄉下住了十多年，現在想到大城裏去住。

8. 我昨天看報，知道上海有兩個男人殺了人，就馬上死了。

9. 漢高祖平定天下，又叫韓信做了大官。

10. 他的祖父母都是生在十九世紀的，死在十九世紀。

C. Render the following into Chinese:

1. What did Hań Hsiǹ do when he returned to his native village after he had realized his ambitions?

2. I cannot endure it any more. I have to tell him that he cannot bully me any longer.

3. You helped him review his lessons in Chinese. His whole heart is full of gratitude.

4. He likes to heǎr the story of Hań Hsiǹ's rewarding the washer-woman.

5. He was so busy yesterday afternoon that he did not have time even to eat his dinner.

6. Every time he fished I sat beside him to read newspapers.

7. That woman is very pitiable. Her husband was killed by a friend three years ago.

8. He is much thinner than before. I don't know whether he is sick or not.

9. Can this be washed away? If it can't, then don't wash it.

10. There are schools in the city; there are also schools in the country.

VOCABULARY CHARACTERS

(Nung)
Agriculture [*]

(T'ien)
Field, farm; (a surname)

(Ch'ien)
To lead along, to pull

(Keng)
To plough, to till

(Hsin)
Bitter, acrid [*]

(Fen)
To give instructions to, to command [*]

(Fù)
To command, to order [*]

(Fei)
The lungs

(Man)
To conceal from

(Cheng)
Upright, right; positive [*]

(Cheng)
First month of the year [*]

(Hui)
Moment

(Tsai)
To govern, to rule [*]; to slaughter

(Hsiang)
Mutual, reciprocal [*]
(Hsiang)
Minister [*]; portrait; physiognomy

(Sung)
(A surname); (name of a Chinese dynasty)

(Hū)
Suddenly [*]; to neglect [*]

(Ping)
And, also, side by side [*]; really [*]

(Liang)
Good, excellent [*]

(Ch'eng)
Sincere, true, honest [*]

348

騙 (P'ien)
To deceive, to swindle

肥 (Feí)
Fat, fleshy

身 (Shen̄)
Body [*]

體 (T'ǐ) Often abbreviated
to 体, or 体.
Body [*]; style [*]; to
show consideration [*]

靠 (K'aò)
To depend on, to lean
on, to rely on

害 (Haì)
To harm; harm; to suffer
from, to be troubled
with [*]

COMPOUNDS

農人 (Nunḡjeń)
農夫 (Nungfū) } Farmer

耕田 (Ken̄g-t'ień) To plough
the fields

辛苦 (Hsiñk'u) Fatigued

吩咐 (Feñfu) To order, to
give instructions to

肺病 (Feìping̀) Tuberculosis of
the lungs, lung disease

正要 (Chen̄gyaò) To be on the
point of, just about to

騙子 (P'ieǹtzu) Swindler

一會兒 (Īhuǎrh) A moment

宋朝 (Sung̀ch'ao) The Sung
Dynasty

欺騙 (Ch'īp'ieǹ) To deceive

害病 (Haì-pinǵ) To be sick, to
suffer from illness

身體 (Sheñt'i) Body; health

老頭兒 (Laŏt'oúrh)
老頭子 (Laŏt'oútzu) } Old man

正月 (Chen̄ḡyüeh) First month
of the year, January

忽然 (Hūjañ) Suddenly, all of
a sudden

瞞得了 (Mańteliaŏ) Possible to
conceal from

瞞不了 (Mańpuliaŏ) Impossible
to conceal from

宰相 (Tsaíhsiang̀) Prime
minister

良心 (Lianǵhsin) Conscience

誠實 (Ch'enǵshih) Honest

實在 (Shih́tsaì) Really, truly

有意 (Yǔ-ì) Intentionally, with
intention

相信 (Hsianǵhsiǹ) To believe

可靠 (K'ŏk'aò) Dependable,
reliable

靠着 (K'aòche) To be depending on, to be relying on

靠得住 (K'aòtechù) Capable of
being depended or
relied on

靠不住 (K'aòpuchù) Incapable
of being depended or
relied on

READING MATERIAL

賣牛的故事

有一個農人在田邊兒吃午飯的時候，看見一個老頭兒牽着一頭牛走過，一頭兒走，一頭兒説，"誰要買牛？誰要買牛？"農人聽見了，心裏就想："我耕田耕得這麼辛苦，不是正要買一頭牛幫自己的忙麼？"他馬上就把老頭兒叫住説，"好朋友，你要賣這頭牛麼？"老頭兒説，"不錯，我要賣這頭牛。你打算買麼？"農人説，"是的，我要買。你肯賣給我，就好極了。"

老頭兒賣了牛就回家去了。走了一會兒，忽然想起，自己説，"主人是過肺病的，吩咐我告訴買牛的人。如果我有意瞞騙，不告訴過路的人，這並不是欺騙人麼？現在我怎麼辦好呢？"他想了一會，就説，"這頭牛一定是害過病的。現在我只要對農人説一聲'這頭牛要買麼？'，他一定説'不要緊，我只買牛了'，我就可以對主人説'我已經告訴買的人了'，就行了。"

然病了。欺騙還欺人。不久，忽然不行，不但欺騙，還欺。

走着路，不久，忽然對自己說，"不行，不但騙還欺人，而且不害良心嗎？"回過頭來，回到農人那裏，牽着牛，望他說去，對很現給，前對明說農人，說，"好朋友，我有一句話，你剛才買的牛，以前是害過病的。你大，可是如果不願意買，我現在給你。"

又來去，不牛，但己馬，農話肥你，還人過，說，"我買的時候，不知道，所以回。病的。現在知道了，請先生把錢給回。"

他起該果，買不自他，對的很的錢，害過。把錢給回農人，就把錢給到家裏，他就把賣牛的主人對他說，"你的主人誠實是個可靠的人。"就是宋朝出名的司馬光。

又我的騙主騙，應如了人，把錢給到家裏，可就把到主實誰？就是宋朝出名的司馬光。

老頭家告訴誠實是司馬兒。回過頭家，老回過一主相。

他起應該，如果買不，自他，很的錢，害過願意。

又來去，不牛但，己馬，農害願意。

想應如了人，緊然把是不罷。

又我的騙主騙家要，雖肺就牛以我了的真的。

ROMANIZED TEXT OF READING MATERIAL

Maì niú te kùshih

Yū īko nunǵjeń tsaì t'ień pièrh ch'iń wǔfań te shiñhou, k'ańchien īko laǒt'oúrh ch'ieñche īt'oú niú tsoūkuò, īt'oúrh tsoǔ, īt'oúrh shuō, "Shuí yaò maï niú? Shuí yaò maï niú?" Nunǵjeń t'inǵchienle, hsiñli chiù hsianǧ: "Wǒ kenḡ-t'ień kenḡte chèma hsiñk'u, pū shiñ chenǧ yaò maï īt'oú niú panḡ tzùchīte manǵ ma?" T'ā māshanǧ chiù pá laǒt'oúrh chiaòchù shuō, "Haǒ p'enǵyu, nǐ yaò maì chèt'oú niú ma?" Laǒt'oúrh shuō, "Pū ts'ò, wǒ yaò maì chèt'oú niú. Ní tǎsuan maï ma?" Nunǵjeń shuō, "Shiñ te, wǒ yaò maì. Ní k'eñ maì keí wo, chiù haǒchí le."

Laǒt'oúrh maìle niú chiù huí-chiā ch'ü le. Lùshang tsoǔle īhuǎrh, hūjań hsianǵch'i chǔjente feñfu, chiù tuì tzùchī shuō, "Chǔjen feñfukuo 'Chèt'oú niú shiñ haìkuo feìpinǧ te, júkuó yǔ jeń yaò maì, ītinǧ yaò kaòsu t'a.' Hsieñtsaì wǒ mańle maì niú te nunǵjeń, pū shiñ wó yǔ-ì ch'īp'ień t'a ma? Hsieñtsaì tseñma pań haǒ ne?"

T'ā hsianǧle ihsiang chiù shuō, "Chè pinǧ pū yaòchiñ, wó chiñ yaò tuì chǔjen shuō, 'Wó iching kaòsule maì niú te nunǵjeń le' chiù hsinǵ le."

T'ā yù wanǧ ch'ień tsoǔche lù. Pū chiǔ, hūjań yù hsianǵch'ilai. T'ā tuì tzùchī shuō, "Pū hsinǵ pu hsinǵ, wǒ yinḡkaī ch'ü shuōminǵpai niú shiñ haìkuo feìpinǧ te. Júkuǒ pū ch'ü shuōminǵpai, wǒ chiù pūtań ch'īp'ieñle maì niú te nunǵjeń, erñch'ieñ haí ch'īp'ieñle chǔjen, pūtań ch'īp'ieñle chǔjen, erñch'ieñ haí ch'īp'ieñle tzùchīte liañghsin ne."

T'ā māshanǧ huíkuo t'oú lai, huítaò nunǵjeń chiāli, tuì nunǵjeń shuō, "Haǒ p'enǵyu, wó yǔ īchù yaòchiñ te huà tuì ni shuō. Nǐ kanǵts'aí maì te niú, suījań heñ feí heñ tà, k'ǒshih ich'ień shiñ haìkuo feìpinǧ te. Nǐ hsieñtsaì júkuǒ pū yüañi maì, wǒ chiù pǎ ch'ień huań keí ni."

Nunǵjeń shuō, "Wó maì te shiñhou, pū chiñtao niú shiñ haìkuo feìpinǧ te. Hsieñtsaì chiñtao le, sǒī pū yüañi maì le. Ch'inǵ hsieñsheng pǎ ch'ień keīhui wo pa."

Laǒt'oúrh chiù pǎ ch'ień keīhuí nunǵjeń, ch'ieñle niú huí-chiā. Huítaò chiāli, t'ā chiù pǎ maì niú te chinḡkuò, kaòsu chǔjen. Chǔjen tuì t'a shuō, "Nǐ cheñ shiñ īko ch'enǵshih k'ǒk'aò te jeń."

Chǔjen shiñ shuí? Chiù shiñ Sunǵch'ao ch'ūminǵ te tsaïhsianǧ Szūmǎ Kuanḡ.

NOTES

1. The Sung Dynasty lasted from A.D. 960 to 1279.

2. 司馬光 was a native of the Hsià (夏) district in modern Honan (河南) province. Born in A.D. 1019, he obtained his Chiñshiñ (進士) degree (a third-degree graduate under the old system of competitive examination) before he was twenty years old and afterward began his public career. In a relatively short time he rose to the position of Minister of State. He was strongly opposed to the reform measures introduced by Wanǵ Añshiñ (王安石). After he left politics he devoted his efforts to the writing of the famous history, the *Tzūchih T'unǵchień* (資治通鑑), or *Universal Mirror of Aids to*

Government, which covers the period from the beginning of the fourth century B.C. to the close of the Five Dynasties, which ended in A.D. 960. This monumental work was finished in 1084. Shortly afterward he returned to public life, but soon fell ill and died in 1086. See No. 1756 in Giles's *Biographical Dictionary*, pp. 669–671.

3. 並, in its adverbial capacity, often assumes the meanings of "by any means, to any extent or degree, really": 並不是, "[It] is not really [so]"; 並不高, "[It] is not really tall "; 並沒有, "There is none really"; etc. Note that it precedes the negative particle 不 or 沒 when so used.

4. 頭 is the classifier for animals. Unlike 隻, which can be used for the same purpose, it is confined to animals alone.

5. 司馬 is one of a small number of double surnames in Chinese. It originated from an ancient official position whose duties were comparable to those of the Minister of War.

6. 肥, the antonym of 瘦, is used only in connection with animals and animal meat. Do not use it with persons. With persons the word to use is 胖 (p'ang̀), "corpulent, fat."

7. 叫住 is a resultative compound meaning "to shout to a stop." 我把他叫住了 means "I shouted him to a stop." The positive and negative variations are 叫得住, "capable of shouting to a stop," and 叫不住, "incapable of shouting to a stop."

ORAL EXERCISES

A. Say the following in Chinese:

1. Please wait a moment. Please wait here for a moment for me.
2. Who is that old man? What does that old man want? What does that old man want to see?
3. Is he dependable? Can that farmer be depended on?
4. He who ploughs the fields is a farmer, not a student.
5. Don't deceive me. Don't deceive anybody.
6. He was sick with tuberculosis five years ago.
7. All swindlers are dishonest. No honest person would be a swindler.
8. He is a man without any conscience. Don't befriend him.
9. What has he commanded you to do? He has commanded me to give this to you.
10. He was not at all afraid of the Prime Minister of the Sung Dynasty.

B. Render the following into English:

1. Chèk'uaì chūjoù t'aì feí le, chiaò t'a pūyaò maǐ pa.
2. T'ā shihtsaì shih wŏte kōko, pū shih wŏte p'engyu.
3. Maì niú te laŏt'oúrh feīch'ang ch'engshih.
4. T'ā tsót'ien keī p'ientzu p'ienle heň tō te ch'ien.
5. Sung̀ch'aote tsaihsiang̀ shih shuí? Shih shen̂ma tìfangte jeń?
6. Shuí kaòsu ni t'ā shih haìkuo feìping̀ te?
7. Nàko laŏt'oúrh tsò-jeń k'aòtechù k'aopuchu?
8. Chèhsieh nunǵjeń t'ient'ieň kenḡ-t'ień, shihtsaì hsiňk'uchí le.

9. Chiñt'ien shih̀ Cheñgyüeh ch'ūsañ, pū shih̀ ch'ūchiŭ.
10. Wŏ k'aǹle īhuǎrh shū chiù keñ nimen taò ch'engli ch'ü.
11. Wŏte sheñt'i haŏ, nīte sheñt'i yeh́ haŏ.

WRITTEN EXERCISES

A. Transcribe Section B, above, in Chinese.

B. Render the following into English:

1. 世界上的騙子都是沒有良心的,都是很靠不住的.

2. 司馬光是中國宋朝的宰相,也是一個很出名的歷史家.

3. 去年他害了肺病,就在山上的醫院裏頭休息了八個多月,他的肺病現在已經好了.

4. 他是前天從中國來的,可是今天早上忽然又到中國去了.

5. 宋先生今晚上要到城裏去聽音樂會,他的女兒吩咐的好朋友住在這兒.

6. 他那件事情你還瞞得了他麼?這兒.

7. 你說得很對,我看一定是瞞不了他的.

8. 昨天牽了兩頭肥牛在我們前頭走過的人,是不是他的兒子?

9. 一頭兒吃飯,一頭兒説話,並不是很容易做得到的.

10. 他 靠 着 自 己 家 裏 有 錢, 就 常
常 做 對 不 起 人 家 的 事.

C.　Render the following into Chinese:

1.　Almost every farmer in America is literate and can read books and newspapers.

2.　The hospitals here are all [hospitals] for people stricken with tuberculosis of the lungs.

3.　As a man he is quite honest and has never deceived anybody.

4.　There are people living in the cities and there also are people living in the country.

5.　I am about to tell you that his master is a very dependable person.

6.　They all say that he is a man without conscience, but he has never deceived any of his friends.

7.　He was not the Prime Minister of the Sung Dynasty really. He was born during the Han Dynasty.

8.　All of a sudden it rained heavily and the whole sky was full of black clouds.

9.　Please wait here for me. I will be back in a moment.

10.　He ordered me to sell his old house to the farmer who came to see you last week.

Lesson FIFTY

A Review Lesson

CHARACTERS

Number of Strokes	Characters	Pronunciation and Tone	Meaning	Lesson Reference
Four	日	Jìh	Sun, day	47
	化	Huà	To transform, to melt	47
	巴	Pā	To hope; (noun suffix)	48
Five	史	Shìh	History; (a surname)	47
	主	Chǔ	Master, chief; to advocate	48
	田	T'ień	Field, farm; (a surname)	49
	正	{Chenġ	Upright, right; positive	49
		{Chenḡ	First month of the year, January	49
Six	死	Szǔ	To die; dead; death	46
	收	Shōu	To receive, to collect	46
	各	Kò	Each	46
	印	Yìn	To print; an official seal	47
Seven	弄	Nunġ	To toy with, to fix, to do something to	46
	伸	Sheñ	To stretch, to extend	46
	助	Chù	To help, to assist	48
	忍	Jěn	To endure	48
	志	Chìh	The will	48
	辛	Hsiñ	Bitter, acrid	49
	吩	Feñ	To give instructions to, to command	49
	身	Sheñ	Body	49

356

Number of Strokes	Characters	Pronunciation and Tone	Meaning	Lesson Reference
Seven	宋	Sung̀	(A surname); (name of a Chinese dynasty)	49
	良	Lianǵ	Good, excellent	49
Eight	性	Hsing̀	Quality, nature, character; sex	46
	泡	P'aò	To steep, to soak; bubble	47
	刷	Shuā	To brush; a brush	47
	爬	P'á	To crawl, to climb	48
	咐	Fù	To command, to order	49
	肺	Feì	The lungs	49
	肥	Feí	Fat, fleshy	49
	忽	Hū	Suddenly; all of a sudden	49
	並	Ping̀	And, also, side by side; really	49
Nine	紀	Chì	Record, order; year; (a surname)	46
	拾	Shih́	To pick up; ten	46
	指	Chih̆	Finger; to point at	46
	帝	Tì	Supreme ruler, emperor	47
	祖	Tsŭ	Ancestor	48
	恨	Heǹ	To hate; hatred	48
	勇	Yunğ	Brave	48
	洗	Hsĭ	To wash	48
	負	Fù	To bear, to shoulder; to lose; to turn one's back on	48
	相	Hsianḡ / Hsiang̀	Mutual, reciprocal / Minister; portrait; physiognomy	48 / 48
Ten	針	Cheñ	Needle, hand (of timepiece); stitch	47

Number of Strokes	Charac-ters	Pronuncia-tion and Tone	Meaning	Lesson Reference
Ten	胯	K'uà	Thigh, leg	48
	殺	Shā	To kill, to put to death	48
	耕	Kenḡ	To plough, to till	49
	宰	Tsaĭ	To govern, to rule; to slaughter	49
	害	Haì	To harm; harm; to suffer from, to be troubled with (illness)	49
Eleven	乾	Kañ	Dry	46
	淨	Ching̀	Clean	46
	清	Ch'inḡ	Pure, clear; the Ch'inḡ (Manchu) Dynasty, 1644–1912	47
	帶	Taì	Belt, bandage, ribbon; to carry along	47
	將	{Chianḡ / Chiang̀}	To take, to be about to / A general	47 / 47
	偉	Weĭ	Great, heroic	47
	產	Ch'añ	To produce; to reproduce; property	47
	連	Lień	To join; to include; even; a company (of soldiers); (a surname)	48
	釣	Tiaò	To fish	48
	牽	Ch'ień	To lead along, to pull	49
Twelve	替	T'ì	To substitute for, to take the place of	46
	無	Wú	Not to have, without	46
	朝	{Chaō / Ch'aó}	Morning / To face; dynasty	48 / 48
	欺	Ch'ī	To deceive; to take unfair advantage of	48
Thirteen	歲	Suì	Year, year of age	46
	羨	Hsień	To envy	46
	楚	Ch'ŭ	Distinct, clear	47

Number of Strokes	Characters	Pronunciation and Tone	Meaning	Lesson Reference
Thirteen	傳	Ch'uań	To pass on, to transmit	47
		Chuaǹ	Biography	47
	照	Chaò	To shine on; to take photographs; according to	47
	鄉	Hsianḡ	Country (opposite of city)	48
	感	Kaň	To affect, to move, to feel	48
	農	Nunǵ	Agriculture	49
	會	Huǐ	Moment	49
Fourteen	種	Chunǧ	Seed; kind; race	47
		Chunǧ	To plant	47
	榮	Junǵ	Glory	47
	瘦	Shoù	Thin, lean	48
	滿	Maň	Full; Manchu	48
	漢	Haǹ	Chinese; brave man; (name of a Chinese dynasty)	48
	誠	Ch'enǵ	Sincere, true, honest	49
Fifteen	窮	Ch'iunǵ	Poor, exhausted, destitute	46
	齊	Ch'í	Even; uniform in length or height; to make even	46
	慕	Mù	To admire	46
	餓	Ò	Hungry	48
	憐	Lień	Pity	48
	靠	K'aò	To depend on, to lean on, to rely on	49
Sixteen	整	Chenǧ	Regular; in good order; whole; to adjust	46
	歷	Lì	To pass through	47
	瞞	Mań	To conceal from	49
Seventeen	雖	Suī	Although	46

Number of Strokes	Characters	Pronunciation and Tone	Meaning	Lesson Reference
Seventeen	韓	Hań	(A surname)	48
	膽	Tǎn	Gall bladder	48
Nineteen	羅	Ló	Gauze, netting; (a surname)	47
	騙	P'ièn	To deceive, to swindle	49
Twenty-three	體	T'ǐ	Body; health	49

ORAL DRILL

A. Say the following in Chinese:

1.
birthday	prime minister	scientist
printing	finger	inventor
culture	thumb	historian
gun powder	little finger	tradition
chemistry	age	God
retribution	character	toothbrush
master	science	thigh
conscience	empire	paternal grandfather
swindler	diary	century
farmer	history	the lungs

2.
to pacify	to conceal from
to restrain one's anger	to be depending on
to kill	to plough the fields
to fish	to make tea
to bully	to brush the teeth
to requite	to produce
to pity	to start and operate (business)
to wash away	to admire
to order (command)	to tidy up
to deceive	to put in working order

3.
clean	poor and wretched
neat	dependable
fatigued	intentional
although	suddenly
to be about to	brave

4.
Japanese history	The twentieth century
American culture	Important inventions
Chinese traditions	The history of science

The history of France in the eighteenth century
My diary of the year 1947
The famous scientists of America
The early years of the fifteenth century
The early years of the nineteenth century
How old is your father this year?
He is fifty-eight years old.
When is your birthday?
My birthday is September 29.
What is a swindler?
A swindler is a person who deceives people.
I believe in God; he, too, believes in God.
What is a farmer?
A farmer is one who ploughs the fields.
Please tidy up the things here.
Although he is clever, he is dishonest.
Although they are reliable, they are not brave.
Yesterday he intentionally harmed you.
He asked me suddenly who they were.
Without a toothbrush I can't brush [my] teeth.
Don't pick up that old hat of mine.
I have already left with them instructions to come home early tonight.
He is depending on his father to teach him how to fish.
Who has put my fountain pen out of order?
Who can help me put my wrist watch in working order?
I want to plant some grass in front of my new house.
Don't bully him! He is my good friend.
I can't for the moment recall his full name.
You have helped him in learning spoken Japanese. He is very grateful.
He has washed clean all my old clothes.
Hań Hsiǹ has helped Liú Pang to pacify China.
By whom was his master killed?
Whom did he kill after he had bullied me?
Is it fatiguing to plough the fields in the daytime?
He is really dependable. You can ask him to do anything for you.
How many fingers are there on a hand?
There are five fingers on a hand.
What are the five fingers called?
They are called the thumb, the forefinger, the middle finger, the
fourth finger, the little finger.
Which is the biggest of the five fingers?
The thumb is the biggest.
Which is the longest?
The middle finger is the longest.
He went to the country very early this morning.
I admire him very much because his temperament is good.

He admires you very much because you speak very clearly.
What did you bring back from China last year?
What did he take back to America year before last?
Gun powder and the compass were both invented by the Chinese.
Do you know what you are going to do in the future?
This drugstore was started and operated by his grandfather during the early years of the nineteenth century.
We are studying the history of the Roman Empire in school.
Did it rain last night? Why is it that the ground here is full of water?
I am not really afraid of him. I am only afraid of God.
Please point out the word you don't know, for me to see.
His health is better than mine; my health is better than yours.

B. Render the following into English:

Nǐ tàile shoūt'iaó huilai meiyu?
Ch'inǵ ni pǎ chèko shench'anǵ itiǎrh.
Pūyaò ts'unǵ chōtzu shangt'ou p'ákuoch'ü!
Chèko weǹt'í wǒ pū hen̆ minǵpai. Ch'inǧ Sunǧ hsiensheng chih̀chiaò-chihchiao.
Chiaò t'a pá ts'aǒtì shangt'ou te huārh toū shihch'ilai!
Ch'inǵ ni kaòsu t'a pǎ tìfang nunǧkanching itiǎrh!
Weìshem̀ma nǐ lieǹ chèko tzù yeh̆ pū jeǹshih?
Aìtìshenǧ [Edison] shih̆ īwei hen̄ yŭ-minǵ te fāminǵchiā, t'ā shih̆ Meǐkuo-jeǹ.
Nǐ chih̆tao chih̆naǹ-chen̄ shih̆ nǎi kuóte jeǹ fāminǵ te ma?
T'ā meìmeite hsinǧch'ing feīch'anǵ haǒ, sóī t'āte naǹ-p'enǵyu yeh̆ tō, nŭ-p'enǵyu yeh̆ tō.
T'ā ch'anǵch'ang ch'īfu wo te, nǐ haí yaò chiaò wo ken̄ t'a tsò haǒ p'enǵyu ma?
Nǐ kanǧts'aí weǹ wo t'ā hsinǧ-shem̀ma, wǒ īshih̆ shuōpuch'ulai.
T'ā chih̆tao wo pū jeǹshih nàko tzù, chiù kùi weǹ wo.
Chunǧkuo Hanch'aote lìshih̆ shih̆ hen̆ ch'anǵ te, hen̄ weītà te.
T'āte waì-tsūfùmŭ toū shih shenǧ tsaì Peǐp'inǵ te.
T'ā yù meí yŭ fùmŭ, yù meí yŭ hsiunǧtì, nǐ shuō k'ŏlieǹ puk'olien?
Nìte tan̄tzu hen̆ tà, tzùchī īko jeǹ ch'ù chiù hsinǵ le.
Wǒ panǧ ni hsüeh̆ Jihweǹ, nǐ panǧ wǒ hsüeh̆ shùhsüeh̆ haǒ puhao?
Nàhsieh jeǹ toū shih p'ieǹtzu, pūyaò ken̄ t'amen tsò p'enǵyu!
Wǒ k'aǹ t'a tsò-jeǹ yù itiǎrh k'aòpuchù.
Shuí shih̆ Chunǧkuo Sunǧch'ao ch'ūminǵ te tsaīhsianǧ?
Chèyanǧ chunǧyaò te shih̆, nǐmen tsem̀ma maǹteliaǒ t'a ne?
T'āmen tsò-jeǹ yù ch'enǵshih, yù k'ŏk'aò, sóī t'āmente p'enǵyu toū feīch'anǵ hsieǹmu t'amen.
Nàko laǒt'oúrh fen̄fule t'amen minǵt'ien tsaǒshang tsaì laí.
T'āte tātzù-chī keī t'ate tìti nunǵhuaì le, chenǧ yaò taò ch'enǵli ch'ü maī ichià hsiñ te.

Nĭ ĭt'oúrhì tsaì hsüeȟhsiaò nieǹ-shū, ĭt'oúrh tsaì yúcheṅg-chú lit'ou tsò-shiȟ, ĭtiṅg heň hsiñk'u le.

Wŏ shiȟtsaì shiȟ ch'ǔnien cheṅgyüeh ch'ūchiŭ laí te, pū shiȟ ch'ieǹnien shiȟerȟyüeh ch'ūwū laí te.

Wŏmente shùhsüeȟ chiaòyüań Suṅg Ch'uñchiaṅg hsiensheng, haì feìpiṅg haìle wŭ nień liṅg pāko yüeȟ, īlaí-ĭch'ǔ yeȟ īpuhaȏ, hoùlaí chiù szū le.

Jiȟpeň tsuì chiǹ sañshiȟ nień ilaí, meī nień ch'ūch'aň te szū, pĭ Chuṅgkuo ch'ūch'aň te yù haȏ yù tō.

Nàko yiǹshuā-sŏ shiȟ pushih nĭte fùch'in sañ nień ĭch'ień k'aīpaǹ te?

Wŏ miṅgt'ien yaò taò ch'eńgli ch'ü maĭ īpă yáshuātzu.

Nĭmen chiaṅglaí yaò taò Ìtàlì ch'ü hsüeȟ yiñyüeȟ puyao?

Nĭ shuō Chuṅgkuote lìshiȟ ch'uańshuō toū shiȟ pū k'ŏk'aò te ma?

Chèpeň jiȟchì shiȟ wŏte, pū shiȟ nĭte, yeȟ pū shiȟ t'āte.

Chèchień wūtzu lit'ou te tuṅghsi, yù kañching, yù cheṅgch'i.

Nĭmen kòjeń chiñt'ien toū yŭ shū, chiȟ, pĭ, mò meiyu?

Shiȟchiehshang meĭiko kuóchiā toū yŭ tzŭchīte weńhuà keñ lìshiȟ te.

T'āte suìshurh haí t'aì hsiaȏ, pū neng tzŭchī tsò-ch'uań taò Yiṅgkuo ch'ü.

Ni tsót'ien keī t'a wŭk'uaì ch'ień, t'ā pă shoūt'iaó keīle ni meiyu?

Ch'iń ni pă yù shoŭ sheñch'ulai keī t'amen k'aǹk'an.

WRITING DRILL

A. Write out in Chinese all the items in Section 1 of Oral Drill above.
B. Transcribe in Chinese all the items in Section 2 of Oral Drill above.
C. Answer the following questions in Chinese:

1. 司馬光是誰？ 我們怎麼知
道他喜歡誠實可靠的人？

2. 韓信是誰？ 他是甚麼時候
的人？

3. 韓信小的時候，誰給過他飯
吃的？ 後來他得了志，就怎樣報
答那個人？

4. 韓信在淮陰怎樣給人家欺
負？ 為甚麼他沒有把那個人殺了？

5. 絲是那一國的人發明的？
是甚麼時候發明的，我們知道麼？

6. 現在有很多絲出產的國家，除了中國以外，是那幾個？

7. 中國人的發明，除了絲以外，還有那幾種？

8. 第四十六課裏頭說的張文英的十個小朋友是甚麼？

9. 他的同學為甚麼都羨慕他？

10. 第四十九課裏頭說的農人，後來為甚麼不願意買牛？

READING DRILL

After reading the following, render it into English:

打石頭¹

從前有一個賣油條²的小孩兒³，有一天他賣完了油條，得了兩百個錢，擱在一塊石頭上頭。他就在這塊石頭上頭坐一坐。後來他正要走的時候，那兩百個錢不見了。他找來找去也找不着，就哭起來。

縣官剛在那兒走過，聽見小孩兒哭，就問他，"你為甚麼哭？"小

---

¹ Adapted from *Jênjên Tú* (人人讀), Vol. I, edited by Chuang Tséhsüan (莊澤宣) (Shanghai: Commercial Press, 1933).

² 油條 means "puffed fritters."

³ 小孩兒 means "a child." Cf. Lesson Fifty-one.

孩兒説,"我賣油條賣了兩百個錢,擱在石頭上頭不見了,所以哭."縣官説,"我明白了,一定是石頭把你的錢偷⁴了去了."他就叫人把石頭拿來打.

大家⁵聽見縣官要打石頭,都走來看.看見縣官真的打石頭,都笑起來.縣官就説,"笑的人不許走.要走的人先得拿三個錢出來."他又叫人拿水來,叫大家把錢扔⁶到水裏去.

後來有一個人扔錢到水裏去的時候,縣官看見水面有油,就説,"偷小孩兒的錢的,就是這個人."

那個人還要不認錢是他偷的.縣官就叫人把他所有⁷的錢都拿出來,一看,剛有一百九十七個錢,個個都是有油的.那個人沒有法子,不能不認他是偷小孩兒的錢的.

---

⁴ 偷 (t'oū) means " to steal." Cf. Lesson Fifty-three.

⁵ 大家, literally " big family," means " everyone, all the people present." Learn this compound by heart.

⁶ 扔 means " to throw." Cf. Lesson Fifty-one.

⁷ 所有 means " all there is, all there are, all." 他所有的錢 may be rendered into English as " all his money, all the money he had."

縣 官 就 叫 他 把 錢 給 回 小 孩
兒, 打 了 他 三 百 下,[8] 還 叫 他 以 後 不
要 再 偷 別 人 的 錢.

---

[8] 下 here means "stroke, time." 打一下 may be rendered into English as "to beat or strike a stroke or time."

VOCABULARY CHARACTERS

少 (Shaò)
Young

秦 (Ch'iń)
(A surname); the Ch'in Dynasty, 221–206 B.C. [*]

滅 (Mieh)
To extinguish, to destroy, to exterminate

仇 (Ch'oú) Also written 讐, 讎.
Enmity, enemy [*]

橋 (Ch'iaó)
Bridge

碰 (P'enǵ) Also written 掽.
To knock, to bump; to meet with, to run into

腳 (Chiaǒ) Also written 脚.
Foot, leg

扔 (Jenḡ)
To throw

跑 (P'aǒ)
To run

兵 (Pinḡ)
Soldier

研 (Yeń)
To grind fine; to study, to do research [*]; study, research [*]

究 (Chiù)
To investigate [*]

軍 (Chüń)
Army [*]

劉 (Liú)
(A surname)

邦 (Panḡ)
State, country [*]

革 (Kó)
To change [*]; to remove from office [*]

命 (Minǵ)
Fate, destiny; life; command, order [*]

陸 (Lù)
Land [*]; (a surname)

戰 (Chàn)
Warfare [*]; to wage war, to contend [*]

長 (Chǎng)
To grow; an elder, a senior [*]; head, chief [*]

脾 (P'í)
The spleen

堅 (Chieñ)
Solid, firm [*]

戌 (Ch'eñg)
To complete [*]; all right!; (to turn) into [*]

孩 (Haí)
Child [*]

末 (Mò)
End [*]

固 (Kù)
Solid, firm, secure [*]

力 (Lì)
Strength, power, ability [*]

COMPOUNDS

小孩子 (Hsiaŏhaítzu) ⎫
小孩兒 (Hsiaŏhárh) ⎭ Child

戰 國 (Chànkuó) The Warring (feudal) Kingdoms (a period in Chinese history, 481–221 B.C.)

志 氣 (Chìhch'ì) Ambition

堅 固 (Chieñku) Firm, secure

滅 掉 (Miehtiao) To destroy utterly, to exterminate

報 仇 (Paò-ch'oú) To avenge a grievance, to revenge

仇 人 (Ch'oújeñ) Personal enemy

碰 見 (P'engchien) To meet by chance, to run into

滿 意 (Mǎnì) To be satisfied; satisfactory

兵 力 (Pinğlì) Military power

孩 子 (Haítzu) ⎫
孩 兒 (Hárh) ⎭ Child (showing more personal interest)

研 究 (Yeñchiù) To study thoroughly; research, study

兵 船 (Pinḡch'uañ) Man-of-war, warship

兵 書 (Pinḡshū) Book on military tactics

長 大 (Chanğtà) To grow up

長 官 (Chanğkuañ) Senior or superior officers

生 長 (Shenḡchanğ) To be born and raised

軍 事 (Chüñshìh) Military affairs

軍 官	(Chüñkuañ) Military officer	聽 話	(T'ïnḡ-huà) To be docile; to be obedient
軍 人	(Chüñjeń) Serviceman	扔 開	(Jenḡk'ai) To throw away
力 量	(Lìliang) Power, ability, strength	扔 出 去	(Jenḡch'uch'ü) To throw out
力 氣	(Lìch'i) Power, strength (physical)	從 小	(Ts'unǵhsiaǒ) Since childhood
軍 服	(Chüñfú) Military uniform	點 頭	(Tieň-t'oú) To nod the head
軍 法	(Chüñfǎ) Military law	知 識	(Chiňshih) Knowledge (from experience)
成 不 成	(Ch'eng puch'eng) Will it do? Is it all right?	成 功	(Ch'enḡkunḡ) To succeed; success
不 成	(Pūch'eng) It wòn't do	海 軍 上 將	(Haǐchüñ shaǹg-chianǵ) Admiral
成 了	(Ch'enǵle) It will do; it is all right	海 軍 中 將	(Haǐchüñ chunḡ-chianǵ) Vice-admiral
半 夜	(Paǹyeh̀) Midnight	海 軍 少 將	(Haǐchüñ shaò-chianǵ) Rear admiral
海 軍	(Haǐchüñ) Navy		
陸 軍	(Lùchüñ) Army	陸 軍 上 將	(Lùchüñ shaǹg-chianǵ) General
空 軍	(K'unḡch'üñ) Air force	陸 軍 中 將	(Lùchüñ chunḡ-chianǵ) Lieutenant general
陸 地	(Lùtì) Land (vs. water)	陸 軍 少 將	(Lùchüñ shaò-chianǵ) Major general
革 命	(Kóminɡ̀) Revolution; to revolt		
起 革 命	(Ch'ǐ kóminɡ̀) To start a revolution	生 氣	(Shenḡ-ch'ì) To be angry
革 命 軍	(Kóminɡ̀-chüñ) Revolutionary army	起 來	(Ch'ǐlai) To rise, to get up
脾 氣	(P'ích'i) Temper, temperament	等 候	(Tenɡ̌hoù) To wait for
末 年	(Mònień) The final years, the last years	天 亮	(T'ieñlianɡ̀) Daybreak, dawn

READING MATERIAL

張 良 跟 老 頭 兒

張 良 是 戰 國 末 年 時 候 韓 國
的 人. 他 的 樣 子 生 得 很 不 錯, 好 像張良是韓國人。秦滅了韓國，張良很想報仇。可是他知道一個人報仇不容易，所以常常想怎麼報仇。他年歲一大，志氣也很大。

有一天，他走到一座橋頭，碰見一個老人。老人故意把一隻鞋脫下來，掉到橋下，叫張良給他撿上來。張良看見是一個老人，就給他撿上來了。老人又把腳伸出來，要張良給他穿上。張良給他穿上鞋。老人笑著走了。

老人走了不遠又回來，對張良說：“你這個孩子可以教。五天以後天亮的時候，你到這橋上來見我。”

五天以後，天剛亮，張良就走到橋上，可是老人已經先到了。老人很生氣，對張良說：“你跟老人見面，怎麼可以遲到？再過五天早點兒來見我罷。”

又過了五天，雞叫的時候，張良就走到橋上，可是老人又已經先到了，很生氣，說：“小孩兒，你來見我。”

張良比老人來得早，在天橋上。老人說：“你以後來見我，我就先到了，你來得太晚了。再過五天早點兒來。”

又過了五天，雞叫的時候，張良就走到橋頭，老人還沒有來。張良在橋上走到橋頭，腳底下來照一照，等著老人。

頭兒又比他先到了，又很生氣的説，“你這一回又來得太晚了．再過五天來，不許再來得晚了！”

五天又很快的過去了．這一回，張良半夜就起來，快快兒的穿好衣裳，就跑到橋上去等候老頭兒．到了天亮，才看見老頭兒走來．老頭兒看見了張良在那兒等着，就笑着説，“這麼樣才對啊！”老頭兒就給了他一本兵書，叫他好好兒的研究．

張良得了那本兵書，就天天研究，得了不少的軍事知識．後來長大了，就幫助劉邦起革命，把秦國滅了，給韓國報了仇．

ROMANIZED TEXT OF READING MATERIAL

Chanḡ Lianǵ ken̄ laŏt'oúrh

Chanḡ Lianǵ shih̀ Chaǹkuó mònień shih́hou Hańkuote jeń. T'āte yang̀tzu shenḡte heň pūts'ò, haŏ hsiang̀ īko nǔjen, k'ŏshih t'ā ts'unǵhsiaŏ chiù yú heň tà te chih̀ch'i, chin̄tao Hańkuo shih̀ keī Ch'ińkuo mieh̀tiao te, sŏï ch'anǵch'ang hsiang̀ fátzu keī tzùchīte kuóchiā paò-ch'oú.

T'ā nień sui haí hsiaŏ te shih́hou, yŭ ī t'ień, tsoŭtaò ītsò ch'iaó shangt'ou, p'enḡchienle īko laŏt'oúrh. Laŏt'oúrh k'aǹchienle t'a, chiù pă tzùchí chiaŏshang te hsień, t'ōle hsialai, kùi jenḡtaò ch'iaó tīhsia ch'ü, heň tàshenḡte chiaò t'a pă hsień shih́ch'ilai. Chanḡ Lianǵ k'aǹle laŏt'oúrh ik'an, chiù tień-t'oú chaòche tsò le. K'ŏshih laŏt'oúrh haí pū mańì, ītiǹg yaò chiaò Chanḡ Lianǵ pă hsień keī t'a ch'uań tsaì chiaŏshang. Chanḡ Lianǵ yù chaòche tsò le.

Laŏt'oúrh chiù tuì Chanḡ Lianǵ shuō, “Nite p'ích'i heň pūts'ò, yeń heň t'inḡ-huà, wŭ t'ieñ ĭhoù, nĭ ītsaŏ chiù yaò taò chèrh lai chieñ wo, wó yŭ huà tuì ni shuō." Shuōwañle chiù tsoŭ le.

Wŭ t'ieñ ĭhoù, Chanḡ Lianǵ heń tsaŏ chiù taòle ch'iaóshang, k'ŏshih laŏt'oúrh pĭ t'a īching hsieñ taò le, heñ shenḡ-ch'ìte shuō, "Hsiaŏhárh, nĭ laíte t'aì wañ le. Tsaì kuò wŭ t'ieñ lai chieñ wo pa."

Tsaì kuòle wŭ t'ieñ, Chanḡ Lianǵ tsaì t'ieñ kanḡ lianḡ chī chiaò te shiñhou, chiù tsoŭtaò ch'iaóshang, k'ŏshih laŏt'oúrh yù pĭ t'a hsieñ taò le, yù heñ shenḡ-ch'ìte shuō, "Nĭ chèi huí yù laíte t'aì wañ le. Tsaì kuò wŭ t'ieñ laí, pū hsŭ tsaì laíte wañ le!"

Wŭ t'ieñ yù heñ k'uaìte kuòch'ü le. Chèi huí, Chanḡ Lianǵ pañyeĥ chiù ch'ĭlai, k'uaìk'uārhte ch'uañhaŏ īshang, chiù p'aŏtaò ch'iaóshang ch'ü tenḡhoù laŏt'oúrh. Taòle t'ieñliaǹḡ, ts'aí k'añchien laŏt'oúrh tsoŭlai. Laŏt'oúrh k'añchienle Chanḡ Lianǵ tsaì nàrh tenḡche, chiù hsiaòche shuō, "Chèmayanḡ ts'aí tuì a!" Laŏt'oúrh chiù keīle t'a īpeñ pinḡshū, chiaò t'a haŏhaŏrhte yeñchiù.

Chanḡ Lianǵ téle nàpeñ pinḡshū, chiù t'ieñt'ieñ yeñchiù, téle pū shaŏ te chünshih chiñshih. Hoùlaí changtà le, chiù panḡchu Liú Panḡ ch'ĭ kóminḡ, pă Ch'iñkuo mieĥle, keī Hañkuo paòle ch'oú.

NOTES

1. 張良 was a native of the feudal state of Hań (韓) (See Note 2 below). Even as a youth he was much perturbed by the fact that his own native state had been destroyed by the state of Ch'iń (秦) and attempted unsuccessfully to assassinate its first emperor. He had distinguished himself for his military prowess and wise counseling in the service of Liú Panḡ (劉邦), who ennobled him. He died in 187 B.C. See No. 88 in Giles's *Biographical Dictionary*, pp. 33–34.

2. 韓 was a feudal state in China during the Period of the Warring Kingdoms (戰國), 481–221 B.C. It came into being as a result of the partition of the older feudal state of Chiñ (晉) into three smaller states in 458 B.C., the other two states being Weì (魏) and Chaò (趙). It was one of the seven overlording states of the period and occupied the modern eastern Shensi (陝西) and northwestern Honan (河南) provinces. It was finally absorbed by the mighty Ch'iń (秦), which unified China into an empire in 221 B.C.

3. For 劉邦, see Note 3 on 漢高祖, Lesson Forty-eight.

4. The state of Ch'iń (秦) was one of the seven overlording states in China during the Period of the Warring Kingdoms. Its site is in modern Shensi (陝西 Shañhsī) province. Under the leadership of its most aggressive ruler, Ch'iń Chenḡ (秦政, 259–210 B.C.), later known as Shiĥ Huanḡtì (始皇帝), it swallowed all the other feudal states and united China into an empire in 221 B.C.

5. 長 (chanḡ), in the sense of "elder, senior," etc., is often used as a suffix to convey the idea of "chief" or "head" of an organization or group: 校長, "principal, president of a school or college or university"; 會長, "president of an association or society"; 連長, "company commander"; 科長,

"head of a department in a government or business office"; 軍長, "army commander"; etc.

    6. 成不成? 不成! and 成了! may be used interchangeably with 行不行? 不行! and 行了! respectively.

ORAL EXERCISES

A. Say the following in Chinese:

    1. Chinese soldiers; American men-of-war; the British army; the Russian navy; the French air force.

    2. To purchase gun powder; to study military law; to be excellent soldiers.

    3. My military uniform; my army uniform; my superior officers; air force officers; Chinese naval officers.

    4. He is satisfied; he is not satisfied at all; he is not quite satisfied; he is not satisfied.

    5. He likes to be an admiral; you like to be an army officer; I like to be an air force officer.

    6. Do you know in which country he grew up? Yes, I do; he grew up in China.

    7. The early years of the period of the Warring Kingdoms; the last years of the Hàn Dynasty.

    8. The state of Hàn was exterminated by the state of Ch'ín; the state of Chaò, too, was exterminated by the state of Ch'ín.

    9. His temper is good; your temper is also good.

    10. Whom did you run into this morning when you were going to school? Where did you run into him?

B. Render the following into English:

    1. Wŏ keí ni paò-ch'oú haŏ puhao? T'ā keí ni paòle ch'oú meiyu?

    2. Chèhsieh shih năi kuóte chünjeń? Nàhsieh shih pushih Yīngkuote chünjeń?

    3. Wŏte fùch'in shih haĭchün chungchiang, pū shih lùchün shaòchiang.

    4. T'ā yeńchiùle pingfă pū chiu, haí yú heñ tō weǹt'í pū mingpai te.

    5. Weìshemma ní pă nàko hsiaŏhárhte shū keñ ch'ieñpĭ jengle ch'uch'ü?

    6. Nàwei haĭchün shangchiang shih pushih hsing-Huang te? T'ā shih pushih Peĭp'ing-jeń?

    7. T'āmen shih nĭte ch'oújeń pushih? Ní yŭ ch'oújeń meiyu?

    8. Nàhsieh toū shih chünshih te weǹt'í, ch'ing ni weǹwen nĭte changkuañ pa.

    9. Chungkuo kóming, Meĭkuo kóming keñ shihchieh kóming, toū shih kóming.

    10. Wŏmente p'engyu toū shih tsaì Chungkuo peĭpù shengchang te.

WRITTEN EXERCISES

A. Transcribe Section B, above, in Chinese.

B. Render the following into English:

1. 那個小孩兒年歲雖然很小, 可是有很大的志氣; 他說將來要給國家報仇.

2. 他告訴我十八世紀的時候, 法國人幫助過美國人革命.

3. 這個美國兵的脾氣非常壞, 所以長官對他很不滿意.

4. 我們做人一定要有志氣, 沒有志氣就沒有成功的希望了.

5. 英國的兵的力比不上美國的, 法國的兵的力也比不上美國的.

6. 你今天早上在街上碰見那兩位軍官是誰? 他們穿的是不是海軍軍服?

7. 一位是姓劉的, 一位是姓宋的, 姓劉的是海軍中將, 姓宋的是海軍少將, 他們穿的是海軍軍服.

8. 中國人在十九世紀就開始革命, 到了二十世紀初年才成功.

9. 韓國是給趙國滅掉的不是? 不是給趙國滅掉的, 是給那一國滅掉的?

10. 中 國 有 海 軍, 陸 軍 跟 空 軍; 美 國 也 有 海 軍, 陸 軍 跟 空 軍.

C. Render the following into Chinese:

1. The officer who ran in from outside to speak to you is a rear admiral.

2. These are all Chinese army uniforms, not American navy uniforms.

3. Although he has been an officer for five or six years, he has never studied military law.

4. Who is your father's personal enemy? Are you going to avenge your father?

5. That lieutenant general was born in America, but grew up in France.

6. When did the American Revolution begin? When did it succeed?

7. Are they satisfied with that child? Is that child satisfied with them?

8. These men-of-war are not only very secure, but also both big and long.

9. Why did you throw away the books which I bought for you last Thursday?

10. I don't quite understand why he says your temper has not been very good since childhood.

VOCABULARY CHARACTERS

岳 (Yüeh)
(A surname)

敵 (Tí)
Opponent [*]; to be a
match for [*]

攻 (Kunḡ)
To attack

危 (Weí)
Danger; dangerous [*]

 (Hsieň)
Danger; dangerous [*]

勝 (Sheng̀)
To conquer, to win [*]

仗 (Chang̀)
Battle

 (Linğ)
Collar [*]; to lead

撼 (Haǹ)
To move, to shake [*]

 (Kueì)
Chinese juniper

 (Tiū) Also written 丢.
To lose; to throw

 (Tsaò)
To build, to manufacture
[*]

反 (Faň)
To turn wrong side out

 (Tseí)
Thief

待 ((Taī)
To stay
(Taì)
To treat

 (Yüań)
Source, origin [*]

 (Hsiunǵ)
Male [*]; heroic [*]

376

士 (Shih̀) Scholar [*]; warrior [*]

拼 (P'iñ) Also written 拼, 拚. To stake or risk; to piece together

動 (Tunğ) To move

失 (Shih̄) To lose, to miss [*]

敗 (Paì) Defeat [*]; to defeat [*]

決 (Chüeh́) To decide [*]

COMPOUNDS

將軍 (Chianḡchüñ) General

兵法 (Pinḡfǎ) Military tactics

兵士 (Pinḡshih̀) Soldier

危險 (Weíhsieǎ) Danger, dangerous

敵人 (Tíjeń) Enemy

敵國 (Tíkuó) Enemy country

敵軍 (Tíchüñ) Enemy troops

仇敵 (Ch'oútí) Enemy

對敵 (Tuìtí) To oppose (as an enemy); opponent

時期 (Shih́ch'í) Period, time

當兵 (Tanḡ-pinḡ) To be a soldier, to enlist

攻打 (Kunḡtǎ) To attack

打仗 (Tǎ-chanğ) To wage war

打勝 (Tǎshenğ) To emerge victorious (in a fight)

領帶兒 (Linğtàrh) Necktie

帶領 (Taìlinğ) To lead, to conduct

對待 (Tuìtaì) To deal with

和氣 (Hóch'ì) Kind, affable

和平 (Hóp'inǵ) Peace, peaceful

同情 (T'unǵch'inǵ) Sympathy

部下 (Pùhsià) Officer and men under a command

原故 (Yüańku) Cause, reason

動撼 (Tunğhan) To move, to shake

收回 (Shoūhuí) To take back, to recover

用意 (Yungì) Intention

主張 (Chǔchang) To advocate, advocacy

造反 (Tsaò-faň) To revolt, to start a revolt

打敗 (Tǎpaì) To be defeated, to defeat (in a fight)

打勝仗 (Tǎ-shenğchanğ) To wage a victorious war, to win a war

打敗仗 (Tǎ-paìchang) To lose a war, to be defeated in war

勝利 (Shenglì) Victory; victorious

英雄 (Yinghsiung) Hero

出力 (Ch'ū-lì) To exert energy, to put forth effort

看重 (K'anchung) / 看得起 (K'antech'ǐ) To look up to, to have great regard for

看不起 (K'anpuch'ǐ) To hold in disregard, to slight

怪不得 (Kuaìpute) No wonder (that)

賣國賊 (Maìkuó-tseí) Traitor (to a country)

拼命 (P'iñ-ming) With all one's might, desperately; to risk one's life

安定 (Anting) Peaceful, quiet, free from disturbances

失敗 (Shihpaì) To fail; failure

決意 (Chüeh-ì) / 決定 (Chüehting) To decide, to resolve, to determine

岳父 (Yüehfù) Father-in-law (wife's father)

岳母 (Yüehmǔ) Mother-in-law (wife's mother)

百戰百勝 (Paìchan-paìsheng) To be ever victorious

愛國 (Aì-kuó) Patriotic

READING MATERIAL

岳飛

岳飛是中國宋朝一個很有名的將軍。他從小就很聰明，最愛研究兵法。

中國在那個時候，很不安定，危險得很。常常有敵人來攻打，危險時期過得很……岳飛生長在這個國家，覺得不是自己的國……心裏頭很難過，替國家出力，沒有願了，所以……岳飛一天看見就以……他決定自己去當兵……

他為着這一部下很得力，打了許多勝仗。敵人碰到岳家軍，都要打敗，不肯和他們打仗。他們說：「撼山易，撼岳家軍難。」意思是說，要搖動一座山容易，要搖動岳家軍很難。

岳飛待他的兵士很好，士兵都肯為他拼命。因為這個緣故，岳家軍個個都是英雄。

那時候宋朝把失地一塊一塊的收回來。可是宋朝的宰相秦檜，主張和敵人講和，不願意打仗。他見岳飛立了大功，心裏不平，就造出「莫須有」的罪名，把岳飛殺了。岳飛死的時候，還很年輕。

岳飛是一個愛國的英雄，到現在人人還都愛他。秦檜害死了岳飛，到現在人人還都恨他。

點兒也看不起, 而且很恨他, 叫他做 "賣國賊."

ROMANIZED TEXT OF READING MATERIAL

Yüeh̀ Feī

Yüeh̀ Feī shih̀ Chun̄gkuo Suǹgch'ao īko heń yŭ-ming te chian̄gchǚn. T'ā ts'un̄ghsiaŏ chiù heň ts'un̄gming, tsuì aì yeńchiù pin̄gfǎ.

Chun̄gkuo tsaì nàko shih̀hou, heň pū antiǹg, ch'aǹgch'an̄g yŭ tíjeń laí kun̄gtǎ, weíhsieňteheň. Yüeh̀ Feī shen̄gchan̄g tsaì chèko shih̀ch'í, hsiñ lit'ou meí yụ̆ ī t'ieñ pū shih̀ chüeh̀te nańkuò te. T'ā pū yüàni k'aǹchien tzùchīte kuóchiā, keī tíjeń mieh̀ le, sói chiù chüeh̀-ì ch'ü tan̄g-pin̄g, t'ì kuóchiā ch'ū-lì.

T'ā tan̄gle pin̄g pū chiŭ, chiù tsòle īko hsiaŏ chǚñkuañ. Houlaí yiñweì tăle pū shaŏ te sheǹgchaǹg, chan̄gkuañ chiù ī t'ieñ pĭ ī t'ieñ k'aǹchuǹg t'a, chiaò t'a taìlin̄g tà chǚñ. T'ā taì pin̄gshih̀ heň hóch'i, yù k'eň keñ t'amen tàchiā ch'iñ-k'ŭ, sói tétaò t'amente t'un̄gch'iǹg. T'ā pùhsiàte pin̄gshih̀, toū k'eň weì kuóchiā p'iñ-miǹg ch'ü tā-chaǹg. Tíchǚñ meī huí p'eǹgche t'amen, toū shih̀ keī t'amen tăpaì te. Yiñweì chèko yüańku, tíchǚñ toū shuō, "Wŏ-men yaò tun̄ghan ītsò tà shañ haí suàn jun̄gi, yaò tun̄ghan Yüeh̀ Feī pùhsiàte pin̄gshih̀, chiù feīch'aǹg nań le."

Yüeh̀ Feī t'ì kuóchiā ch'ū-lì, ch'iñkuo pū shaŏ te k'ŭ, yù pá ĭch'ieñ tiūle te tìfang, shoūhuíle pū shaŏ. T'ā chih̀ yŭ īko yüàǹwaǹg, chiù shih̀ pă tíjeń mieh̀ le, k'ŏshih shuí yeh̀ hsian̄gputaò, Suǹgch'aote tsaīhsiàǹg Ch'iñ Kueì, pieh̀ yŭ yuǹgì. T'ā k'aǹchienle Yüeh̀ Feī paīchaǹ-paīsheǹg, chiù chŭchang hóp'iǹg, t'un̄gshih̀ pă Yüeh̀ Feī chiaòhuilai, shuō t'a yŭ-ì tsaò-fañ, chiù pă t'a shāszu le.

Yüeh̀ Feī szŭle ihoù, Suǹgch'aote pin̄glì chiù pīpushaǹg ts'un̄gch'ieñ le, tiūle te tìfang, yeh̀ ī t'ieñ pĭ ī t'ieñ tō le. Kuaìpute Chun̄gkuo-jeń taò hsièntsaì haí heň k'aǹchuǹg t'a, shuō t'a shih̀ īko aì-kuó te yin̄ghsiuǹg, k'ŏshih tuìyú Ch'iñ Kueì, chiù ītiărh yeh̀ k'aǹpuch'ĭ, erhch'ieh̀ heň heǹ t'a, chiaò t'a tsò "maìkuó-tseí."

NOTES

1. 岳飛, a native of T'an̄gyiñ (湯陰) in Honan (河南) province, was born in A.D. 1103. In his youth he devoted considerable attention to athletic exercises as well as to the reading of history and Suñ Wŭ's (孫武, sixth century B.C.) *Art of War* (兵法). He began his military career as a lieutenant and finally rose to the rank of general; in 1136 he tried to restore to the Sung Dynasty the Chinese territory held by the Tartars. His efforts were frustrated by Ch'iñ Kueì, who finally accused him of treason and executed him in 1141. See No. 2501 in Giles's *Biographical Dictionary*, pp. 945–950.

2. 秦檜 was born in A.D. 1090 in Chian̄gning̀ (江寧) in Kiangsu (江蘇) province, and began his public career in 1115. He had been a censor and

president of the Board of Rites before he was made a duke. He concluded a peace between China and the Tartars in 1134, ceding to the latter north China. He escaped assassination in 1150. He died in 1155 on the verge of being made a prince. For having killed Yüeh Feī, he has been an object of scorn in the eyes of Chinese historians and people alike. See No. 392 in Giles's *Biographical Dictionary*, pp. 153–154.

3. 大軍 means a "large army."

4. 誰也想不到 is to be taken in the sense of "no one would have thought of the fact that" or "no one would have anticipated that." The object of 想不到 is 宋朝的宰相秦檜別有用意.

5. 別有用意, literally "in other ways to have intentions," may be rendered into English as "to have other intentions or ideas." Note that 別 qualifies 有 in the Chinese, whereas in the English rendering of it, "other" qualifies "intentions."

6. 待, in the sense of "to stay, to remain," is also written 獃.

7. The variant form, 拚, is not to be used for 拼, meaning "to piece together."

ORAL EXERCISES

A. Say the following in Chinese:

1. A necktie; my necktie; to lose a necktie; success; failure.

2. To be a soldier; he wants to be a soldier; why does he want to be a soldier? Because of this reason, he wants to be a soldier.

3. Our enemy; their superior officers; our country's victory; the intention of the troops under his command. Will it do? It won't do! It will do!

4. We defeated the enemy troops three months ago in that place.

5. There is danger ahead. Don't walk forward any more.

6. As a person he is extremely affable, so almost everyone likes him.

7. Hań Hsiǹ was a famous general during the early years of the Han Dynasty.

8. The people of an enemy country are not permitted to stay here.

9. Do you hold him in high regard? Why don't you hold him in high regard?

10. Who advocated peace? Who advocated selling [his] country?

B. Render the following into English:

1. Jeńte lìch'i meí yú mǎte lìch'i tà.

2. Wǒ heň yüaìni panḡ nite manḡ, k'ǒshih wǒte lìliang heń hsiaǒ.

3. T'āmen tsót'ien ǐching chüehtìnḡle mínḡnien pū taò waìkuo ch'ü.

4. Chunḡkuote yinḡhsiung ǐtinḡ shih haǒhaǹ, haǒhaǹ pū ǐtinḡ shih Chunḡkuote yinḡhsiunḡ.

5. T'ā taì p'enḡyu feích'ang hóch'i, sóí heň tétaò t'amente t'unǵch'inḡ.

6. Wǒmen tàchiā toū k'anchunḡ t'a, yīnweì t'ā heń yunḡkaň.

7. Nǐmente kuóchiā k'uaìyaò keñ Jihpeń tǎ-chanḡ le.

8. Jeńjeń toū aì hóp'inḡ, pū aì tǎ-chanḡ.

9. Nǐ pū hsǔ t'a laí, kuaìpute t'ā meí laí.

10. T'ā chiaò ni tsò haǒ shih, nǐ chiù yinḡkaī p'iń-minḡ ch'ü tsò.

WRITTEN EXERCISES

A. Transcribe Section B, above, in Chinese.

B. Render the following into English:

1. 世界上有很多人是愛成功,怕失敗的;這些人都不明白沒有失敗,就沒有成功.

2. 我昨天看見張先生領了很多學生去當兵,替國家出力.

3. 中國跟日本打過好幾回仗,有時候日本打勝,有時候日本打敗.

4. 宋秋光先生不是他的父親,是他的岳父.

5. 我今天要把我送給你的領帶兒,借給他用成不成?

6. 那位將軍很愛研究兵法,可是他部下的兵士都很看不起他,因為他做人很不和氣.

7. 他雖然主張和平,可是他並不是賣國賊.

8. 中國打了十多年仗,就得到最後的勝利.

9. 敵軍的長官,常常叫他們部下的兵士,拼命去打仗,不要怕危險.

10. 中 國 在 宋 朝 的 時 候, 因 為 常
常 跟 敵 人 打 仗, 所 以 很 不 安 定.

C. Render the following into Chinese:

1. A person who is willing to risk his life in fighting for his country is not afraid of danger.

2. He advocates that we should all love our own country.

3. What is the intention of his superior officers in advocating the starting of a revolt at this time?

4. Can you tell me how he dealt with the officers and men under my command?

5. His mother-in-law [wife's mother] has decided to ask him not to befriend traitors.

6. The enemy troops attacked the territory of our country from the northeast.

7. Those soldiers are truly very brave because they are not the slightest bit afraid of danger.

8. He studies diligently in school, so he succeeds; you don't study diligently in school, so you fail.

9. Do you know of any person in our country who does not admire heroes?

10. If I have the strength, I will certainly help you.

VOCABULARY CHARACTERS

(Wang)
King [*]; (a surname)

(Yen)
(A surname)

(Chiaō)
To join; to deliver; to pay

(Chenḡ)
To fight over, to argue about

(K'oŭ)
Mouth, opening [*]

(Ts'aí)
Talent [*]

(Taŏ)
To fall down, to collapse [*]
(Taò)
To pour; to invert [*]

(Aī)
Low, short of stature

(Ch'iang) Also written 墙.
Wall

(Tsé)
Pattern, rule, principle [*]

(Fù)
To return, to recover [*]; to repeat, to renew [*]

(Fan)
To offend, to violate; a criminal [*]

(Tsuì)
Crime, sin

(T'oū)
To steal; stealthily [*]

(Chú)
Tangerine [*]

(Huaí)
(Name of a river)

(Pien)
To change

(Hsì)
Relation, consequence [*]

384

洞 (Tǔnǧ) Cave, hole	貓 (Maō) Also written 猫. Cat
狗 (Koǔ) Dog	鼠 (Shǔ) Rat, mouse [*]
派 (P'aì) To dispatch, to appoint; a "school," a clique	土 (T'ǔ) Earth, soil, dust; local, native [*]
耗 (Haò) To waste, to consume [*]	次 (Tz'ù) Time, occasion

COMPOUNDS

外交 (Waìchiaō) Diplomacy

外交史 (Waìchiaō-shih̆) Diplomatic history

外交家 (Waìchiaōchiā) Diplomat

外交官 (Waìchiaō-kuañ) Diplomatic official

體面 (T'ìmien) Honor; honorable

人才 (Jeńts'aí) Talented persons; personnel

口才 (K'oǔts'ai) Eloquence

才能 (Ts'aíneng) Ability, talent

矮子 (Aïtzu) Man of short stature; dwarf

立刻 (Lìk'ò) At once; immediately

得罪 (Tétsui) To offend

橘子 (Chǔtzu) Orange, tangerine

橘子水 (Chǔtzu-shuǐ) Orange juice

變成 (Pieǹch'enǧ) To change into, to turn into

變化 (Pieǹhuà) To change, to transform; change, transformation

發生 (Fāsheṅǧ) To arise, to take place, to occur

人口 (Jeńk'oǔ) Population

原則 (Yüańtsé) Fundamental principle

關係 (Kuañhsi) Relation; relationship; consequence, importance

報復 (Paòfu) To get even with, to revenge

淮河 (Huaíhó) The River Huai

國王 (Kuówanǵ) King

犯罪 (Faǹ-tsuì) To commit a crime; to sin

犯法 (Faǹ-fǎ) To violate the laws

犯人 (Faǹjen) Criminal

罪人	(Tsuìjen) Sinner
土地	(T'ŭtì) Land, territory
土人	(T'ŭjeń) Natives, aborigines
土話	(T'ŭhuà) Local dialect
城門	(Ch'eńmeń) City gates
官員	(Kuańyüań) Officials (of a government)
水土	(Shuít'ŭ) Climatic conditions
反倒	(Fańtaò) On the contrary
想不到	(Hsiangˇputaò) Unable to think of or anticipate
想得到	(Hsiangˇtetaò) Able to think of or anticipate
難道	(Nańtaò) Do you mean to say? Is it conceivable that?
辦理	(Pànlĭ) To transact, to do
山洞	(Shañtunˇg) Cave
耗子	(Haòtzu) ⎫ Rat, mouse
老鼠	(Laóshŭ) ⎭
沒關係	(Meí kuańhsi) It doesn't matter; never mind
千萬	(Ch'ieńwań) By all means; ten million

READING MATERIAL

晏子跟楚王

晏子是齊國的一個很有名、很有體面的外交家。他每次替齊國說話，所以別的國家的人都很爭重他。

有一次晏子到楚國去，楚國的人都知道晏子立刻叫晏子從城牆那頭一個狗洞進到城裏。晏子想不到，就說：「這是狗國才從狗洞進去。只有狗跟狗才到狗洞……」

楚王意一頭洞走進一個城裏……外交說的，所以有一國王意一頭洞……的會面的就是上個是……

……是外交官。外交官是代表國家的，所以一定要派最好的人去。我本國……

「齊國是不是沒有人了呢？只好請你來呢？」外交原則，不是也是……國的狗進去。」知道好請齊派外交的家小國去，我本國來。

齊國是大國，楚國是小國，本國一定要笑自己跟楚國，出他們，有王故，想了很久才想出一個法子。楚王們知道晏子是個子很矮的人，要笑他。他候，楚王們請到高興的人吃飯時來。小官。

晏子到了楚國，楚王叫人在城門旁邊開了一個狗洞，請晏子從狗洞進去。晏子沒有進去，他說：「難道我們到一個國家是笑了，難為你們楚國要笑我，本晏子生氣，想報復。」

晏子說：「我們齊國派人，是派好的人到好的國家去，是派最好的矮你們本晏子生復。有一天，楚王拿了酒請晏子喝了一……」

晏子進了狗洞，狗應該從狗洞進去。楚王聽了這話，就才到晏國去，是派我到楚倒就有人，小官拿了一國的人？」

才是應該好好理門，問了到晏國去，才人，子去，是到好又你們本……好的外交官。我不不有了下人的，外好到身派反以一個小官，喝酒拿了一國的人？

的官。我很高興坐有樣，到是派的，所以是了。兩個幾問：「這是那一國的人？」小官……

意回答説,"是齊國人." 楚王又問,"他犯了甚麼罪了?" 小官們回答説,"犯了偷東西的罪." 楚王就問晏子説,"齊國的人都喜歡做賊的麼?"

晏子慢慢兒的説,"我聽說橘是淮河的果子,因齊國的地方種的橘子很好吃,可是種在壞地方就關係不同,這也是因為水土不同的原因。把橘子變成枳,就會水土不同,東西不做賊了,這也是因為水土不同的緣故。齊國的人在齊國就不偷東西,到了楚國就偷東西,這也是因為水土的關係。各人在楚國、齊國的關係,可是晏子的話,長的北了,子好以子為國了,為故子慕晏子。"

楚王聽了晏子的話,心裏頭又恨晏子,又羨慕晏子的口才,就沒有話。

ROMANIZED TEXT OF READING MATERIAL

Yeǹtzŭ keñ Ch'ŭ-wang

　　Yeǹtzŭ shih̀ Ch'íkuote īko heń yŭ-míng te waìchiaōchiā. T'ā meǐ tz'ù taò waìkuo ch'ü, toū heň huì shuō-huà, heň huì t'ì tzùchīte kuóchiā chenǧ t'imien te, sói Ch'íkuote jeń toū heň k'aňchunǧ t'a.

　　Yŭ ī tz'ù, Yeǹtzŭ taò Ch'ukuo ch'ü. Ch'ŭkuote kuówang t'ingshuō Yeǹtzŭ shih̀ heń yú k'oǔts'ai te, chiù kuì yaò nań t'a inan. T'ā chiňtao Yeǹtzŭ shih̀ īko aītzu, chiù chiaò jeń lìk'ò tsaì ch'engch'iang shangt'ou k'aīle īko hsiaǒ tunǧ, chiaò Yeǹtzŭ ts'ung nàko tung tsoǔchin ch'engli. Hsiangp̌utaò

Yentzŭ shuō, "Chè shih īko koŭtung, chih yú koŭ ken taò koŭkuó ch'ü te
jeń, ts'aí chin koŭtung. Wŏ shih Ch'íkuote waìchiaō-kuan, pū shih koŭ,
Ch'ŭkuo yeh pū shih koŭkuó, sói wŏ pū yinḡkaī ts'uń chèko koŭtung
chinch'ü."

Ch'ŭ-wang t'inḡle Yentzŭte huà, chihtao shih hen yŭ taòli te, meí yŭ
fátzu, chihhaŏ chiaò jeń k'aīle ch'enḡmeń, ch'inḡ t'a chinch'ü. Ch'ŭ-wang
ch'inḡ Yentzŭ tsòhsia, chiù wen t'a shuō, "Nantaò nimen Ch'íkuo meí yŭ
jeńts'aí le ma? Weìshehma yaò p'aì ni chèyang te jeń, taò women Ch'ŭ-kuo
lai ne?"

Yentzŭ shuō, "Wŏmen Ch'íkuo p'aì waìchiaō-kuan taò waìkuo ch'ü, shih
yŭ ītinḡ te yüańtsé te, chiù shih haŏ te p'aìtaò haŏ te kuóchiā ch'ü, pū haŏ
te p'aìtaò pū haŏ te kuóchiā ch'ü. Wŏ shih tsuì pū haŏ te, shent'i yù aī yù
hsiaŏ, penshih yeh meí yŭ, sói p'aì wo taò nimen Ch'ŭkuo lai."

Ch'ŭ-wang penlaí shih yaò hsiaò Yentzŭ te, k'ŏshih fantaò keī Yentzŭ
hsiaòle tzùchi ken Ch'ŭkuo, sói chiù hen shenḡ-ch'ì, hsianḡle heń chiù ts'aí
hsianḡch'ule īko paòfu te fanḡfā.

Yŭ ī t'ien, t'ā ch'inḡ Yentzŭ ch'ih-fan. T'āmen liangko jeń hō-chiù hōtaò
kaōhsing te shihhou, yú chīko hsiaò kuan nále īko jeń chinlai. Ch'ŭ-wang
wen, "Chè shih nǎi kuóte jeń?" Hsiaŏ kuanmen kùi huítá shuō, "Shih
Ch'íkuo-jeń." Ch'ŭ-wang yù wen, "T'ā fanle shehma tsuì le?" Hsiaŏ kuanmen huítá shuō, "Fanle t'oū tunḡhsi te tsuì." Ch'ŭ-wang chiù wen Yentzŭ
shuō, "Ch'íkuote jeń toū hsīhuan tsò tseí te ma?"

Yentzŭ manmārhte shuō, "Wŏ t'inḡshuō chútzu chang tsaì Huaíhó īnań
te tìfang, penlaí shih hen haŏ te kuŏtzu, k'ŏshih pǎ chútzu chunǧ tsaì
Huaìhó ípeī te tìfang, chiù huì piench'enḡ hen huaì te kuŏtzu le. Chè
shih shehma yüańku ne? Chiù shih yinweì kòtìfangte shuít'ŭ pū t'uń te
kuanhsi. Ch'íkuo-jeń tsaì Ch'íkuo pū huì tsò tseí, k'ŏshih ī taòle Ch'ŭkuo
chiù t'oū tunḡhsi le, chè yeh pū shih yinweì Ch'íkuo ken Ch'ŭkuote shuít'ŭ
pū t'uń te yüańku te kuanhsi ma?"

Ch'ŭ-wang t'inḡle Yentzŭte huà, chiù meí yŭ huà k'ói shuō, hsiñ lit'ou yù
hen Yentzŭ, yù hsienmu Yentzŭte k'oŭts'ai.

NOTES

1. 晏子 or 晏嬰 (Yen Yinḡ) is also known under his style, 平仲 (P'inḡ-
chung). He was an official of the feudal state of Ch'í (齊) during the second
half of the sixth century B.C. He was noted for his thrifty habits in life
as well as for his quick wit and eloquence. He died in 493 B.C. See No.
2483 in Giles's *Biographical Dictionary*, p. 943.

2. 楚 was a feudal state during the Spring and Autumn (春秋) period,
721–481 B.C. It grew much larger and more powerful during the period of
the Warring Kingdoms, 481–221 B.C., but was finally swallowed by the
military giant, the state of Ch'iń (秦). Its site is in modern Hunan, Hupeh,
Anhui, Kiangsu, and Chekiang (湖南, 湖北, 安徽, 江蘇, 浙江) provinces.

3. 齊 was another strong feudal state during both the Spring and
Autumn and Warring Kingdoms periods. Like Ch'ŭ, it was conquered by
Ch'iń. Its site is in modern Shantung and Hopei (山東, 河北) provinces.

4. 淮河, or Hwai Ho, is the principal stream between the Yellow River and the Yangtze River and is noted for not having a mouth. It now empties into Lake Hungtse (洪澤湖, Hunǵtsé-hú) and other lakes nearby.

5. 難 as used in paragraph 2 of the Reading Material is a verb meaning "to create difficulty for, to embarrass."

6. Note that the subject of the verb 想不到 is not stated and therefore could be anyone.

7. 難道, literally "difficult to say," is to be understood in the sense of "Do you mean to say, could it be conceivable that . . . ?" It is used only in interrogative statements to express grave doubt or surprise on the part of the speaker.

8. Note that 矮 is the opposite of 高, "tall (in stature)," while 低 is the opposite of 高, "lofty, high."

9. 立刻 and 馬上 may be used interchangeably.

10. The classifier for 牆 is either 道 or 面.

11. 耗子 is more commonly used in conversation in Peiping than 老鼠, which is more commonly used elsewhere.

ORAL EXERCISES

A. Say the following in Chinese:

1. To commit a crime; a criminal; the criminal has committed a crime.

2. Diplomacy; China's diplomacy; the diplomacy of the United States of America; British diplomacy in the Far East; the history of diplomacy.

3. To offend other people; to offend them; don't offend those foreigners; don't offend their friends.

4. A wall; a high wall; a principle; a diplomatic principle; those three scientific principles.

5. England's territory; China's territory; the king of England; French diplomatic officials.

6. Eloquence; those people's eloquence; an eloquent person; they are exceptionally eloquent.

7. Our country's honor; to strive for honor; to strive for our country's honor; to strive for our own honor.

8. Is there any relation? What relation? The teacher-student relation.

9. Oranges; orange juice; to drink orange juice; to eat oranges; to like to eat oranges; to love to drink orange juice.

10. Who is that short person? Do you see that short person over there?

B. Render the following into English:

1. T'ā shih̀ nǎi kuóte kuówanǵ? Shuí tétsuile t'a?

2. Nàko jeń suījań shih̀ ko aītzu, k'ǒshih t'āte k'oūts'ai heň pūts'ò.

3. Chèhsieh shih sheḿma tìfangte t'ǔjeń? T'āmen shuō te shih sheḿma t'ǔhuà?

4. Ch'á wó ǐching p'aòhaǒ le, taò ǐpeī keí ni hō haǒ puhao?

5. Nǐ shih̀ t'āte tìti, t'ā shih̀ pushih waìchiaǒ-kuaň, nańtaò ní yeň pū chih̀tao ma?

6. Wŏ cheñ hsiangˇputaò t'ā huì p'aì ni taò Meǐkuo ch'ü tsò waìchiaō-kuañ.

7. Nà pū shiȟ heń t'ȋmien te shiȟ, chiaò t'a ch'ieñwan pūyaò tsò.

8. Wó peñlaí shiȟ yaò t'a lai chieñ wo te, k'ǒshih hsieñtsaì faňtaò yaò wo-tzùchȉ ch'ü chieñ t'a.

9. T'ā pū shiȟ yŭ-ì nań ni te, wŏ k'aǹ ni yeȟ pū yungˋ hsiangˋ t'a paòfu le.

10. Chèko huàhsüeń yüańtsé wŏ shiȟtsaì pū heň mingˊpai.

WRITTEN EXERCISES

A. Transcribe Section B, above, in Chinese.

B. Render the following into English:

1. 昨天我清清楚楚的告訴了他我要買中國橘子,想不到他今天給我買了這些美國橘子.

2. 中國跟美國的土地都非常大,不過中國的人口,比美國的多三倍.

3. 我昨天看的書,叫"最近五十年來的中國外交史";看完了可以借給你看看.

4. 貓看見了老鼠跑進一個洞裏去,也想跑進去,可是洞太小,貓跑不進去.

5. 他又高又大,別人一定以為他不是在中國長大的.

6. 我知道他們是中國西南部的土人,可是他們說的土話,我一句也聽不懂.

7. 研 究 外 交 的 人, 我 們 叫 "外 交 家"; 辦 理 外 交 的 官 員, 我 們 叫 "外 交 官."

8. 劉 先 生 上 禮 拜 買 的 新 汽 車, 昨 天 晚 上 不 知 道 給 誰 偷 了.

9. 有 口 才 的 人, 不 一 定 有 學 問; 有 學 問 的 人, 不 一 定 有 口 才.

10. 剛 從 那 個 山 洞 跑 出 來 的 黃 狗, 是 不 是 你 妹 妹 的?

C. Render the following into Chinese:

1. If you have offended him, he will certainly get even with you.

2. A sinner is one who has sinned; a criminal is one who has violated the laws.

3. A good person can become a bad one, and a bad person can become a good one.

4. The American government has most recently sent two hundred students to China to study in Chinese universities.

5. Have you paid your tuition? I haven't paid it yet.

6. During the last five years he has been studying America's diplomatic history.

7. The relationship between him and me is that of son and father.

8. I admire him because he is both learned and eloquent.

9. Can you tell me what changes have taken place here since last Tuesday?

10. The present population of our country is almost twice that of fifty years ago.

VOCABULARY CHARACTERS

(Lìn)
(A surname)

(Tài)
To substitute [*]; a generation

(Chaò)
(A surname)

(Ch'iaǵ)
Strong

(Jò) Usually printed 弱.
Weak

(Keñ)
Root [*]; (classifier for pillars, strings, sticks, etc.)

(Yǜ)
Jade

(T'uì)
To retreat, to withdraw, to regress

(Ch'eń)
Minister, official (of a monarchy) [*]

(Shuaī)
To smash [*]; to fall, to stumble

(Suì)
To break into fragments; fragmentary; fragment

(Paǒ)
Something of great value; precious

(T'aǒ)
To ask for; to send a punitive expedition against [*]; to be a nuisance [*]

(Lùn)
To discuss [*]

(Shanḡ)
Commerce; commercial [*]; to deliberate, to consult [*]

(Kuaň)
Tube, pipe [*]; to control, to take charge of; to mind; (a surname)

(Janǵ)
To yield; to allow, to let, to cause to

(Huó)
To live, to be alive; alive

393

議 (Ì)
To discuss, to criticize
[*]

席 (Hsí)
A mat, a banquet [*]

柱 (Chù)
Pillar [*]

神 (Shén)
Spiritual being, deity;
expression [*]

責 (Tsé)
To blame [*]; duty,
responsibility [*]

備 (Peì)
To prepare [*]

COMPOUNDS

交戰國 (Chiaōchaǹ-kuó) Belligerent countries

戰 事 (Chaǹshih) }
戰 爭 (Chaǹcheng) } War

大 戰 (Tàchaǹ) Big war

世界大戰 (Shihchieh-tàchaǹ) World war

時 代 (Shiǹtaì) Era, period, epoch

朝 代 (Ch'aótaì) Dynastic period

代 數 (Taìshù) Algebra

代 理 (Taìli) To act as an agent

代理人 (Taìli-jeń) Agent

代 替 (Taìt'ì) To substitute

退 步 (T'uì-pù) To regress; regression

臣 子 (Ch'eńtzu) Minister (of a monarchy)

會 議 (Huiì) Conference

開會議 (K'aī huiì) To hold a conference

毛 病 (Maóping) Flaw, defect

商 議 (Shangì) } To deliberate, to
商 量 (Shangliang) } consult

寶 玉 (Paŏyǜ) Precious jade

寶 貴 (Paŏkueì) Valuable, precious

討 論 (T'aŏluǹ) To discuss; discussion

聲 明 (Shengmiń) To state clearly; declaration

商 人 (Shangjeń) Merchant

買 賣 (Maǐmai) Buying and selling, trade, business

責 備 (Tsépei) To chastise, to rebuke

不 管 (Pūkuaň) No matter whether, regardless of whether

包 管 (Paŏkuan) To guarantee that

假 如 (Chiǎjú) Supposing

根 兒 (Kērh) Root

根 本 (Keńpeň) Foundation, basis; fundamental, basic

過得去 (Kuòtech'ǜ) Passable, tolerable

過不去 (Kuòpuch'ǜ) Impassable, intolerable

出席 (Ch'ū-hsí) To be present at or attend a meeting

主席 (Chǔhsí) Chairman or presiding officer of a meeting

主意 (Chúi) Intention, decision

打定主意 (Tǎtìng chúi) To make a decision

柱子 (Chùtzu) Pillar

誠意 (Ch'engì) Sincerity, earnestness

摔碎 (Shuaīsuì) To smash to pieces

零碎 (Lingsuì) Fragments, odds and ends; fragmentary, miscellaneous

工人 (Kungjeń) Laborer

寶石 (Paǒshiń) Precious stones

紅寶石 (Hung-paǒshiń) Ruby

根本上 (Keñpeńshang) Basically, fundamentally

神氣 (Sheńch'i) Expression, expressive

活動 (Huótunğ) Active; activities

快活 (K'uaìhuo) Happy

生活 (Shenğhuo) Livelihood

會長 (Huìchanğ) President of a society or organization

校長 (Hsiaòchanğ) Principal or president of a school or college or university

部長 (Pùchanğ) Head or minister of a government department

市長 (Shińchanğ) Mayor

罷工 (Pà-kunğ) To strike; strike

決不 (Chüehpū) On no account; certainly not

交換 (Chiaōhuàn) To exchange

READING MATERIAL

藺相如

藺相如是戰國時代的趙國人。那時候，秦國強，趙國弱，秦國就常常欺負趙國。

有一回，趙國得了一塊寶玉，是很寶貴的。不知道怎樣給秦國的國王知道了，就寫信給趙國的國王說，"我願意把秦國的十五個城的地方，送給趙國，來交換這塊寶玉。"趙王接到了信，不知道怎麼辦才好。如果他答應秦王，就恐怕給了秦國，秦王不肯把地方給他；如果不答應，又恐怕得罪秦國。真是進退兩難。他立刻叫他的臣子們來開一個會議，討論這件要事。

出席的臣子都不敢說話，只有藺相如說，"讓我拿這塊寶玉到秦國去見秦王罷。我包管跟他交換地方回來的。假如秦王不把地方給趙國，我決不會把玉給秦國的。"

趙王聽了藺相如的話，就很快活，派相如帶了寶玉去見秦王。相如到了秦國，就把玉拿給秦王看。秦王喜歡得很。相如站在旁邊兒，看見秦王的神氣，知道他並沒有把地方送給趙國的誠意，就說，"大王，這塊寶玉還有一點兒毛病，我很想指出來給大王看。"秦王以為是真的，就把寶玉交給相如。相如拿着玉，退了幾步，身體靠着柱

送玉，怕五就一趟就交把的方王弱，大
方把恐十後他回如有人真地大小又要殺
地要樣把以叫玉天是經大先送又的
有了他應五就把一王已如以玉國來把很
把還這了天，把玉先送把趙玉先不如好是放
沒完見答明來，那大我假可把趙玉先不如只好
他說看好聲出的道以了就定強玉先
說意王只國了去的國交換國大把就一又寶請
秦誠秦了趙走國交換國大把就
王，說意秦如秦了意趙方趙大又不
備國子送相到到王誠回地國又不敢怪
秦的摔碎送兒去秦的帶把趙秦不要頭不
責趙柱玉城塊國向換玉要給的決王裏子，
子，給向把個交

ROMANIZED TEXT OF READING MATERIAL

Lìn Hsiangjú

Lìn Hsiangjú shìh Chànkuó shìhtàite Chàokuo-jén. Nà shìhhou, Ch'ínkuo ch'iang, Chàokuo jò, Ch'ínkuo chiù ch'angch'ang ch'īfu Chàokuo.

Yǔ ī huí, Chaòkuo téle īk'uaì paǒyù, shìh heń paǒkueì te. Pū chìntao tsem̆yang keĭ Ch'ińkuote kuówang chiħtao le, chiù hsieħ-hsiǹ keĭ Chaòkuote kuówang shuō, "Wǒ yüaǹi pǎ Ch'ińkuote shiħwŭko ch'eńgte tifang, sunġ keĭ Chaòkuo lai chiaōhuaǹ chèk'uaì paǒyǜ." Chaò-wang chieħtaòle hsiǹ, pū chiħtao tsem̆ma paǹ ts'aí haǒ. Júkuǒ t'ā tāying Ch'iń-wang, chiù k'unġp'à Ch'ińkuo téle paǒyǜ, pū k'eń pǎ tifang keĭ Chaòkuo, júkuǒ pū tāying, yù k'unġp'à tétsuile Ch'ińkuo, cheñ shiħ chiǹt'uì liang-nań le. T'ā lìk'ò chiaò t'ate ch'eńtzumen lai k'aī īko huiì, t'aǒluǹ chèchieǹ yaòshiħ.

Ch'ü-hsí te ch'eńtzu toū pū kǎn shuō-huà, chiħ yü Liǹ Hsiangjú shuō, "Janġ wo ná chèk'uaì paǒyǜ taò Ch'ińkuo ch'ü chieǹ Ch'iń-wang pa. Wǒ paōkuan keñ t'a chiaōhuaǹ tìfang huilai te. Chiǎjú Ch'iń-wang pū pǎ tìfang keĭ Chaòkuo, wǒ chüeħpū huì pǎ yǜ keĭ Ch'ińkuo te."

Chaò-wang t'inġle Liǹ Hsiangjúte huà, chiù heň k'uaìhuo, p'aì Hsiangjú taìle paǒyǜ ch'ü chieǹ Ch'iń-wang. Hsiangjú taòle Ch'ińkuo, chiù pǎ yǜ ná keĭ Ch'iń-wang k'aǹ. Ch'iń-wang hsīhuanteheň. Hsiangjú chaǹ tsaì p'ang-pierh, k'aǹchien Ch'iń-wangte sheńch'i, chiħtao t'a pinġ meí yú pǎ tìfang sunġ keĭ Chaòkuo te ch'enġì, chiù shuō, "Tà wang, chèk'uaì paǒyǜ haí yü ītiǎrh maóping, wó heń hsiang chiħch'ulai keĭ tà wang k'aǹ." Ch'iń-wang īweí shiħ cheñ te, chiù pá paǒyǜ chiaō keĭ Hsiangjú. Hsiangjú náche yǜ, t'uìle chĭ pù, sheńt'i k'aòche chùtzu, tsépei Ch'iń-wang, shuō t'a meí yú pǎ tìfang sunġ keĭ Chaò-kuo te ch'enġì. Shuōwańle haí yaò pǎ yǜ hsianġ chùtzu shuaī. Ch'iń-wang k'aǹchien t'a chèyang, k'unġp'à pǎ yǜ shuaīsuì le, chiħ-haǒ tāyingle pǎ shiħwŭko ch'eng sunġ keĭ Chaòkuo, shengmíng wŭ t'ieñ ihoù chiù chiaōhuaǹ.

Hsiangjú tsoŭle ch'ulai, chiù chiaò keñ t'a īk'uàrh taò Ch'ińkuo ch'ü te jeń, pǎ yǜ taìhui Chaòkuo ch'ü. Taòle chiaōhuaǹ te nài t'ieñ, Hsiangjú chiù hsianġ Ch'iń-wang shuō, "Wǒ chiħtao tà wang shiħ meí yü chiaōhuaǹ te ch'enġì te, sóí wó īching chiaò jeń pǎ yǜ taìhui Chaòkuo ch'ü le. Chiǎjú tà wang cheñte yaò pǎ tìfang chiaōhuaǹ, chiù k'ói hsieñ pǎ tìfang keĭ Chaò-kuo, Chaòkuo ītinġ pǎ yǜ sunġ keĭ tà wang te. Ch'ińkuo yù tà yù ch'iang, Chaòkuo yù hsiaǒ yù jò, chüeħpū kǎn pū pá paǒyǜ sunġlai te. Yaòshih tà wang yaò kuaì wo, chiù ch'inġ hsieñ pá wo shāle pa."

Ch'iń-wang suījań pū heń hsīhuan, k'ǒshih hsiǹ lit'ou haí chiħtao Hsiangjú shiħ Chaòkuote haǒ ch'eńtzu, pū jeń shā t'a, chiħhaǒ fanġ t'a hui Chaòkuo ch'ü.

NOTES

1. 藺相如, who lived in the third century B.C., was a native and official of the feudal state of Chaò (趙) and finally became its prime minister. His chief interest as a statesman of Chaò was to protect his own state from the wiles of the powerful state of Ch'iń. See No. 1256 in Giles's *Biographical Dictionary*, p. 484.

2. The Period of Warring Kingdoms (戰國時代) is a historical period in China lasting from 481 to 221 B.C. In general, it was characterized by keen rivalry and subtle intrigue among the various feudal states as a result of the breakdown of the feudal system. Chaos and unrest grew while suffering spread among the people. This period witnessed the raipd growth

of China, primarily as a result of some of the states' ambitions to expand territorially. The period came to an end when the mighty state of Ch'iń eliminated all its rivals and unified China into an empire in 221 B.C.

3. 趙 was a feudal state created as a result of partition of an older state, Chiǹ (晉), into three states. Chaò was one, and the other two were Haǹ and Weì (韓, 魏). The partition occurred in 453 B.C. (cf. Note 2 of Lesson Fifty-one). Chaò was absorbed by the state of Ch'iń, which unified China in 221 B.C. It occupied parts of modern Shansi (山西), Hopei (河北), and Honan (河南) provinces.

4. 進退兩難 (chiǹt'uì liaňg-naǹ), literally "to advance to retreat both difficult," is to be taken in the sense of "in a dilemma" or "unable to go forward or backward."

5. The classifier for 柱子 is 根, which is also used for the same purpose for 頭髮; 繩子 (sheńgtzu), "string, rope"; 管子; etc.

6. 碎 may be joined to other verbs to form resultative compounds to indicate a "broken" or "fragmentary" state: 打碎, "to break into pieces or fragments," 摔碎, "to smash to pieces or bits."

7. 代 is frequently prefixed to titles to indicate an "acting" status: 校長, "principal or president of a school, college, or university," and 代校長, "acting principal or president," etc. Get used to the following: 部長 and 代部長; 主席 and 代主席.

8. Note that the tone of 主 in 主意 is changed from the third to the second.

ORAL EXERCISES

A. Say the following in Chinese:

1. A conference; to hold a conference; to attend a conference.

2. A dynasty; a period; a pillar; a minister [of a monarchy]; a merchant; a chairman.

3. To discuss; to discuss a problem; to discuss the problem of war and peace.

4. Decision; to make a decision; my decision; whose decision; the decision is made; has the decision been made?

5. Suppose he comes; suppose he discusses that question with me; suppose they mind my affairs.

6. What period was that? That was the Period of the Warring Kingdoms. That was not the Period of the Three Kingdoms.

7. What dynasty was that? That was the Haǹ Dynasty. That was the Suǹg Dynasty. That was the Miǹg (bright) Dynasty. That was the Ch'iňg (pure, clear [that is, the Manchu]) Dynasty.

8. Have you deliberated on what to do? Do you want to deliberate on what to say?

9. He is a very active person. What activities have they been having recently?

10. Is there any flaw? Whose place is he taking?

B. Render the following into English:
    1. Chèhsieh hunǵ-paŏshiń shiĥ pushih heń paŏkueì te?
    2. Ní kuaň t'amente shiĥ tsò sheńma? T'āmen pū shiĥ nīte p'enǵyu, pūyaò kuaň pa.
    3. Pūkuaň t'a-men hsĭhuan puhsihuan, nĭmen chiñt'ien ītinǵ yaò tsoŭ le.
    4. Nà pū shiĥ keñpeň te weìt'í, nĭmen hsieìtsaì pūyaò t'aŏluì pa.
    5. Shuí pă t'ate pōlí-peī shuaīsuì le? Shiĥ nĭ pushih?
    6. Wŏmen hsieìtsaì yū faň ch'iĥ, yū īshang ch'uañ, yeĥ yū fanǵtzu chù, sóĭ shenḡhuo haí kuòtech'ù.
    7. Chèhsieh linḡsuì te tunḡhsi nĭmen haí yaò puyao?
    8. Nàweì Chaò hsiensheng shiĥ wŏmen hsieìtsaì te shiĥchanǧ.
    9. Wŏ tsuì chiì t'inḡshuō pū chiŭ chiù yaò fāsheñḡ chaìshiĥ le.
    10. Wŏ chüeĥte t'ā shiĥ meí yū ch'enǵì te, pūyaò tsaì weì t'a nàko weìt'í le.

WRITTEN EXERCISES

A. Transcribe Section B, above, in Chinese.
B. Render the following into English:

1. 因為他沒有念過中國歷史,所以張良是誰,是那一個時代的人,他一點兒也不知道.

2. 世界和平會議下禮拜要在中國開會,美國政府已經決定派官員出席.

3. 第一次世界大戰是在一九一四年發生的,中國,美國,英國,法國,日本,俄國,意大利都是交戰國.

4. 我們看看他的神氣,就可以知道他心裏頭很不快活了.

5. 耕田的是農人,做工的是工人,做買賣的是商人.

6. 我 們 的 學 問, 要 一 天 比 一 天 進 步, 不 進 步 就 要 退 步 了.

7. 世 界 上 的 國 家, 沒 有 一 個 不 是 喜 歡 和 平, 沒 有 一 個 不 恨 戰 爭 的.

8. 他 昨 天 晚 上 說 的 話, 根 本 上 沒 有 一 句 是 有 道 理 的.

9. 我 們 的 校 長 宋 文 江 先 生, 去 年 到 英 國 去 了 以 後, 石 志 堅 先 生 就 做 代 校 長.

10. 他 們 已 經 打 定 了 主 意, 明 年 到 中 國 去 出 席 遠 東 和 平 會 議.

C. Render the following into Chinese:

1. Don't mind him. If he wants to go home, let him go.

2. Suppose he wants us to discuss that basic question; what shall we say?

3. We deliberated for a long time without finding any good way to manage it.

4. I have already told you very many times not to do it. Why don't you rebuke yourself?

5. Those laborers will have a conference tomorrow to discuss the question of calling a strike.

6. Which is the strongest nation in the world? Which is the weakest nation in the world?

7. Who is the American Secretary of State[1] at present? Do you know the name of the present American Secretary of the Navy?

8. Suppose the chairman doesn't come; then who will be the acting chairman?

9. If you tell him not to attend the conference, I can guarantee that he won't attend.

10. I have already told them not to discuss those things at next week's conference.

---

[1] Translate it as though it were "Minister of Diplomacy."

Lesson FIFTY-FIVE

A Review Lesson

CHARACTERS

Number of Strokes	Characters	Pronunciation and Tone	Meaning	Lesson Reference
Two	力	Lì	Strength, power, ability	51
Three	士	Shih̀	Scholar, warrior	52
	土	T'ŭ	Earth, soil, dust; local, native	53
	口	K'oŭ	Mouth, opening	53
	才	Ts'aí	Talent	53
Four	仇	Ch'oú	Enmity, enemy	51
	少	Shaò	Young	51
	反	Faň	To turn wrong side out	52
	王	Wanǵ	King; (a surname)	53
Five	扔	Jenḡ	To throw	51
	末	Mò	End	51
	仗	Chang̀	Battle	52
	失	Shih̄	To lose, to miss	52
	犯	Faǹ	To offend, to violate; a criminal	53
	代	Taì	To substitute; a generation	54
	玉	Yù̀	Jade	54
Six	危	Weí	Danger, dangerous	52
	丢	Tiū	To lose; to throw	52
	交	Chiaǒ	To join; to deliver; to pay	53

402

Number of Strokes	Characters	Pronunciation and Tone	Meaning	Lesson Reference
Six	次	Tz'ù	Time, occasion	53
	臣	Ch'eń	Minister, official (of a monarchy)	54
Seven	兵	Pinḡ	Soldier	51
	究	Chiù	To investigate	51
	邦	Panḡ	State, country	51
	成	Ch'enǵ	To complete; all right; (to turn) into	51
	攻	Kunḡ	To attack	52
	決	Chüeń	To decide	52
Eight	命	Minɡ̀	Fate, destiny; life; command, order	51
	長	Chanɡ̆	To grow; an elder, a senior; head, chief	51
	固	Kù	Solid, firm, secure	51
	岳	Yüeh̀	(A surname)	52
	爭	Chenḡ	To fight over, to argue about	53
	狗	Koŭ	Dog	53
Nine	軍	Chüń	Army	51
	革	Kó	To change, to remove from office	51
	孩	Haí	Child	51
	待	⌠Taī	To stay	52
		⌡Taì	To treat	52
	洞	Tunɡ̀	Cave, hole	53
	派	P'aì	To dispatch, to appoint; a "school," a clique	53
	則	Tsé	Pattern, rule, principle	53
	係	Hsì	Relation, consequence	53

Number of Strokes	Characters	Pronunciation and Tone	Meaning	Lesson Reference
Nine	柱	Chù	Pillar	54
	活	Huó	To live, to be alive; alive	54
	神	Sheń	Spiritual being, deity; expression	54
Ten	秦	Ch'iń	(A surname); the Ch'iń Dynasty, 221–206 B.C.	51
	拼	P'iñ	To stake or risk; to piece together	52
	原	Yüań	Source, origin	52
	晏	Yeǹ	(A surname)	53
	倒	Taǒ / Taò	To fall down, to collapse / To pour, to invert	53 / 53
	耗	Haò	To waste, to consume	54
	弱	Jò	Weak	54
	根	Keñ	Root; (classifier for pillars, strings, sticks, etc.)	54
	退	T'uì	To retreat, to withdraw, to regress	54
	席	Hsí	A mat, a banquet	54
	討	T'aǒ	To ask for; to send a punitive expedition against; to be a nuisance	54
Eleven	研	Yeń	To grind fine; to study, to do research; study, research	51
	陸	Lù	Land; (a surname)	51
	堅	Chieñ	Solid, firm, secure	51
	動	Tuṅg	To move	52
	造	Tsaò	To build, to manufacture	52
	敗	Paì	Defeat; to defeat	52
	偷	T'oū	To steal; stealthily	53
	淮	Huaí	(Name of a river)	53

Number of Strokes	Characters	Pronunciation and Tone	Meaning	Lesson Reference
Eleven	商	Shanḡ	Commerce; commercial; to deliberate, to consult	54
	責	Tsé	To blame; duty, responsibility	54
Twelve	跑	P'aǒ	To run	51
	脾	P'í	The spleen	51
	雄	Hsiunǵ	Male; heroic	52
	復	Fù	To return, to recover; to repeat, to renew	53
	強	Ch'ianǵ	Strong	54
	備	Peì	To prepare	54
Thirteen	滅	Mieh̀	To extinguish, to destroy, to exterminate	51
	碰	P'eng̀	To knock, to bump; to meet with, to run into	51
	腳	Chiaǒ	Foot, leg	51
	勝	Sheng̀	To conquer, to win	52
	賊	Tseí	Thief	52
	矮	Aǐ	Low, short of stature	53
	罪	Tsuì	Crime, sin	53
	鼠	Shǔ	Rat, mouse	53
	碎	Suì	To break into fragments; fragmentary, fragment	54
Fourteen	領	Lǐng	Collar; to lead	52
	趙	Chaò	(A surname)	54
	摔	Shuaī	To smash; to fall, to stumble	54
	管	Kuǎn	Tube, pipe; to control, to take charge of; to mind; (a surname)	54
Fifteen	劉	Liù	(A surname)	51

Number of Strokes	Characters	Pronuncia- tion and Tone	Meaning	Lesson Reference
Fifteen	敵	Tí	Opponent; to be a match for	52
	論	Lùn	To discuss	54
Sixteen	橋	Ch'iaó	Bridge	51
	險	Hsieň	Danger; dangerous	52
	撼	Hàn	To move, to shake	52
	戰	Chàn	Warfare	52
	橘	Chű	Tangerine	53
	貓	Maō	Cat	53
Seventeen	檜	Kueì	Chinese juniper	52
	牆	Ch'iang	Wall	53
Nineteen	寶	Paǒ	Something of great value; precious	54
Twenty	藺	Lìn	(A surname)	54
	議	Ì	To discuss, to criticize	54
Twenty- three	變	Pièn	To change	53
Twenty- four	讓	Jàng	To yield; to allow, to let, to cause to	54

ORAL DRILL

A. Say the following in Chinese:

1. diplomacy	peace	pillar	army	talent
flaw	reason	soldiers	navy	population
activities	enemy	children	air force	jade
ruby	hero	happy	land	man-of-war
algebra	traitor	success	honor	mayor
chairman	victory	failure	king	thief
business	revolution	knowledge	rat	conference
discussion	necktie	learning	dog	agent
war	intention	midnight	cat	sincerity
eloquence	dangerous	secure	intolerable	expression

2. belligerent countries
    diplomatic history
    world war
    to hold a conference
    to make a decision
    to be in a dilemma
    orange juice
    to be ever victorious
    It doesn't matter.
    to have great regard for
    major general
    to nod the head
    senior officers
    to destroy utterly
    to start a revolution

to become a soldier
to be victorious in war
to be defeated in war
no wonder that
Do you mean to say...?
to risk one's life
admiral
rear admiral
vice-admiral
lieutenant general
to be angry
to be satisfied
Will it do?
military uniform
to advocate

3. The early years of the Han Dynasty
    The last years of the Sung Dynasty
    The history of the early years of the Warring Kingdoms Period
    The history of the last years of the Spring and Autumn[1] Period
    To do research in the diplomatic history of France in the eighteenth century
    To do research on the population of Japan in the early years of the nineteenth century
    Who started the revolution in China during the early years of the twentieth century?
    Will it do for him to lead these soldiers?
    He was born and raised in Russia.
    In the world there is a lot of water, but there is little land.
    What kind of relationship is there between this question and that one?
    We have discussed that question for almost three hours; however, we have not yet decided who should be the chairman of the conference tomorrow.
    Can't you even see the pillar in front of you?
    The enemy troops are already gone. You can tell him about it.
    If you were pleased, why didn't you tell them last night?
    If you should ever run into him, please ask him to come.
    He has been like this since childhood.
    His temper is extremely bad; don't talk with him.
    I don't know how to deal with those foreigners.
    Here the place is quite free from disturbances.
    Have you decided yet to send him to England as our diplomatic official?
    This is wartime! You mustn't strike now.

---

[1] Say "Ch'un-ch'iū."

Why did the laborers strike? How long have they been on strike?

My wife's father advocates that we should all love our country.

Have you ever met his wife's mother? She is a native of Peiping.

He is a man of great eloquence; therefore, the soldiers under his command all have great regard for him.

As a person he is not affable. Don't mind him! Don't mind his affairs!

Your success is also my success; your failure is also my failure.

England in the nineteenth century was often victorious in war.

Do you mean to say that even such a person of talent as he is would do such a dishonorable thing?

When a country's population is too numerous, many important questions will arise.

If he has any sincerity he will come back tomorrow to see us.

After Mayor Martin went to Nanking to attend the conference, who served as acting mayor?

Several months ago the American Secretary of the Army went to Japan. He stayed there for several weeks.

Supposing he didn't attend next week's conference, whom would you send?

Regardless of whether he is in business, he should have consulted you.

Whom are those children waiting for? Are they waiting for their parents?

Don't be angry! He didn't offend you intentionally.

War and Peace is a famous novel;[2] it was written by a nineteenth-century Russian novelist.

I truly couldn't anticipate that he could have turned into such a person.

B. Render the following into English:

Wŏmen kuóchiāte jeńts'aí

T'āmen kuóchiāte t'ūtì

Chèhsieh toū shih̀ Chungkuote waìchiaō kuañyüań.

Shuí kaòsu ni haŏ te waìchiaòchiā ītinğ shih̀ haŏ te waìchiaō-kuañ?

Nǐmen tătinğle chúi meiyu? Nà shih̀ shuíte chúi? Shih̀ nǐte ma?

T'āmen chiǹlaí feīch'ang huótunğ, tseḿma ní yeh̀ pū chih̀tao?

Júkuó nǐ pū laí, t'ā ītinğ pū kaǹ tzùchǐ īko jeń ch'ù.

Liú t'aìt'ai ch'ieńt'ien shuō te huà, toū shih̀ keńpeńshang pū tuì te.

T'ā tsòle Weńhsüeń-yeńchiùhuìte[3] huìyüań, taò hsieǹtsaì īching yǔ sañ nień le.

Ní maǐ nàpeň shū, wŏ chiù paōkuan t'a yeh̀ maǐ īpeň.

T'ā pū shih̀ yǔ-ì shuō nàchù huà te, ch'inğ ni pūyaò tsépei t'a pa.

Wŏmen minğt'ien yaò k'aī te huìì, wó k'ung̊p'à pū neng ch'ū-hsí le.

T'ā shih̀ Meīkuo-ch'ìch'ē-kung̊szūte taìlǐ-jeń, wŏ pū shih̀.

---

[2] Say "hsiaŏshuō," although strictly speaking a "novel" is "ch'angp'ień hsiaŏshuō" (lengthy fiction), 長篇小説.

[3] "Yeńchiùhuì" means "research society or association."

Chèko k'ōhsüeń yüańtsé wŏ pū heň minǵpaì, nǐ ne?

Yú heň tō jeń hsīhuan chiaò hsieǹtsaì te shiȟtaì tsò "Tà shiȟtaì".

Nǐmen toū chiȟtao Szūmă Kuaṅ shiȟ Chuṅḡkuo sheḿma shiȟtaìte jeń puchihtao?

Shiȟchieh-tàchaǹ shiȟ tsaì năi nień fāsheṅḡ te?

Wŏ tsót'ien īching chiaŏle hsüeȟfeì le, īkuṅ̀ chiaŏle sañpaì szùshihwŭk'uaì ch'ień.

T'ā shaṅ̀-lĭpaì paǹlĭ nàchieǹ shiȟ te faṅḡfă, yŭ jeń shuō haŏ, yeȟ yŭ jeń shuō pū haŏ.

Nàko shaňtuṅ̀ lit'ou yú heň tō haòtzu, shiȟ pushih t'āmen tsót'ien waňshang kaòsu ni te?

T'ā pūtaǹ heń yú k'oùts'ai, erȟch'ieȟ heń yŭ hsüeȟweǹ.

T'ā ts'uṅ́ch'ień tsò-jeń heń laŏshih, heń k'ŏk'aò, k'ŏshih chiǹlaí pieǹ le, yù pū laŏshih, yù pū k'ŏk'aò.

Nĭ miṅ́t'ien tsaŏshang ch'ǜ puch'ü, keń t'a yŭ sheḿma kuañhsi ne?

Wŏ t'iṅ̀ḡshuō womente cheṅ̀ḡfú yaò p'aì t'a taò Chuṅḡkuo ch'ü tsò waìchiaŏ-kuañ.

Kuañyú nimen hsià-lĭpaì yaò k'aī te huiì, wó īching keń nimente hsiaŏ-chaṅ̀ shaṅ̀liangkuo le.

Wŏ miṅ́nien yaò chiǹ năisŏ hsüeȟhsiaò, yaò nieǹ ná chīmeń kuṅḡk'ò, toū īching tātiṅ̀ḡle chúi le.

Yaòshih ní yŭ ch'eńgì, chiù k'ói keń t'a t'aŏluǹ nàko weǹt'í. Nĭ meí yŭ ch'eńgì, chiù pū yuṅ̀ḡ tō shuō-huà le.

Wŏmen ch'iú hsüeȟweǹ, ītiṅ̀ḡ yaò ī t'ień pĭ ī t'ień chiǹ-pù, yiñweì meí yŭ chiǹ-pù, chiù yaò t'uì-pù le.

Wŏ k'aǹ ni chiaò t'a-tzùchī īko jeń taò waìkuo ch'ü, shiȟ ītiṅ̀ḡ yŭ weí-hsieň te.

Wŏmen īching chüeȟtiṅ̀ḡle ch'iṅ́ nite yüeȟfù miṅ́t'ien taò womente chiāli lai ch'iȟ chuṅḡfaǹ.

WRITING DRILL

A. Write out in Chinese all the items in Section A of Oral Drill above.

B. Transcribe in Chinese all the items in Section B of Oral Drill above.

C. Answer the following questions in Chinese:

1. 張 良 是 那 一 個 朝 代 的 人？
為 甚 麼 他 要 給 國 家 報 仇？

2. 老 人 怎 麼 知 道 張 良 的 脾 氣
好？ 後 來 他 把 甚 麼 送 給 張 良？

3. 岳 飛 是 誰？ 為 甚 麼 他 部 下
的 兵 士，都 肯 為 國 家 拼 命 去 打 仗？

4. 秦檜是誰？他做了甚麼對不起岳飛的事？

5. 晏子是那一國的外交官？楚王為甚麼要難他？

6. 藺相如是那一個時代，那一國的人？秦王想把甚麼給趙國來交換寶玉？後來秦王為甚麼不把藺相如殺了？

READING DRILL

After reading the following, render it into English:

兩個朋友爭牛[4]

有一個人，家裏有一隻牛，這隻牛有一天病了．病了很多天也沒有好．那個人以為牛的病，是不會好的，就把牛送給他的一個朋友．

他的朋友一看，就知道牛的病是會好的，要是好好兒的養[5]牛，病好了，還可以用的，就天天養牛．後來牛的病真的好了，很有用．牛的主人看見牛已經病好了，又想要回去．

可是養牛的人說，"牛有病的

---

[4] Adapted from 人人讀，Volume 1.

[5] (Yang) means "to nourish, to care for, to support (as dependents); to give birth to."

我現在把牛養在那裏？世界上那裏有這樣的道理：你的牛生病，送給你養；病好了，你又要道理，要牛回去呢？"

人說，"牛本來是我的，沒生過病也好，生過病也好。"他們兩個人，爭這隻牛，爭起來了，就去見縣官。縣官對他們說，"我要問你們兩個：第一，牛是誰的？第二，甚麼是很要緊的？你們可以回答我。誰回答得好，我就把牛給他。"

他們兩個人，就回家去想。想了三天。到了第四天早上，就再去見縣官。

牛的主人對縣官說，"我的牛很大；我會耕田，是很要緊的。我要牛。"養牛的人說，"我的器量[6]很大；我的朋友是很要緊的。我要朋友，不要牛。"

縣官聽完了就說，"養牛的人，牛是他的。"牛的主人沒有話可以再說，只好不要牛，自己回家去。

[6] This means "natural capacity for understanding people."

VOCABULARY CHARACTERS

(Lań)
Orchid [*]

(Mā)
Mama [*]

(Wù)
Matter, thing [*]

(Chinğ)
Scenery [*]

(Kŭ)
Ancient; (a surname)

(T'ińg)
Courtyard [*]

(T'ināg)
Hall

(Ch'uanḡ)
Window [*]

(Hù)
Door [*]; household

(Mù)
Stage curtain; act of a play

(Chenḡ) To draft, to recruit

(Tań) Also 担.
To carry (with pole on shoulder)

(Yū)
Grief [*]; to be worried [*]

(Yeň)
To perform (as a play, music, etc.)

(T'ieň)
Placard, notice, invitation [*]
(T'ieh)
Rubbing from inscription [*]

(Pì)
Necessary, must [*]

(Leì)
Tired, weary

(Hsì)
Play (drama)

(Chiȟ)
To weave (as cloth, etc.)

(Yǐng)
Image, shadow [*]

(T'àn) Also written 嘆.
To sigh [*]

(Ch'ū) Also written 出.
(Classifier for plays)

(Pà)
Papa [*]

(Lìng) Also written 令.
Command, order [*]; to cause

COMPOUNDS

男孩子 (Nań-haítzu) ⎫
男孩兒 (Nań-hárh) ⎬ Male child; son

心 事 (Hsiñshiȟ) Mental cares, worries

徵 兵 (Chengֿ-pīngֿ) To draft men for military purposes

年 輕 (Nieńch'ingֿ) Young in years

蘭花兒 (Lańhuārh) Orchid

從 軍 (Ts'ungֿ-chün) To enlist, to join the ranks

人 物 (Jeńwù) Men and things; dramatis personae

生 物 (Shengֿwù) Animate objects

死 物 (Szŭwù) Inanimate objects

動 物 (Tungֿwù) Animals

相 同 (Hsiangֿt'ungֿ) Same, similar

物 理 (Wùlì) Physics

布 景 (Pùchingֿ) Stage scenery

有機物 (Yŭchī-wù) Organic matter

女孩子 (Nŭ-haítzu) ⎫
女孩兒 (Nŭ-hárh) ⎬ Female child; daughter

帖 子 (T'iehֿtzu) Placard, notice, invitation

字 帖 (Tzùt'iehֿ) Rubbing from inscription for calligraphic purposes

擔 憂 (Tanֿ-yū) To be worried

難 得 (Nańté) Rare, difficult to find or get

吃不起苦 (Ch'iȟpuch'í k'ǔ) Unable to suffer hardship

戰 場 (Chanֿch'angֿ) Battlefield

去 得 (Ch'ùte) Able to go

去不得 (Ch'ùpute) Unable to go

到 底 (Taòtǐ) At bottom, after all

底 子 (Tǐtzu) Bottom; sole (of shoes); foundation

不 必 (Pūpì) Not necessary

必 定 (Pìtingֿ) Certainly, positively

無機物 (Wúchī-wù) Inorganic matter	爸 爸 (Pàpa) Papa
古 代 (Kŭtaì) The ancient period; antiquity	媽 媽 (Māma) Mama
近 代 (Chìntaì)	戲 院 (Hsìyüàn) Theatre
現 代 (Hsièntaì) } The modern period; modern	影 子 (Yĭngtzu) Image, shadow
家 庭 (Chiāt'ing) The family (as an institution)	電 影 (Tièiyĭng) Motion pictures
客 廳 (K'òt'ing) Parlor	電影院 (Tièiyĭng-yüàn) Motion-picture theater
飯 廳 (Fàit'ing) Dining room	看 戲 (K'àn-hsì) To see a play
窗 戶 (Ch'uanghu) Window	片 兒 (P'ièrh) Calling card; motion-picture film
織 布 (Chīn-pù) To weave cloth	演 説 (Yĕn-shuō) To make a speech
織布機 (Chīnpù-chī) Loom	演説家 (Yĕnshuōchiā) Orator
開 幕 (K'aī-mù) To raise the curtain; to begin	生 命 (Shēngmìng) Life
歎 氣 (T'àn-ch'ì) To sigh	命 令 (Mìnglìng) Command, order
歎一口氣 (T'àn ī k'oŭ ch'ì) To heave a sigh	美 京 (Mĕichīng) Washington, D.C.

笑 話 (Hsiàohuà) Joke

READING MATERIAL

木 蘭 從 軍
第 一 幕　　　離 家 (一)

人 物: 木 蘭, 木 蘭 的 父 親, 母 親, 姐 姐,
　　　弟 弟.

布 景: 普 通 古 代 家 庭 的 客 廳, 窗 戶
　　　的 旁 邊 兒 有 一 架 織 布 機.

開 幕: 木 蘭 的 父 親 坐 在 椅 子 上 看
　　　書, 母 親 跟 弟 弟 坐 在 旁 邊 兒.

木蘭織了一會兒布，忽然停了，歎了一口氣，接着又歎了一口氣。

1. 父親：木蘭，你今天怎麼歎了一口氣，又歎一口氣啊？你心裏頭有甚麼事啊？是不是有甚麼事？

2. 木蘭：爸爸，沒有甚麼事。

3. 弟弟：二姐姐，是不是大姐姐欺負了你，所以你歎氣？大姐姐她怎麼會說笑話！她今天欺負你，昨天不在，是老是欺負人的？

4. 木蘭：弟弟，你真是很愛我呢？大姐姐很愛我的，她怎麼會欺負我？你知道大姐姐今天你怎麼訴我起來，昨天不在做難。

5. 母親：女兒，你有甚麼心事，告訴我就得了。（一頭兒說，一頭兒站起來，向織布機走去。）

6. 木蘭：媽媽，我告訴你罷。我們現在頭打仗，不覺得爸爸給國家打仗，怎麼會不覺得？上爸爸的名字當頭，怎麼會？我晚上看見爸爸的徵兵帖子，還要心裏難過，兒的呢！

7. 父親：木蘭，你年歲這麼小，而且是個女孩兒，也會替爸爸擔憂，

（父親續）……去給國家。這一點，我已經想得很明白了。那麼，假如人家好，太……當然，這就罷了。更年輕的弟弟，不是更年輕……我已經當過兵，打過仗了，年紀大了。現在不比當兵的爸爸，打不了仗了。爸爸吃不了這個苦，心裏頭就……難過了。真打你，難過……

8. 木蘭：爸爸，現在不比當兵打仗，哥哥去！爸爸吃不了，沒有替爸爸去。爸爸恐怕別人去，我不能過。不了，不過恐怕有爸爸……明白，大概替爸爸，太小，說不出來。

9. 母親：（很想說話，可是沒有說出來。）

10. 父親：你說的話，句句都很有道理。除了我自己去以外，我就沒有別的法子了。你們不要擔憂，將來我們大家都……打了勝仗，回來，我們大家都很快樂的。萬一我死在戰場，也是一件非常光榮的事。將來我一定也……

11. 木蘭：（站起來。）我很願意替爸爸去當兵打仗。

12. 父親：你是女孩兒，怎麼去得？

13. 木蘭：男孩兒也是人，女孩兒……

也 是 人, 怎 麼 去 不 得? 爸 爸, 我 的
主 意 已 經 打 定 了, 我 一 定 要 去.

14. 父 親: 木 蘭, 你 的 用 意 很 不 錯,
可 是 到 底 你 還 是 個 女 孩 兒, 天 下
那 兒 會 有 女 兒 去 當 兵 的 道 理?
假 如 你 是 男 人, 我 當 然 讓 你 去. 要
是 你 不 喜 歡 去, 國 家 也 要 把 你 徵
去 的.

15. 木 蘭: 爸 爸, 你 不 必 多 管, 女 兒
自 有 道 理... 我 現 在 累 極 了, 要 進
去 休 息 休 息. (走 進 去.)

ROMANIZED TEXT OF READING MATERIAL

Mùlań ts'uńg-chün

Tìi mù   Lí-chiā (Ī)

Jeńwù: Mùlań, Mùlańte fùch'in, mǔch'in, chiehˇchieh, tìti.

Pùchińg: Pǔt'uńg kǔtaì chiāt'ińgte k'òt'ińg, ch'uańghute p'ańgpierh yǔ īchià chiħpù-chī.

K'aī-mù: Mùlańte fùch'in tsò tsaì ītzushang k'aǹ-shū, mǔch'in keń tìti tsò tsaì p'ańgpierh. Mùlań chiħle īhuǎrh pù, hūjań t'ińg le, t'aǹle īk'oǔ ch'ì, chiehˇche yù t'aǹ īk'oǔ ch'ì.

1. Fùch'in: Mùlań, nǐ chiñt'ien hsiñ lit'ou yǔ sheḿma shiħ? Tseḿma t'aǹle īk'oǔ ch'ì, yù t'aǹ īk'oǔ ch'ì a?

2. Mùlań: Pàpa, meí yǔ shemma shiħ.

3. Tìti: Erħ-chiehˇchieh, shiħ pushih Tà-chiehˇchieh chiñt'ien ch'īfule ni, sóǐ yaò t'aǹ-ch'ì a?

4. Mùlań: Tìti, nǐ cheń huì shuō hsiaòhuà! Nǐ chiħtao Tà-chiehˇchieh shiħ heǎ aì wo te, t'ā tseḿma huì ch'īfu wo ne?

5. Mǔch'in: Nǔerh, ní yǔ sheḿma hsiñshiħ, kaòsu wo chiù té le. (Ītoúrh shuō, ītoúrh chaǹch'ilai, hsiaǹg chiħpù-chī tsoǔch'ü.)

6. Mùlań: Māma, wǒ kaòsu ni pa. Wǒmen tsót'ien waǹshang k'aǹchien te cheńg-pińg t'iehˇtzu, shaǹgt'ou pū shiħ yǔ Pàpate mińgtzu ma? Pàpa hsieǹtsaì laǒ le, haí yaò ch'ü tańg-pińg, keī kuóchiā tǎ-chaǹg, tsò nǔerh te hsiñ lit'ou, tseḿma huì pū chüeħte naǹkuò ne?

7. Fùch'in: Mùlań, nǐ nieńsui chèma hsiaǒ, erħch'ieħ shiħ ko nǔ-hárh,

yeȟ huì t'ì pàpa tañ-yū, cheñ shih̓ nańté le. K'ŏshih tanḡ-pinḡ ch'ü keȋ kuóchiā tǎ-chang̓, shih̓ nańjen pū neng̓ pū tsò te. Chèi tień nĭ ming̓paile, hsiñ lit'ou chiù pū huì tsaì chüeȟte nańkuò le.

8. Mùlań: Pàpa, nài tień wŏ tanḡjań ming̓pai, pūkuò Pàpa hsieȟtsaì nieńchi ȋching chèma tà le, k'ung̓p'à ch'iȟpuch'ȋ tanḡ-pinḡ te k'ŭ pa. Chiǎjú yŭ pieȟiko pĭ Pàpa nieńch'inḡ te nańjen, t'ì Pàpa ch'ü tanḡ-pinḡ tǎ-chang̓, pū shih̓ keng̓ yaò haŏ ma? Wŏ meí yŭ kōko, Tìti nieńchi yù t'aì hsiaŏ, pū neng̓ t'ì Pàpa ch'ü!

9. Mŭch'in: (Heń hsiang̓ shuō-huà, k'ŏshih meí yŭ shuōch'ulai.)

10. Fùch'in: Nĭ shuō te huà, ch̓uch̓u toū heń yŭ taòli. Ch'úle wo-tzùchĭ ch'ü ȋwaì, wŏ k'aȟ chiù meí yŭ pieȟte fátzu le. Nimen pūyaò tañ-yū, chianḡlaí wó tǎsheng̓le chang̓ huílai, wŏmen tàchiā toū ȋting̓ heň k'uaȋlo te. Waȟî wó szū tsaì chaȟch'ang̓, yeȟ shih̓ ȋchień feȋch'ang̓ kuanḡjung̓ te shih̓.

11. Mùlań: (Chaȟch'ilai.) Wó heň yüaȟi t'ì Pàpa ch'ü tanḡ-pinḡ tǎ-chang̓.

12. Fùch'in: Nĭ shih̓ nŭ-hárh, tsem̓ma ch'ùte?

13. Mùlań: Nań-hárh yeȟ shih̓ jeń, nŭ-hárh yeȟ shih̓ jeń, tsem̓ma ch'ù-pute? Pàpa, wŏte chúi ȋching tāting̓ le, wŏ ȋting̓ yaò ch'ù.

14. Fùch'in: Mùlań, nȋte yung̓ì heň pūts'ò, k'ŏshih taòtí nĭ haí shih̓ ko nŭ-hárh. T'ieñhsià nǎrh huì yú nŭerh ch'ü tanḡ-pinḡ te taòli? Chiǎjú nĭ shih̓ nańjen, wŏ tanḡjań jang̓ ni ch'ù. Yaòshih nĭ pū hsīhuan ch'ù, kuóchiā yeȟ yaò pá ni cheng̓ch'ü te.

15. Mùlań: Pàpa, nĭ pūpì tō kuǎn, nŭerh tzù yŭ taòli ... Wŏ hsieȟtsaì leìchí le, yaò chiȟch'ü hsiūhsihsiuhsi. (Tsoȟchinch'ü.)

NOTES

1. 木蘭 was a Chinese heroine known for having taken the place of her aged father as a soldier and fought for twelve years on the frontier in male disguise without revealing her own sex. Other than the fact that this great adventure of hers has been treated in a poem (木蘭篇, Mùlań P'ieñ) of uncertain authorship, not much is known about her. Some scholars say that she lived in the fifth century, A.D.; others think that she was born either in the 隋 (Suí) Dynasty, A.D. 589–618, or early in the 唐 (T'ang̓) Dynasty, A.D. 618–907. No one is sure of her birthplace; one source claims her to have been a native of modern Hopei province, another claims her to have been a native of modern Honan province, a third maintains that she was a native of modern Kansu (甘肅) province. Differences of opinion with regard to her surname still exist. Authorities cannot agree as to whether her surname is 朱 (Chū), 花 (Huā), or 魏 (Weì).

2. 開幕 and 閉幕 (cf. Lesson Fifty-seven), although primarily dramatic terms, may be used to designate the beginning and end, respectively, of a memorable occasion, special event, or impressive ceremony: 遠東和平會議 明天要開幕了, "The Far Eastern Peace Conference will begin tomorrow"; 遠東和平會議今天已經開了幕沒有, "Has the Far Eastern Peace Conference already begun today?"

3. Note that 做女兒的 in Number 6 of the Reading Material above is

a relative clause with its subject (人) understood. It means "the person who is the daughter," that is, Mùlań herself. It can be rendered into English as "I, his [or the] daughter."

4. 吃不起做兵的苦 means "unable to stand (or suffer) the hardship of (being) a soldier."

5. 女兒自有道理 means something like "(your) daughter has her own way of reasoning."

6. 爸爸 and 媽媽 are both intimate terms of address, and their use resembles that of "papa" and "mama," respectively.

7. 美京 stands for 美國(的)京城, "the national capital of the United States of America," hence, Washington, D.C. Another name for Washington in Chinese is 華盛頓 (Huáshengtuǹ).

ORAL EXERCISES

A. Say the following in Chinese:

1. A play; a good play; to see a play; to see a moving picture; physics; to study physics.

2. A window. Please open the window. Do you see the window there? How many windows are there in this room?

3. Where is the parlor? Where is the dining room? The parlor is to the left of the dining room. The dining room is at the back of the parlor. Whose order is that? That is the order of my superior officer.

4. To weave cloth; to learn how to weave cloth. I don't know how to weave cloth. He teaches me how to weave cloth.

5. He likes to make speeches. I don't like to make speeches. I like to make jokes. He doesn't like to make jokes.

6. Has the curtain been raised yet? When is the curtain going to be raised?

7. Please don't worry. Please don't worry about him. Please don't worry about me.

8. What [kind of] flower is this? Is it [an] orchid?

9. Is there any theater in this city? How far is the theater from here? How many people can the theater seat?

10. Who has sent you this invitation card? Is my name written on the invitation card?

B. Render the following into English:

1. Chungkuo chiāt'ińg; Meǐkuo chiāt'ińg; tà chiāt'ińg; hsiaǒ chiāt'ińg; Chungkuote tà chiāt'ińg; Meǐkuote hsiaǒ chiāt'ińg.

2. Nǐ ch'ùte ch'üpute? T'ā tseṁma ch'ùte? Ní yǔ kungfu, tseṁma ch'ùpute?

3. T'ā t'ańle ik'oǔ ch'ì le, nǐ meí t'ińgchien ma?

4. Nimen hsǐhuan k'ań-hsì ne, haíshih hsǐhuan k'ań tieǹyiňg ne?

5. Ch'ińg ni pǎ ch'uanghu k'aik'ai. Pūyaò pǎ nàko ch'uanghu kuańshang.

6. Chèchià chiṅpù-chī shiḣ shuí maǐ te? Shiḣ ní maǐ te pushih?

7. Chèyanġ meī te lańhuārh, cheń shiḣ nańté le.

8. T'āmen p'ingshih pū tsaì faǹt'ing ch'ih-faǹ te.
9. Nàko ch'uanghu tīhsia yú ītzu keñ chōtzu meiyu?
10. Jeń shih tungwù, niú, koǔ, maō yeh toū shih tungwù.

WRITTEN EXERCISES

A. Transcribe Section B, above, in Chinese.
B. Render the following into English:

1. 有生命的東西,我們叫"生物,"也叫"有機物";沒有生命的東西,我們叫"死物,"也叫"無機物."

2. 木蘭是中國古代的女人,替他父親去從軍,過了十二年才回家.

3. 這兒的電影院今天晚上演的片兒,一個叫"戰爭跟和平,"一個叫"自從你去了以後."

4. 演說家都是很有口才的,沒有口才的人,必定不能做演說家.

5. 中國現代的家庭跟古代的家庭,有相同的地方,也有不相同的地方.

6. 你們家裏的客廳真漂亮,地方又大,窗戶又多,我們家裏的客廳,老實說比不上.

7. 我聽說世界和平會議,不久就要在美京開幕了,你怎麼不知道?

8. 要 是 你 心 裏 頭 沒 有 覺 得 難 過, 怎 麼 你 昨 天 晚 上 要 歎 氣 呢 ?

9. 他 近 來 看 書 看 不 到 一 個 鐘 頭, 就 覺 得 很 累 了, 我 很 替 他 擔 憂.

10. 昨 天 晚 上 我 們 看 的 戲, 叫 "木 蘭 從 軍." 那 齣 戲 一 共 有 兩 幕, 很 有 意 思.

C. Render the following into Chinese:

1. Do you know what difference there is between animate objects and inanimate objects?

2. How can you stand the hardship of being a merchant? How can he stand the hardship of being a diplomat?

3. Although he is a famous orator, he likes to make jokes with other people.

4. You have your own life; he, too, has his own life; your life and his are not the same.

5. Although he is now sick, he will get well very soon. Please don't worry about him.

6. What kind of notice is that in your hand? Is it a draft notice?

7. A man as frank and capable as he is certainly is very difficult to find now.

8. You need not ask him to tell you where the theater is. I can tell you.

9. Although you like to go, if you are busy now, how can you go?

10. After all, he is a person of great learning; hence he can answer all our questions.

VOCABULARY CHARACTERS

(Hsī)
To pity [*]

(Ch'í)
Flag [*]

(Chīng)
To alarm, to startle [*]

(Pàn)
To dress up as, to disguise as

(Chū)
To reside (literary Chinese); (a surname) [*]

(Mèng)
Dream

(Chí)
To gather, to collect [*]

(Hó)
To join together [*]; fit, suitable [*]

(Pì)
To shut, to close [*]

(Ch'üán)
Power, authority, right

(Lì)
Profit, interest [*]; strong, fierce [*]

(Ì)
The right thing to do [*]; meaning, significance [*]

(Wù)
Affair, business [*]

(Jèn)
Duty, responsibility [*]

(Hsiǎng)
To enjoy [*]

(Huá)
China; splendor; flowery (literary Chinese) [*]

(Tsú)
Clan

(Yú)
Cause [*]; to permit, to allow; from

(Shoù)
To receive [*]; (sign of the passive voice)

 (Chaō)
To beckon with the hand; to recruit; to attend to [*]

 (Miń)
People, citizens [*]

 (Hsiaŋ̆)
To sound; to be heard

 (Ch'üań) Usually written
全.
Complete, completely [*]

(Piaŏ)
External, outside [*]; list, table, schedule [*]; meter [*]

COMPOUNDS

表同情 (Piaŏ t'unǵch'inǵ) To sympathize

老人家 (Laŏjenchia) An aged person; (title of respect)

可惜 (K'ŏhsī) What a pity! Too bad that...; it is a pity that...

從來 (Ts'unǵlaí) Hitherto, up to now

得意 (Téì) Elated, exultant

認出 (Jeǹch'u) To recognize

現出 (Hsieǹch'u) To show, to manifest, to reveal

驚奇 (Chinǵch'í) Astonished and amazed

原來 (Yüańlaí) The truth is

扮做 (Paǹtso) To dress up as, to disguise as

打扮 (Tăpan) To dress up

居然 (Chūjań) Indeed, actually

代表 (Taìpiaŏ) To represent; representative

外表 (Waìpiaŏ) Exterior, outside; outward, external

外表上 (Waìpiaŏshang) Outwardly, externally

旗子 (Ch'ítzu) Flag

人民 (Jeńmiń) People (of a country or region)

國民 (Kuómiń) People, citizens

民國 (Mińkuó) Republic

國旗 (Kuóch'í) National flag

民主國 (Mińchŭ-kuó) Democratic country; democracy

中華民國 (Chunǵhuá-mińkuó) The Chinese Republic

民族 (Mińtsú) Nation

中華民族 (Chunǵhuá-mińtsú) The Chinese nation

權利 (Ch'üańli) Rights

權力 (Ch'üańlì) Power, authority

政權 (Chenǵch'üań) Political power

兵 權 (Pingch'üan) Military power

主 權 (Chǔch'üan) Sovereign rights, sovereignty

民 權 (Minch'üan) People's rights

表姐妹 (Piaó-chiehmeì) Female first cousins of another surname

表兄弟 (Piaǒ-hsiungtì) Male first cousins of another surname

做 夢 (Tsò-meng̀) To dream, to have a dream

夢 見 (Meng̀chien) To dream of, to dream that

夢 想 (Meng̀hsiangˇ) To daydream; daydream

夢想不到 (Meng̀hsiangˇputaò) Not to have dreamed of (or that)

信 號 (Hsinhaò) Signal

集 合 (Chíhó) To assemble

招 手 (Chaō-shoǔ) To wave the hand, to beckon with the hand

閉 幕 (Pì-mù) To lower or drop the curtain; to conclude

軍 樂 (Chünyüeh) Military music

音樂家 (Yinyüehchiā) Musician

決 心 (Chüehhsin) Decision

下決心 (Hsià chüehhsin) To make a decision

義 務 (Ìwu) Obligation

意 義 (Ìì) Significance, meaning

責 任 (Tséjen) Duty, responsibility

負 責 (Fù-tsé) To be responsible

擔 負 (Tanfù) To bear on the shoulder, to shoulder; to assume (as duty)

享 受 (Hsiangˇshoù) To enjoy

自 由 (Tzùyú) Liberty, freedom

理 由 (Lǐyú) Reason, ground

平 等 (P'ingtengˇ) Equal rank, equality

完 全 (Wanch'üan) Complete, entire; completely, entirely

利 錢 (Lìch'ien) Profit, interest

利 害 (Lìhai) Severe, fierce; severely, fiercely

READING MATERIAL

木 蘭 從 軍

第 一 幕　　離 家 （二）

1. 母 親: 木 蘭 這 個 女 孩 兒, 會 替
老 人 家 擔 憂, 真 是 難 得, 可 惜 到 底
還 是 個 女 孩 兒.

2. 弟弟：媽媽,我不很明白.難道女孩子就不能去當兵,給國家出力了麼?

3. 母親：我從來沒聽見過女孩兒去當兵的.

4. 弟弟：二姐姐要去當兵,爸爸媽媽都說他是個女孩兒,不能去.我是男孩兒,那麼我替爸爸去就好了.

5. 父親：你去也不行.你雖然是男孩兒,可是你年歲太小,沒有力氣打仗.

6. 弟弟：爸爸,我年紀雖然小,可是…(木蘭穿了軍服,從外頭進來,非常得意.)

7. 父親：(站起來,樣子很客氣.)請問這位青年軍官是誰,是從那兒來的?

8. 母親：先生,請坐請坐.

9. 木蘭：(一頭兒摘下軍帽,一頭兒笑起來.)你們真的認不出我是誰麼?那麼我可以替爸爸去打仗了.

10. 弟弟：(現出驚奇的神氣。)啊！二姐姐，你不是穿了軍服，真像個青年男子！原來是二姐姐啊！

11. 母親：木蘭，你穿了軍服，我一時認不出你是誰。

12. 父親：你剛才從外頭進來，女子穿上軍服，居然瞞得我，怎麼會在男人屋子裏？一定當兵了。頭裏人穿到給了瞞的，我休息一時。

13. 木蘭：爸爸就在屋子裏說，男人穿軍服，我扮了這看，也當一兵了。當兵，衣裳買了，給媽媽，人能……你們別怕，到底去也是一樣的，外頭還當一話。我一去能你們爸爸們別怕，然到底去也是一樣的。

14. 父親：你穿上軍服，像個男孩兒，我再夢想的意見多說，那上軍官我決不想，可不會了。你很像女孩子，你上個的，軍服雖然是讓見那樣的，那樣了。表是兵樣。

15. 母親：爸爸，我不必再說；木蘭，你不必再……(軍樂忽然響起來。)

16. 木蘭：爸爸，媽媽，這就是集合

的信號了．我雖然是個女孩兒，可是我已經下了決心，替爸爸去從軍，現在我要立刻去了．（姐姐從裏頭走出來．木蘭大聲説．）爸爸，媽媽，姐姐，弟弟，我去了．再見再見！（説完了就從大門走出去．）

17. 父親，母親：木蘭，木蘭，好女兒，再見！

18. 姐姐：妹妹，再見！

19. 弟弟：（招手．）二姐姐，再見！

（閉幕）

ROMANIZED TEXT OF READING MATERIAL

Mùlań ts'uńg-chüñ

Tìi mù   Lí-chiā (Erh̀)

1. Mǔch'in: Mùlań chèko nǔ-hárh, huì t'ì laǒjenchia tañ-yū, cheñ shih̀ nanté, k'ǒhsī taòtī haí shih̀ ko nǔ-hárh.

2. Tìti: Māma, wǒ pū heñ mingpai. Nañtaò nǔ-hárh chiù pū neng ch'ü tang-pinḡ, keī kuóchiā ch'ü-lì le ma?

3. Mǔch'in: Wǒ ts'unǵlaí meí t'inḡchienkuo nǔ-hárh ch'ü tang-pinḡ te.

4. Tìti: Erh̀-chieh̀chieh yaò ch'ü tang-pinḡ, Pàpa Māma toū shuō t'a shih̀ ko nǔ-hárh, pū neng ch'ü. Wǒ shih̀ nań-hárh, nèma wǒ t'ì Pàpa ch'ü chiù haǒ le.

5. Fùch'in: Nǐ ch'ü yeh̀ pū hsinǵ. Nǐ suījań shih̀ nań-hárh, k'ǒshih nǐ nienśui t'aì hsiaǒ, meí yǔ lìch'i tā-chanḡ.

6. Tìti: Pàpa, wǒ nienchi suījań hsiaǒ, k'ǒshih ... (Mùlań ch'uanle chüñfú, ts'ung waìt'ou chinlai, feīch'anḡ téi.)

7. Fùch'in: (Chanch'ilai, yanḡtzu heñ k'òch'i.) Ch'inḡ weǹ chèweì ch'inḡ-nień chüñkuañ shih̀ shuí, shih̀ ts'unǵ nǎrh lai te?

8. Mǔch'in: Hsieñsheng, ch'inḡ tsò ch'ing tso.

9. Mùlań: (Īt'oúrh chaīhsia chüñmaò, īt'oúrh hsiaòch'ilai.) Nimen cheñte jeǹpuch'ū wo shih̀ shuí ma? Nèma wó k'ói t'ì Pàpa ch'ü tā-chanḡ le.

10. Tìti: (Hsieǹch'u chinḡch'í te sheńch'i.) Ā! Yüánlaí shih̀ Erh̀-chieh̀chieh, pū shih̀ shemma ch'inḡnień chüñkuañ. Erh̀-chieh̀chieh, nǐ ch'uanle chüñfú, cheñ hsianḡ ko nańjen a!

11. Mǔch'in: Mùlań, nǐ ch'uañle chünfú, wǒ īshih̄ jeǹpuch'ū ni shih̄ shuí.
12. Fùch'in: Nǐ kanḡts'aí chiǹle lit'ou ch'ü hsiūhsi, tseḿma huì ts'unḡ wait'ou chiǹlai a?
13. Mùlań: Pàpa shuōle nǔjen pū neng ch'ü tanḡ-pīng, wǒ chiù tsaì wūtzu lit'ou ch'uañle nite īshang, paǹtso nańjen, ts'unḡ houmeń taò wait'ou ch'ü maǐle chèt'aò chünfú, ch'uañshangle keī Pàpa Māma k'añk'an. Hsieǹtsaì wǒ chūjań mańle nimen, piehjen wó yeh̄ ītinḡ mańteliaǒ te, wǒ pū p'à pū neng ch'ü tanḡ-pīng le.
14. Fùch'in: Nǐ ch'uañshangle chünfú, suījań waìpiaǒshang heń hsianḡ ko nań-chünkuañ, k'ǒshih taòtǐ haí shih̄ ko nǔ-hárh. Wǒ chüehp̄ū huì janḡ nǐ ch'ü tanḡ-pīng te. Nǐ pūpì tsaì menḡhsianḡ le.
15. Mǔch'in: Pàpa, wǒte ìchien yeh̄ shih̄ īyanḡ. Mùlań, nǐ pūpì tsaì tō shuō nàyanḡ te huà le. (Chüñyüeh̄ hūjań hsianḡch'ilai.)
16. Mùlań: Pàpa, Māma, chè chiù shih̄ chíhó te hsiǹhaò le. Wǒ suījań shih̄ ko nǔ-hárh, k'ǒshih wó ìching hsiàle chüehhsiñ, t'ì Pàpa ch'ü ts'unḡchün, hsieǹtsaì wǒ yaò lìk'ò ch'ǜ le. (Chiehchieh ts'unḡ lit'ou tsoǔch'ulai. Mùlań tàshenḡ shuō.) Pàpa, Māma, Chiehchieh, Tìti, wǒ ch'ǜ le. Tsaì chieǹ tsai chien! (Shuōwańle, chiù ts'unḡ tàmeń tsoǔch'uch'ü.)
17. Fùch'in, Mǔch'in: Mùlań, Mùlań, haó nǔerh, tsaì chieǹ!
18. Chiehchieh: Meìmei, tsaì chieǹ!
19. Tìti: (Chaō-shoǔ.) Erh̄-chiehchieh, tsaì chieǹ!

(Pì-mù)

NOTES

1. 老人家 is a title of respect used in addressing persons who are advanced in years irrespective of sex.
2. 認出, "to recognize," implies identifying or differentiating the thing in question by the process of recognition. The positive and negative forms of this resultative compound are 認得出 and 認不出.
3. 居 is primarily a literary word meaning "to reside" (cf. 住). 居然, "indeed, actually," implies that the situation following it is more or less contrary to or beyond expectation.
4. The classifier for 夢 is either 個 or 場.
5. 權 is frequently used as a suffix to mean "right" or "power." Thus, 政權 is "political power"; 兵權, "military power"; 主權, "sovereign rights"; 民權, "the people's rights"; etc.
6. 對 or 對於 is used in connection with 負責 to bring out the idea of being answerable for something. Thus, 對於你昨天說的話,他應該負責, "For what you said yesterday he should be responsible."
7. The classifier for 旗子 is 面.
8. 原來, "the truth is," is used to indicate that the speaker's earlier impression or conclusion is erroneous or does not tally with the fact discovered. Thus, 原來你不是江先生的父親 implies that the speaker must have thought that the person addressed was the father of Mr. Chianḡ, but the truth, which has now been revealed to the speaker, is that he is not.

ORAL EXERCISES

A. Say the following in Chinese:

1. A republic; the Chinese Republic; the government of the Chinese Republic; the people of the Chinese Republic; the people's representatives.

2. A nation; the Chinese nation; a flag; the Chinese national flag; the liberty of a nation; the equality of a nation.

3. A dream; to have a dream; to dream of; to dream of you; to dream of you waving [your] hands.

4. To enjoy; to enjoy rights; to enjoy liberty; to enjoy equality.

5. Is he responsible? Is he irresponsible? It is too bad that he is so irresponsible! It is a pity that he can't come today!

6. What grounds do you have? What grounds does he have? What good reasons does he have for sending you to attend our conference?

7. I can shoulder my responsibilities. His responsibilities are very heavy.

8. The truth is that he did not like military music.

9. Up to now I haven't been there. Up to now I haven't told him.

10. He is quite elated; he is not quite elated; he is quite downcast.

B. Render the following into English:

1. Nà shih̀ năi kuóte kuóch'í? Shih̀ Chunḡkuote kuóch'í pushih?

2. Ch'üańli shih̀ wŏmen k'ŏi hsianḡshoù te, tséjeǹ shih wŏmen yaò tañfù te.

3. Nimen tsót'ien wańshang k'aǹ te hsì, shih̀ chítieň chunḡ k'aī-mù te?

4. Paǹtso kunḡjeń te jeń shih̀ shuí? Shih̀ t'āte tìti pushih?

5. Nĭ k'aǹ, t'ā tăpanch'ilai, cheń p'iaòliang le.

6. T'ā laŏjenchia leìchí le, pū neńg ch'ǜ le, jang̀ wo tsò t'ate taìpiaŏ pa.

7. T'ā chèma k'uaì chiù huílai, wŏ meǹghsianḡputaò le.

8. Kanḡts'aí tsaì waìt'ou hsiang̀ ni chaō-shoù te, shih̀ pushih t'āte erh̀tzu?

9. Nĭ waìpiaŏshang heň hsiang̀ ko yiñyüeh̀chiā, t'ā waìpiaŏshang heň hsiang̀ ko waìchiaōchiā.

10. Wŏmen tsò-jeń toū yaò fù-tsé, pū fù-tsé te jeń shih̀ pū k'ŏk'aò te.

WRITTEN EXERCISES

A. Transcribe Section B, above, in Chinese.

B. Render the following into English:

1. 中華民國是一個民主國;中華民國的政府,是一個民主政府. "民主"就是人民做主人的意思.

2. 民主國家的人民,個個都能

享受自由跟平等的.

3.每一個國家的國民,都有他們自己應該享受的權利,也有他們自己應該擔負的責任.

4.世界上的國家,都有自己的主權的.中國有中國的主權,美國有美國的主權.

5.他昨天早上對我們說的話,沒有一句是有理由的.

6.他本來是要跟你們一塊兒去看電影的,可惜後來沒有工夫去.

7.政權是一種權力,兵權也是一種權力.

8.我現在認得出他是誰了.他就是前天代表你出席和平會議的.

9.他說過不喜歡做外交官,可是他現在居然做起外交官來了.

10.啊!我夢想不到他昨天才回來,明天又要走了!

C. Render the following into Chinese:

1. We are the citizens of the United States of America; they are the citizens of the Republic of China.

2. We enjoy liberty and equality; they, too, enjoy liberty and equality.

3. The Chinese nation is a very old nation and has a very lengthy history.

4. I had a dream last night and dreamed of you coming home from America.

5. What reason do you have for asking him to disguise [himself] as an old musician?

6. He was quite elated this morning when I saw him in front of the motion-picture theater

7. I couldn't recognize him when he disguised [himself] as a merchant from the Orient.

8. We shall assemble in front of the theater at nine o'clock tomorrow morning.

9. When he is dressed up he actually looks quite like an old man of seventy or eighty years of age.

10. To enlist is our obligation to our country. It is a responsibility which all good citizens should shoulder.

VOCABULARY CHARACTERS

(Chan)
(Classifier for lamps)

(Teng) Also written 灯.
Lamp

(Í)
To doubt, to suspect [*];
doubt, suspicion [*]

(Ch'í)
To ride astride

(P'i)
(Classifier for horses)

(Ts'ai)
To guess

(Hsiao)
To diminish, to consume

(Ch'ui)
To blow

(Yeh)
Old gentleman [*]; (a
term of respect for
men) [*]

(Yíng)
Military camp [*]; bat-
talion

(Chiă)
Armor [*]; (first of the
"Heavenly Stems")

(Ĭ) or (Ĭ)
(Second of the "Heavenly
Stems")

(Hā)
(Sound of laughter)

(Maò)
Appearance [*]

(Huò) or (Hò)
Either, or [*]

(Tz'ú)
Gentle, compassionate [*]

(Chung)
To hit the center, to hit
the mark [*]

(Tù)
Stomach, abdomen [*]

432

(K'anḡ)
Peace, repose [*]; health [*]

(Chièn)
Healthy [*]

(Fañ) Usually printed 翻.
To turn over; to translate

(Ì)
To translate

福
(Fú)
Good luck, good fortune [*]

COMPOUNDS

驚疑 (Chīngí) To be amazed and doubtful

疑心 (Íhsin) To doubt, to suspect

消息 (Hsiaōhsi) News, information

一起 (Īch'ī) All together

騎馬 (Ch'í-mǎ) To ride a horse

騎兵 (Ch'ípinḡ) Cavalry

步兵 (Pùpinḡ) Infantry

自行車 (Tzùhsinḡ-ch'ē) Bicycle

電燈 (Tièntenḡ) Electric light

油燈 (Yútenḡ) Oil lamp

點燈 (Tień-tenḡ) To light a lamp

吹燈 (Ch'uī-tenḡ) To blow out or extinguish a lamp

開電燈 (K'aī tièntenḡ) To turn on an electric light

關電燈 (Kuañ tièntenḡ) To turn off or shut off an electric light

軍營 (Chūnyinḡ) Military camp

營長 (Yinḡchanǧ) Battalion commander

大本營 (Tàpeǹyinḡ) Military headquarters

面貌 (Mièmaò) Looks, face

禮貌 (Límaò) Good manners, courtesy

馬力 (Mǎlì) Horsepower

或是 (Huòshih) Either, or

猜中 (Ts'aīchunǧ) ⎫
猜着 (Ts'aīchaó) ⎭ To guess accurately

猜得中 (Ts'aītechunǧ) ⎫ Able to guess accurately
猜得着 (Ts'aītechaó) ⎭

猜不中 (Ts'aīpuchunǧ) ⎫ Unable to guess accurately
猜不着 (Ts'aīpuchaó) ⎭

慈愛 (Tz'úaì) Loving, compassionate, kind

老太爺 (Laŏt'aìyeń) Old gentleman

老太太 (Laŏt'aìt'ai) Old lady

福氣 (Fúch'i) Good luck; lucky, fortunate

健康 (Chieǹk'anḡ) Health

康健 (K'anḡchieǹ) Healthy

奶奶 (Naĭnai) Grandma

爺爺 (Yeńyeh) Grandpa

翻譯 (Fañi) To translate; translation

翻成
譯成 (Fañch'eńg) (Ìch'eńg) } To translate into

難怪 (Nańkuaì) No wonder

肚子 (Tùtzu) Stomach, abdomen

餓死 (Òszu) To starve, to die of hunger

當中 (Tanḡchunḡ) In the midst of, among, in the course of

回頭 (Huí-t'oú) To turn the head back

READING MATERIAL

木 蘭 從 軍

第 二 幕　　回 家

人物: 木蘭, 父親, 母親, 姐姐, 弟弟, 兵甲, 兵乙.

布景: 跟第一幕一樣.

開幕: 木蘭的父親坐在客廳的左邊兒, 母親跟姐姐坐在右邊兒. 弟弟從外頭跑進來.

　　1. 弟弟: 爸爸, 媽媽, 大姐姐, 二姐姐回來了.

　　2. 母親: (驚疑的樣子.) 真的麼? 真的麼?

　　3. 父親: (驚疑的樣子.) 你怎麼知道啊?

……時，剛騎着馬回來的那個軍官，住在那位姐姐家裏，我就猜。那二姐消息不來，那一定是她還活着回來了。頭一着他，以了；一着他，以了。從外頭跟説的姐姐，一年不見，現在今天到了，也許是今天到的，是她還活着回來了。也許不如到外頭去。

4. 弟弟説：我剛騎着白馬從門外回來，走東頭，安定城裏一條街。一進城，聽説這軍官……着要我們軍……候，要我們軍罷。

5. 父親：恐怕十……實在説，我老實不敢夢想。他有不是，沒也真，不定也真不看。

6. 母親：爸爸，（站起來。）我們不如到外頭去看看罷。

7. 父親：（點頭，也站起來。）好罷，我們出去看看。

8. 母親：（望前走了兩步，回頭對弟弟説。）你們坐在這兒等等，我跟爸爸出去看看就回來。姐姐跟弟弟等，我跟爸爸出去。（走出去。）

9. 姐姐：弟弟，你聽清楚了麼？那騎着馬的軍官，真是二姐麼？那個了。

10. 弟弟:我聽得很清楚了,那個軍官是住在東安街的.

11. 姐姐:可是住在東安街的人,除了我們一家以外,還有不少別的人,怎能説那個軍官就是二姐姐了呢?(外頭有人説話的聲音.)

12. 弟弟:(從窗戶向外頭看了一看,就大聲説.)大姐姐,你別疑心了.你自己來看看罷.二姐姐跟爸爸媽媽一起走進來了.(站起來用手指着.)

13. 姐姐:啊! 弟弟,你猜中了,真是二姐姐回來了.(木蘭,父親,母親跟兩個兵都進來.)

14. 弟弟:(很喜歡的説.)二姐姐,你回來了.

15. 姐姐:(一頭兒笑,一頭兒説.)妹妹,你回來了真好了! (兵甲兵乙都很驚疑.)

16. 木蘭:姐姐,弟弟,我回來了.姐姐還是跟十二年以前差不多一樣,可是弟弟就比從前長得又高又大了.

17. 兵甲:（對兵乙說.）我們長官的老太爺,老太太,還是這樣康健,真是難得,真好福氣了!

18. 兵乙:是的,有這麼慈愛的父母,跟這麼好的姐姐,弟弟,難怪他大官也不肯做,只要回家來.

19. 木蘭:（對父母說.）這兩位弟兄,是跟我一起打仗,打了十二年的.我們在十二年當中,不知道吃了多少苦,殺死了多少敵軍了.

20. 父親:你們兩位請坐請坐.

21. 兵甲,兵乙:老太爺,別客氣.

22. 木蘭:（對兵甲,兵乙說.）這是我的家,不是軍營,你們不必客氣.我進去一會兒就出來.（兵甲,兵乙坐下.木蘭跟姐姐進去.）

23. 父親:（對弟弟說.）孩子,這兩位哥哥,走了不少的路,肚子一定餓了.你去弄一點兒酒菜來罷.

24. 弟弟:爸爸,好,我去弄酒菜來.

25. 兵甲,兵乙:老太爺真客氣!（木蘭穿上了女人的衣裳出來.兵甲,兵乙看見了,覺得十分驚奇.）

26. 木蘭:(笑着對兵甲,兵乙説.)你們知道我是誰麼?

27. 兵甲:小姐的面貌,很像我們的長官,我想一定是他的姐姐,或是妹妹了.

28. 兵乙:不但面貌像,而且聲音也差不多一樣.

29. 木蘭:我就是他了.(兵甲,兵乙説不出話來.)我本來是個女人,因為父親老了,所以替他去打仗,穿上了軍服,跟你們一起打了十二年仗,沒有一個人看得出我是個女人.你們説好笑不好笑?哈哈!哈哈!

30. 父親,母親,兵甲,兵乙:哈哈!哈哈!

(閉幕)

ROMANIZED TEXT OF READING MATERIAL

Mùlań ts'uń-chün

Tìerh̀ mù   Huí-chiā

Jeńwù: Mùlań, Fùch'in, Mǔch'in, Chiehchieh, Tìti, Pinɡ-Chiā, Pinɡ-Ĭ.
Pùchinɡ̀: Keñ tìi mù iyanɡ̀.
K'aī-mù: Mùlańte fùch'in tsò tsaì k'òt'inɡ̀te tsŏpierh, mǔch'in keñ chiehchieh tsò tsaì yùpierh. Tìti ts'uń waìt'ou p'aŏchinlai.

1. Tìti: Pàpa, Māma, Tà-chiehchieh, Erh̀-chiehchieh huílai le.
2. Mǔch'in: (Chinɡ̌í te yanɡ̀tzu.) Cheñ te ma? Cheñ te ma?
3. Fùch'in: (Chinɡ̌í te yanɡ̀tzu.) Ní tsem̌ma chih̀tao a?
4. Tìti: Wǒ kanɡ̄ ts'uń waìt'ou huílai te shih̀hou, t'inɡ̄shuō ch'enɡ̀meń waìt'ou yǔ īko chünkuañ, ch'íche īp'ī paí-mǎ, hoùt'ou keñche lianɡ̌ko

pinḡ, kanḡ yaò chiṅ-ch'enḡ lai. Jeṅchia toū shuō t'a shiḣ chù tsaì wŏmen chèt'iaó Tunḡañ-chieḣ te, sóí wŏ ts'aī nàweì chüṅküañ ītinḡ shiḣ Erḣ-chieḣchieh le.

5. Fùch'in: K'unḡp'à pū ītinḡ shiḣ Erḣ-chieḣchieh pa. T'ā ch'ùle shiḣerḣ nień, ītiārh hsiaōhsi yeḣ meí yŭ. Laŏshih shuō, t'ā hsieṅtsaì haí huóche pu, wó yeḣ pū kaṅ shuō. Yaòshih t'ā chiṅt'ien huílai, nà chiù cheñ shiḣ wŏ menḡhsianḡputaò te le.

6. Mŭch'in: Pàpa, yeḣhsü shiḣ Mùlań yeḣ shuōputinḡ. (Chaṅch'ilai.) Wŏmen pūjú taò wàit'ou ch'ü k'aṅk'an pa.

7. Fùch'in: (Tieṅ-t'où, yeḣ chaṅch'ilai.) Haŏ pa, wŏmen ch'ūch'ü k'aṅ-k'an.

8. Mŭch'in: (Wanḡ ch'ień tsoūle lianḡ pù, huí-t'oú tuì chieḣchieh keñ tìti shuō.) Nimen tsò tsaì chèrh tenḡiteng, wŏ keñ Pàpa ch'ūch'ü k'aṅk'an chiù huílai. (Tsǫuch'uch'ü.)

9. Chieḣchieh: Tìti, nĭ t'inḡ ch'inḡch'ule ma? Nàko ch'íche mǎ te chüṅkuañ, cheñ shiḣ Erḣ-chieḣchieh le ma?

10. Tìti: Wŏ t'inḡte heń ch'inḡch'u le, nàko chüṅkuañ shiḣ chù tsaì Tunḡañ-chieḣ te.

11. Chieḣchieh: K'ŏshih chù tsaì Tunḡañ-chieḣ te jeń, ch'úle women īchiā īwaì, haí yŭ pū shaŏ pieḣte jeń, tseḿ nenḡ shuō nàko chüṅkuañ chiù shiḣ Erḣ-chieḣchieh le ne? (Waìt'ou yŭ jeń shuō-huà te shenḡyin.)

12. Tìti: (Ts'unḡ ch'uanḡhu hsianḡ waìt'ou k'aṅle ik'an, chiù tàshenḡ shuō.) Tà-chieḣchieh, nĭ pieh íhsin le. Nĭ-tzùchĭ lai k'aṅk'an pa. Erḣ-chieḣchieh keñ Pàpa Māma īch'í tsoūchinlai le. (Chaṅch'ilai yunḡ shoú chiḣche.)

13. Chieḣchieh: Ā! Tìti, nĭ ts'aīchunḡ le, cheñ shiḣ Erḣ-chieḣchieh huílai le. (Mùlań, Fùch'in, Mŭch'in keñ lianḡko pinḡ toū chiṅlai.)

14. Tìti: (Heń hsīhuante shuō.) Erḣ-chieḣchieh, ni huílai le.

15. Chieḣchieh: (Īt'oúrh hsiaò, īt'oúrh shuō.) Meìmei, nĭ huílai le cheñ haŏ le! (Pinḡ-Chiā Pinḡ-Ĭ toū heń chinḡí.)

16. Mùlań: Chieḣchieh, Tìti, wŏ huílai le. Chieḣchieh haì shiḣ keñ shiḣerḣ nień ich'ień ch'àputō īyanḡ, k'ŏshih Tìti chiù pĭ ts'unḡch'ień chanḡte yù kaō yù tà le.

17. Pinḡ-Chiā: (Tuì Pinḡ-Ĭ shuō.) Wŏmen chanḡkuañte laŏt'aìyeń, laŏt'aì-t'ai, haí shiḣ chèyanḡ k'anḡchień, cheñ shiḣ nańté, cheñ haŏ fúch'i le!

18. Pinḡ-Ĭ: Shiḣ te, yŭ chèma tz'úaì te fùmŭ, keñ chèma haŏ te chieḣchieh, tìti, nańkuaì t'a tà kuañ yeḣ pū k'eñ tsò, chiḣ yaò huí chiā lai.

19. Mùlań: (Tuì fùmŭ shuō.) Chè lianḡweì tìhsiung, shiḣ keñ wo īch'í tāchanḡ, tāle shiḣerḣ nień te. Wŏmen tsaì shiḣerḣ nień tanḡchunḡ, pū chiḣtao ch'iḣle tōshaó k'ū, shāszule tōshaŏ tíchüñ le.

20. Fùch'in: Nĭmen lianḡweì ch'inḡ tsò ch'ing tso.

21. Pinḡ-Chiā, Pinḡ-Ĭ: Laŏt'aìyeń, pieh k'òch'i.

22. Mùlań: (Tuì Pinḡ-Chiā, Pinḡ-Ĭ shuō.) Chè shiḣ wŏte chiā, pū shiḣ chüṅying, nĭmen pūpì k'òch'i. Wŏ chiṅch'ü īhuǎrh chiù ch'úlai. (Pinḡ-Chiā, Pinḡ-Ĭ tsòhsia. Mùlań keñ chieḣchieh chiṅch'ü.)

23. Fùch'in: (Tuì tìti shuō.) Haìtzu, chè lianḡweì kōko, tsoūle pū shaŏ te lù, tùtzu ītinḡ ò le. Nĭ ch'ü nunḡ ītiǎrh chiùts'aì lai pa.

24. Tìti: Pàpa, haŏ, wŏ ch'ü nunḡ chiùts'aì lai.

25. Pǐnḡ-Chiǎ, Pǐnḡ-Ĭ: Laŏt'aìyeń cheñ k'òch'i! (Mùlań ch'uańshangle nǚjente īshang ch'ūlai. Pǐnḡ-Chiǎ, Pǐnḡ-Ĭ k'ańchienle, chüeh̀te shih̀feń chinḡ-ch'í.)

26. Mùlań: (Hsiaòche tuì Pǐnḡ-Chiǎ, Pǐnḡ-Ĭ shuō.) Nǐmen chih̀tao wo shih̀ shuí ma?

27. Pǐnḡ-Chiǎ: Hsiaóchiehte mieǹmaò, heń hsiaǹg womente chanğkuañ, wó hsianğ ītinğ shih̀ t'āte chieh̀chieh, huòshih̀ meìmei le.

28. Pǐnḡ-Ĭ: Pūtaǹ mieǹmaò hsiaǹg, erh́ch'ieh́ shenḡyin yeh́ ch'àputō īyanğ.

29. Mùlań: Wŏ chiù shih̀ t'ā le. (Pǐnḡ-Chiǎ, Pǐnḡ-Ĭ shuōpuch'ū huà lai.) Wó peńlaí shih̀ ko nǚjen, yiñweì fùch'in laŏ le, sóǐ t'ì t'a ch'ü tā-chanğ, ch'uańshangle chüñfú, keń nimen ich'í tăle shih̀erh̀ nień chanğ, meí yǔ īko jeń k'aǹtech'ū wo shih̀ ko nǚjen. Nǐmen shuō haŏhsiaò puhaohsiao? Hāhā! Hāhā!

30. Fùch'in, Mǔch'in, Pǐnḡ-Chiǎ, Pǐnḡ-Ĭ: Hāhā! Hāhā!

(Pì-mù)

NOTES

1. 甲 is the first of the 天干 (T'ieñ-kañ, "Heavenly Stems"), of which there are ten (甲; 乙; 丙, Pǐnğ; 丁, Tinğ; 戊, Wù; 己; 庚, Kenḡ; 辛, Hsiñ; 壬, Jeń; 癸, Kueí), and which are used as symbols, like "1, 2, 3, 4" or "A, B, C, D," etc., for indicating serial order. In Chinese, besides the "Heavenly Stems," there are also the 地支 (Tìchih̀, "Earthly Branches"), of which there are twelve (子; 丑, Ch'oǔ; 寅, Yiń; 卯, Maŏ; 辰, Ch'eń; 巳, Szù; 午, Wǔ; 未, Weì; 申, Sheñ; 酉, Yǔ; 戌, Hsǚ; 亥, Haì), and which are also used for indicating serial order as well as the hours (one hundred twenty minutes each) of the day. The combination of the ten 天干 and twelve 地支 together constitutes the 干支 system, which makes the cycle of sixty, used for reckoning the years, sixty being the lowest common multiple of ten and twelve. The cycle begins with the combination 甲子, which is followed by 乙丑, 丙寅, 丁卯, etc., until it ends with 癸亥; and then another 甲子 begins a new cycle. In some modern schools in China the four "Heavenly Stems," 甲, 乙, 丙, 丁, are used for grading purposes corresponding to our letter grades of A, B, C, D, respectively. 兵甲 and 兵乙 in the Reading Material above may well be rendered into English as "Soldier A" and "Soldier B," respectively.

2. 老太爺, "the old gentleman," and 老太太, "the old lady," are both polite terms used for "father" and "mother," respectively. When used in direct address, they can be sometimes rendered into English as "Venerable Sir" and "Venerable Madam."

3. The difference in usage between 還是 and 或是, as both may be used to mean "or," is that the former is used exclusively in disjunctive questions —that is, questions involving a choice of alternatives—whereas the latter is used in nondisjunctive questions. Examples: 你要中國錢還是美國錢?, "Do you want Chinese money or American money?", implying "Which of the two kinds of money do you want?" 你要中國錢或是美國錢不要?, "Do you

want Chinese money or American money?", implying "Of the two kinds of money, do you want either or not?" Observe that in answering the former type of disjunctive question, the choice between the alternatives offered must be stated. Thus, we may say: 我要中國錢, or 我要美國錢. However, in answer to the latter type of nondisjunctive questions, we have to give only a "yes" or "no" answer, depending on whether we want either. In declarative statements, unless they contain an indirect disjunctive question, 還是 cannot be used to translate "or." Instead we must use 或是. Example: "He doesn't like to eat beef or drink cow's milk" becomes 他不喜歡吃牛肉或是喝牛奶.

　　4. The classifier for "horsepower," by analogy of 馬, is also 匹.

　　5. 中 (chung) may be used with action verbs to form resultative compounds to indicate accuracy or correctness. Thus, 猜中 means "to guess accurately or correctly"; 打中, "to hit accurately."

　　6. When 翻 is used in the sense of "to translate," it may also be written 繙. 翻成 is more colloquial than 譯成.

ORAL EXERCISES

A. Say the following in Chinese:

　　1. A lamp; an oil lamp; an electric light; to light an oil lamp.

　　2. Our military headquarters; the military headquarters of the revolutionary troops; the military headquarters of the enemy troops.

　　3. Is this an oil lamp or an electric light? Do you want an oil lamp or an electric light? I want an oil lamp. I don't want an oil lamp or an electric light.

　　4. News; good news; bad news. Have you any news? Is the news good or bad? Have you any good or bad news? No, I haven't any.

　　5. Please guess a little; please don't guess. What do you want me to guess? Did he guess it right?

　　6. What do you suspect? Whom do you suspect? Why do you suspect him?

　　7. To ride a horse; to ride a bicycle. I can ride a horse; he can ride a bicycle.

　　8. A battalion of soldiers; a battalion of cavalry; battalion commander; Battalion Commander Huang.

　　9. As a person he is quite kind; his friends all love him.

　　10. One horsepower; a six-horsepower machine; a two-thousand-fifty-eight-horsepower machine.

B. Render the following into English:

　　1. T'ā tsò-jeń feīch'áng yú lǐmaò, sói wǒmen toū heń hsǐhuan t'a.

　　2. Chè shih chünyíng, pū shih hsüehhsiaò, yeh pū shih Ch'ingnień-huì.

　　3. Chèliang tzùhsing-ch'ē suījań shih wǒte, k'ǒshih wǒ pū huì ch'í.

　　4. Chèrh t'aì heī lě, nǐmen tsemma pū k'aī tientēng ne?

　　5. T'āte mienmaò shengte heň pūts'ò, ǐk'aǹ nǐ chiù chihtao t'a shih k'ŏk'aò te.

6. T'ā tsót'ien tuì nimen shuōle shemma, wǒ ts'aīlaíts'aīch'ù yeh ts'aīpuchaó.

7. T'ā heń hsiang pǎ chèko Yinḡweń chùtzu fañch'enǵ Chunḡweń.

8. T'ā shuō huòshih nǐ huòshih wǒ toū k'ói ch'ü maǐ chiñt'ien te paò.

9. Jeń pū ch'ih̄ tunḡhsi, heń k'uaì chiù yaò òszu le.

10. Nimen hsieǹtsaì k'ói ích'i huích'ü, mingt'ien ích'i tsaì laí.

WRITTEN EXERCISES

A. Transcribe Section B, above, in Chinese.

B. Render the following into English:

1. 張先生是在政府機關裏頭做翻譯的, 他的中文跟英文都很好.

2. 他雖然長得又高又大, 可是他的健康很平常, 他每年最少病三四回.

3. 騎兵跟步兵都是兵, 不同的地方就是騎兵騎馬, 步兵走路.

4. 革命軍的軍營離火車站不很遠, 最多不過兩英里到三英里.

5. 馬國光營長雖然是我們的長官, 可是他待我們很和氣. 有這麼好的房子住, 又有這麼漂亮的汽車開.

6. 你真福麼

7. 哈哈! 你心裏頭有甚麼話想說, 我都猜中了.

8. 我今天早飯跟中飯都沒吃過, 現在肚子餓得很利害了.

9. 怎 麼 你 父 親 上 禮 拜 坐 飛 機
到 上 海 去 了 以 後, 到 現 在 一 點 兒
消 息 都 沒 有 呢?

10. 他 騎 了 兩 個 鐘 頭 自 行 車, 難
怪 他 覺 得 累 了.

C. Render the following into Chinese:

1. Please translate the following three sentences from English into French.

2. I put out the electric light just now, but I didn't put out the oil lamp.

3. Do you know when his birthday is going to be? If you don't, please guess.

4. Why do you suspect that he wanted to steal your typewriter last night?

5. He knows how to light an oil lamp, but doesn't know how to turn on an electric light.

6. Although my grandmother is eighty-six years old, she is very healthy.

7. Do you know what he has eaten? He says his stomach aches terribly.

8. The windows of my house were blown open by the strong wind last night.

9. This old bicycle was lent to me by his younger brother three weeks ago.

10. When you go home this evening, please turn off all the electric lights.

VOCABULARY CHARACTERS

(Yeń)
Word; to speak (literary Chinese) [*]

(Shih̄)
Poem, poetry

(Chüeń)
To cut short, to break off [*]; absolutely, by no means, on no account [*]

(Shoŭ)
Beginning, head [*]; (classifier for poems)

(Mień)
Sleep; to sleep (literary Chinese) [*]

(Weń)
To hear (literary Chinese); to smell, to sniff at

(T'í)
To cry, to caw (literary Chinese) [*]

(Niaŏ)
Bird [*]

(Shuanḡ)
Frost

(Shuaī)
To decay, to decline

(T'uń)
Boy, child, youth (literary Chinese) [*]

(Hó)
What? How? Why? Which? (literary Chinese) [*]; (a surname)

(Pó)
To moor (literary Chinese) [*]

(Laò) Reading pronunciation is (Lò).
To drop, to fall, to alight

(Wū)
Crow [*]

(Fenḡ)
Maple [*]

(Yű)
To fish; fisherman (literary Chinese) [*]

(Ch'oú)
To worry; grieving [*]

444

 (Ch'uang) Also written 床. Bed, couch

 (Chǔ) Also written 舉. To lift, to raise

 (Kaǐ) To alter, to correct

 (Pìn) Hair on the temples

(Hsiaǒ) Dawn; to understand, to know [*]

 (Kū) Paternal aunt; husband's sister; maiden [*]

 (Sū) (Name for Soochow and Kiangsu provinces) [*]; (a surname)

 (Szù) Buddhist temple, Buddhist monastery [*]

 (Yǔ) Speech, dialect, language [*]

(Hsièn) Also written 綫. Thread, line, wire

COMPOUNDS

詩 家 (Shiḣchiā) ⎫
詩 人 (Shiḣjeń) ⎬ Poet

做 詩 (Tsò-shiḣ) To write poetry

五言詩 (Wǔyeń-shiḣ) Five-syllable-line poetry

七言詩 (Ch'īyeń-shiḣ) Seven-syllable-line poetry

語 言 (Yǔyeń) Languages

天 才 (T'ieńts'aí) Genius; natural talent

漁 夫 (Yǘfū) ⎫
漁 人 (Yǘjeń) ⎬ Fisherman

寺 院 (Szùyüàn) Buddhist monastery

姑 爹 (Kūfu) Husband of paternal aunt

姑 母 (Kūmǔ) Paternal aunt

落下來 (Laòhsialai) To fall down

下 落 (Hsiàlò) Whereabouts

下 霜 (Hsià-shuaṅ) There is frost

鳥 兒 (Niaǒrh) Bird

改過來 (Kaǐkuolai) To correct (as a mistake)

改 良 (Kaǐliaṅ) To improve; improvement

修 改 (Hsiūkaǐ) To revise

兒 童 (Erħt'uṅ) Children (collectively)

童子軍 (T'ungtzŭ-chüñ) Boy Scouts

紅十字會 (Hungshihtzù-huì) Red Cross Society

舉起來 (Chŭch'ilai) To lift up, to raise

舉手 (Chŭ-shŏu) To raise the hand

光線 (Kuanḡhsièn) (Ray of) light

無線電 (Wúhsièn-tien) Radio, wireless telegraphy

無線電報 (Wúhsièn-tiènpaò) Radiogram

收音機 (Shoūyiñ-chī) Radio, receiving set

寒暑表 (Hañshú-piaŏ) Thermometer

時間表 (Shiñchieñ-piaŏ) Time-table, schedule

絕對 (Chüeñtuì) Absolutely

絕句 (Chüeñchù) Four-line poem or poetry

聞一聞 (Weñiwen) To take a sniff at

聞見 (Weñchien) To (actually) smell

聞得見 (Weñtechièn) Able to (actually) smell

聞不見 (Weñpuchièn) Unable to (actually) smell

改正 (Kaĭcheñg) To correct

文言 (Weñyeñ) Literary language

白話 (Paíhuà) Vernacular language

曉得 (Hsiaŏte) To understand, to know

死人 (Szŭjeń) Dead person

國語 (Kuóyŭ) National language

楓樹 (Fenḡshù) Maple (tree)

READING MATERIAL

(甲) 五 言 絕 句 兩 首

一. 春 曉 (孟 浩 然 Menḡ Haòjañ)

春 眠 不 覺 曉; 處 處 聞 啼 鳥.

夜 來 風 雨 聲, 花 落 知 多 少？

二. 夜 思 (李 白 Lĭ Pó)

牀 前 看 月 光, 疑 是 地 上 霜.

舉 頭 望 山 月, 低 頭 思 故 鄉.

(乙) 七言絶句兩首

一. 回鄉 (賀知章 Hò Chiĥchanḡ)

少 小 離 家 老 大 回;
鄉 音 無 改 鬢 毛 衰.
兒 童 相 見 不 相 識,
笑 問 客 從 何 處 來.

二. 楓橋夜泊 (張繼 Chanḡ Chì)

月 落 烏 啼 霜 滿 天;
江 楓 漁 火 對 愁 眠.
姑 蘇 城 外 寒 山 寺,
夜 半 鐘 聲 到 客 船.

ROMANIZED TEXT OF READING MATERIAL

(Chiă) Wŭyeń chüeĥchŭ lianǵshoŭ

Ĭ. Ch'uñ Hsiaŏ (Menḡ Haòjań)

Ch'uñ mień pū chüeń hsiaŏ;
Ch'ùch'ù weń t'íniaŏ.
Yeĥ laí feñgyŭ shenḡ,
Huā lò chiĥ tōshaŏ?

Erĥ. Yeĥ Szū (Lĭ Pó)

Ch'uanǵch'ień k'aǹ yüeĥkuanḡ,
Ĭ shiĥ tìshanḡ shuanḡ.
Chŭ-t'oú wanǵ shăñ yüeĥ,
Tī-t'oú szū kùhsianḡ.

(Ĭ) Ch'ıyeń chüeĥchŭ lianǵshoŭ

Ĭ. Huí-hsianḡ (Hò Chiĥchanḡ)

Shaòhsiaŏ lí-chiā laŏtà huí;
Hsianḡyiñ wú kaī piǹmaó shuaī.
Erĥt'unǵ hsianḡchień pū hsianḡshiĥ,
Hsiaò weǹ k'ò ts'unḡ hóch'ù laí.

Erh̀. Fenḡch'iaó yeh̀ pó (Chanḡ Chì)

Yüeh̀ lò wū t'í shuanḡ mañ t'ieñ;
Chianḡfenḡ yúhuŏ tuì ch'oú mień.
Kūsū ch'enḡwaì Hańshañ-szù,
Yeh̀pañ chunḡshenḡ taò k'ò ch'uań.

NOTES

1. 孟浩然, A.D. 689–740, was a native of 襄陽 (Hsianḡyanǵ) in Hupeh province, and decidedly a poet of first rank of the 唐 (T'anǵ) Dynasty, 618–907. See Giles's *Biographical Dictionary*, No. 1518, p. 581.

2. 李白 (Lĭ Pó) or 李太白 (Lĭ T'aìpó), A.D. 705–762, was a native of 昌明 (Ch'anḡminǵ) in Szechuan province and one of the most outstanding poets of the T'ang Dynasty. He was named after the planet Venus, of which his mother was said to have dreamed prior to the poet's birth. His poetic genius made such a lasting impression on 賀知章 (see Note 3 below), a contemporary poet, that the latter described him as a "banished immortal" and introduced him to 玄宗 (Hsüańtsunḡ), the reigning monarch, who was a great patron of the arts and literature and who appointed the poet to the 翰林院 (Han̄liń-yüaǹ), or Hanlin Academy. After a period of court life, the poet returned to wandering, and during the rebellion, of 755 he got himself involved in it, though unintentionally. His life was saved by the intercession of his influential friend 郭子儀 (Kuò Tzŭí). It was said that his death came as a result of his attempting to embrace the reflection of the moon on the water. See Giles's *Biographical Dictionary*, No. 1181, pp. 455–456.

3. 賀知章 (Hò Chih̄chanḡ), A.D. 659–744, a native of 山陰 (Shañyiñ) of Chekiang province, was a contemporary and great admirer of Lĭ Pó. Gifted as a poet, he was also famous for his skill in calligraphy. See Giles's *Biographical Dictionary*, No. 643, pp. 259–260.

4. 張繼 (Chanḡ Chì), a poet of the eighth century A.D., was a native of 襄州 (Hsianḡchoū) in Hupeh province. He became a 進士 (Advanced Scholar, a graduate of the third degree, roughly equivalent to the Ph. D.) in 753. Later he served as Secretary of the Board of Revenue. See Giles's *Biographical Dictionary*, No. 25, p. 11.

5. Chinese poetical compositions fall into six categories: (1) 詩, or poetry usually with five or seven characters or syllables to the line, with its own set rules for rhymes and tone sequence and rhetorical devices; (2) 詞 (Tz'ú), or poems with lines of varying length and with rigid patterns for line division, use of rhymes, and tone sequence for the entire composition; they were originally meant to be sung but their melodies have been irrevocably lost; (3) 歌 (Kō), or songs to be sung, usually more rhythmic and repetitious than 詩 or 詞; (4) 賦 (Fù), or unrhymed but metrical poems in prose, descriptive and lyrical in nature; (5) 曲 (Ch'ŭ), or operatic verse; (6) 彈詞 (T'ańtz'ú), or ballad poetry, to be recited with musical accompaniment.

詩 may be subdivided into the 古詩 or 古體詩 (ancient style) and

今體詩 or 近體詩 (modern style). The term "ancient style" is used to refer to the poetry written before the T'ang Dynasty. Its lines may have three, four, five, six, or seven syllables each. It uses only thirty-four rhymes. Words in the "even" (平) as well as "oblique" (仄, Tsè) tones may be used as rhymes. It permits the change of rhymes within the same poem. There is no set requirement at all for tone sequence. The "modern style" was originated in the sixth century and perfected during the seventh and eighth centuries. It includes the 律詩 (Lùshih), "regulated poèm," and the 絕句, "cut-short (or stop-short) poem." It uses one hundred and six rhymes instead of the thirty-four of the ancient style. It prefers rhymes in the "even" tone to those in the "oblique" tone. The unrhyming line in it must end with a word in the opposite tone. In a "regulated" poem, which is primarily an eight-line poem, lines three and four, and five and six, must be verbally parallel: i.e., each part of speech must be fully matched throughout the lines, and the tones have a tendency to run in pairs within the same caesural unit. In a five-syllable line the caesura is between the second and third syllables, and in a seven-syllable line it is between the fourth and fifth syllables. As to the "cut-short" or "stop-short" poem, invariably a four-line poem, its lines may be (1) the first four lines of a "regulated" poem, in which the lines of its closing couplet will be verbally parallel to each other (cf. 夜思 by 李白, above); (2) the last four lines of a "regulated" poem, in which case the lines of its opening couplet will be verbally parallel to each other; (3) the middle four lines of a "regulated" poem, in which case verbal parallelism will affect the entire poem; (4) the first two and last two lines of a "regulated" poem, in which case the whole poem will be free from verbal parallelism.

Speaking of rhymes in Chinese prosody, they are more accurately vowel assonances, i.e., they stress similarity of vowel sounds. The rhymes used in Chinese prosody have gone through considerable phonetic changes since the eighth century, when they were standardized, so that some of them as they are pronounced in Mandarin at present no longer sound rhyming. In Chinese prosody there are two tones to deal with: "even" and "oblique." Words which are "even" in tone in the classical language remain "even" in prosody, while words which are "rising," "departing" (or falling), and "entering" (or abrupt) in tone in classical Chinese become "oblique." These four tones of classical Chinese upon which the classification of tones in prosody is based must not be confused with the four tones of Mandarin, which are quite different in quality.

    6. 眠, "to sleep, sleep," is primarily a literary word. It should not be used interchangeably with 睡覺. Its use in modern Chinese is limited to certain compounds, such as 失眠症 (Shihmień-chenğ), "insomnia," 安眠藥, "hypnotics," etc.

    7. 聞, "to hear," is a literary word. Don't use it interchangeably with 聽見.

    8. The classifier for 牀 is 張.

    9. 楓橋 or "Maple Bridge" is in the western suburb of Soochow (蘇州),

now also known as 吳縣 (Wúhsien). It is in southern Kiangsu province.

   10. 火 in 漁火 is to be taken in the sense of 燈火, "lamplight."

   11. 姑蘇 is another name for Soochow.

   12. 寒山 is the name of a Buddhist monastery supposedly named after 寒山子, a noted Buddhist monk and poet of the first half of the seventh century, who had sojourned there. It is east of Maple Bridge.

ORAL EXERCISES

A. Say the following in Chinese:

   1. A poem; a long poem; a short poem; a five-syllable-line poem; a seven-syllable-line poem.

   2. Can you actually smell? Yes, I can. No, I can't. Please take a sniff at this.

   3. What is falling down? An airplane is falling down. A leaf is falling down. A flower is falling down.

   4. Please raise your hand. Please raise your left hand. Don't raise your right hand.

   5. My paternal aunt; my paternal aunt's husband; my paternal aunt's children.

   6. What [kind of] bird is this? Whose bird is that? There is a bird on the tree.

   7. Chinese Boy Scouts; American Boy Scouts. These are Chinese Boy Scouts; those are American Boy Scouts.

   8. Was there any frost yesterday morning? There was frost every morning last autumn.

   9. Where is the radiogram? Is that radiogram yours? Do you know who has sent it to you?

   10. This piece of rock is too heavy; I can't lift it up myself. Will you be able to help me a little?

B. Render the following into English:

   1. Hó hsiensheng shih̀ Peǐp'ing̀-jeń haíshih Shang̀haǐ-jeń a?

   2. Ní hsieh̀ts'ò te tzù, ikung̀ yǔ shih̀ch'ìko, wǒ toū iching keí ni kaǐcheng̀ le.

   3. Chèko shoūyiñ-chī shih̀ t'ā chieh̀ keí wo te, pū shih̀ wǒ-tzùchí maǐ te.

   4. T'ā kang̀ts'aí tuì women shuō te huà, toū shih̀ chüeh̀tuì meí yǔ taòli te.

   5. T'āte fùch'in shih̀ iko heń yǔ-ming̀ te shih̀jeń, pū shih̀ p'ing̀ch'ang̀ te shanḡjeń.

   6. Chèko hańshú-piaǒ cheñ haǒ a, shih̀ shuí sung̀ keí ni te?

   7. Ni huì tsò-shih̀ puhui? Ni huì tsò sheḿma shih̀?

   8. Nàko yǔfūte hsiàlò, taò hsientsaì haí meí yǔ jeń chih̄tao.

   9. Yǔ jeń shuō tsò wǔyeń-shih̄ heň nań, yeh̀ yǔ jeń shuō tsò ch'īyeń-shih̄ heň nań.

   10. Chè shih̀ pushih nǐmen hsüeh̀hsiaò shang̀-k'ò te shih̀chieñ-piaǒ a?

C. Learn the four poems in this lesson by heart so that you can recite them from memory.

WRITTEN EXERCISES

A. Render the following into English:

1. 這個屋子的窗戶,又多又大,所以光線非常好,你們滿意麼?

2. 去年秋天的天氣很冷,差不多每夜都下霜,到了早上,房子前頭的草地都白了.

3. 每句都有五個字的詩,是五言詩;每句有都七個字的詩,是七言詩.

4. "絕句"是每首都有四句的詩;每句都有五個字的詩,叫"五言絕句",每句都有七個字的詩,叫"七言絕句".

5. 他很有學語言的天才,所以法文他學得很好,俄文也學得很好.

6. 你們都知道無線電是那一國的人發明的,是甚麼時候發明的麼?

7. 今年放寒假的時候,沒有書念,我打算到紅十字會去做事.

8. 我們姑父姑母的兒子,是我

們 的 表 兄 弟, 姑 爻 姑 母 的 女 兒, 是
我 們 的 表 姐 妹.

　9. 詩 我 已 經 做 好 了, 裏 頭 也 許
有 用 字 用 得 不 好 的 地 方, 請 你 給
我 修 改 一 下.

　10. 不 好 的 東 西, 我 們 一 定 要 想
法 子 改 良 才 好.

B. Make your own translation in English of the poems in this lesson. Before beginning your attempt, it may be helpful and interesting to compare the following easily available translations:

　1.　For 春曉:

　　a)　Jenyns, Soame. *Selections from the Three Hundred Poems of the T'ang Dynasty.* London: John Murray, 1940, p. 26.

　　b)　Ts'ai, T'ing-kan. *Chinese Poems in English Rhymes.* Chicago: University of Chicago Press, 1932, p. 1.

　　c)　Bynner, Witter. *Jade Mountain* (6th printing). New York: Alfred A. Knopf, 1945, p. 108.

　　d)　Fletcher, W. J. B. *Gems of Chinese Verse.* Shanghai: Commercial Press, 1926, p. 135.

　2.　For 夜思:

　　a)　Ts'ai, T'ing-kan. *Op. cit.*, p. 29.

　　b)　Bynner, Witter. *Op. cit.*, p. 53.

　　c)　Obata, Shigeyoshi. *The Works of Li Po* (3d printing). New York: E. P. Dutton and Company, 1928, p. 55.

　　d)　Ayscough, Florence, and Amy Lowell. *Fir Flower Tablet.* Boston: Houghton Mifflin, 1926, p. 74.

　　e)　Fletcher, W. J. B. *Op. cit.*, p. 25.

　　f)　Giles, H. A. *Gems of Chinese Literature: Verse.* London: Bernard Quartrich, 1926, p. 77.

　3.　For 楓橋夜泊:

　　a)　Bynner, Witter. *Op. cit.*, p. 4.

　　b)　Jenyns, Soame. *Op. cit.*, p. 26.

　　c)　Ts'ai, T'ing-kan. *Op. cit.*, p. 114.

　　d)　Fletcher, W. J. B. *Op. cit.*, p. 159.

Lesson SIXTY
A Review Lesson

CHARACTERS

Number of Strokes	Characters	Pronunciation and Tone	Meaning	Lesson Reference
One	乙	Ĭ, Ì	(Second of the "Heavenly Stems")	58
Four	戶	Hù	Door; household	56
	匹	P'ĭ	(Classifier for horses)	58
	中	Chunğ	To hit the center, to hit the mark	58
Five	古	Kŭ	Ancient; (a surname)	56
	必	Pì	Necessary, must	56
	令	Lìnğ	Command, order; to cause	56
	民	Mín	People, citizens	57
	由	Yú	Cause; to permit, to allow; from	57
	甲	Chiă	Armor; (first of the "Heavenly Stems")	58
Six	合	Hó	To join together; fit, suitable	57
	任	Jèn	Duty, responsibility	57
	全	Ch'üán	Complete, completely	57
	寺	Szù	Buddhist temple or monastery	59
Seven	扮	Pàn	To dress up as, to disguise as	57
	利	Lì	Profit, interest; strong, fierce	57
	吹	Ch'uī	To blow	58
	肚	Tù	Stomach, abdomen	58
	言	Yén	Word; to speak	59

453

Number of Strokes	Characters	Pronunciation and Tone	Meaning	Lesson Reference
Seven	何	Hó	What? How? Why? Which?; (a surname)	59
	改	Kaĭ	To alter, to correct	59
Eight	物	Wù	Matter, thing	56
	爸	Pà	Papa	56
	帖	{T'ieȟ / T'ieȟ}	Placard, notice, invitation / Rubbing from inscription	56 / 56
	居	Chǖ	To reside; (a surname)	57
	招	Chaō	To beckon with the hand; to recruit; to attend to	57
	享	Hsianǧ	To enjoy	57
	表	Piaŏ	External, outside; list, table, schedule; meter	57
	受	Shoù	To receive, etc.	57
	或	{Huò / Hò}	Either, or	58
	牀	Ch'uanǵ	Bed, couch	59
	泊	Pó	To moor	59
	姑	Kū	Paternal aunt; husband's sister; maiden	59
Nine	哈	Hā	(Sound of laughter)	58
	首	Shoŭ	Beginning, head; (classifier for poems)	59
Ten	庭	T'inǵ	Courtyard	56
	務	Wù	Affair, business	57
	消	Hsiaō	To diminish, to consume	58
	眠	Mień	Sleep; to sleep	59
	衰	Shuaī	To decay, to decline	59
	烏	Wū	Crow	59

Number of Strokes	Characters	Pronunciation and Tone	Meaning	Lesson Reference
Eleven	累	Leì	Tired, weary	56
	惜	Hsī	To pity	57
	閉	Pì	To shut, to close	57
	族	Tsú	Clan	57
	猜	Ts'aī	To guess	58
	康	K'anḡ	Peace, repose; health	58
	健	Chieǹ	Healthy	58
	鳥	Niǎo	Bird	59
Twelve	景	Chǐnḡ	Scenery	56
	窗	Ch'uanḡ	Window	56
	華	Huá	China; splendor; flowery	57
	絕	Chüeń	To cut short, to break off; absolutely, by no means, on no account	59
	啼	T'í	To cry, to caw	59
	童	T'unǵ	Boy, child, youth	59
Thirteen	媽	Mā	Mama	56
	集	Chí	To gather, to collect	57
	義	Ì	The right thing to do; meaning, significance	57
	盞	Chǎn	(Unit of measure for lamps)	58
	爺	Yeh́	Old gentleman; (term of respect for men)	58
	福	Fú	Good luck, good fortune	58
	詩	Shih̄	Poem, poetry	59
	楓	Fenḡ	Maple	59

Number of Strokes	Characters	Pronunciation and Tone	Meaning	Lesson Reference
Thirteen	愁	Ch'oú	To worry; grieving	59
Fourteen	幕	Mù	Stage curtain; act of a play	56
	演	Yeň	To perform (as a play, music, etc.)	56
	旗	Ch'í	Flag	57
	夢	Meng̀	Dream	57
	疑	Í	To doubt, to suspect; doubt, suspicion	58
	貌	Maò	Appearance	58
	慈	Tz'ú	Loving, compassionate	58
	聞	Weń	To hear; to smell, to sniff at	59
	漁	Yú	To fish; fisherman	59
Fifteen	歎	T'aǹ	To sigh	56
	徵	Chenḡ	To draft, to recruit	56
	憂	Yū	Grief; to be worried	56
	影	Yiň	Image, shadow	56
	線	Hsieǹ	Thread, line, wire	59
Sixteen	擔	Tañ	To carry (with pole on shoulder)	56
	燈	Tenḡ	Lamp	58
	舉	Chǔ	To lift, to raise	59
Seventeen	戲	Hsì	Play (drama)	56
	營	Yiń	Military camp; battalion	58
	霜	Shuanḡ	Frost	59
Eighteen	織	Chiñ	To weave (as cloth, etc.)	56

Number of Strokes	Charac-ters	Pronuncia-tion and Tone	Meaning	Lesson Reference
Eighteen	騎	Ch'í	To ride astride	58
	翻	Fań	To turn over; to translate	58
Twenty	齣	Ch'ū	(Classifier for plays)	56
	譯	Ì	To translate	58
	蘇	Sū	(Name for Soochow and Kiangsu province); (a surname)	59
Twenty-one	蘭	Lań	Orchid	56
Twenty-two	權	Ch'üań	Power, authority, right	57
	響	Hsiǎng	To sound, to be heard	57
Twenty-three	驚	Chīng	To alarm, to startle	57
Twenty-four	鬢	Pìn	Hair on the temples	59
Twenty-five	廳	T'īng	Hall	56

ORAL DRILL

A. Say the following in Chinese:

1. news
   health
   duties
   interest
   signal
   citizens
   representative
   good luck
   family
   joke

   motion picture
   Boy Scouts
   fisherman
   poet
   (ray of) light
   paternal aunt
   stage scenery
   animal
   equality
   monastery

   antiquity
   dining room
   parlor
   bottom
   battlefield
   worries
   whereabouts
   obligation
   sovereign rights
   liberty

2. elated
   fiercely
   difficult to find
   externally
   astonished and amazed
   able to go
   to make a speech
   to disguise as

   loving
   all together
   no wonder
   in the midst of
   after all
   to light a lamp
   to assemble
   to weave cloth

to heave a sigh   to have a dream
to ride a horse   to beckon with the hand

3. a flag   a radiogram
   a radio receiving set   a theater
   an orchid   a play
   a loom   one horsepower
   a bicycle   a lamp

4. To like military music
   To write poetry
   To write Chinese poetry
   To be a famous poet
   To enjoy the rights of citizens
   To enjoy political power
   To shoulder responsibilities
   To shoulder the responsibilities of citizens
   A citizen of the Chinese Republic
   A citizen of the United States of America
   Completely equal in rank
   Completely correct
   Completely wrong
   The history of the ancient period
   They are very lucky.
   Is their health good?
   Do you doubt them?
   Ask him to turn on the electric lights.
   No wonder he wasn't pleased!
   No wonder he wasn't willing to go!
   What is there beneath the chair?
   Whose books are beneath the desk?
   Would you like to see a play today?
   Why does he like to see motion pictures?
   Has he ever seen this film?
   They have bought an oil lamp.
   Do they know how to light an oil lamp?
   He can ride a horse; I can ride a bicycle.
   Is this your superior officer's command?
   Our battalion commander is a native of Shanghai.
   How many windows can you see in this room?
   These windows here are both big and tall; the windows there are
both small and low.
   There are two flags here; one is large, one is small.
   Translate this sentence from English into Russian.
   The translation made by him is entirely wrong.
   There was no frost here at all last autumn.

He absolutely can't go this evening because his father is coming here to see him.

Have you ever studied poetry?   Are you fond of studying poetry?

Can you guess accurately what he has in his hand?

Please guess what the meaning of the Chinese word is.

Which is brighter, an electric light or an oil lamp?

Is the military camp very far from the train station in the city?

China has infantry troops and cavalry; Japan also has infantry and cavalry.

Birds can fly; airplanes also can fly;

He says he is very hungry and wants to know if you have anything to give him to eat.

Have you a train schedule here?   I want to know when the train will leave.

These poems were written by three very famous poets of the early years of the nineteenth century.

Almost everybody here says that he is a genius and that he can do many things.

Last night he went to Washington, D.C., by airplane. He will be back day after tomorrow.

B.   Render the following into English:

Fàṅt'inḡte ch'uanḡhu

K'òt'inḡ lit'ou te jeń

Chaṅch'anḡshang yú heň tō pinḡ.

Chunḡhuá-mińkuóte lìshih̀

Chunḡhuá-mińtsúte lìliang

Wùlite chung̀yaò yüańtsé

Wǒmente piaǒ-hsiunḡtì

T'āmente piaó-chieh̀meì

Yüańlaí t'ā tsót'ien meí ch'ù.

Yüańlaí t'ā shih̀ heń yü-ch'ień te.

Nǐ ch'ih̀tech'ì ch'ihpuch'i k'ǔ ne?

T'ā meí laí, nǐ pūpì ch'ù le.

T'ā meí ch'ù, nǐ pìting̀ yaò ch'ù.

Taòtǐ t'ā weìsheḿma meí kaòsu ni ne?

Wǒ taòtǐ shih̀ shuí, nǐ kaòsule t'a meiyu?

Nà shih̀ pushih wǒmen chíhó te hsiṅhaò?

Weìsheḿma t'āmen chüeh̀tuì pū hsīhuan chūnyüeh a?

Tieǹ yinḡ k'aīle mù tó chiǔ le, nǐmen chih̀tao ma?

"Mùlań ts'unǵ-chüń" shih̀ pushih īch'ū lianǧmù te hsì?

Nǐmen laǒt'aìyeh̀te fúch'i feīch'ang haǒ.

Yaòshih nǐ minǵt'ien t'aì mang, wǒ chiù k'ói taìpiaó ni ch'ü.

Nàhsieh toū shih̀ Meǐkuote taìpiaǒ, pū shih̀ Chunḡkuote taìpiaǒ.

Chèrh yǔ chèma liang̀ te tieǹtenḡ, nǐmen haí yaò shuō kuanḡhsieṅ pū koù ma?

Wŏ chiaò t'a pūyaò ch'ǜ, t'ā yeȟ ch'ǜ le, chè cheñ shiȟ wŏ menġhsiang-putaò te shiȟ.

T'ā t'ient'ien yeȟli toū tsò-menġ, yǔ shiȟhou menġchien ni, yǔ shiȟhou menġchien wo.

Hó hsiensheng taòle Meīkuo iȟoù, wó chiȟ k'aȟchienkuo t'a ī huí, sóȉ t'āte hsiàlò, wŏ waȟch'üaȟ pū chiȟtao.

Wŏte kūmǔ tsò-jeń heȟ tz'úaì, sóȉ t'āte erȟnǔ keñ p'enġyu toū heȟ aì t'a.

Wŏte haŏ p'enġyu tsót'ien keī chenġfǔ chenġle ch'ü tanḡ-pinḡ, hsieȟtsaì shuōputinġ t'ā shemma shiȟhou k'ói huílai.

Wŏ chiȟt'ien tsoūle heñ tō lù, hsieȟtsaì leìchí le, heñ hsianġ hsiūhsihsiuhsi.

Wŏmen tsót'ien waȟshang k'aȟ te hsì, yeȟte heń haŏ.

T'ā tăpanch'ilai, chūjaȟ hsianġ īko shihpā-chiǔ suì te nǔ-hsüeȟsheng.

Wŏmente yinḡtzu shiȟ ch'angch'anġ keñ women tsaì īk'uàrh te. Wŏmen tsoǔ, yinḡtzu yeȟ tsoǔ; wŏmen tsò, yinḡtzu yeȟ tsò.

Chèhsieh Meīkuo hsüeȟshengte līmaò heȟ pūts'ò, chèrh te jeń toū heń hsīhuan keñ t'amen tsò p'enġyu.

Meī t'ieñ t'ienliang te shiȟhou, niaǒrh toū chiaò, yǔ te chiaòte haŏt'inḡ, yǔ te chiaòte pū haŏt'inḡ.

Wŏmen yaò chiȟtao t'ieñch'i lenḡ puleng, huòshih jè puje, k'aȟk'an haȟshú-piaǒ chiù hsinġ le.

Chèhsieh hunḡ-huārhte hsianḡch'ì, nǐmen tsaì nàrh weȟtechieȟ wenpuchien?

Wó keī t'amen hsieȟ te ch'anġ hsìn, īching hsieȟhaǒ le, ch'inġ ni k'aȟk'an, yǔ shemma ts'ò tzù, toū ch'inġ ni kaīchenġ pa.

Chèko shoūyiñ-chī shiȟ wó wǔ nieȟ ich'ieȟ tsaì Meīchinḡ nieȟ-shū te shiȟhou maǐ te.

T'ā kanḡts'aí kaòsu wo, chè pū shiȟ Meīkuo Hunḡshiȟtzù-huì, yeȟ pū shiȟ Yinḡkuo Hunḡshiȟtzù-huì, shiȟ Chunḡkuo Hunḡshiȟtzù-huì.

WRITING DRILL

A. Write out in Chinese all the items in Section 1 of Oral Drill above.

B. Transcribe in Chinese all the items in Section 2 of Oral Drill above.

C. Retell in story form in Chinese the tale of "Mùlaȟ ts'unġ-chün" on the basis of Lessons Fifty-six, Fifty-seven, and Fifty-eight.

D. Paraphrase in modern Chinese the four poems in Lesson Fifty-nine.

INDEX
of Characters and Compounds

The characters are arranged alphabetically according to romanized pronunciation. The compounds are grouped in the order of their appearance immediately under the character which is their first component element. The arabic figure at the right of each column indicates the lesson number.

M

Mā 媽	56
Māma 媽媽	56
Mǎ 馬	29
Mǎlù 馬路	29
Mǎch'ē 馬車	29
Mǎshàng 馬上	34
Mǎlì 馬力	58
Ma 麼	2
Mǎi 買	12
Mǎitaò 買到	32
Mǎitetaò 買得到	32
Mǎiputaò 買不到	32
Mǎimai 買賣	54
Mài 賣	22
Màikuó-tseí 賣國賊	52
Mán 瞞	49
Mánteliaǒ 瞞得了	49
Mánpuliaǒ 瞞不了	49
Mǎn 滿	48
Mǎnì 滿意	51
Màn 慢	17
Mànch'ē 慢車	17
Mànmārhte 慢慢兒的	18
Mang 忙	21
Maō 貓	53
Maó 毛	3
Maópǐ 毛筆	3
Maóī 毛衣	32
Maó-wàtzu 毛襪子	32
Maóping 毛病	54
Maò 帽	32
Maòtzu 帽子	32
Maò 貌	58
Meí 沒	1
Meí kuañhsi 沒關係	53
Meí 眉	37
Meímao 眉毛	37
Meǐ 美	4
Meǐkuo 美國	4
Meǐkuo-jén 美國人	4
Meǐkuo-huà 美國話	4

Meǐkuo-shū 美國書	4
Meǐkuo-chiň 美國紙	4
Meǐkuo-pǐ 美國筆	4
Meǐkuo-ch'ień 美國錢	9
Meǐkuo-fàn 美國飯	13
Meǐkuo-ts'aì 美國菜	13
Meǐkuo-ch'á 美國茶	13
Meǐkuo-chengfǔ 美國政府	36
Meǐchingͫ 美京	56
Meǐ 每	29
Meì 妹	33
Meìmei 妹妹	33
Mén 門	26
Ménp'aí 門牌	31
Men 們	1
Mengͫ 夢	57
Mengchien 夢見	57
Menghsiangͫ 夢想	57
Menghsiangͫputaò 夢想不到	57
Mǐ 米	43
Mieh 滅	51
Miehtiao 滅掉	51
Mień 眠	59
Mièn 麵	14
Miènpaò 麵包	14
Mièn 面	37
Mín 民	57
Mínkuó 民國	57
Mínchǔ-kuó 民主國	57
Míntsú 民族	57
Mínch'üań 民權	57
Ming 明	4
Mingpai 明白	4
Mingt'ien 明天	7
Minghsiǹ-p'ièrh 明信片兒	28
Ming 名	31
Mingtzu 名字	31
Mingͫ 命	51
Mingͫling 命令	56
Mò 墨	34
Mòshuǐ 墨水	34
Mò 末	51

Helpful Hints for Using a Dictionary Arranged According to the Radical System

1. Determine the radical of the character. A radical may form the upper portion, the lower portion, the left portion, or the right portion of a character. Sometimes it is even spread out in a character. A character may retain its own basic form or it may assume a variant or modified form. A little actual experience in this task is worth more than pages of generalization. The student should at the earliest possible moment learn the list of radicals for this purpose. Following the hints here, the list of 214 radicals is given for his convenience.

2. Count the strokes of the radical after it has been determined.

3. Locate the radical in the Radical Index, which every good dictionary has. Then note the page indication given for it.

4. Count the strokes of the character exclusive of the radical.

5. Locate the character in the group of characters having that specific number of strokes under the same radical.

6. In the case of characters whose radical is either diffused or difficult to determine, consult the Stroke Index, which any good dictionary also provides. In consulting this index it is necessary to count the strokes of the entire character. By the page reference given in the Stroke Index, the character can be reasonably easily located in the dictionary.

THE 214 RADICALS OF A CHINESE DICTIONARY

Number of Strokes	Order in Dictionary	Radical	Pronuncia-tion	Meaning	Modified Form or Forms in Compounds
One	1	一	Ī	One; unity	
	2	丨	Kuň	Vertical line	
	3	丶	Chŭ	Dot, point	
	4	丿	P'ieh̄	Left curving strokes	
	5	乙	Ĭ, ì	Second of "Heavenly Stems" (numbers)	
	6	亅	Chüeh̄	Barb of a hook	
Two	7	二	Erh̀	Two	
	8	亠	T'oú	Head, cover	
	9	人	Jeń	Man, human	亻
	10	儿	Jeń	Man (depicted by his legs)	

489

Number of Strokes	Order in Dictionary	Radical	Pronunciation	Meaning	Modified Form or Forms in Compounds
Two	11	入	Jù	To enter	
	12	八	Pā	Eight; to divide	丷
	13	冂	Chiŭng	Wilderness; space	
	14	冖	Mì	To cover, a cover	
	15	冫	Pinğ	Ice, icicle	
	16	几	Chī	Table, stool	
	17	凵	Kǎn	Open vessel; receptacle	
	18	刀	Taō	Sword, knife	刂
	19	力	Lì	Forearm; strength	
	20	勹	Paō	To wrap	
	21	匕	Pǐ	A man turned around; spoon	
	22	匚	Fanğ	Chest	
	23	匸	Hsǐ	To cover, to conceal	
	24	十	Shih́	Ten	
	25	卜	Pǔ	To divine	
	26	卩	Chieh́	Seal; trust	㔾
	27	厂	Haǹ	Projecting cliff	
	28	厶	Szū	Selfish; private	
	29	又	Yú	The right hand; again	
Three	30	口	K'oǔ	Mouth	
	31	囗	Weí	Enclosure; country	
	32	土	T'ǔ	Soil; earth	圡

Number of Strokes	Order in Dictionary	Radical	Pronunciation	Meaning	Modified Form or Forms in Compounds
Three	33	士	Shih̀	Scholar	
	34	夂	Chih̆	To follow; end	
	35	夊	Suī	To walk slowly	
	36	夕	Hsí	Moon; evening	
	37	大	Tà	Man; big	
	38	女	Nǔ	Woman; female	女
	39	子	Tzǔ	Child, son; seed	子
	40	宀	Mień	Shelter; roof	
	41	寸	Ts'uǹ	Standard; rule; inch	
	42	小	Hsiaǒ	Small	
	43	尢,兀	Wanḡ	Feeble, weak	
	44	尸	Shih̆	Corpse, carcass	
	45	屮	Ch'è	Germinating plant, sprout	
	46	山	Shañ	Mountain	
	47	巛	Ch'uañ	Stream, river	川
	48	工	Kunḡ	To work; work	
	49	己	Chǐ	Self	
	50	巾	Chiñ	Kerchief, towel	
	51	干	Kañ	Weapon, shield	
	52	幺	Yaō	Tiny; one	
	53	广	Yeň	Eaves	
	54	廴	Yiň	To journey afar	

Number of Strokes	Order in Dictionary	Radical	Pronunciation	Meaning	Modified Form or Forms in Compounds
Three	55	廾	Kunğ	To join and hold up hands	
	56	弋	Ì	To tie arrow with string; to take	
	57	弓	Kunḡ	A bow	
	58	彑	Chì	Head of a boar	彐, 且
	59	彡	Shañ	Long hair	
	60	彳	Ch'ih̀	Short step; to walk	
Four	61	心	Hsiñ	Heart; mind	忄, 小
	62	戈	Kō	Halberd; spear	
	63	戶	Hù	Door; family	
	64	手	Shoŭ	Hand	扌
	65	支	Chih̄	Branch; hold; draw	
	66	攴	P'ū	Hand with weapon; to tap	攵
	67	文	Weń	Pattern; writing	
	68	斗	Toŭ	Measuring vessel; a bushel	
	69	斤	Chiñ	Ax; a catty	
	70	方	Fanḡ	Square; direction	
	71	无	Wú	Not; no	旡
	72	日	Jih̀	Sun; day	
	73	曰	Yüeh̀	To say, to speak	
	74	月	Yüeh̀	Moon; month	
	75	木	Mù	Wood; tree	
	76	欠	Ch'ieǹ	To stretch and yawn; to owe	

Number of Strokes	Order in Dictionary	Radical	Pronunciation	Meaning	Modified Form or Forms in Compounds
Four	77	止	Chiň	The foot at rest; to stop	
	78	歹	Taĭ	Broken bones; bad, evil	歺, 卢
	79	殳	Shū	A lance; to kill	
	80	毋	Wú	Do not!	
	81	比	Pĭ	Two men standing side by side; to compare	
	82	毛	Maó	Hair; wool	
	83	氏	Shiḧ	Surname; family	
	84	气	Ch'ì	Vapor	
	85	水	Shuĭ	Water	氵
	86	火	Huŏ	Fire	灬, 灬
	87	爪	Chaŏ	Claw; hand	爫
	88	父	Fù	Father	
	89	爻	Yaó	Divination sign; to mix	
	90	爿	Ch'ianǵ	Left half of a tree; a piece of wood	
	91	片	P'ien	Right half of a tree; a slip, chip, bit	
	92	牙	Yá	Tooth, tusk	
	93	牛	Niú	Ox, cow, bull	牛
	94	犬	Ch'uaň	Dog	犭
Five	95	玄	Hsüań	Black; profound	
	96	玉	Yǔ	Jade	王
	97	瓜	Kuā	Melon	

Number of Strokes	Order in Dictionary	Radical	Pronuncia-tion	Meaning	Modified Form or Forms in Compounds
Five	98	瓦	Wǎ	Pottery; tile	
	99	甘	Kañ	Sweet	
	100	生	Shenḡ	Birth; life; growth	
	101	用	Yunḡ	To use; use	
	102	田	T'ień	Field	
	103	疋	Shū / P'ĭ	Foot in motion / A bale	疋
	104	疒	Nì	Disease; illness	
	105	癶	Pò	To stretch out the legs	
	106	白	Paí, Pó	White; clear	
	107	皮	P'í	Skin; hide; rind	
	108	皿	Miň	Vessel	
	109	目	Mù	Eye; index; chief	
	110	矛	Maó	Spear, lance	
	111	矢	Shiň	Arrow, dart	
	112	石	Shiń	Stone, rock	
	113	礻,示	Shiǹ	Earth god; to show	礻
	114	禸	Joŭ	Traces of animal footsteps	
	115	禾	Huó	Growing grain	禾
	116	穴	Hsüeh̀	Hole; cave; pit	
	117	立	Lì	To stand upright; to set up	
Six	118	竹	Chú	Bamboo	竹
	119	米	Mĭ	Uncooked rice	米

Number of Strokes	Order in Dictionary	Radical	Pronuncia-tion	Meaning	Modified Form or Forms in Compounds
Six	120	糸	Mì / Szū	Silk	糹
	121	缶	Foŭ	Earthenware	
	122	网	Wăng	Net	罒, 罓 / 冈, 罓
	123	羊	Yańg	Sheep, goat	羊, 芊
	124	羽,羽	Yŭ	Feathers	
	125	老	Laŏ	Old, aged	耂
	126	而	Erh́	Whiskers; you; etc.	
	127	耒	Leĭ	Plow handle	
	128	耳	Erh̆	The ear	耳
	129	聿	Yù̆	Then, forthwith	
	130	肉	Joù	Flesh, meat	月
	131	臣	Ch'eń	Vassal; minister	
	132	自	Tzù	The nose; self; from	
	133	至	Chih̀	To extend to; to arrive	
	134	臼	Chiù	Mortar	
	135	舌	Shé	The tongue	
	136	舛	Ch'uaň	To oppose	
	137	舟	Choū	Boat	
	138	艮	Keǹ	Hard, obstinate	
	139	色	Sè	Color	
	140	艸	Ts'aŏ	Grass; herb	艹, 艹

Number of Strokes	Order in Dictionary	Radical	Pronunciation	Meaning	Modified Form or Forms in Compounds
Six	141	虍	Hū	Tiger's stripes	
	142	虫	Ch'unǵ	Insect, worm	
	143	血	Hsüeh̀	Blood	
	144	行	Hsinǵ	Crosswalk; to walk	
	145	衣	Ī	Clothes	衤,衣
	146	襾	Hsià	A cover	
Seven	147	見	Chieǹ	To see	
	148	角	⎰Chüeh́ ⎱Chiaǒ	Horn; corner	
	149	言	Yeń	To say; a word	
	150	谷	Kŭ	Valley, ravine	
	151	豆	Toù	Sacrificial vessel; beans	
	152	豕	Shih̀	Pig, hog	
	153	豸	Chaì	Worm; released	
	154	貝	Peì	Shell, money, treasure	
	155	赤	Ch'ih̀	Red; flesh-colored	
	156	走	Tsoǔ	To walk briskly	
	157	足	Tsú	Foot, leg	
	158	身	Sheñ	Body, trunk; self	
	159	車	⎰Chŭ ⎱Ch'ē	Cart, vehicle	
	160	辛	Hsiñ	Acrid; grievous	
	161	辰	Ch'eń	Time; hour	
	162	辵	Chò	To go fast and stop suddenly	辶,辶

Number of Strokes	Order in Dictionary	Radical	Pronunciation	Meaning	Modified Form or Forms in Compounds
Seven	163	邑	Ì	Town, city	(right) 阝
	164	酉	Yǔ	Wine vessel	
	165	釆	Pień	To distinguish	
	166	里	Lǐ	Village; Chinese mile	
Eight	167	金	Chiń	Metal; gold	
	168	長	Ch'ań	Long	
	169	門	Meń	Door, gate	
	170	阜	Foù	Hill	(left) 阝
	171	隶	Taì	To reach	
	172	隹	Chuī	Bird with short tail	
	173	雨	Yǔ	Rain	𠨧
	174	靑,青	Ch'iń	Green	
	175	非	Feī	No, not	
Nine	176	面	Mień	Face, surface	
	177	革	Kó	Hide; to flay	
	178	韋	Weí	Leather, thong	
	179	韭	Chiǔ	Leeks	
	180	音	Yiń	Sound	
	181	頁	Yeh̀	Head of a person; page	
	182	風	Fenḡ	Wind	
	183	飛	Feī	To fly	
	184	食	Shiń	To eat	

Number of Strokes	Order in Dictionary	Radical	Pronunciation	Meaning	Modified Form or Forms in Compounds
Nine	185	首	Shoŭ	The head	
	186	香	Hsiāng	Fragrant; incense	
Ten	187	馬	Mă	Horse	
	188	骨	Kŭ	Bone	
	189	高	Kaō	High, tall	
	190	髟	Piaō	Long hair	
	191	鬥	Toù	To fight, to contest	
	192	鬯	Ch'anǵ	Sacrificial wine	
	193	鬲	Lì / Kò	Caldron	
	194	鬼	Kueĭ	Spirit, ghost	
Eleven	195	魚	Yŭ	Fish	
	196	鳥	Niaŏ	Bird	
	197	鹵	Lŭ	Earth containing salt	
	198	鹿	Lù	Deer	
	199	麥	Maì	Wheat	
	200	麻	Má	Hemp	
Twelve	201	黃	Huanǵ	Yellow	
	202	黍	Shŭ	Glutinous, paniculate millet	
	203	黑	Heī	Black	
	204	黹	Chiȟ	Needlework	
Thirteen	205	黽	Miȟ	Frog; to exert	
	206	鼎	Tinǧ	Tripod	

Number of Strokes	Order in Dictionary	Radical	Pronuncia-tion	Meaning	Modified Form or Forms in Compounds
Thirteen	207	鼓	Kŭ	Drum	
	208	鼠	Shŭ	Rat, mouse	
Fourteen	209	鼻	Pí	The nose	
	210	齊	Ch'í	Level, even	
Fifteen	211	齒	Ch'ĭh	Tooth, notch	
Sixteen	212	龍	Lunǵ	Dragon	
	213	龜	Kueī	Tortoise	
Seven-teen	214	龠	{Yüeȟ {Yaò	Musical pipes; flute	

Simplified Chinese Characters
and Their Traditional Equivalents

The following list of simplified Chinese characters and their traditional equivalents is provided solely for the convenience of users of this textbook who may on various occasions have been baffled by the simplified characters encountered in publications from the Chinese mainland. It includes the 230 forms officially adopted by the Communist regime in February 1956 for all publications, the 285 to be similarly adopted at a later date, and many others yet to be extensively tried out before being adopted on a nation-wide basis. As time goes on, undoubtedly there will be additional simplified characters devised. Therefore the following list should in no way be considered final or complete. For ease of reference the simplified characters are grouped according to the number of strokes each contains. Their traditional equivalents are placed in parentheses immediately to their right. Items marked * are found in this book in their traditional forms.

Two Strokes

*飞(飛)　*双(雙)　阝(鄧)　务(務)

*几(幾)　广(廣)　丑(醜)　队(隊)　冬(鼕)

厂(廠)　亏(虧)　*气(氣)　*厅(廳)　*叶(葉)

卜(蔔)　*羽(習)　*开(開)　历(曆,　尔(爾)

了(瞭)　*乡(鄉)　斗(鬥)　歷)　帅(帥)

*儿(兒)　亿(億)　羊(豐)　专(專)　*出(齣)

厶(私)　卫(衛)　*办(辦)　*书(書)　*处(處)

Three Strokes　尸(屍)　劝(勸)　仓(倉,　*只(祇,

　　　*于(於)　区(區)　艙)　隻)

*万(萬)　与(與)　*边(邊)　艺(藝)　迈(邁)

*义(義)　*个(個)　辽(遼)　忆(憶)　*过(過)

才(纔)　**Four Strokes**　币(幣)　*无(無)　达(達)

千(韆)　匹(疋)　仆(僕)　韦(韋)　迁(遷)

*干(乾,　*云(雲)　仅(僅)　元(圓)　归(歸)

幹)　*为(為)　*风(風)　火(伙)　*旧(舊)

*么(麼)　*从(從)　凤(鳳)　**Five Strokes**　去(墼)

501

*号(號)	髮)	*伤(傷)	*权(權)	厌(厭)
厉(厲)	*写(寫)	吁(籲)	执(執)	*产(產)
*东(東)	式(貳)	*当(當,	扫(掃)	扩(擴)
*乐(樂)	汙(潑)	噹)	庄(莊)	亚(亞)
台(檯,	*召(招)	妇(婦)	压(壓)	网(網)
臺,	氷(冰)	*灯(燈)	*欢(歡)	曲(麯)
颱)	付(副)	夺(奪)	师(師)	回(迴)
*头(頭)	仟(儒)	団(團,	*阳(陽)	*爷(爺)
*对(對)	*布(佈)	糰)	阴(陰)	*杀(殺,
电(電)	占(佔)	*关(關)	阶(階)	煞)
灭(滅)	礼(禮)	巩(鞏)	*进(進)	庆(慶)
汇(匯,	长(長)	*后(後)	*岁(歲)	伞(傘)
彙)	Six Strokes	尽(盡,	尘(塵)	夹(夾)
*叹(嘆)		儘)	岂(豈)	买(買)
宁(寧)	*会(會)	*齐(齊)	戏(戲)	连(連)
*兰(蘭)	朱(硃)	乔(喬)	忏(懺)	扞(捍)
卢(盧)	众(眾)	*兴(興)	吓(嚇)	穵(挖)
龙(龍)	还(還)	冲(衝)	尧(堯)	尪(尷)
汉(漢)	*这(這)	向(嚮)	杂(雜)	奸(姦)
节(節)	迟(遲)	虫(蟲)	寻(尋)	匈(胸)
刍(芻)	运(運)	*刘(劉)	妆(妝)	坏(壞)
圣(聖)	*远(遠)	划(劃)	壮(壯)	*刚(剛)
术(術)	伙(夥)	*动(動)	夸(誇)	交(繳)
丛(叢)	*价(價)	协(協)	华(華)	*并(併,
业(業)	优(優)	孙(孫)	毕(畢)	並)
*发(發,	伪(偽)	朴(樸)	导(導)	异(異)

疠(疫)	际(際)	园(園)	*坊(塲)	瀰)
屿(嶼)	*怀(壞)	状(狀)	劳(勞)	*担(擔)
Seven Strokes	系(係,繫)	*县(縣)	苇(葦)	拥(擁)
		*穷(窮)	苍(蒼)	拟(擬)
困(睏)	余(餘)	启(啟)	粤(聘)	*刮(颳)
沈(瀋)	*条(條)	卤(鹵,滷)	兎(兔)	环(環)
*报(報)	灵(靈)	*两(兩)	*皃(貌)	艰(艱)
*体(體)	灶(竈)	亩(畝)	陈(陳)	参(參)
犹(猶)	层(層)	沤(漚)	陇(隴)	*备(備)
*苏(蘇,嗉)	庐(廬)	佣(傭)	邹(鄒)	庙(廟)
寿(壽)	芦(蘆)	彻(徹,澈)	韧(韌)	舍(捨)
歼(殲)	迭(疊)	严(嚴)	补(補)	卷(捲)
乱(亂)	*块(塊)	龟(龜)	*医(醫)	*实(實)
谷(穀)	坛(壇,罎)	吨(噸)	Eight Strokes	帘(簾)
*声(聲)	坟(墳)	灿(燦)	制(製)	*宝(寶)
应(應)	*来 来	伯(佰)	板(闆)	画(畫)
*听(聽)	麦(麥)	*床(牀)	松(鬆)	国(國)
克(剋)	沪(滬)	弃(棄)	态(態)	矿(礦)
护(護)	沟(溝)	*荟(薈)	征(徵)	疟(瘧)
*农(農)	*忧(憂)	沧(滄)	郁(鬱)	拣(揀)
折(摺)	扰(擾)	扞(捍)	丽(麗)	极(極)
别(彆)	*陆(陸)	抡(擅)	*罗(羅,囉)	枪(槍)
*里(裏)	邻(鄰)	扳(攀)	衰(褰)	胁(脅)
时(時)	壳(殼)	肖(蕭)	弥(彌,)	郑(鄭)
*邮(郵)	疗(療)			肿(腫)
				齿(齒)

逊(遜)   迹(蹟,跡)   **Nine Strokes**   面(麵)   虾(蝦)

适(適)   肴(餚)   标(標)   显(顯)

审(審)   变(變)   复(復,複,覆)   *帮(幫)   宪(憲)

枣(棗)   炖(燉)   *带(帶)   *赵(趙)

肃(蕭)   泽(澤)   觇(覘)   递(遞)   昼(晝)

肮(骯)   泼(潑)   荐(薦)   恼(惱)   毡(氈)

构(構)   *枫 楓   *虽(雖)   垒(壘)   浊(濁)

拦(攔)   注(註)   洒(灑)   娄(婁,嘍)   疮(瘡)

炉(爐)   拢(攏)   总(總)   胜(勝)

泸(瀘)   虱(蝨)   尝(嘗)   拦(欄)   *树(樹)

图(圖)   择(擇)   *种(種)   烂(爛)   *认(認)

凭(憑)   采(採)   *战(戰)   浏(瀏)   哑(啞)

录(錄)   *果(菓)   *响(響)   炼(煉)   洼(窪)

虏(虜)   帜(幟)   *咸(鹹)   临(臨)   衬(襯)

岭(嶺)   岩(巖)   秋(鞦)   俩(倆)   荅(答)

*怜(憐)   侄(姪)   窃(竊)   栋(棟)   厘(釐)

籴(糴)   肾(腎)   荞(蕎)   柜(櫃)   讥(譏)

单(單)   坚(堂)   *举(舉)   胡(鬍)   险(險)

苹(蘋)   *咀(嘴)   姜(薑)   洁(潔)   济(濟)

肤(膚)   劲(勁)   垦(墾)   茧(繭)   匦(匭)

隶(隸)   侩(儈)   类(類)   *将(將)   象(像)

卖(賣)   苐(第)   独(獨)   奖(獎)   柒(漆)

矾(礬)   瓮(甕)   垫(墊)   *牵 牽   荣(榮)

周(週)   泻(瀉)   *点(點)   纤(纏,纖)   栈(棧)

迟(遲)   *胆(膽)   蚁(蟻)

幸(倖)   *亲(親)   挡(擋)

挂(掛)	致(緻)	烬(燼)	涌(湧)	惨(慘)
茬(藏)	牺(犧)	浆(漿)	*桔(橘)	偿(償)
荞(蕎)	剧(劇)	竞(競)	晋(晉)	旋(鏇)
弯(彎)	借(藉)	窍(竅)	悮(悮,	据(據)
茎(莖)	家(傢)	斋(齋)	誤)	盖(蓋)
脉(脈)	恳(懇)	烛(燭)	尃(敷)	累(纍)
剐(剮)	赶(趕)	掂(摣)	蚝(蠔)	盘(盤)
皇(凰)	*难(難)	硷(礆)	敆(微)	*梦(夢)
*矦(侯,	淀(澱)	讧(讓)	席(蓆)	麸(麩)
候)	*敌(敵)	脏(臟,	脐(臍)	堕(墮)
*荨(等)	党(黨)	髒)	脍(膾)	葉(耀)
炮(砲)	宾(賓)	纵(縱)	渎(瀆)	猎(獵)
疯(瘋)	坝(壩)	涩(澀)	纬(緯)	练(練)
	*笔(筆)	恶(惡,	纲(綱)	秽(穢)
Ten Strokes	毙(斃)	噁)	*祘(算)	轰(轟)
	涂(塗)	艳(艷)	皱(皺)	讲(講)
*样(樣)	脑(腦)	*盐(鹽)	疖(癤)	*惊(驚)
*罢(罷)	砾(礫)	痈(癰)	捞(撈)	惧(懼)
养(養)	虑(慮)	袄(襖)	*袜(襪)	悬(懸)
*爱(愛)	获(獲,	壶(壺)		质(質)
随(隨)	穫)	酝(釀)	Eleven Strokes	兽(獸)
蚕(蠶)	饥(饑)	逻(邏)		渗(滲)
*热(熱)	积(積)	崔(鶴)	衅(釁)	啬(嗇)
晒(曬)	胶(膠)	*议(議)	*离(離,	隐(隱)
称(稱)	监(監)	涝(澇)	璃)	跃(躍)
准(準)	紧(緊)	涨(漲)	御(禦)	酝(醞)
症(癥)			痒(癢)	

渊(淵)	织(織)	*象(像)	膛(膛)	摆(擺,
购(購)	络(絡)	须(鬚)	绘(繪)	襬)
萤(螢)	*线(綫,	滞(滯)	*经(經)	摊(攤)
讳(諱)	綫)	装(裝)	粝(糲)	滩(灘)
竖(豎)	笼(籠)	钟(鐘)	筛(篩)	誊(謄)
轮(輪)	笺(箋)	属(屬)	蔫(蔫)	龄(齡)
贤(賢)	断(斷)	錾(鏨)	窝(窩)	顾(顧)
*猫(貓)	躯(軀)	钥(鑰)	*钢(鋼)	鸡(鷄,
飡(餐)	矫(矯)	*药(藥)	祸(禍)	雞)
*营(營)	账(賬)	窜(竄)	痨(癆)	舰(艦)
龛(龕)	阎(閻)	硷(鹼)	畴(疇)	鉴(鑒)
讽(諷)	讴(謳)	释(釋)	牍(牘)	寝(寢)
论(論)	铇(鉋)	游(遊)	犊(犢)	搅(攪)
袭(襲)	Twelve Strokes	践(踐)	*贱(賤)	摄(攝)
敛(斂)	证(證)	趋(趨)	Thirteen Strokes	铄(鑠)
捻(撚)	湿(濕)	鬧(鬭)		钻(鑽)
脓(膿)	惩(懲)	喂(餵)	碍(礙)	雾(霧)
*萝(蘿)	筑(築)	译(譯)	辞(辭)	誉(譽)
欲(慾)	飓(颶)	*识(識)	触(觸)	酱(醬)
麻(蔴)	确(確)	谄(諂)	献(獻)	签(簽,
遍(徧)	联(聯)	勋(勳)	粮(糧)	籤)
寐(寢)	粪(糞)	然(燃)	*铁(鐵)	继(繼)
*脸(臉)	椭(橢)	裆(襠)	蒙(朦,	轿(轎)
聋(聾)	腊(臘)	裢(褳)	濛,	轻(輕)
职(職)	琼(瓊)	蛮(蠻)	懞)	跷(蹺)
绎(繹)	亵(褻)	蛳(螄)	辟(闢)	馋(饞)

腭(齶)	*车两(車兩)	瘫(癱)	缕(縷)	龌(齷)
韵(韻)	秽(穢)	嘱(囑)	篓(蔞)	箫(簫)
雏(雛)	*愿(願)	驿(驛)	瘪(癟)	
*钱(錢)	踊(踴)	赎(贖)	潜(潛)	Eighteen Strokes
睹(覩)	绳(繩)	赞(贊,	鸥(鷗)	
携(攜)	驴(驢)	讚)		镊(鑷)
蜗(蝸)	飓(颶)	读(讀)	Sixteen Strokes	缆(纜)
筹(籌)	飔(颸)	飘(飄)		锁(鎖)
钼(鉬)	踌(躊)	颈(頸)	缠(纏)	攒(攢)
痴(癡)	铲(鏟)	溅(濺)	莺(鶯)	
畺(疆)	龈(齦)	铸(鑄)	骄(驕)	
绣(繡)	蛏(蟶)	锈(鏽)	锣(鑼)	鳖(鱉)
驱(驅)	续(續)	锅(鍋)	蛊(蠱)	
	绷(繃)	僵(殭)	缤(繽)	Twenty-two Strokes
Fourteen Strokes	萝(蘿)	龊(齪)	篮(籃)	
	漏(瘻)	搅(攪)	穑(穡)	
蝠(虫畐)		蝎(蠍)		
蔑(衊)	Fifteen Strokes	揽(攬)	Seventeen Strokes	
酿(釀)		蝼(螻)		
蜡(蠟)	霉(黴)	耧(耬)	篱(籬)	
蔷 薔	*聪(聰)		谗(讒)	
			验(驗)	

When the State Council of Communist China ordered the adoption of simplified characters in February 1956, the following 54 simplified character components which might form the top, bottom, left, or right portion of characters were included in the official list. They are grouped according to number of strokes for ease of reference.

Two Strokes

讠(言)
几(幾)

Three Strokes

纟(糸)
门(門)
饣(食)
马(馬)
义(義)

Four Strokes

见(見)
贝(貝)
车(車)

仑(倫)
冈(岡)
収(臤)
韦(韋)
风(風)
匆(昜)
乌(鳥)
区(區)
专(專)

Five Strokes

圣(巠)
钅(金)
长(長)
东(東)

戋(戔)
刍(芻)
芈(兟)
发(發)
只(戠)
罕(睪)
兴(興)
临(臨)
龙(龍)

Six Strokes

页(頁)
师(師)
产(產)
乔(喬)

尧(堯)
当(當)
会(會)
齐(齊)
亦(䜌)

Seven Strokes

呙(咼)
鱼(魚)
佥(僉)
农(農)
寿(壽)

Eight Strokes

单(單)

肃(肅)
齿(齒)
卖(賣)
罗(羅)

Nine Strokes

娄(婁)

Ten Strokes

宾(賓)
监(監)

508